Pricing Guide
for
Desktop
Publishing
Services

Third Edition

STREET SMART PRICING
FOR THE
SMALL BUSINESS ENTREPRENEUR

by

Robert C. Brenner, MSEE, MSSM

With U.S. Regional & Canadian
Billing Rates

Pricing Guide for Desktop Publishing Services
Third Edition

Printed in the United States of America
Second Printing - January 1995

ISBN 0-929535-13-8

Published by

Brenner Information Group
9282 Samantha Court
San Diego, CA 92129
(619) 538-0093

TABLE OF CONTENTS

Pricing Guide
for
Desktop Publishing Services

Introduction

"Price, not timing, can be everything."
- Normal Dolph, Success Magazine

Congratulations on making a good decision. This is the third edition of a guide that has become the de facto pricing standard for the small business DTP entrepreneur. Since its inception three years ago, thousands of new and aspiring business owners have used this guide to develop sound pricing strategies and successful price quotes. It can help you, too.

Whether you're selling a product or offering a service, the price you set is critical to business success. Sometimes raising your prices will increase sales. At other times, cutting prices will stimulate sales. Pricing is a complex, yet exciting part of business. It's comprised of many factors, and the more you know about what affects price and a customer's willingness to let go of hard-earned cash, the more business you'll get and the more money you'll make.

Research consistently indicates that few small business owners really understand operating costs and how to determine what prices to charge. Many owners fail to consider factors such as the time spent with customers as a cost. Many are reactive and establish prices based on what everyone else seems to be charging—the "going rate." They're slow to raise prices when appropriate and don't test each price for its affect on sales. Most owners just don't know how to analyze and establish optimum prices.

Pricing is a skill. It can be successfully applied only if you have the tools necessary to analyze and make good decisions.

This reference book was written to provide those tools. As a guide to product and service pricing, this book focuses on desktop publishing shops and service bureaus, although once you've learned the "basics," you can apply the techniques in this guide to any business venture.

There are seven chapters to the *Pricing Guide for Desktop Publishing Services - Third Edition.* Chapter 1 covers the meaning of price. In Chapter 1, you'll learn about costs, what's behind a selling price and how the consumer thinks.

Chapter 2 covers pricing strategy. In this chapter, you'll learn ways to analyze your business, understand your customer, and outfox your competition. You'll discover techniques for establishing price and how various market conditions can affect what you charge. By studying this chapter, you'll be able to generate your own pricing strategy.

Chapter 3 explains how shop owners charge for their services. It covers both pricing by the unit (character, line, page, etc.) and pricing by time expended (minutes, hours, etc.). This chapter describes how to come up with your shop's hourly rate and how productivity affects this value. It also covers flat rate pricing and describes how you can use a budgeted hourly rate to develop a price to quote for a complete job.

Part of your success is determined by how well you estimate and bid. Chapter 4 shows you how to respond to a request for quote (RFQ) or request for bid (RFB). It describes techniques for selecting the optimum price to quote and shows you how to negotiate a win-win solution with your client. This chapter also describes estimating software that can help make your tactical decisions better and your response to opportunities faster and more successful.

Chapter 5 helps you convert strategic planning into tactical operations. It's where the "rubber meets the road." This chapter describes the operational tricks of the trade used by successful shop owners. It includes finding your break-even point, dealing with cut-throat competitors, and techniques for breaking out top profits. The chapter also includes samples of forms and worksheets that you can adopt for making your business work better and more productive.

Chapter 6 provides table listings of the results of research into current pricing across North America. This chapter was produced through extensive surveys, personal interviews, analyzing numerous price sheets and display advertisements and the synthesis of countless articles, books, and trade journals. Each facet of desktop publishing and prepress has been addressed. Based on the research results described in Chapter 5, you can compare your pricing strategy with that of competitors all over the country. You can also use Chapter 6 to recognize and analyze other potential products or services that you might want to offer.

In the Appendix, you'll find useful information about the profession of desktop publishing. This chapter presents survey results on the profile of the DTP and prepress shops located all over North America. It will help you understand what the competition looks like, what businesses structure is most popular, how many employees a typical shop has, what hardware and software they use, and where they get their best business leads. This chapter will give you an insight into the operational strategies of those "in the business."

The Appendix also provides other useful information to help you succeed in your business. This includes a tabulated list of the publications regularly read by professionals who are operating DTP and service bureau shops. By knowing what these owners read, you can determine what they feel are the most useful publications for their business.This chapter also describes what professional associations that the our survey respondents feel are worth joining. The chapter concludes with the addresses of associations mentioned by a majority our survey participants or worthy of your consideration.

Our world is a kaleidoscope of text and colorful graphics. And we are being lifted up by information wave that will change our lives forever. Some people call this wave an "information highway" or "data highway." Whatever we choose to call this revolution, there are more opportunities for desktop publishers today than ever before in history. To succeed in this business, you need comprehensive information. This guide was written to help you win—to help you meet your pricing concerns.

In producing this book, our goal is to elevate desktop publishing as a profession by helping struggling DTPers set better prices. Shop owners work hard to succeed in business. And few professions have the consistent intense learning requirement as the profession you have chosen. It is our desire to recognize your efforts and to do our part to bring the fee structure of desktop publishing and prepress more in line with the education and skills required—and with the work actually performed by today's DTP professional.

Chapter 1

The Concept of Pricing

"This is not a let's-just-wing-it operation."

An effective business strategy cannot be developed without a clear understanding of price. Yet pricing cannot occur in a vacuum. It requires the careful consideration of several important and interrelated factors. This chapter introduces the concept of price and explains why pricing is a dynamic business activity.

Terms to Remember

Discount - Refers to a percentage reduction from retail price. A $2,000 product purchased at 40% discount [2000 - (2000 * .4)] has a wholesale cost of $1,200.

Fixed Costs - Costs that don't vary with the level of business activity. They exist whether you have little or lots of business.

Gross Profit Margin - The percentage of what's left over after taking the cost of goods sold out of a sale price. Thus a product that sells for $100 with an $85 cost of goods sold would produce a gross profit of $15 and a gross profit margin of 15% (.15). An $85 product with a $65 cost of goods yields a gross profit of $20 and a gross profit margin of 23.53% (20 divided by 85).

Markup - Refers to a percentage increase from wholesale price. You mark up the wholesale price to cover the cost of sales and to provide a certain profit. Markup is equal to the discount divided by 100 less the discount all multiplied by 100. Therefore a discount of 40 percent is proportional to a markup of [40/(100-40)] x 100 = 66.7%. A $1,200 wholesale product can be marked up by 66.7% [(1200 X .667) + 1200] to achieve a selling price of $2,000. Customers buy at discount. Retailers sell at markup.

Profit Margin - A decimal value describing the amount of reward a company gets for offering a product or service. Profit margin is usually expressed as a decimal. To get profit margin, subtract the cost of goods from the sales income and then divide this result by the sales. A $100 sales price with a cost of goods of $85 yields a .15 profit margin [(100-85)/100 = 0.15].

Price is the money (or other consideration) that a customer pays for a product or service. It's a statement of value. Price is usually expressed in dollars and cents.

Variable Costs - Costs that vary with the level of business being conducted.

What's Included in a Price?

A fixed price is composed of a "standard" rate for that product or service, plus some time and materials pricing for the customized elements, and some value pricing based on the perceived value that a solution represents to a customer. Businesses charge the most for those things that have the most value to the buying public.

Markup - What's in Their Price?

Full retail prices can be roughly partitioned into two equal halves—the cost to produce, and the cost to sell. The second half is called *"markup."* This incorporates a selling cost plus projected profit. It could also include a return on your investment in the hardware and software required to make the product. Markup varies from product to product and from business to business.

Trying to find out a competitor's markup is like trying to find out what new toys are being developed by Hasbro. This information is kept proprietary. But you can calculate it based on knowing the wholesale cost, the selling costs, and an idea of their operating costs. One rule of thumb is that how often a product sells (inventory turns over) directly affects the product's markup. A fast turnover suggests a lower markup—say 20%. A high price product with a low turnover typically has a high markup—say 55%.

Retail department stores typically charge two times the wholesale price (100% markup). This is called a *"keystone markup."* Sometimes they tack on an additional 10% to the selling price if the product is imported or private-label. This lets them sell it at "half off" and still make money.

A discount store has a lower selling cost so they typically use a 40% markup. An "off-price" retailer typically marks up its products by about 35%. Although these are typical, markup can vary within the same store.

When a store offers a "Percent-Off" sale, the fun really begins. The initial markup is never as important as the final selling price.

The difference between the actual selling price and the wholesale price is called *"gross margin" or "gross profit."* The wholesale price includes the cost to produce that product. Gross margin is expressed as a percent of revenue. Out of this, you pay expenses such as sales, marketing, and general and administrative costs.

It's a closely held secret by most retail outfits, but we have clues to what it should be by studying the trade publications. Computer manufacturers operate at approximately 50% gross margin. Software companies typically achieve gross margins in the 80% area. Desktop publishers and prepress service bureaus typically operate in the 30% - 40% range.

Gross margin is a way to isolate profitability regardless of other costs that may cloud the profit picture. Gross margin is also an indicator of the value of a product or service. A gross margin can tell you when you're selling a service that has become a commodity product in the market.

As more shops offer a service and prices settle at some nearly uniform level, the gross margin decreases. When it drops below 30%, you're service is becoming a commodity. Many shops focus on higher margin products and services.

Factors Affecting Price

Price is affected by many related factors—the type and size of the market, customer demand, the competition, government regulations, and so on.

Market Type

How you decide to price your product or service often depends on the type of market in which you will compete. If there are many DTP shops and service bureaus in your locale, you adopt a different pricing strategy than if you operate in a community in which you are the only business of your type. Basically, there are four types of markets in which you may operate—monopolistic, oligopolistic, purely competitive, and monopolistic competitive. It's important to know where you stand before you decide where you want to stand.

One Seller, Many Buyers, No Price Competition

In the jargon of economists, this is a "monopolistic" market. You operate the only shop in your area and you have many customers. The nearest competitor is in the next town so you don't really have a price competitor to deal with.

When you're the "only game in town" you must price carefully so you don't cause buyers to select other alternatives to get the service they need (e.g., hire students, hire support from out of town, etc.). You also don't want another entrepreneur to see value in starting a competitive business in your neighborhood. Therefore, you price your products and services to cover costs and return good profit without encouraging competition.

Few Sellers, Many Buyers, Pricing Based on Competitor's Action

This is called an "oligopolistic market." In this market, the high cost to get set up keeps the participants low. So, few people operate this type of business. For those that do, all the competitors will offer a very similar product, so the pricing strategy depends on not only what the customers prefer, but also on what the competitors do.

If this is your market type, reducing your prices will cause your competition to reduce theirs. Raise your prices, and they may or may not raise theirs. If they don't, you may have to retract your price increase just to keep customers.

Many Sellers, Many Buyers, Same Price

In this "purely competitive" market, the product is the same, so you can't charge more than your competitor because a customer knows that the same product is available for a lower price elsewhere in town. This makes both buyer and seller price-takers rather than price-makers.

The inability to offer a different product, means that all of the sellers must price the same. Your only advantage is to be where most of the customers go to shop. The only way to get away from a purely competitive market is to offer additional products or services to make you different. The homogeneous product becomes essentially a lost leader. You make your money on differentiation. And this puts you into the fourth type of market—monopolistic competitive.

Many Sellers, Many Buyers, Many Prices

In economic terms, a "monopolistic-competitive" market. Here's a market in which you can succeed and have the most fun. This market has product and service differentiation. You try for maximum differentiation so you can achieve maximum profit. The customer determines price so pricing analysis and strategy become important. This is where goodwill, advertising, capability, and all the other aspects of business can have the most affect. For most of us, this is the market in which we operate.

Market Size

If you plan to operate in a small town, your local market may be too small to make your business successful. Four sales a week at $20 a pop won't pay the rent and feed the family too. You will have to draw business to you from outlying areas by advertising outside the county or state. Every entrepreneur seeks the largest market with the least competition.

With our world rapidly becoming a global sales floor, don't be afraid to seek business from across the state (or country). One colleague that I met operates a graphics design and desktop publishing business in Hawaii. She advertises in a national publication and draws business from all over the U.S., yet she operates from a island thousands of miles from the mainland. The world is literally an open door market for desktop publishing businesses today.

Demand

A capability to generate a really nice product is useless if no-one cares. Without demand for your products and services, your business cannot survive. Nor can you make it if your products are obsolete. A typing service using manual typewriters will fall on its face trying to compete with a computer-based shop providing the same service. Offering to produce newsletters using dot-matrix print output will never successfully compete with a shop providing the same service but based on laser print output. You must find and develop products and services that are unique and that customers want.

The adage for success is simple: Find a need and fill it. Doing it may be less simple. Only by knowing the marketplace and your business can you be sensitive and recognize opportunity. If you can provide a product or service that meets a high demand, your business can grow significantly.

Economy

Fifty years ago, Abraham Maslow developed a hierarchy of needs to describe people and what they perceive as important. A similar hierarchy of needs can be developed based on the economy. Buyers look at a product based on perceived value. This value can rise or fall depending on personal need, future plans, current finances, and the economic outlook.

As the economy sours, most people conserve more and reduce spending. They increase bargain shopping, select less expensive solutions, and put off major purchases. Many businesses cut prices, extend credit, and offer more for less as they try to stimulate sales. They alter their products or services to provide lower-cost alternatives. They cut the frills, unbundle the services, and may also offer self-directed document generation opportunities.

As the rate of inflation increases, buying power declines and shoppers become even more price sensitive. So businesses stress lower prices and better values. The rate of inflation strongly influences how customers perceive price.

Competition

If your service isn't selling, you can always consider lowering your prices to create volume. But cutting your price by 50 percent won't increase your sales volume by 400 percent (which is usually what you'll need to net the same profit).

Let's say you get customers who want laser-printed sheets. Some shops use several pricing grids. One is based on the total number of sheets handled. Another is based on the total number of pages per original. And a third is based on the amount of toner coverage on each sheet. These pricing grids are based on the time to print and the toner expended. The total number of pages printed per original provides volume discounts and is more favorable to the large-volume customer.

Customers who want special features such as color printing have expectations that this will cost more and price doesn't seem to be a major factor to them. Therefore, the average cost for a color output page is $10—far more than the $1.66 per page average for black and white laser printouts.

Combining competitive pricing with quality products is hard to beat.

Perceived Value

A service product can command a higher price if it's marketed as different and of premium quality. Marketing executive, Purchasing decisions are often driven by the emotional and psychological character of the buyer. After commiting to a sale, many buyers use logic to rationalize the wisdom of their decision. They were drawn to your shop by the value that they perceived in your products and services.

By being considered preeminent in your field, you can successfully charge a "premium price" for your service. In this case, your "premium price" is an aggressive advertisement for quality. However, you must deliver on the perception. If you get tainted with a bad job, your image and prestige will suffer. So will your sales.

When a customer falls in love with a product, you can increase its price and they'll still buy. This added price is the "WOW" content. Price is really what a customer is willing to pay. If they'll pay more, then most retailers charge more. The McDonald's fast food restaurant chain calls this *"value pricing."* They generate a "value menu" as a long term phenomenon rather than simply use it as a tactic to meet competition. McDonald's knows what products customers really prefer. They set higher margins on french fries and soft drinks because these are the most common sales that accompany combination meals and sandwich orders.

Esthetics and Location

There is a distinct difference in how some customers perceive a business that operates out of a garage, out of a "hole-in-the-wall" strip center, or out of a professional business complex.

When a customer comes to you, esthetics and location become important in how you price your products and services. Each of these three locations can be a successful business. But each will cater to a different customer mix. That "mix" may include customer location.

Therefore, decide what customer base you want to target. Then learn all you can about your customer. Based on this knowledge, organize and operate your business accordingly.

Law and Government

Pricing directly affects both consumers and businesspeople, so local, state, and federal regulations have been implemented to keep customers and competitors from being served unfairly. Before you start a business, and certainly while you operate your business, you must be aware of the laws and ordnances that affect how you can function.

Your local Chamber of Commerce and government offices can help you determine the local, state, and federal regulations that you must follow. Each state has its own version of an Unfair Sales Practices Act that limits the mark-ups you can place on certain items. You can charge more, but not less than specified mark-ups allow. These "minimum mark-up" laws still allow sales of old or out-dated products, but they are designed to protect small businesses by forcing discounters to apply at least a minimum mark-up to their products. This lets a small operator remain competitive with a larger operation.

In 1936, the federal government passed the Robinson-Patman Act to prevent price discrimination. This act makes it illegal to charge a lower price to one customer than you charge to another similar customer. You should not induce, give, or receive discriminatory prices. What you charge (or pay) must be consistent for all. For example, you can't give a discount to one party without offering the same discount to everyone else. This helps you when large retailers demand a wholesale discount even though they may purchase in small quantity.

The Robinson-Patman Act does enable cooperative advertising and promotions as long as the same opportunities are offered to all customers on proportionally the same terms.

There are two provisions in the Act that may appear discriminatory, but are accepted. The first allows you to charge one customer a lower price if your purpose is to meet the same low price offered by a competitor. Thus, a customer who brings you an ad for the same services offered by a competitor at a lower price can realize a savings if you are wiling to lower your price to match the competitor's price. You can meet a competitor's lower price without violating the intent of the Act.

The second provision lets you price a product differently between buyers if you can prove that the difference represents a pass-through of costs saved by selling to one buyer over another (e.g., one buyer is local and doesn't require products to be packaged and shipped).

The Federal Trade Commission Act established a watchdog agency to monitor how businesses operate in the United States. Both the Robinson-Patman Act and the Federal Trade Commission Act were designed to protect consumers and small businesses. Congress also passed the Sherman Antitrust Act to deal with price.

Only by keeping current on local, state, and federal business legislation can you operate with some assurance that you will avoid legal troubles.

In addition, groups of similar businesses must not organize to set "standard" prices on products and services. The Sherman Antitrust Act, the Clayton Antitrust Act, and the Federal Trade Commission Act all make it illegal for a group of competing businesses to collectively set prices. Each must price independently.

Many owner/operators simply have not learned how laws, ordnances, and regulations can affect their business. Many are operating in gray areas of legality. And some are actually conducting business in violation of law.

If you notice a competitor "operating outside the law," rather than sending "the feds" to catch this person, give the competitor a call and let them know that they may be breaking the law. Most small business owners do not intentionally violate the law. They simply have so much to learn and handle, that unintentional oversights or improper activities occur. However, ignorance is no excuse. It's better for all of us to look out for each other, than for us to look out for the law. We should not be in this to drive each other out. We should be in this so all of us can win and enjoy our business adventures.

Your Profit Objectives

The only way you can increase your profit margin is to lower your percentage of costs. A business with the largest market share should also have the lowest cost. Both material and labor costs are directly proportional to market share.

Trading short-term profit (through lower prices) to gain market share may be a good long-term strategy if your material costs decrease as sales volume increases. If not, be careful of quick profits with long term losses.

Cost of Goods or Services Sold

No consideration of pricing should occur without a clear understanding of the cost basis that is unique to your own shop. Each time you purchase new equipment or a new application program, there are two costs involved—the purchase cost and the ownership cost.

We can negotiate various purchase prices depending on where and how we buy. Once the purchase is concluded, the cost becomes the basis for any tax-related depreciation we are able to assume.

The cost of ownership is different. It includes those expenses related to operating and maintaining the system. It takes time and energy to learn and exploit the power in the hardware and software used in your business. With software becoming more complex and hardware becoming more powerful, you cannot assign operating tasks to just anyone. You must first become proficient yourself. Then you must teach those who support you. With processing power dispersed throughout your shop, the functions and capabilities can become more than one person can handle well. This means that you may have to hire expertise to help cover unfamiliar tasks. You'll have to rely on others to perform. This will require management, leadership, and education. Each of these factors has an associated after-purchase cost.

Maintenance cost is another direct expense that you must understand and control. Hardware and software each have an associated maintenance cost. For hardware, it includes cleaning, diagnostic check-ups, and repair actions when necessary. It could include a service agreement for third party support. Software maintenance can include paying for on-line technical support or the cost to customize a program for your business. An accounting package needs modifications to incorporate changes to the staff, to add new benefits, to change the tax and social security structure. A database used for market analysis and customer contacts needs update and clean-up. A spreadsheet needs modification to incorporate new information or to produce a different output. Each action has an associated cost.

Then there are the less-obvious costs—the indirect costs. These include upgrade, trade-in and system availability. We upgrade our hardware and software to keep at the forefront of technology, or to increase our capability as business grows. Sometimes we trade in older equipment for new hardware. And sometimes we wait for advertised hardware or software that never becomes a reality. We call this "vaporware." In the past two years, a growing number of products have been touted, hyped, and promised. But delivery was woefully late, or nonexistent. Basing your business plan on hardware or software that becomes vaporware has a cost. Don't believe the optimistic schedules of marketeers. Plan implementations far enough ahead that you can work out the bugs and operational idiosyncrasies (or implement alternatives) long before you put your new system on line.

Pricing Techniques

There are basically four reference baselines for pricing your products and services—demand-oriented, cost-oriented, competition-oriented, and profit-oriented pricing. Some businesses develop a composite of two or more of these approaches to pricing.

Demand-Oriented Pricing

This approach places more emphasis on customer tastes and preferences than it does on cost, competition and profit. There are six types of demand pricing— skimming, penetration, prestige, lining, odd-even, and demand-backward.

Price Skimming

In *price skimming*, a high initial price is charged for a new product. Customers who want the product will be less sensitive to price because they perceive high value in the product. As demand by this group is satisfied, the price is reduced to attract the next (more price-sensitive) consumer group.

Skimming is effective when customers line up to buy the moment a product is released. The product is perceived to have high quality. However, the high initial price must not be so high that it attracts competitors. The early appearance of competition can prevent you from using a higher initial price to offset high startup production and marketing costs and from achieving lower follow-on production costs with lower selling prices later in the product life cycle.

Penetration Pricing

In *penetration pricing*, a low introductory price is used to generate large mass appeal. The intent is to gain as much market share as possible before competitors move in. This strategy works when the market place is price sensitive. Production costs can be dramatically lower as sales volume increases. The low initial price acts to discourage competition.

Some businesses implement price skimming when a product is first released to recoup initial development and promotion costs. Then, some months later, they implement penetration pricing to attract a larger segment of the market. The electronics industry follows this strategy.

Pricing the Prestige

Perceived value can demand a higher sales price. When a product or service is perceived as high quality or a "status " purchase, a high price works well. In fact, lowering the price can reduce demand because the customer may perceive the change as a lowering in quality. If your customers expect to pay more for your services, why deny them the satisfaction?

This form of psychological pricing matches perceived value to selling price. When service is seen as having added value, demand rises and the price is adjusted upward. Customers who don't place a high value on service are offered a lower-priced service product. This is a form of "price discrimination" that can be used effectively as long as you have a solid understanding of the marketplace.

Differential Pricing (Price Lining)

A business with a line of products can partition the products into categories with specific prices for each category. Each line of products is targeted to a specific type of customer. Even when products are purchased at the same cost, they may be marked up differently based on color, style and expected demand.

For example, when I was a teenager, I worked at a salt company where standard salt and Kosher salt both came from the same raw material bin. Both products received the same processing, yet the Kosher salt was poured into a container with a different packaging label. This enabled the company to sell Kosher salt to distributors for almost twice the price of the regular salt. Yet both came from exactly the same raw material source.

Price lining can also be applied when demand varies in different markets. Here you typically sell at a higher price to those markets in which a lower price won't increase bottom line revenue. You then sell at a lower price in those markets that are sensitive to price. U.S. manufacturers often sell products overseas for much more than the added cost for doing business internationally simply because U.S. products are perceived as having higher quality.

A business applies *differential pricing* by considering each product or service relative to time, season, location, and customer. For example, a custom Christmas newsletter service could be introduced in the fall and priced at maximum in November and December. Then you can offer special prices for DTP jobs placed during off-times and off-days. You can change the packaging of a product (e.g., fancy covers on reports designed for large corporate customers), and you can offer different prices to outlying areas or locales.

Odd/Even Pricing

The *odd/even* approach uses the cents (or points) to promote a lower price than reality. Selling a product for $2.99 instead of $3 gives the impression that the customer is paying "just over two dollars." You'll learn more about this in the strategy section.

Demand-Backward Pricing

Here, a company estimates a price that customers will be willing to pay. Then it works backwards through the calculations to arrive at an acceptable manufacturing quality and production cost that enables the pre-determined selling price.

This is what happened in the modem industry. Modem manufacturers knew that they needed to get the selling price of the 9600 bps modem below $1,000 to increase sales. So they backed into the price and designed a product that could be built at a cost that would allow sales at $995 or less and still produce acceptable profit.

If you know that short-run publishers are growing at a rapid rate yet they consistently face "large run" prices, why not develop a product and service that you can offer at a production cost low enough to meet the price they are willing to pay?

Cost-Oriented Pricing

Establishing price based on cost is the most frequent pricing method used in business. Usually, minimal consideration is given to the effect price will have on demand. The focus is on cost, not demand. There are three forms of cost-oriented pricing—mark-up, cost-plus, and cost-volume.

Mark-Up Pricing

In this form of cost-oriented pricing the sales figure is established by adding a predetermined percentage to the cost of a product. This amount can be a percentage of the selling price, or a percentage of the cost. The total markup represents operating expenses, overhead and profit.

Mark-ups differ based on the product, competition, turnover, and sales risk. However, many businesses use a "standard" mark-up for each product category. Clothing is typically marked up by 40-60%. Staple food items such as bread and milk are marked up by 10-23%. Snack foods receive a 27-47% mark-up, and so on. In reality, there's a mark-up at each stage in the development of a product—manufacturing, distribution, and final sales. The net result is a product or service that has been marked up several hundred percent over its initial raw material cost as it passes through each stage in the manufacturing-to-customer process.

If a product cost $10 from a wholesale supplier, a business owner will add a portion of overhead costs (rent, utilities, insurance, salaries, etc.) and profit to this base cost to arrive at a selling price. To arrive at this selling price, divide the wholesale cost by one minus the percent overhead plus percent profit (both expressed in decimal) as shown in the formula below. If overhead represents 25% of your costs and you want a 10% profit, you would mark up a $10 product by 53.8% to achieve a selling price of $15.38.

$$\text{Selling Price} = \frac{\text{Wholesale Cost}}{1 - (\text{overhead} + \text{profit})}$$

Thus

$$\text{Selling Price} = \frac{10}{1 - (.25 + .10)}$$

$$= \frac{10}{1 - 0.35}$$

$$= \frac{10}{.65}$$

Selling Price = \$15.38

To get the markup percentage, apply the formula

$$\% \text{ Markup} = \frac{\text{Selling Price} - \text{Wholesale Cost}}{\text{Wholesale Cost}} \times 100$$

$$= \frac{15.38 - 10.00}{10.00} \times 100$$

$$= \frac{5.38}{10} \times 100$$

Percent Markup = 0.538 x 100

= 53.8%

Several variations of mark-up pricing exist—a calculated mark up for each product or service, a standard mark up on all products, and a markup based on some accepted reference. Basing your price on covering total costs, including overhead, with a pre-determined mark up for profit is called *full cost pricing*. If your price covers the variable costs of doing business with a predetermined mark-up for profit but not all of your overhead, you are applying *incremental cost pricing*. This method assumes that your mark-up will cover overhead and provide a fair profit. It is only effective for those skilled in pricing.

The following formula can be used to calculate price using cost plus mark-up:

$$\text{Price} = (\text{Direct Matls} \times \text{Mark-up}) + (\text{Est. Time} \times \text{Hourly Rate})$$

$$= (\text{Total Production Costs}) \times (\text{Mark-up})$$

Calculated Mark-Up

In the calculated mark-up approach, each product and service is analyzed to determine its associated costs. Then a mark-up is applied to each product or service based on demand, perceived value, and similar factors. *Mark-up* or *cost-based* pricing is often used on time and materials contracts.

Standard Mark-Up

In this method a business owner partitions the products and services into specific categories. Each category is assigned a *"standard"* mark up. The appropriate mark-up is then applied to each element in a category.

One form of the standard mark-up approach is to allocate a basic rate to each cost center in the shop and then uses these rates and the productive hours available to estimate a job. This approach is called *budgeted hourly rate* pricing.

Accepted Reference Mark-up

There are two versions of the *accepted reference mark-up* approach. One is to establish base prices for all products and services by analyzing the actual operating costs and then adding the appropriate mark-up. The final "standard" prices are then published in an "in-house" price list. The retail price list page is shown to customers. Some shops call this the "counter price sheet."

The second approach is to purchase a book of industry standard rates for the products and services that you offer. This book is then consulted each time a job estimate is required. The Industry Standard Rate book is most useful when it accommodates location and market conditions.

Except for competitive bid situations, mark-up pricing is probably not appropriate because it doesn't maximize profit when the possibility exists to charge as much as the market will bear. In addition, the cost basis for service is often difficult to determine. Nevertheless, mark-up pricing is often considered the fairest pricing method for both buyer and seller.

Cost-Plus Pricing

In *cost-plus pricing*, the customer pays for the cost of developing a product plus some percentage or fixed amount above cost. For example, a customer brings a complex and inter-dependent project to you. There are elements in the project whose costs are uncertain. Instead of trying to "guesstimate" your costs, you offer to do the job for your costs plus a percentage. I've successfully implemented this strategy when a customer wants services that I don't provide. I subcontract the job and provide my client with a copy of the actual invoice from the subcontractor. On my invoice, I add a percentage to the subcontractor charge for my administration of the job.

Cost/Volume Pricing

In this approach, a cost/volume curve such as that shown in Figure 1-1 is generated to equate the volume of sales income to manufacturing and overhead costs. It shows graphically that as you increase sales, the net unit manufacturing costs decrease. A percentage of the cost of sales will expense out as overhead, so as volume increases, the cost of goods or services sold (per unit of product or service) actually decreases. This suggests that if you lower your sales price, more people should buy, and the added volume should further increase your profit.

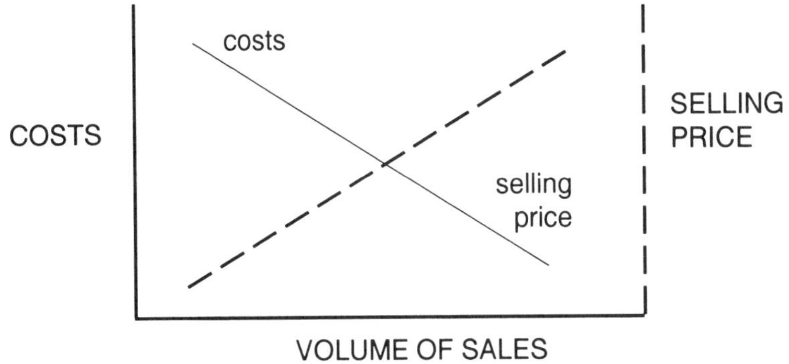

(Fig 1-1. A typical cost/volume curve.)

Some people call this approach *"doing yourself in."* It's risky because it presumes that your competition will sit still while you manipulate prices in the marketplace. This approach is based on your having an accurate assessment of the customer base and of your competition. And it assumes that you clearly understand your costs on a product-by-product and service-by-service basis.

The Cost/Volume approach is often a trap, because as you lower your price, your competition usually lowers theirs in response. You effectively become a price leader on the way down toward insolvency. The inherent risks are simply too great for most shop owners to attempt. Trying to optimize sales using a cost/volume curve is risky.

Profit-Oriented Pricing

There are three forms of profit-based pricing—targeted profit, targeted return-on-sales, and targeted return-on-investment. In all three methods, you balance revenues and costs to establish a selling price.

Targeted Profit Pricing

In this method, you set an annual profit target of a specific dollar amount. You determine your fixed and variable costs. Then you estimate how many units of a product or service you can sell and how sensitive demand is to price. Next, you set a target profit value and decide what price you can charge.

Since profit equals revenue less costs, we can use the following formula to derive a price.

$$\text{Targeted Profit} = \text{Total Revenue} - \text{Total Cost}$$

where

$$\text{Total Revenue} = (\text{Price}) \times (\text{Quantity})$$

$$\text{Total Cost} = \text{Fixed Cost} - (\text{Variable Costs} \times \text{Quantity})$$

Therefore,

$$\text{Profit} = (\text{Price})(\text{Qty}) - [\text{Fixed Cost} - (\text{Variable Costs} \times \text{Qty})]$$

Solving for price, we get:

$$\text{Price} = \frac{\text{Profit} + \text{Fixed Cost} + (\text{Variable Costs} \times \text{Quantity})}{\text{Quantity}}$$

This simplistic formula assumes that the price you select will not change the quantity of sales realized from those estimated. It also doesn't account for the investment needed to achieve the sales volume (cost of goods sold).

By knowing your cost of goods, the revenue you want and the profit you want to earn, you can back into this formula and determine the best quantity and the best selling price to use by changing the variables in your "what if" cost/price breakdown spreadsheet.

Targeted Return-on-Sales Pricing

This method focuses on achieving a minimum percent return on each sale. In this case, you use the same fixed and variable prices established for the Targeted Profit pricing method, with the same quantity of sales. Then apply this data to the following formula:

$$\text{Targeted Return} = \frac{\text{Targeted Profit}}{\text{Total Revenue}}$$

$$= \frac{\text{Price x Qty - [Fixed Cost + (Vble Costs x Qty)]}}{\text{Price x Quantity}}$$

Solving for price we get:

$$\text{Price} = \frac{\text{- Fixed Cost - (Variable Costs x Quantity)}}{\text{Quantity (Targeted Return - 1)}}$$

The negative values in the top and bottom of the formula cancel out, resulting in a positive price value.

Targeted Return-on-Investment Pricing

The *targeted return-on-investment* pricing method assumes that you can obtain at least as good a return on the money that you invested in a business as you can by investing in financial securities. If you feel that you can get a 15% return by investing in stocks, bonds, mutual funds, etc., then you can develop a business model that relates price, quantity, unit variable costs, fixed costs, overhead, taxes, etc. to yield the same 15% return on investment for a number of variable business options.

In this method, you select a profit and then work backward to determine what pricing will cover your expenses and still yield your desired return.

This is a sophisticated version of cost-plus pricing. The profit-oriented pricing methods are ideally suited for computer spreadsheet analysis.

Competition-Oriented Pricing

In *competition-oriented pricing*, you establish prices based on what your competition is doing. Referencing your prices to what the competition charges is a common business practice.

This approach includes price matching and percent-above or percent- below pricing strategies. The options that you can use include accepted customary pricing, subjective (at, above, or below market) pricing, and loss-leader break-even pricing.

Accepted Customary Pricing

Here, the customer expects to pay a "standard" fee for certain products or services. For years, black and white copies cost 10¢ each. To raise your price to 15¢ would exceed the accepted price threshold of your customers and they would shop elsewhere. When paperback books were priced at $3.95 each, and printing costs increased, a publisher would change the quality of the paper, or the quality of the binding to keep manufacturing costs low so they could hold the $3.95 price constant for the buying public.

Bucking the accepted standard price can also be risky.

Going-Rate Pricing

This method is common. It's based on charging what the competition is charging. It doesn't require analysis to determine the best prices for a profit objective. And it assumes that your competition is being successful by charging the prices that they charge.

There's a risk involved when you assume that your competition knows what they're doing. They could be selling at a loss or below acceptable profit levels without your knowing it. If all the competitors begin matching each other, everyone can lose money together. Some say "misery loves company," but this is taking the adage too far.

Subjective Pricing

After years in the business, owners get a "feel" for what a price should be. Using this subjective feeling, they then can price their products and services at, below, or above this benchmark.

Businesses that target their products and services for a specific market, will price accordingly. If you want to sell to the high-end corporate customer, you will price your products and services to meet the expectations of this market. You will base your prices on your opinion of what is acceptable.

Loss-Leader Pricing

In *loss-leader* pricing, a product or service is sold at break-even or just below cost to attract customers to your business and to sell them on your other products and services. Your goal is not to increase sales of that "no-profit" product, but to attract sales of other higher-margin products and services.

Composite Pricing

You can combine several pricing methods to produce your own composite. For example, you can establish one set of prices for established products and another for new products. You can price for flexibility, for a particular market niche, bundle your products, price for leadership, and price for market share.

Each method assumes different goals, objectives, assumptions, and requirements. Each method also has its own deficiencies. The optimum way to price is to develop a composite that includes the best things from each approach.

Use the industry standard rates. Consider the competition's pricing. Do a cost analysis on your own business. Determine the time it takes you to perform certain tasks. Place a value on your skills and your experience. Then, wrap all this into a custom pricing book that works for you.

Once your draft price book is complete, adjust and fine tune the basis for each price to create your own final rates. By developing a custom rate book, you can quickly and accurately provide an estimate without having to spend a lot of time re-constructing your business cost basis. With your composite pricing guide, you can bid on jobs with full confidence that a desired profit margin is already integrated into each price quote. A computer spreadsheet program can be used to develop pricing models that you can adjust to find the optimum strategies for each product and service.

Estimating Demand

Demand for your products and services is directly influenced by the customers that you target — their tastes and preferences, their income, the size of this market, and the price and availability that you establish. These demand factors can be represented in a curve that graphically shows the maximum number of products and services that you believe customers will buy at a given price. In the demand curve shown in Figure 1-2, the vertical axis is price. The horizontal axis represents quantity of sales. The curve shows how changes in price affect changes in the quantity of a product or service demanded by the customer base.

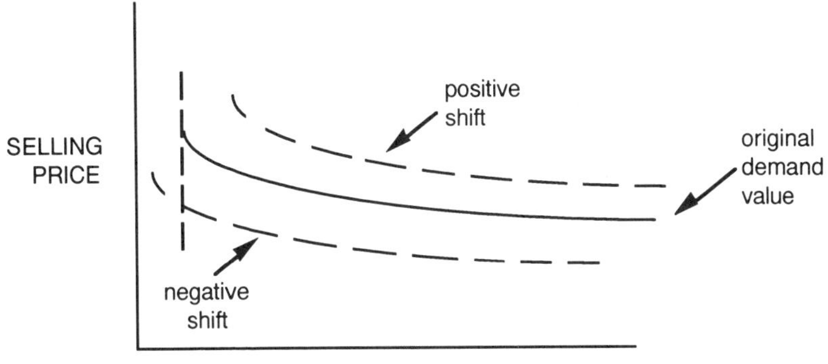

Fig. 1-2. A typical demand curve.

The trick here is to determine where the curve should be on the graph — selling price versus quantity sold. An increase in the size of the market causes the curve to shift to the right (positive). An increase in competition causes it to shift to the left (negative). An increase in the income level of your customers causes a positive shift to the right—more products are demanded. An introduction of new technology can cause a negative shift of the curve (to the left). An increase in the need for desktop publishing and prepress services will cause a positive shift of the curve (to the right).

Therefore, as you encourage the corporate and private users to buy more DTP and prepress services, our profession as a whole will benefit. This is why associations and other organizations are so important in making business better for the good of an industry or profession.

Elasticity

The slope of the demand curve is called its *"elasticity factor."* If the market for a product or service is price sensitive, demand is said to be *"elastic."*

A decrease in price can generate enough additional sales to increase the total revenue because the product demand is elastic. If a change in price has no effect on total revenue, the demand curve is said to have *"unitary elasticity."*

And if a reduction in price actually results in a decrease in revenue, the demand is said to be *"inelastic."* In this case, raising the price would generate more revenue because of the higher price received for each unit sold.

Figure 1-3 describes the elastic, unitary elastic, and inelastic demand conditions.

Fig.1-3a. Elasticity of demand (Elastic).

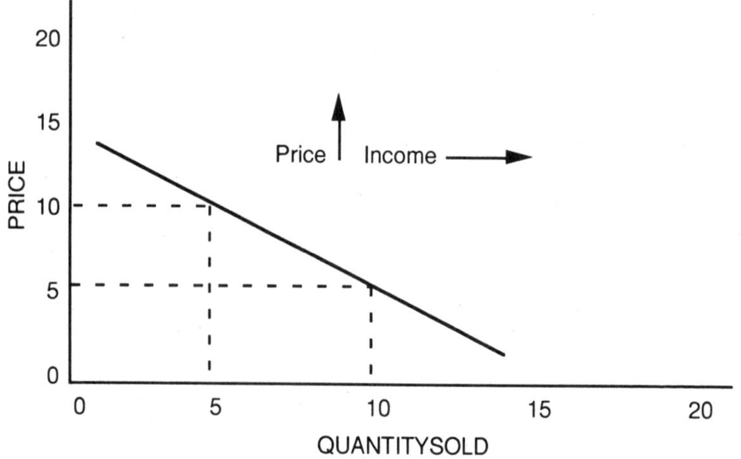

Fig.1-3b. Elasticity of demand (Unitary Elastic).

Fig.1-3c. Elasticity of demand (Inelastic).

The shape of the elasticity curve varies by product or service and by time. A product with a wide customer-base appeal is more price elastic than one with a limited appeal.

What Affects Elasticity of Demand?

Two factors have the most influence on elasticity—the relative importance of the product to the customer's budget, and the availability of alternative products. A high-cost job can make a customer price sensitive (demand becomes elastic), but an inexpensive job such as getting a 3-page letter printed out on a laser printer has little impact on a budget, so price sensitivity does not play an important role in their buying decision. This is why there are more promotions for support on larger projects than there are for relatively minor sales such as disk copying, data conversion, and simple hard copy printouts.

However, the availability of alternative products and services has a significant influence on demand. When there are dozens of DTP and prepress shops offering the same products and services, the customer will shop for the lowest price. This elasticity makes them price sensitive and they will have little or no shop loyalty. To hold these customers, you must be price vigilant and offer to renegotiate if a customer discovers a competitor offering lower fees. However, be cautious that you aren't being duped by the customer. And, also be careful that you don't accept a job at a loss.

How to Evaluate Elasticity

Elasticity is difficult to measure. The key here is to tap every available resource to determine all you can about the shape of the demand curve for those products and services that you offer.

Typical resources include market analysis, special reports, statistical analysis, market surveys, experimentation, and experience. Use your modem to access relevant on-line services. Contact your local libraries to get research support. Work through your local and national business organizations to gather information. Ask your colleagues. Ask your customers. Ask your competitors. Attend business lunches and networking groups. Gather intelligence wherever you are and whenever you can.

A recent study found that a price increase between 10% and 20% had little affect on reduced purchases, but an increase of 40% or more prompted customers to seek alternatives, including going out of town for support.

Actions in Each Demand Elasticity Situation

If demand is elastic, make every effort to price competitively. If demand changes little as price is varied, change your product or service to make it more elastic. If revenue decreases as price is increased (inelastic), consider raising your prices to generate more revenue (even with fewer sales). You could also compete based on nonprice factors such as the expertise of your staff or the speed of your response.

Perspectives on Pricing

The Changing Complexion of Pricing

The way service is being priced is changing. The mood is away from selecting a winning proposal based on the lowest bid. Although price will always be important, the buyer's perception of your ability to perform at an agreed price is becoming paramount.

In the past, many businesses earned a reputation for taking a loss on the first contract to "get their foot in the door." After the contract was awarded, they then tried to "get well" by promoting changes for which they could charge higher fees.

In our profession, as competition increases, customers look critically at differentiating factors such as quality, professional attitude, and value-added service. These factors should be considered part of your total pricing package.

Customers want to know how your service will be implemented. Will you use quality paper? What is your best print resolution? Will the layout be easy to modify? Can you expand your support as a need develops for other services? Are you able to consistently provide outstanding service?

The concept of quality is beginning to sink into the minds of buyers. The trend is for customers to make price a secondary issue. Many will be willing to spend more to get quality products and service. This phenomenon will be affected by economic downturns, but the trend strongly suggests that customers will gravitate to businesses that consistently offer quality service.

Notes on Pricing Service

In-house hourly service rates vary from $20 to $95 (prepress system work is often billed out at over $150 an hour). Few owners (18%) charge for travel time if they have to go out to a customer's site. Most shop owners place no value on the difference between a client bringing a job to them or to their sending someone out to pick up the job. They are accepting added costs without adding income at the other end.

A sad commentary is that few DTPers and service bureaus understand why they should charge a different rate for different types of service. Many owner/operators leave a lot of money on the table when they price a job.

Take a hard look at all the services that you provide. Assess the worth associated with the value of each function or output. Then review, implement, and adjust your rates accordingly. Recognize and then consciously decide if you still want to provide a service free.

Is Price King?

How much value do your customers place on your level of service? Depending on the type of customers to which you focus your marketing and advertising, the value can be significant.

Some DTP shops and service bureaus openly list prices 15 to 20 percent higher than competitors. But, usually these shops have earned a reputation for providing the best customer service in the area. Corporate customers will pay more when you make them feel that they're important to you and that your service is high quality and fast.

What Customers Really Want

The service and support provided by your business is rated by your customers based on the responsiveness and quality of your shop and the knowledge that your team has of the customer's business. Many customers want to know how your service and support can give them an edge over their competitors. If you can show them good designs—brochures, covers, etc.—that you've produced and that have won design awards, or that have been touted as among the top response-pulling ads in a publication, you'll win their business. Consistently strive to be the best.

Then, find out what your customers really want. Develop an organization that can listen well and is consistently sensitive for market intelligence. Go to great extremes to learn the business of each client. Many of them operate on a minute-to-minute schedule and can't afford delays. Discover their concerns, problems, and frustrations. See if you can provide solutions to part of their needs. Understand their document generation problems and then make a sincere effort to help them solve each problem.

Customer surveys suggest that the most important factors driving purchase decisions are price, quality, and commitment to customer service—in that order.

Looking Beyond Price

Once a prospect gets attracted by your price, other factors come into play.

1. *Shop image.* This is produced by the way your people answer the telephone, how they react when customers enter your shop, and how you and your people treat each customer during and after a sale.

2. *Ability to meet specification.* Don't advertise or suggest capabilities that you don't have. Focus on what you can do best given the people, the equipment, and the time that you actually have.

3. *Work samples.* Have a portfolio of samples to show your prospect. If possible show them how they were produced. (e.g., Let them watch you prepare a sample application in the computer and then print it on your laser printer or imagesetter. Let them see you cut, trim and bind some workbooks for a local company.) Not only does this give them an idea of your operation, it may spark ideas of other projects they may want to have you do for them.

4. *Pick-up and delivery.* Time is money. If a client can hand off a job to you and then focus on what they do best, everyone wins. Explain to them that their time may not be well spent driving across town to bring a job to

you or to drive over to pick up completed work. Suggest that you pick up and deliver the work (for a modest fee).

5. *Distance from customer.* Increasingly, businesses are seeking local support. Therefore, concentrate the majority of your marketing and advertising in your own neighborhood.

5. *References.* You may convert a reluctant prospect to a solid customer by offering to let them talk to other companies to whom you've provided products or services. Be sure to get permission from each reference before you suggest that a prospect call them.

6. *Quoted versus actual delivery date.* Delivering a product 10 days early may be as bad as delivering it 10 days late. An early response could introduce possible storage and loss or damage problems for the customer. It's best to negotiate a delivery date and then to deliver on that date or a day earlier. Avoid late deliveries. These can cause the loss of repeat business.

7. *Payment terms.* We all want cash up front, but America is a country based on credit. So, develop a "terms and conditions" strategy that is comfortable for everyone. On small jobs, let them pay in full upon delivery. On larger jobs, get a percentage up front, a percentage upon completion of some agreed milestone event, and a final percentage upon completion and sign-off of the job. For loyal repeat customers, work out a net payment time for your work, but be open and up front with them regarding the need for working capital to do the best job you can for them. Since most of your customers will likely be small business entrepreneurs, they will understand cash flow and are usually easy to work with on payments. Frank and honest communication is the key.

Will Customers Pay for Added Value?

Everyone wants more value added to a product or service. But few seem willing to pay for it.

Those companies that boast many forms of added value—free pickup and delivery, overnight response, special document design classes, etc. will find a ready market for the "free" part of their service. But, with desktop publishing becoming so common, some customers perceive that the availability of desktop design makes document layout a commodity form of service. They have difficulty accepting that good layout doesn't just magically occur. As more and more of them actually attempt DTP on their own, they begin to realize that a lousy design on a powerful computer with very capable software is still a lousy design. Education and experience make believers (and ready customers) out of these people. However, many of them become quite adept at spotting the new business offering "added value" at little or no cost. They swoop in on inexperienced business owners and literally suck the energy and capability out of these unsuspecting operators, leaving a broke and broken relic, milked into giving quality work at pauper-producing prices.

The High Price Myth

Some perceptions about your business are complimentary and can work to your advantage. If a competitor describes you as aggressive, your best response may be to simply thank them. If you're known as high priced, this can be bad. It can also be very good.

Being labeled as expensive is not bad as long as you provide plenty of value for what you do. If your fees are among the top in your area, you can only affect this perception by lowering your prices. However, if you do this, you risk suggesting a reduction in service or quality.

Actually, customers will grumble, but they'll pay more if you're perceived as providing the best products and services available. The best restaurants are expected to charge top rates. Yet, they don't lack for customers.

A printing industry rule of thumb is that if you don't get at least 20 percent of your customers complaining about your prices, you've probably set your rates too low.

Keeping your fees high means that competition can challenge you with lower rates, but they may not be able to survive the extremely low profit margins. After all, just like in retail, business success in DTP is based on margin. We can purchase the same types of equipment and hire the same type of support. What makes us different is our operating location, how we perceive and apply customer service, and what margin of profit we are willing to accept.

Easing "Sticker Price" Shock

An article in *ThePage* described how to add clarity to a job and help customers overcome the shock of seeing a large project price. The article suggested that you generate an "Instructions to the Customer" sheet describing the things that the client can do to prepare and format text and graphics so your job is easier and faster and their bill is lower. Provide this suggestion guide prior to the start of a job.

The way a client prepares the work for delivery to you can directly save you time and your customer money. Explain to the customer that they can reduce job costs by carefully preparing the work before they bring it to you. Ask them to provide their input in the formats that your equipment can easily handle. Some shops provide the use of screen fonts so a customer can design their document in a form as close to final as possible.

If you must take raw text files and flow them into a page layout template, explain to your customer that they can reduce their costs substantially by giving you files in a form that makes your layout work easier and faster. Suggest that they provide text without any formatting. Have them use a tab or extra blank line to indicate new paragraphs. Ask them to use an agreed code such as [1], [2], [3], etc. to designate different levels of heads and subheads. Ask them to provide hard copy art in a size that you can easily scan into the computer.

For art and photographs that you will strip into the document, explain that the cleaner they make their graphics, the less time you will spend cleaning them up for the stat process.

Explain how they can make the importing of text and graphics smoother and faster and directly affect the bottom line of their invoice. Show them how they can save project costs by considering a different paper or a lower resolution output. Suggest the use of clip art in place of custom art. Suggest different ways to handle color. Explain the cost implications of each approach. Describe your discount programs and how a customer can save by bundling work or purchasing work in quantity. Not only will they save project dollars, but you will be gaining a loyal return customer and likely several referrals in the process.

Summary

Price and pricing is a fascinating and dynamic area of business. Now that you understand price and how it affects the success of your business, you can see that many factors are involved in the prices that you set. In the next chapter, you'll explore pricing strategies and discover how to develop your own hourly rates. You'll also learn how to generate your own counter price list.

Chapter 2

Developing Your Own Pricing Strategy

Pricing has been described as one of the most challenging parts of business operation. To succeed in business, as to succeed in sports, you must develop goals, objectives, and a strategy. In your business plan, you established your goals and objectives. This chapter will help you establish a strategy. Besides learning how to develop a strategic plan for successful pricing, you'll be exposed to creative pricing techniques currently being used by shop owners around the country. You will also learn when and how to raise prices, and when and how to reduce prices while continuing to grow a profitable business.

Terms to Remember

Break-even - That point at which income equals costs. Beyond this point, your company starts making profit.

Direct Costs - Those costs that can be allocated to a specific job or project.

Indirect Costs - Costs that cannot be directly associated with a job or project. These include both fixed and variable costs. Indirect costs are also called *overhead costs*.

Marginal - The change in producing just one more unit.

Marginal Costs - The addition to total cost caused by producing one more unit of a product or service.

Marginal Revenue - The addition to total revenue caused by selling one more unit of a product or service.

Overhead - Indirect costs that are allocated against each job. These include a portion of the fixed and variable costs associated with a project.

Price Points - The cents numbers that are included with a dollar amount in a price figure.

Pricing Objectives - The overall pricing goals or targets for your business.

Pricing Strategies - A framework in which your pricing objectives can be translated into specific (tactical) pricing actions.

Pricing Tactics - The actions or decisions that enable you to carry out your pricing strategies.

Developing a Pricing Strategy

Pricing decisions are often the result of hunch, gut feel, intuition, or "let's charge that price, too" reactions. Yet there are practical ways to make good pricing decisions. These methods become tools that a business owner uses to conduct market analysis and to develop business strategies.

Each prospective customer has a need that requires intelligent response to price, quality, and schedule. You add value by the way that you handle these factors. If you can offer the greatest value in at least one of these three areas, you should get more than your share of the available business.

There are two distinctly different types of customers that you must deal with in pricing your products and services—the *commodity customer* and the *solutions customer.* The commodity customer wants to buy a product at the lowest cost and neither wants nor desires hand-holding. The solutions customer wants the best price but also wants a source for answers when operations become too complex and confusing. There are many businesses that offer basic products without technical support. There are others who thrive on the premise that the customer needs information and place customer service and support paramount in their strategic decisions.

In today's economic climate, most customers seem motivated only by price. They'll quickly take their business elsewhere when problems arise or your quoted price exceeds their threshold. Although little customer loyalty exists (or business-to-customer loyalty, for that matter), the customer's expectations and attitudes still lag whatever business loyalty that may exist.

However, contrary to what you may now feel, the solutions-oriented business will likely supersede the commodity-oriented business within the next four or five years. Technology and information transfer are becoming too complex for simple solutions. The company that can guide a customer through a project will likely earn respect and more business. For customers only interested in price and output, you can establish a special rate structure for them (differential pricing). Or, let them seek out and purchase from the "canned-product" low price shops.

To develop your strategy, you must think like a customer. This means that you've truly got to know your customer. What first attracts them to a business? Price? Quality? Response time?

If it's price, then you must be competitive. I didn't say charge the lowest price in the area. Nor did I say be the most expensive (although there's much to be said for being among the higher priced companies). The key is to provide sufficient perceived—as well as real—value to warrant the prices that you charge.

A pricing strategy that encourages higher sales volume in an elastic market can produce stronger profits. If you adopt a pricing strategy based on maintaining a high margin, you may find your customers moving to another competitor. This causes some DTP shops to focus on unique and special services. With something distinct to offer, your margins are higher and the competition is reduced. The personal computer industry once enjoyed this position, but high margins brought in more competitors until price cutting erupted. Today, the PC is simply a hardware commodity. Their profit margins have gone into the tank.

A similar thing is happening in laser printing and imagesetting services. Some businesses have reduced their prices to a point that, although their volume is high, their margin is so low that profit is minimum. These businesses use the laser and imagesetter services as "loss leaders" while pushing other (added) services to recoup a healthy net margin.

One school of thought suggests that shops bundle services to minimize the complexity that the customer can perceive, offering a "total" solution to any job. Some customers prefer that they not get involved in the difficult stages of document design and printing. Anything that you can do to help in this process lends value to your business.

Typically, larger companies prefer a "bundled solution" approach. Small businesses will likely opt for the unbundled approach and purchase only those services that they can't provide themselves. They are reluctant to pay for services that they don't need or can do themselves.

Talk to any customer, and they'll say that quality is very important. Yet, when push comes to shove, many customers are willing to accept lower quality to get a better price or response time. It's up to you to find what quality they will accept and then produce to this standard.

To many business people, fast response is key. They are typically rushed on most projects and appreciate a support organization that can work evenings and weekends (if necessary) to get out a job that is well done and meets their harried schedule. Some DTP shops find that over 60% of their business involves rush jobs.

Critical Factors in Your Price Strategy

As shown in Figure 2-1, five factors define the range of options that you have in setting price —real costs and profits, the customer's perceived value of your products and services relative to alternative choices, the differences in the various segments of your market, likely reactions from competitors, and your company's marketing objectives. Each of these issues should be considered when you develop your strategy for pricing.

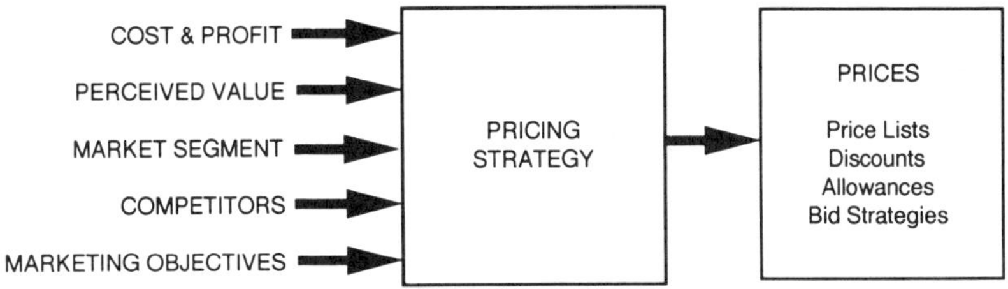

Fig. 2-1. Five factors affect the prices you charge.

Notice I said strategy. Many businesses are followers. They price their goods and services based on what competitors charge. But what happens when all DTP shops are doing the same thing? There is no leader, just price confusion. You need a logical way to determine what your prices ought to be. Then you can decide what you want them to be. At least you'll know the difference. And you will feel comfortable that you are pricing for profit, not for paucity (scarceness, or meager income).

You need to clearly understand why you are in business. Is your goal to build a retirement nest egg? Is it to build a large, thriving business to turn over to your kids? Is it to just have fun in life? Is it to earn all the money that you can by a certain age? Is it to return good service to a country that has served you so well? Whatever the reason, you need to recognize and accept why you are operating your business.

Next, you must decide the real nature of your business. Is your business to provide solutions? It is to provide time for others to do different things? Are you offering a profit opportunity for your customers? Are you selling layout and design, or are you selling worry-free publishing?

Consider the "Gillette safety razor" strategy. Gillette made his profit by selling blades, not by selling razors. He sold his razor at a loss so he could really sell the patented blades at a comfortable mark-up. What the customer wanted was simply a cheaper shave. Gillette sold a way to get a one penny shave—substantially less than going to a barber at the time.

Xerox adopted the Gillette razor pricing strategy and developed a huge market by selling a copy of a document, not by selling a copying machine. There could be a Gillette razor in your business too.

From your analysis you can develop a mission statement that explains why you are operating your business. Take time to write a brief mission statement describing what kind of company you are and where you intend to go. Chart your course.

With this statement clearly in mind, gather your staff and begin an analysis process leading to goals and objectives. Look at your products and services. Are you providing the right products and services to the right markets in the right time frame? What about your competitors? What products and services are they offering? What is their market position? What can you determine about the area they cover, the prices they charge, and the extent of their business? Can you spot any weaknesses in their strategy?

Based on this assessment, establish short term and long term goals for your business. Decide where you plan to go, what you plan to do, and where you plan to be three years from now. Do you want to improve efficiency? Quality? Market share? This self-introspection process is best accomplished as a team—all of your full time staff should be involved.

The goals that you establish form the basis for your marketing plan—your road map for operations. A key to surviving a competitive market is good planning followed by good plan execution.

After a look at the long range, take a shorter view and answer the same questions for the near term. What do you want to accomplish each year between now and three years from now? This is the basis for your tactical plan.

Based on the strategic (long term) plan and your tactical (short term) plan, carefully establish business objectives. These objectives should be specifically expressed and be not only achievable, but measurable. Each objective should have an associated responsible person and deadline for accomplishment.

Part of these objectives address pricing. Based on these, develop a pricing strategy that represents a framework in which your pricing objectives can be translated into pricing tactics. These tactics become the specific decisions or actions that you'll follow to carry out your formula for success.

Once you've clearly defined the goals and objectives for your business, communicate these to your staff. It is from these goals and objectives that you establish specific tasks for each of your employees.

As you implement your plan, monitor the daily operations and periodically measure quantitatively how you and your team are doing in meeting your objectives. When an objective has been met, tell your staff. Then reward everyone for their part in making success happen.

If your goals become unrealistic, change the formula, change the ground rules, or change the players (if necessary). It's important to accept change in your formula for success. Change will occur. And only by revising your goals and objectives can you keep everything on a known path.

Eight Steps to Setting Price

There are eight steps that you must perform to arrive at the price for a product or service.

1. Identify the constraints and objectives in your pricing strategy.
2. Estimate the demand for your services.
4. Estimate the possible sales revenue.
4. Estimate the demand elasticity associated with your product or service. You need to know the pros and cons of each of your products and services. You need to know how customers and your competitors will react to any price change you may make. To help, get input from people outside your company—customers, vendors, colleagues, and your competitors.
5. Determine the cost, and analyze its relationship to sales volume and profit.
6. Select an initial set of prices based on demand, cost, profit, and competition.
7. Establish the pricing policy on which you base your list or quotable prices. This can be a single price policy, a flexible price policy, or an incremental cost-revenue balancing policy.
8. Make adjustments to your list of quotable prices based on discounts, or special allowances.

Establishing Pricing Objectives

Pricing objectives are the overall goals or targets that you want to reach.

Typically, short term objectives focus on achieving some level of profit, surviving a down economy, protecting your market share, discouraging or weakening competition, preventing a rival with a cash flow problem from disrupting the market, getting a specified return on investment, or achieving some level of personal satisfaction and reward.

Long term objectives can include becoming a recognized leader in the marketplace, achieving top quality in a particular area, reaching some specified sales volume, or positioning your business for a financially rewarding sellout.

Whatever you decide, be sure to make your objectives consistent with the mission statement that describes your business. Some businesses use return-on-investment (ROI) as a measurement. Others use inventory turnover and number of sales to help decide if an objective has been met.

If you decide that you want to target the upscale and more sophisticated customer, then design your shop and your business forms to reflect this ambience. But don't then set your rates to appeal to the price-sensitive customers. If you want to be unique, then your prices should reflect this. They also should be in line with your expenses.

Study the Market

Make a thorough study of the potential in the market that you've selected.

How many people are buying your products and services? How many are located in your immediate area? What's the demographic trend for the future? What is the purchasing power of your market? What prices are customers willing to pay right now? Who are your customers? What businesses are they in? What businesses will they be operating in five years?

Determine Demand

Use the tools described in the previous section to determine market demand. Estimate the demand elasticity of each of your products and services. With this information, develop your own strategy for pricing.

Study the Competition

Take a long, hard look at your competitors. What are they doing right? What are they doing wrong? How are they pricing their products and services? What "extras" are they offering? Who are they? Where are they? How successful do they seem? Where do they advertise? How often? How large an ad do they place? What professional groups or organizations do they join? What does their financial statement (10-K financial report) tell you about how successful they are? What markets do they seem to be serving?

Then make some strategic decisions based on your findings. Should you price to match your competition? This serves to stabilize prices and avoid costly price wars. But it can stagnate your business. Is a niche market developing that is not being served? Should you focus on this niche market and then price to avoid competition? This action lets you make a reasonable profit without attracting new competitors.

If your products and services are in strong demand and there's a shortage of businesses like yours, you could maximize your profits by raising prices to "the most the market can bear." Be aware that this high pricing could be perceived as "gouging" and "unethical" by customers and business colleagues. Bear in mind that the customer eventually dictates price. And if a competitor is attracted to your niche, those over-charged customers have memories like an elephant. The trick is to set your prices high enough to keep customers, but not so high that you attract new competitors, or so high that the legality of your pricing becomes an issue with government or other local businesses. Remember, if you charge very high prices over a short term, you risk losing market share to competitors who are willing to offer the same or similar services at lower prices.

Study the Economy

Make an assessment of current economic conditions. What is the business climate? What is it expected to be next year? Who are the winners in this economy? Which businesses are growing? Which are stagnating? Which are declining? Who's reducing staff—laying off and offering early retirements? Are there opportunities for short term business with those companies that have reduced staff yet retained document-generation requirements? What are the current governmental fiscal policies expected to do to businesses in your state? Which companies are headed toward Chapter 11 bankruptcy? Which are already there?

During uncertain times, there are several actions that you can take to ease the economic affects on your business. You can eliminate credit. You can modify your discount policies so your customers get a larger discount for paying early. You can even reduce the discount that you offer. You can reduce the net payment due time. You can unbundle products and services to offer more selection to price-sensitive customers. You can also price for delivery from your shop and not include shipping or free pick-up and delivery as part of your own cost of doing business.

Estimate Your Costs

Few shop owners know their actual costs. In fact, when owner-operators calculate their true costs, some have discovered to their dismay that their operating costs exceed revenue. They are actually paying more to earn less.

But what is cost? And how does cost relate to productivity and profit?

There are several types of costs that you must incorporate in your pricing strategy. These include wages, overhead expenses, return on investment, and profit. Your costs are also influenced by the productivity of your shop. Each of these will be discussed in some detail.

Essentially, your costs of doing business must be partitioned into fixed costs, variable costs, direct costs, indirect costs, and overhead. These terms are related and are often confused.

Fixed costs are those expenses that you must pay whether you have little or lots of business. Fixed costs don't vary with sales volume. They exists just because you are in business. Fixed costs include:

- rent	- most utilities	- grounds keeping
- parking	- salaries	- insurance
- taxes	- depreciation	- etc.

For example, you must pay someone to produce service income. It doesn't matter if you perform design and layout or another person does the work. One or both have to perform billable work to generate income. Some shop owners fool themselves by not considering their own direct labor production in calculating costs. However, most DTP shop owners are also designers and technicians. They should charge their time to the business and be paid for their efforts.

Variable costs are those expenses that change with the level of business activity. They include:

- cost of goods sold
- supplies
- fringe benefits
- commissions
- marketing
- advertising
- wages (part-time help)

If you take on more projects, you'll use more paper, more toner, and more electricity. The additional electricity is a variable cost. Part of your utility bill is a fixed cost. Thus, some expenses are semi-variable—part fixed, part variable. You should separate these into the fixed and variable components for good cost analysis.

Direct costs can be directly related to a job or project. These costs can be related to a unique project number or work order. Direct costs include:

- Salaries of employees who directly work on a project (direct labor)
- Equipment leased or rented to do a job
- Materials used on a specific project
- Consultants hired to support a project
- Computer and software costs associated with a specific job
- Documentation purchased to support a job

Anything that can be charged directly to a job work order (direct labor, direct materials, etc.) is a direct cost. Commissions or finders fees paid for activities that result in a job can also be considered a direct cost.

Indirect costs are those expenses that can not be directly charged to a specific job or project. Indirect costs become overhead expenses to your business. Indirect costs can include both fixed and variable costs.

We collect the indirect expenses that we must pay whether or not we sell a product or service and call these our *overhead costs*. Indirect or overhead costs include:

- rent	- utilities	- management salaries
- marketing	- advertising	- secretary/clerk pay
- insurance	- taxes	- vacation expenses
- supplies	- depreciation	- vehicle expense
- maintenance		

Overhead costs do not include designer and technician wages. The overhead for a shop is pro-rated — partitioned into a cost per hour and then distributed — to each service that the shop performs. Typically, you calculate your annual overhead costs and then allocate a portion of your overhead costs to the total hours worked during a year. The total hours worked depends on your staffing and how many hours each person worked. One person working 40 hours a week with two weeks vacation equals 2,000 hours of work a year.

A DTP shop or service bureau will typically have overhead costs that equal 40-50% of the shop's income. A reasonable amount of your overhead costs should be allocated to each job or hour of billable time.

If the more expensive hardware and software are typically used by the higher paid employees, your overhead costs closely track your labor costs. If everyone uses all the equipment and software, your overhead costs will track with the shop's billable labor rate.

Therefore, overhead can be expressed as a percentage or as an hourly rate.

There are two ways to calculate overhead. In shops where pay can be directly associated with the equipment used, overhead is expressed as a percent.

$$\text{Overhead (\%)} = \frac{\text{Total Overhead Costs}}{\text{Total Direct Labor COSTS}}$$

Conversely, in shops where there's little difference between the hourly wages for the employees, and everyone works on all the equipment, you can calculate an overhead rate based on the actual costs and hours billed.

$$\text{Overhead (Hourly Rate)} = \frac{\text{Total Overhead Costs}}{\text{Total Direct Labor HOURS}}$$

Figure 2-2 is a composite drawing showing the various components that comprise total costs. General and administrative costs are often called *"G&A."*

Your monthly billable hours vary based on many factors. For example, a freelance DTPer working out of a home office will only bill about 150 days a year—100 hours a month. The rest of the month is spent on market-

Direct material costs	Direct labor costs	Shop overhead costs		
Shop costs			Selling expense	
Total shop and sales costs				G & A costs
Total costs				

Fig. 2-2. The various components of total cost.

ing and non-earning follow-up. This will affect the daily labor rate and the fees that are charged.

A monthly $6,000 overhead expense and a 22 days-a-month billing factor results in a daily overhead cost of $272.73— $34.09 an hour ($6,000 a month divided by 22 days a month divided by 8 hours a day equals $34.09 an hour). If you earn $100,000 a year and bill 264 days each year, your daily labor rate is $378.78 [100,000 / (22 x 12)]. This equates to $47.35 an hour.

Dividing the hourly overhead cost by your hourly income yields an *overhead factor* of 72% (34.09/47.35 = .72). This is how much of your hourly labor rate is allocated to paying for overhead.

Obviously, overhead costs can be significant. They can easily eat up more than 70% of your gross income. An overhead of 40-50% of your gross income is typical. The *labor rate* that you establish must cover your overhead expenses.

Some shops calculate overhead by combining both direct and indirect costs (total annual expense). Then they convert this overhead into a *burden rate* by subtracting direct labor from the total annual expense and dividing this result by the direct labor expense.

Burden rates can exceed 200%. The burden rate is added to the hourly fee to generate a *burdened hourly rate*. This means that each employee has a portion of overhead allocated to their billable work whenever they bid a job. A DTP designer making $15 an hour could have an overhead load of 125% ($18.75) making their bid labor rate $33.75 for that person's support on a job. Large companies often use accounting systems that apply the burden rate concept.

Return on Investment

Not many shop owners take time to think about or calculate the amount of money that they've invested (poured) into their business. But if you borrowed money to buy computer equipment or software, you would surely pay interest on the loan. The same holds true if you were to "loan" money to a business—your business. You deserve at least the same interest earnings on your loan. This is called "return on investment" or simply ROI. If you put money into your business, but don't consider it a loan that earns interest, you're cheating yourself.

Even a modest return of 4% on your investment will just keep up with inflation. You should calculate the ROI "cost of seed money" to capitalize your business, and include ROI as a repayment cost factor when you establish your prices and service rates.

Business Profit

This is not the same as the money that your shop makes and that you put into your pocket. There are cycles of activity in every business, and you need some reserve to pay the bills when job opportunities are slow. This lets you avoid borrowing from the bank (or your personal savings account) during economic down-turns.

Typically, a shop will factor in a business profit of 5-10% of total sales income. This profit should be considered a cost and should be factored into your prices.

When you analyze the cost factors associated with your shop, you'll probably find that your labor and direct expenses make up 30-40% of the total expense. Marketing will eat up another 20-30%. And nonmarketing costs will chew up another 20-30%. Return on investment will fall between 5-10%, and expected profit should be between 10% and 20%. Each time one of these cost factors increases, you must take some action to reduce another cost factor to maintain your desired return on investment and profit percentage. Everything you do to reduce your overhead expense adds that much more to your bottom line profit.

Calculating Shop Productivity

For smaller shops, overhead is probably the best approach for tracking costs. But productivity plays a major part in the formula. Using overhead and expected productivity, you can calculate what you could charge per hour for your services. Productivity impacts your shop billing rates because your calculated hourly rate must be divided by a productivity percentage to establish your actual budgeted hourly rate.

Not all employees are as productive, and you yourself will not be as productive each day of the week. Besides working on income-producing tasks, you'll also be answering the telephone, sorting mail, making out invoices, performing maintenance, and a myriad of other non-billable tasks.

According to the so-called "30-60-10 Rule" for small business, you will spend 30% of your time marketing, 60% of your time actually performing billable work, and 10% of your time handling paperwork and chasing after payment. When you consider the time spent preparing for a job and cleaning up after a job, you will probably bill out only 50% of your available time. Your shop will be 50% productive at best.

Productivity is directly affected by the number of employees in your shop. While productivity is usually between 30% and 60%, most shops seldom exceed 40%

productivity. A "one-person operation" typically achieves no more than 30% productivity. Two or more people in a shop can achieve 40% at best. And it takes about five employees to reach a productivity level of 50% or more.

Productivity doesn't relate directly to costs. But if you establish a billable rate for service, you can determine how productive your shop is and then determine what hourly rate you need to charge to be profitable. If your shop is 50% productive, you can divide the income needed each hour of operation by a productivity factor to determine how much you really need to charge for each hour of service just to keep your doors open. For example, if you calculate that your hourly rate should be $15, at 50% productivity, you should actually charge $30 an hour to effectively make $15 for each hour that you work.

I you pay a designer $8 an hour, your overhead is $4 an hour, and you want to earn 10% ROI on your startup investment and 10% in profit, you may decide that you need $15 an hour coming in. Dividing the $15 by a 50% productivity factor (expressed as 0.50) yields a $30 per hour rate. This is what you must charge to realize the $15 an hour average net income that is actually desired.

A shop billing out at $25 an hour and 30% productive actually brings in $7.50 an hour—$300 in an average 40-hour week. It's critical that you know the productivity of your shop. The higher the productivity, the lower you can set your hourly rate to make the same return.

There are two ways to determine productivity. First, you can compare the labor billed by an employee each week with the hours worked and the hourly rate that the shop charged for those services that the employee provided. This productivity formula is shown below.

$$\text{Productivity} = \frac{(\text{Labor Income Produced}) / (\text{Hours Worked})}{\text{Shop Hourly Rate}}$$

If one of your people earned $500 in labor charges for the shop, worked 40 hours that week with a shop hourly rate of $25, that person's productivity is 50% [(500/40) / 25 = 0.50].

A second way to structure the productivity formula is to multiply the shop's hourly rate by the number of hours worked and then divide this figure into the labor billed (the income) as shown below.

$$\text{Productivity} = \frac{\text{(Labor Income Produced)}}{\text{(Shop Hourly Rate) (Hours Worked)}}$$

Thus $25 an hour for a 40 hour week yields $1,000. Dividing 1,000 into the $500 earned yields 0.5 or 50% shop productivity.

Some shop owners skew their productivity percentages by working 12 or more hours each day. If they were to work the numbers correctly, some of them could discover that they are actually paying their customers just so they can perform work for them. Productivity is a hidden hazard to profit.

Calculating Individual Productivity

If you measure the productivity of each employee, you can determine what each person contributes to the total required income. Based on this you can compare the skill level and performance of employees who routinely perform the same tasks.

By combining the billable hours generated by all of your employees, you can derived a productivity figure for the shop. Many owners also calculate the productivity for each employee as a basis for pay and promotion opportunity. A basic rule of thumb is that each direct labor person should bring in about 2.5 times their wages. This works most of the time, but a better measurement is to compare the labor income for services rendered with the actual hours billed at the shop's hourly rate.

For example, assume that a designer worked 40 hours and brought in $400 in labor charges. Your shop rate is $35 an hour. But 40 hours at $35 an hour should have generated $1,400. Dividing $400 by $1,400 yields a productivity of 28.6%. If another designer could generate $500 in the same 40 hours, this person's productivity would be 35.7%. Assuming each spent an equal amount of time answering the telephone, filling out forms, and handling other administrative functions, the second designer would be worth more to your shop than the first. The pay that they earn should reflect this. Be willing to pay for performance.

However, any measurement of productivity should be balanced with factors that take time and effort away from income-generating tasks. Resolving a customer problem and improving customer satisfaction should be considered in providing a balance between productivity and adequate customer service.

Factors Affecting Productivity

Most of us have found ourselves assigning selective tasks to certain people. Consciously, or unconsciously, we've judged the ability and productivity of our staff. When we combine certain individuals, we can sometimes realize an increased productivity due to the effect of synergy—their joint efforts produce a result greater than what each individual could achieve if they worked alone.

However, several factors can directly affect the productivity of an individual or a team. Interruptions play a significant role in productivity. So does a "down" day, when people are at the low ebb on their biorhythm curves. A full 8-hour "person day" doesn't mean an 8-hour "productive day."

A significant portion of time is spent refocusing after unscheduled interruptions. In fact, studies suggest that refocusing after an interruption can take as long as 20 minutes. And this is for EACH interruption! If you get interrupted six times a day, you could lose two hours of productive time. Interruptions directly affect job schedule and worker performance. However, you can affect how and when interruptive activities are handled.

A fully focused worker in a larger shop is typically 70-90% productive. This output is reduced by the number and severity of interruptions.

Four types of interruptions affect productivity—telephone calls, co-worker interruptions, visual interruptions, and sound interruptions. If you can relieve your people of the need to hear and respond to customer telephone calls and spontaneous questions, their productive day will approach a full person day. A quiet and private working environment is the single, most effective thing you can provide to directly improve productivity.

Associated with these productivity factors is the impact of a request to "expedite" a job. As people are pushed, the risk of error increases. When you measure the actual time spent on a job, you must include the time needed to rework mistakes. You should mark up jobs that a customer wants "expedited."

How Costs Vary During a Project

There's no question that your cost basis changes during a project. As you use more time on the equipment, your electrical and telephone (and possibly water) use increases. You also incur additional costs in paying for part time help. Work pick up and delivery and trips to buy materials adds to your gas and vehicle expense. Then you'll use more paper, film, toner, chemicals, or other materials in conjunction with a project. This will increase your project costs. These variable costs should be charged directly to the appropriate project.

If you obtain new equipment or upgrades to software, be aware that installation and checkout costs average between 2.5% and 10% of a system's total cost. The actual costs depend on system complexity, the hardware and software mix required, and staff involvement. These costs should be amortized over the life of your equipment and be charged to each job proportionately. Be aware that Congress is trying to extend the "useable life" of software so you'll have to amortize your expense over several years rather than sooner, even when updates typically occur annually. Be certain to charge fixed costs associated with work on a particular project directly to that project. The more fixed costs that you can legitimately bill out to a project, the easier the pain when you evaluate your overhead costs.

Break-Even Analysis

One of the best ways to understand the relationships between cost, sales and profit is by performing break-even analysis. This business technique helps you identify the point at which cost equals income. It is the sales volume or quantity point where your costs are covered and profit begins.

There are two ways to approach break-even analysis—by comparing total sales volume with costs or by comparing total items (units) produced and sold with cost. In both methods, you must understand all of the expenses associated with your business. Part of your costs are fixed and don't change with the volume of sales made—rent, utilities, salaries, insurance, and taxes. Other costs vary with the job—hourly wages, the costs of raw materials and additional utility expenses to produce the goods or services that you sell. To make a profit, you must pay both your fixed and variable expenses and then have some income left over. These residual dollars go into profit and return-on-investment (if you loaned money to your company).

The challenge is to find the point at which your costs are covered and profit can begin to accrue. This is break-even analysis. Your inspection can be made on a grand scale (looking at your total business sales and costs) or on a product-by-product basis.

Whether you choose a sales volume method or total units sold method of break-even analysis, your first step is to determine your fixed and variable expenses.

Sales Volume Method

This technique relates income to cost. First determine your total fixed costs. This becomes a reference baseline to both forms of break-even analysis. Then calculate your total variable costs. Divide the total variable costs by the total number of sales to get an *average variable cost per sale*. You can also determine your *average dollar per sale* by dividing the total revenue by the total number of sales. Then by dividing the average variable cost per sale by the average dollar income per sale, you can find the percentage of variable costs in each transaction.

An average variable cost of $9 and an average selling price of $14 yields 64.3% *variable cost percentage*. Each time you earn one dollar, 64 cents goes to pay for your variable costs and your business keeps about 36 cents. But this is not profit. Not yet. You need to apply this money to pay your fixed costs before you get to count your profit.

$$\text{Avg Variable Cost per Sale} = \frac{\text{Total Variable Costs}}{\text{Total Number of Sales}}$$

$$\text{Avg Dollars per Sale} = \frac{\text{Total Revenue}}{\text{Total Number of Sales}}$$

$$\text{Variable Cost Percentage} = \frac{\text{Avg Variable Cost per Sale}}{\text{Avg \$ per Sale}}$$

To determine how much sales volume you need before you get to keep the 36 cents earned on each dollar of sale, you need to find the break-even point. Express the percent as a decimal and subtract it from one (1 - 0.643 = 0.357, the 36¢ extra on each sale). Then divide this result into your total fixed costs. If your fixed costs are $36,000 annually, you will need $100,840 in sales income before all of your fixed and variable costs are covered (1-.643 = 0.357 and 36,000/0.357 = $100,840). Sales above this point will generate profit.

$$\text{Break-Even Point} = \frac{\text{Total Fixed Costs}}{1 - \dfrac{(\text{Average Variable Cost per Unit})}{(\text{Average Selling Price per Unit})}}$$

$$\text{Break-Even Point} = \frac{36{,}000}{1 - (9/14)} = \frac{\$36{,}000}{0.357} = \$100{,}840$$

If you assume that changes in sales volume don't affect your average selling price, that your fixed costs remain constant, and that your variable costs change in direct proportion to sales, you can plot costs versus sales volume as shown in Figure 2-3 on the next page.

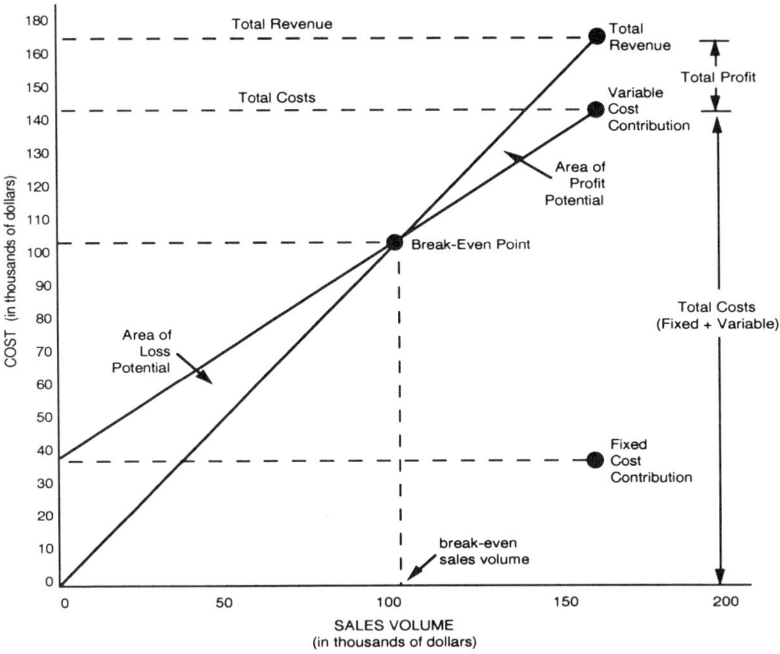

Fig. 2-3. Break-even analysis chart based on the total sales volume method.

In this case, the horizontal axis represents the volume of sales. The vertical axis represents dollars in costs and revenue. Break-even occurs at $103,000 dollars in sales.

Total Units Sold Method

Another way to perform break-even analysis is to determine how many sales are required before costs are covered and profit can accrue. To do this, you need to determine the margin of contribution made by the average sale and the average variable cost per sale. The *contribution margin* is the difference between the average price per sale and the average variable cost per sale.

$$\text{Break-Even Point} = \frac{\text{Total Fixed Costs}}{\text{Unit Selling Price - Unit Variable Cost}}$$

Dividing the total fixed cost by the contribution margin yields a break-even quantity. Using the same numbers in the previous method, we see that an average sale of $14, less an average variable cost of $9, yields a contribution margin of $5. Dividing our total fixed cost of $36,000 by the $5 contribution margin, we get 7,200 units of sale. This means that we must sell 7,200 units at an average price of $14 to cover our fixed and variable costs.

$$\text{Break-Even Point} = \frac{\text{Total Fixed Costs}}{\text{Contribution Margin}} = \frac{\$36,000}{5} = 7,200 \text{ units}$$

To get the break-even point in dollars, multiply the break-even point in units by the unit average selling price. This will check the arithmetic of the first method (7200 x $14 = $100,800).

By using the same assumptions as we did for the total sales volume method, we can plot costs versus units of sale to show graphically when break-even occurs (Figure 2-4).

The $5 made on each sale is applied first toward the fixed costs and then toward profit. If we lower our average sale price, we contribute less toward paying for fixed costs and less remains for profit. This also means that we push the break-even point further out to the right.

Typically, the smallest 20% of your orders account for less than 5% of your sales income. It may not be worth making these sales . There's a point at which your fixed costs exceed your income and you should decline the sale. The break-even chart shows you graphically

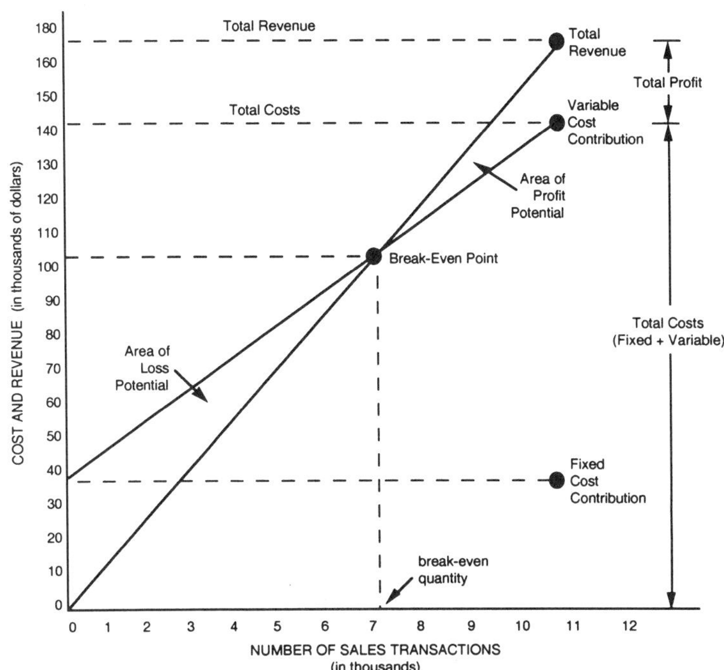

Fig. 2-4. Break-even analysis chart based on the total units of sale method.

why some sales just don't make financial sense. A pallet of low quantity sales may generate revenue that is consistently below your fixed costs with a small variable cost added. This suggests that you should decline these sales, or add a surcharge (charge a higher price) for low dollar sales. This is why many shops have a sliding scale of prices for laser printing and imagesetting output. A lower per unit price is charged for larger volume jobs.

The ideal way to perform break-even analysis is to develop a model using a computer spreadsheet. This lets you dynamically change the variables and determine new break-even points based on different selling prices and costs. It's particularly helpful when you begin changing the per item price.

Break-even analysis can help you decide the viability of a prospective new product. It can show you when it's too costly to produce and sell at a selected price. To increase the income generated, you may have to raise your prices. But this is not always possible. Competition may hold your prices too low to make this product or service worth selling. Your costs can also vary.

Break-even analysis isn't perfect. It doesn't consider discounting, customer demand (elasticity) and the actions of competitors. Nevertheless, it can help you quickly see the impact of various pricing strategies. It's one of the tools that you have for managing your business. By knowing the break-even point, you can determine which products or services to offer. It helps you decide if making an unprofitable sale to gain a long term customer is really worth the sacrifice. And it helps you highlight excessive fixed overhead expenses such as rent, leased equipment, and staff.

To succeed in this business, you must consider every analytical tool that might help you make better pricing decisions. Break-even analysis is one of the better tools.

Margin Analysis

Another management tool is a technique called *"margin analysis."* This tool evaluates the cost and expected income associated with producing and selling more of a product or service. It focuses on profit maximization rather than break even. In margin analysis, the cost associated with producing "one more" unit of a product or service is called its *"marginal cost."* The added revenue associated with selling just one more unit of a product or service is called its *"marginal revenue."*

As shown in Figure 2-5, a Margin Curve can be constructed showing the relationship between price, quantity, cost, revenue and demand. As more units are produced and sold, the average cost decreases, pulling the marginal cost down. The marginal revenue also declines because the most recent sale becomes a comparatively smaller portion of the total income.

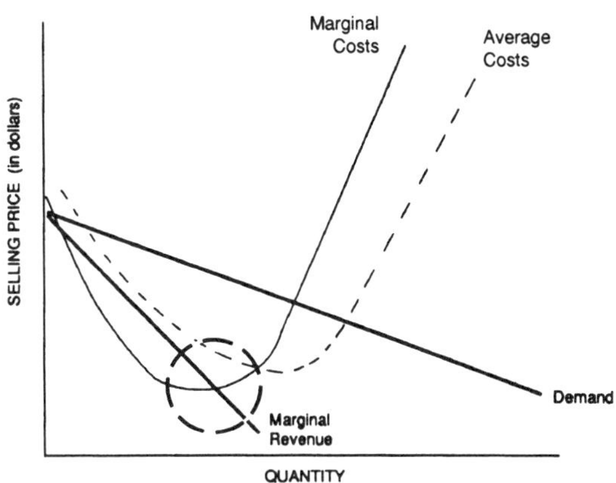

Fig. 2-5. A Margin Curve showing the relationship between costs and revenues as demand and quantity increase.

A point is reached when you must expand your facilities and increase your equipment and staff to handle additional business. This added expense makes the marginal cost and average cost curves bend upward. The key here is that maximum profit is realized at the point where marginal cost exactly equals marginal revenue.

If we then focus on the area where marginal costs and marginal revenue intersect on the margin curve (Figure 2-6), we can identify a point where more business won't generate additional revenue for the company.

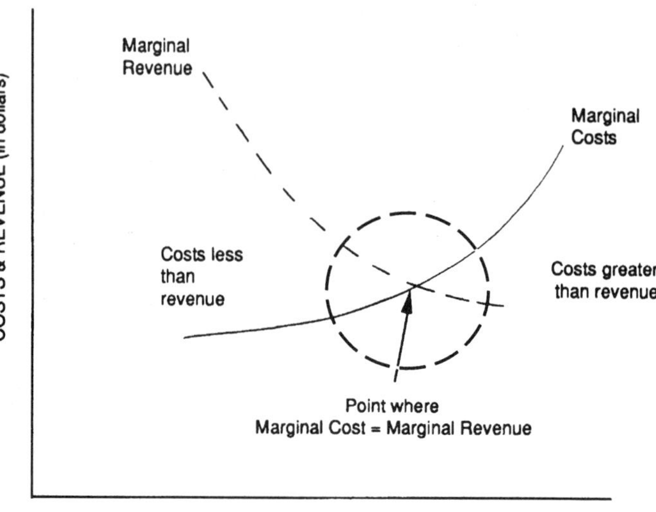

Fig. 2-6. A Margin Curve showing the relationship between marginal costs and marginal revenue.

The idea is to find the margin crossover points for each product or service that you offer and then strive to hold sales of each item at the point where marginal revenue exactly equals marginal cost.

Finding Optimum Order Size Using Margin Analysis

An interesting technique for determining if marginal orders are really worthwhile is to find your optimal order size. This requires knowing your cost per order and your *gross profit margin*. The process works like this:

First, find the spread of your orders by sales size. Some will be less than $25, others will be between $25 and $100, others $100 to $500, and so on.

Second, for each spread category, determine the total number of sales, the total sales dollar value, the percent these sales are of the total sales, and the average sales dollar per order.

Third, find your gross profit margin. Subtract the total cost of goods sold (all categories combined) from total sales (all categories combined) to get a *gross profit*. The *cost of goods sold* represents the total costs to produce the products or services that you sell. This includes inventory raw materials such as paper, toner, film, etc., and direct labor charged to the jobs. By dividing the gross profit by the total sales, you can calculate your gross profit margin. Multiply the gross profit margin by 100 to get the *percent gross profit.* This is the percent of revenue left over to manage the business, sell the products and services, and provide profit and return on your investment.

Fourth, determine your *distribution costs.* These costs include order handling, billing, and salaries for everyone involved in fulfilling the order (but not directly involved in producing the order). A customer calls in. Someone handles the call, takes the order, places the order, adds the order to the job queue, receives the completed job, packages the order for delivery, delivers the order, bills the customer, and processes the payment. The monies expended to do these things become your distribution costs.

Fifth, determine your *average distribution cost per order.* Divide the distribution costs incurred over a year with the number of orders handled. Even though some orders will be large and some small, this estimate provides a fair assessment of what it costs to fill an order.

Finally, calculate your *break-even order size.* Divide the distribution costs per order by the percent gross profit to find the order size needed to break even on the sale. If it costs you $14 to handle an order and your gross profit margin is 35%, you need an average order size of $40 (14 /0.35 = 40) just to match your costs—to break even. On a $36 order, you can expect to earn $12.60. But if it cost you $14 just to handle the order, and you only earn $12.60, you would be losing money just by accepting the order. However, if you got a $250 order to design a newsletter, the cost to process and distribute the order is still $14, but your expected gross profit is $87.50. So after you subtract the $14 processing cost, you have $73.50 as a contribution to overhead and profit.

Break-even and margin analysis provide a valuable picture of your business and help you develop an optimum pricing strategy. Cost analysis gives you a clear picture of the margin possible, but your competitors' price lists still influence the price strategy that you eventually adopt. A good market-driven strategy considers both the internal cost issues and the external customer and competitor marketplace in setting price.

Tactical Pricing Actions

Armed with all the market intelligence you can collect, and both break-even and margin analysis, you can determine the tactical actions that will let you reach or exceed the strategic pricing objectives that you established earlier.

For example, if part of your strategic pricing objective is to achieve a 20% return-on-investment, you could implement tactical actions that identify those price levels that yield this desired return. A strategic pricing objective of surviving an economic downturn could mean that you set prices at a level that will keep business coming in while allowing your shop to scrape by with enough income to cover costs. A strategic objective of avoiding competition could include tactical actions that set prices to discourage competition.

Pricing Problems

There are three primary problems with the way that many DTP and prepress businesses price products and services. First, they under-rate the real value of their products and services. They don't realize how much they freely give away. Second they don't understand how the marketplace perceives DTP products and services. A perception of quality should command a higher price. The trick is to find a niche where your products and services are acceptable and perceived as valuable.

The third problem occurs when owners assume that all DTP and prepress products and services are alike. If you have a unique product or service, price it to what the market will bear—especially if you've invested time and money into its development.

Taking Time to Price It Right

Pricing is one of the most important tasks you have in business. You should evaluate demand, determine all your costs, and then decide what profit is acceptable. These are not trivial issues. Actions by your competitors, the government, and technology all affect how you operate.

The value associated with your pricing also depends on the perception of the customer. This perception is based on what other options your customers feel are available and their expectation of benefit by purchasing from you rather than a competitor. Customers have a feeling of what a price should be. This becomes their basis for acceptance. They also have a threshold above which they simply won't buy. Above this point, they will accept lower quality or choose another option.

Your business will earn a reputation as it grows. This image has much to do with what a customer expects to pay. If your shop is perceived as providing good, high quality service, your prices can be higher. If your business is perceived as a cut-rate job shop, your prices should reflect this too. You must decide the image that you want to create. Then you must work hard to develop and maintain this image.

Observe the retail department stores. Some stores are considered expensive price leaders. Others are perceived as low-cost, low-price outlets. Yet the low-price store doesn't always have a lower product price than a high-price store.

Sometimes, a higher price stimulates demand because a customer perceives added value. Yet, on other occasion, the same product sold at a lower price can also stimulate sales demand. Pricing is an art. There are too many fickle variables to make it a science. Yet we use as much science as possible to make the art of pricing easier to comprehend and apply.

When pricing products and services, some shops incorporate flexibility in their list prices so they can hold occasional sales. They add 15-25% to their initial prices, then lower the "retail" price by some percent while shouting "SALE" in their ads.

Real estate people recommend adding about 10% to the expected selling price of a house so you can negotiate down and arrive at a final price that seems a win for both buyer and seller.

Urgency also plays a factor in your pricing formula. If you have a product or service that suddenly comes into strong demand, apply the "WOW" formula and increase your prices to meet what the market will bear. Just remember, if you set your prices too high, competition will appear and challenge your sales success. Pricing takes skill, patience, and luck.

You must price for profit, and this means consistently evaluating the success of your strategy and readjusting your pricing as necessary. By taking the time to price right, you create the opportunity to profit more.

Pricing Your Services

Much of today's pricing is still done by the "seat of the pants." An acquaintance recently confessed, "I'm swamped with business designing one page flyers for $10 a pop, but I just can't seem to make any money at it." Of course not! This person didn't do a cost analysis and integrate a value for her own time and experience into her price formula. Intuitive and reactionary pricing decisions are dinosaurs in today's dynamic fast-paced world.

The same factors that you consider in arriving at a price for your products—costs, perceived value, market segment, and marketing objectives also apply to pricing your service. By systematically addressing each issue, you can clarify your own business goals and objectives and select a pricing strategy that best fits your situation. Only through logical, sound, and consistent decisions can you establish profitable prices.

The top factors determining your price are the competition that you face and the price your customers are willing to pay. Price is therefore strongly influenced by external forces, not strictly your own costs. Your customers don't care what it cost you to provide service. They care only what you charge them, the quality of your work, and how soon you can deliver.

This means that you'll have a tough up-hill struggle raising your prices unless you can develop a perceived difference in the mind's eye of your customers. If you can't, or you're the new kid on the block, you must adopt a "community standard" pricing strategy. This is essentially a *"going rate"* pricing format. It pays less attention to your costs or to marketplace demand and more to the prices that your competitors are charging.

Pricing Service in a Competitive Market

Pricing can be both a challenge and a source for headaches. Pricing is usually considered the main tool to gain new business. Often pricing strategies center around reactive formulas such as scurrying to match a competitor's price change.

There is a better way—combine cost-based pricing, competition-oriented pricing, and demand-pricing. Adding a desired margin to a cost basis to come up with a price is *"cost-based"* pricing. This is a no-strategy method to establish price.

When we set our price 10-15% lower than the competition to lure price-sensitive buyers into our fold, we are applying *"competition-oriented"* pricing. This method accepts a lower margin. But what do you do when your competition already has their prices set for minimum margin? You could sell yourself right out of business.

Basing your strategy primarily on competitive pricing can work in the short run. But it can also generate a downward spiral that causes competitors to match each other's lower price on the way down and out. This can also cause buyers to perceive your product or service as just another commodity.

By developing a marketing strategy, you make pricing a pro-active event and not a defensive activity. A typical marketing strategy addresses product, place, price, and promotion — what will be sold, where it will be sold, at what price, and how it will be promoted. Solutions to these issues define the strategy of your business. Your marketing strategy becomes a plan that identifies the goals and objectives for the company. A pricing strategy is then developed to support the marketing plan.

Countless pricing formulas are hypothetically possible. You picture yourself as a shop owner who wants to be known as a high volume service-oriented operator, so you price your services 15% less than the leading service bureau in the area.

The price leader retaliates by selectively discounting its services to meet your lower price. This causes you to lose business.

You realize that you can't develop any lasting competitive advantage by price alone. You decide to reposition yourself away from a strategy based only on price. Analyzing your strengths and weaknesses, you decide that magazine and catalog publishing is where you are strongest. You develop a marketing strategy based on premier support to businesses that seek help designing and printing magazines and catalogs. You build on your expertise and offer experienced support, fast response time, and quality output. Your prices reflect the premier concept. You develop a promotional strategy that is consistent with your business focus. Sales build, and your shop thrives.

In another scenario, you envision yourself as a shop owner who wants to provide service to the city, county, state, and federal government customers in your area. You know that laws make government buyers very price sensitive, so you develop a low-price strategy based on product cost. However, you discover that low price by itself won't guarantee sales and long term success. Your service product must be packaged so it exactly meets the government specifications. It should provide nothing more, nor anything less. You redesign your service offering so it can be delivered at minimum cost in the exact form the buyer expects. You restructure your business to be profitable based on this service offering. You down play promotion and focus on getting on every qualified bidders list you can. You ignore the public market and limit your activity to government organizations. Your business grows.

A flash of insight later, you imagine yourself a service center with expertise in a unique field or in producing a unique product. For example, you have a particular expertise in working with prepress color. You invest in the equipment and software to exploit this expertise. Then you focus your promotion on those companies who use color documents. You build a capability to handle any type and form of color input and to produce any type and form of color output. You build a reputation for having every support and service tool available related to color work. By becoming the dominant provider of color services, you develop a business that is almost insensitive to price. You set your pricing based on perceived value. But you don't set your prices so high that others are tempted to enter your market niche. While providing high quality service, you set your prices moderately higher than your major competitors.

You conclude that market-driven pricing is the best way to go. You accept the hard work associated with gathering market intelligence. Rather than basing your price solely on historical production standards, experience, and on reference tables of standard costs, you decide to integrate all of these into a strategy unique to your particular market.

The amorphous mass of intelligence data that you gather begins to coagulate into a pricing strategy. You test the strategy against your estimated costs to see if the margins are acceptable for quoting a particular job. If the margins are too low, you pass on the job. Or, if you decide you still want the contract, you work even harder to improve the efficiency of your operation. You consider better equipment, better working techniques, and reduced overhead expenses. Combining cost and market-driven pricing fosters more efficient operation.

Through the preceding scenarios, the consistent theme is that a pricing strategy is based on a marketing plan. And the marketing plan is consistent with the objectives of the business. Just as a marketing plan shouldn't be established in a vacuum, your pricing strategy should have input from all aspects of the business. And it should reflect the goals and strategies of your company.

Once a marketing plan and a pricing strategy have been developed, build a system to implement these business decisions. Establish procedures for pricing new products and services, and for modifying existing prices as market conditions change.

Pricing actions are governed by state and federal laws. Besides the restrictions on collusion and price fixing, you must be concerned about perceived price discrimination. Competitive pricing is a key component in your business plan, but it should not conflict with law.

Discounting

Another way to approach pricing is to sell your products and services at discount. This approach is based on the "high volume gets discount" concept. The risk here is that you must cover not only the cost of your goods and labor, but you must also account for basic selling expenses such as marketing, advertising, and commissions.

If customers base their buying decision on price alone, you can always be late, as long as you offer the same quality and service as your competitor, but at a much lower price—20 percent is a much lower price.

The *list price* is that price that you quote when you get a call. This price can be adjusted based on a discount or allowance. *A discount* is a reduction from the list price that you apply to a customer's purchase when they meet certain conditions. These conditions include paying cash instead of using a credit card or asking for a net payment schedule, paying early, buying a large quantity of work or service from you, buying during a seasonal promotion, and a trade discount if the customer is reselling the work to another client.

A customer may also qualify for a reduction from the list price for performing some activity. This *allowance* works like a discount. It can be a special markdown for including your promotional flyer in the customer's catalog. It can be a reduced price for participating in a community service project or becoming a member of a certain club or organization.

In some shops, the list price is really just a fictitious number—a wish price—from which to discount. In these businesses, products are rarely sold at list price. If this is how you operate, you're bound to encounter prospective customers who only care about the difference between what you list and what they actually pay.

In some businesses, list price is only important if you put it in your advertising. And publications like this that list comparative prices have no choice but to use each company's list price. It would be better if we had a "price tolerance" gauge that measures what a buyer will pay for a product or service. Then we could use this gauge to evaluate what DTP and prepress shops are willing to charge.

Once desktop publishing shops and prepress service bureaus become more sophisticated in developing pricing strategies, actual prices will adhere closer to published prices. Immediate discounting from your list prices can make a buyer wonder it they're really getting the best deal. As we become better at pricing our products and services, the buyer will not be offered (and expect) discounts, and the confusion that arises between listed prices and actual prices will disappear.

Discounting and the Law

You must be careful if you're considering discounting. A deep discount may constitute unlawful price discrimination. Section 2(a) of the Robinson-Patman Act relates retailer pricing policies to distributors and resellers. It says that it's illegal for a retailer in commerce to sell commodities of like grade and quantity at different prices for use, consumption, or resale, where the effect of the discount difference will substantially lessen competition or create a monopoly. Software publishers sometimes get into trouble on this when they discount to their authorized dealers more than they do to a standard distributor. The differences must be "cost-justified" to the extent of the seller's actual cost savings incurred in making, selling, or delivering the product to a particular reseller.

Services are also considered a product. You can discount to one customer if that customer uses your output, but assumes a higher marketing cost.

Creative Pricing Strategies

There's pricing, and then there's pricing. In this section I'll share some of the creative ways that others are pricing their products and services.

Floor Price Plus Some

Determine the minimum price at which you are willing to sell a product or service. This becomes the *floor price*. Then establish a target sales price. Any sale that is less than the floor price will result in a loss. So by clearly defining your "must-sell-at" and "want-to-sell-at" levels, you can determine how each sale impacts the profitability of your shop. This lets you sell at different price levels and still have a feel for profit per sale. You can accept lower margins on some sales and higher margins on those sales in which you enjoy a market niche. The trick is to avoid tying up valuable resources on jobs that contribute little to your bottom line. Each sale must be evaluated relative to your available capacity and where the sale income falls in your floor/target price range.

Calculated Cost Plus 70%

In this strategy, you calculate your job cost and add 70% more, disregarding any discount. This becomes your selling price—simple to calculate and simple to apply.

Percent Capacity Plus Margin

Here you calculate your standard costs as if your shop is operating at 70% of capacity. Then you add a specific "margin" equal to your standard costs to arrive at a price.

Net Revenue, Inventory Sell Off

Also called *net revenue marginal analysis*, this approach is used to determine when the last item in an inventory lot has been sold. It lets you reduce the selling price for remaining inventory so you can eliminate dated inventory.

This technique is typically used for retail products such as disks of clip art, toner cartridges, etc. It can also be used to meet aggressive sales tactics by your competition.

Competing with the Competition

Shop owners occasionally implement creative pricing techniques, such as adding a "fair" margin of profit to their costs to arrive at a selling price. Then they compare this price with that being charged by other shops to see if their prices are competitive.

Another technique is to find out what a competitor is charging and then to charge five percent less.

Single Price, Any Customer Pricing

In this strategy, you apply a fixed price schedule to every customer. No customer gets special treatment. The high-end corporate customer pays the same fee as the non-profit, low-budget customer.

Tiered Pricing

You've unbundled your products and services. You've tweaked all of your charges. You found discounting a fast way to eat into profits, so you minimize offering discounts and allowances. And still your margins continue to squeeze your bottom line. You decide to go after the big accounts using a variable (*tiered*) pricing strategy. This means that you bill larger companies more for your products and services than you would charge a smaller business customer.

Your variable pricing strategy applies different prices to different customers. A high-end corporate client is charged a premium price while a non-profit organization or home-office entrepreneur is charged a much lower fee. There is a risk here for price discrimination so be sure to work costs and margins carefully.

Research indicates that large companies are often less fazed by higher fees than the smaller companies. These larger organizations are more concerned with your survival, availability and service support than they are with what you charge. They take longer to get signed up to your products and services, but they don't dicker over "nickles and dimes." Therefore, the larger they are, the better your chance of increasing your fees on everything you offer. These customers appreciate the value your shop has to offer and are willing to pay more for your support.

Some shops find that business from the larger accounts gives a strong boost to their net profit. However, you must factor in the additional effort required to realize the sale. The after-the-sale support can also increase significantly.

Often, large accounts will pay a consulting fee up front, but your cost-of-sale can also be larger because they may insist on a lengthy multi-page proposal before any contract is signed and billable work can begin..

Then, there's the specter of discounting. It never really goes away. It looms on the horizon even with large companies. If they make a volume buy, they will likely expect a discount.

This means that your pricing strategy for larger accounts takes as much analysis as your strategy for the average accounts. You can't just pull a price out of thin air because your prospect is a large company. The buyer is usually quite sophisticated, and they talk to others in the business.

One form of tiered pricing is to unbundle all of your products and services so you can sell each item individually. This lets a customer pick and choose the amount of product or service that they want. This strategy maximizes your ability to offer something for everyone.

When you consider tiering your products and services, carefully establish the size and scope for each pricing level. Some shops partition the prices of their products and services into essentially equal different levels—say 10 percent pricing packages. Each level of service and support includes a specific level of hand holding and type of support. For example, you could have one price for taking a document file and importing it into a "standard" style sheet layout. No alterations or other design changes can be made without incurring "extra" charges. There also will be no design consulting or suggestions for improvement. The input is simply converted into pages based on a fixed format.

For those who want a dialogue with the designer and who want to optimize the design, another tier of prices will kick in. This means that those who have the most experience can get a job done for the least cost. It also means that you and your staff will be paid for the work you actually do. This minimizes the "giving" without "receiving" syndrome so prevalent in DTP shops today.

New Product Pricing

Consider an early introduction pricing strategy that sets a relatively high price during the initial stages of the life of a product or service. This skimming strategy makes good sense when the demand for your service is uncertain, you've invested large sums of money in developing the capability, there isn't any known competition, and the service is expected to grow slowly.

If you want to build market share rapidly, adopt a penetration pricing strategy that sets a relatively low price during the initial stages of the life of a product or service.

Leadership Pricing

A *price leader* is a company that is able to make a change in their pricing based on cost and demand conditions without starting a competitive price war. This company can make a price change announcement and others will follow (not undercut) the new price.

If you intend to become a price leader, your business must develop and possess certain characteristics. Your shop must service a large share of the market. You must be committed to a particular product or service line and have a large share of the service capacity in your immediate area. You must have new, cost-effective equipment and support software. You need a closely controlled distribution system that can get price change information out quickly.

Be sensitive to the price and profit needs of your industry. Know pricing strategies intimately and have a sense of timing to correctly know when price changes are necessary. Good marketing research can help you forecast market response. You must maintain good customer relations and gain a reputation for providing superior customer service. With effective project management controls in place (and operational), and clearly understanding the legal issues surrounding any pricing decision, you can position yourself to be a price leader.

Operating as a price leader is perfectly legal as long as you don't conspire with another firm in making your pricing decisions. A price leader sets rates independently of the competition, although the prices that competitors charge are certainly considered during strategic analysis.

"One-Half" Pricing

Some small businesses have found a simple way to set rates. They adopt a modest pricing strategy in which they find out what the most expensive competitor charges and then cut these rates in half.

This pricing strategy sometimes works in systems integration environments where the markup is extremely high. But this "Power of One-Half" strategy presents high risk for the desktop publisher and service bureau. The simple solution may actually be no solution. In fact, it may convert all of your products and services into price loss leaders.

"2X" Pricing

Canadian DTPer, Don McCahill, uses a "two-times" (2X) rule to establish his fee. He takes what he wants to earn and then doubles this figure to come up with a budgeted hourly rate to charge.

If he wants to make $25 an hour after expenses, he'll mark up his services to $50 an hour.

"2.5X" Pricing

If you currently earn $50,000 a year, you're making about $24 an hour. Some DTPers apply a 2.5X multiplier to determine their budgeted hourly rate. To net $24 an hour, they charge $60 an hour (24 x 2.5). This rule of thumb lets them earn what they desire while covering overhead, fringes, administration, and marketing.

If you have a good handle on your overhead and capital investment, you can adopt a lower 2.1 multiplier. This reduces your fee basis to $50 an hour and still lets you net about $24 an hour after expenses.

"3X" Pricing

As a new kid on the block, many of your prospective customers wonder if you'll succeed and question why they should switch. They also question how your products and services will support their own operation.

Don Jones, president of four successful startups, was interviewed in *Success* magazine regarding his formula for taking on the large, entrenched market leaders.

He feels that you first need a product or service that's unique.

Then you need better resources and a significantly better product offering if you want to go after the business of an entrenched competitor. Jones says that you must provide products or services that are at least three times as good as the market leader.

This means that you must analyze your competition. Learn those qualities of the market leader that customers appreciate most. What are the things that make these customers take their business to that competitor?

There are two factors that you can address—product and price. You can take leadership away by developing a "goodness factor" of at least three. Sell a product or service that is three times better than anyone else. To address price, sell your products or services for one-third what the largest competitor charges. This can be difficult.

Only Pricing With Commas Accepted

A recent article in *Home Office Computing* described.how a technical writing and desktop publishing business successfully adopted a pricing strategy that focuses only on high price jobs.

According to the article, if a job does not price out to over $1,000 (has a comma in the number), the job is declined or passed on to another shop.

The strategy here is that jobs with small income potential do not leave room for negotiation. They also do not provide the profit potential that a bigger project can. The idea is to pursue the big dollars and leave the scraps — the business job tailings —to the low price shops.

A Penny Here, A Penny There ...
Adding Cents to Your Pricing Strategy

The cents numbers appended to advertised prices is an area where added profit can be made with little or no added cost.

Advertising a price of $5.36 probably won't generate any more sales than you would get by advertising a price of $5.95. But the higher price can add 59¢ of pure profit to the sale. Natural price points occur in business. Using these points lets you increase your asking price without changing a customer's perception of worth.

These price points have enormous influence on the buying patterns of the public. Mathematically, they represent discontinuities in a price elasticity demand curve. You can sell much more product at $5.95 than you can at $6.05, but not much more at $5.85 than you can at $5.95. Customers consider the 10¢ difference between $5.95 and $6.05 a major hurdle but hardly notice the difference between $5.85 and $5.95. This difference represents 10¢ of direct profit. Making an additional 10¢ on high volume sales can add up fast. Supermarkets make a business by working with pennies of profit.

Natural price points are more frequent at lower prices. Abrupt shifts in demand (price elasticity) are also more frequent at lower prices. Knowing these points of discontinuity can help you act to significantly affect your bottom line.

Eric Mitchell, publisher of *The Pricing Advisor* offers good advice on how you should use price points in your pricing strategy. He partitions product pricing into categories—less than $1, $1 to $10, $10 to $100, and more than $100. Each price category should be handled differently. Mitchell suggests that you can effectively add to your profit by pricing products less than a dollar at a value ending with 9—39¢, 79¢, 99¢ etc. When most customers consider a product selling for "less than a dollar," they notice the tens value, but not the cents value. Therefore, rather than pricing your product at 96¢, make it 99¢ and your customer won't care. The extra 3¢ income passes directly to your bottom line profit.

He further suggests that you avoid ending your product pricing with 1s, 2s, or 4s (e.g., 21¢, 42¢, 64¢), although ending in 5 is acceptable (e.g., 95¢). Just remember, you're trying to focus on profit. The more you can get for your product without changing the perception of value for cost, the better your profit picture.

For products priced between $1 and $10, Mitchell suggests ending the price with the digit 5 or 9 (e.g., $1.15, $1.39, etc.). Avoid using any other digit. A price presentation at $2.75 is equally as attractive as one at $2.79. And, a few cents here, a few cents there—pretty soon you've got real money. Especially if you're handling thousands of pages of data or graphics each week.

When the price exceeds $10, use increments of 25¢ or round off to a whole dollar value without cents (e.g., $11.50, $12, $24.25, $37.75, etc.). Between $10 and $100, he suggests that you avoid using the .99 digits (e.g., $11.99, $24.99, etc.). Mitchell feels that endings of $.25, $.50, and $.75 are preferable because they suggest fair pricing.

Above $100, Mitchell suggests that we stick with whole dollar amounts and never display the $.00 ending. A price of $110.00 looks much larger than a price of $110. It's all in the way we as customers view price.

This strategy is currently used in the pricing of trade and paperback books. Since 1965, publishers had priced their books using a $.95 point level to distinguish them from other consumer goods. This has changed. The decimal point prices have been raised from $.95 to $.99. Some publishers now round off to the next highest dollar point. Hardcover books are being sold with prices rounded off to the nearest dollar or the $.50 price point. None of the publishers have reported consumer resistance to this new pricing strategy.

Many other products are also being introduced with prices that end with .99 rather than .95. Mass market prices are rapidly being converted to the .99 point over the .95 point.

Since most publishing and service bureaus charge a round number fee, you may be missing out on a lot of added profit. There's little need to give up profit.

On Reducing Prices

Cutting prices can be dangerous. Value—not price—sells products and services. Cutting your prices introduces a risk of encouraging cut-throat competition.

If you've claimed to provide high-quality service and then cut your prices, some customers will suspect that you've been gouging them. Customer want quality, but at a cheap price. This forces you to walk a "value-quality-efficiency" tightrope. Your pricing strategy requires special skills and a mindset that can relate clearly to the customer.

IBM and Compaq drastically cut the prices of their PCs in the summer of 1991. Normally, during a sluggish economy, price cuts would stir increased sales. However, the cuts by IBM and Compaq were not enough to stimulate demand in a recession when resellers were consolidating. Sales remained relatively flat and conservative buyers stuck with the clone computers, believing that clones still offered a better deal (perception). As sales stagnated, these two computer giants experienced huge losses in revenue.

Cutting your prices to a point that it costs you money to sell your products and services just so you can "build or regain market share" may be foolhardy. You'll attract the "el cheapo" bargain hunters, but when you must raise your prices to make a profit, you'll find them moving on to the next "cut-throat" vendor. Everybody loses except the low-price bargain buyers.

You must decide if your business should provide more than "mail order" service. Do you really want to target "customers" who aren't willing to pay for solutions and quality work? Perhaps you should let them go and focus on customers who appreciate value and are willing to pay for understanding, empathy, and solution performance.

A shop with excess capacity typically considers price cutting as a way to keep the equipment active. This occurs openly, or is disguised as discounting.

"Shotgun" price-cutting — making price reductions "across the board" — can seal a company's doom. In this strategy, the listed price for every product and service is reduced by a set percent. The owner uses experience and guesswork rather than surgically-precise analysis to re-define the selling price of goods and services.

Cost analysis is not a discretionary activity. It's critical. You must know the exact cost for each product or service that you sell. Improperly calculating your cost factors can drive you into liquidation or bankruptcy.

Never reduce prices across the board. If you cut prices, cut them surgically, cut them intentionally, and know the effect of each action on your break-even profit point.

When Price Cutting Works

Reducing prices to build market share often results in a short-term reduction in profits. You can minimize this effect by moving to increase market share only when one or more of the following conditions exist.

1. *Customers only care about price.* These customers will shift to another shop just to get the lower price. They have the least loyalty of all the customer types. To attract and keep these customers, you need to offer a permanent price advantage. This is why some shops have a special price sheet for "corporate accounts" and a "counter" price sheet for walk-ins. You can make superficial changes in the style or brand of materials that you use, but you risk affecting the quality of your output product. You also risk upsetting current customers when the larger volume of added business means that they get less of your attention.

2. *The total market is growing.* Here, you don't have to "steal the sheep" from your competitors. You concentrate instead on inexperienced buyers of DTP and prepress services. A lower price attracts this segment of the market as they carefully dip their toes into the document generation and printing market for their first time.

3. *Your reputation for quality won't suffer.* If buyers measure quality by your response time and how you communicate, or by some other criteria, cutting the price of your product or services can attract more business.

4. *Your competition probably won't retaliate.* When your competitors are preoccupied with fighting off "alligators"—funding deficits, cash flow, unmet regulations, lower capable equipment, management and employee disputes—you can make a price move without their noticing, or being able to respond in like manner.

5. *Your current market share is small.* If you already have 50% of the market in your area, there's not much advantage in cutting prices. But, if you only hold 5% of the market, the potential for additional sales activity is significantly improved.

6. *Your resources are under-utilized.* There's an economy of scale when you can make every square foot of your shop and every piece of equipment work to generate money. Idle equipment and idle employees are costly.

7. *The margin will remain high.* If reducing prices to increase sales volume will reduce your variable cost per sale—the contribution margin (revenues less variable costs) should remain high.

If a majority of these conditions are present, it's likely that your price-cutting strategy will succeed.

How to Handle the Price Cut

Here are some suggestions on how to handle a price cut.

Look at past history. If you didn't raise your prices when your competitors did, determine if your sales volume and profit increased or decreased.

Offload excess capacity with "two-for-one" offers.

Consider occasional discounting, but watch the effect on positioning. You don't want a price cut to "cheapen the image" of a product or service.

Experiment with formal price cutting in just a few products or services. Don't make across-the-board cuts.

Cite the actual dollar savings rather than the percentage of savings in a price cut, so customers who know the prices will be attracted to your special offer.

Don't automatically follow the price moves of your competitors. They may not have done their homework.

Keep the new break-even point clearly in mind when you consider a lower price.

A Price Reduction Strategy that Worked

One company developed an effective strategy for holding market share while cutting prices. Every time demand rose by 10-20%, the company cut prices. This increase was not enough to make it attractive for the competition to enter that market niche.

On Raising Prices

Most shops are reluctant to raise prices. They feel that it's much harder to raise a price than it is to lower a price. This feeling is supported by studies suggesting that about 72 percent of all consumer buying decisions are based on price alone. With these statistics, you must be very careful when raising prices. You probably shouldn't implement added features or time-saving devices if doing so will increase your list prices by 20 percent or more. This could exceed the "threshold of worth" of your customer base. They'll find your actions unacceptable and seek other alternatives.

On the other hand, many shops literally "give away" labor income because they are afraid customers will balk if they increase their rates to a profitable level. You can only be generous if it doesn't curtail achievement of business goals. You are in business to make a profit. If not, close the doors and sell out. Otherwise, raise your prices so you can make a profit and get a decent return on any financial investment that you've made.

But be careful when considering a price increase. Besides alienating some customers, there is another risk to raising prices. The higher you raise your prices, the more you'll entice competitors to enter your type of business.

Keeping your prices high holds an "umbrella" of temptation over your competitors. If the temptation becomes too strong, they may add resources to compete in your market niche and unseat your leadership position. So when you consider a price increase, make each increase small.

A handy rule of thumb suggests that a 1% increase in price can produce a 10% increase in profit. This is usually a close approximation to reality because once you've developed your products or services, there's little added cost in raising your price, and any increase is applied immediately to the bottom line.

Your best approach is to conduct a product-by-product, service-by-service analysis. Then selectively raise those prices that warrant the action. Just don't raise prices excessively, or you'll alert your competition to a potential opportunity.

How Some Shops Handle Price Increases

Dealing with new customers is relatively easy when you plan to raise your prices. But for your current client base, many shops struggle with the mechanics of a price increase.

Some owners send a warm, personal letter to each current customer reminding them of the successful projects that they've shared in the past. Then they tell them that they are upgrading several capital items (software, hardware, etc.) to provide better, faster service, that inflation is causing higher operating costs, or that they are experiencing higher materials costs from suppliers. Next, they hit them with a small (typically no more than $5 an hour) rate increase. They set the effective date for the price increase about four weeks ahead to give their customers time to take advantage of the current low price. They reassure their customers that they will continue to bill at the old rate for any projects started before the price increase takes effect. Then they assure their customers that they value their business and look forward to new and challenging assignments in the future. Some shop owners include a paragraph that mentions projects that a client has talked about and may want to get accomplished right away.

Another school of thought suggests that you avoid advising your clients of a new hourly rate. This group feels that most shops give customers a quote based on more than just an hourly rate (including a flat fee for work paid up front or added charges for changes), so focusing on a higher hourly rate is unimportant. They also suggest that you not worry about what new clients will think of your higher rates. Most will not be aware of the old rates (as long as you change the signs and paperwork properly). If they are referred by another client, explain why your rate increase was necessary.

Quoting your new rate in a price increase letter may turn away major clients who are not comfortable paying $70 an hour, but who can accept a flat-rate estimate or a daily or weekly rate. Quoting an hourly rate instead of a flat rate to these customers can scare them away. Some people are simply not comfortable working with professionals who charge by the hour. For these folks, it's better to put a job into perspective by expressing project costs as a total package price.

There are other advantages to quoting a flat rate. This approach lets you build in fees and charges that would stand out like a sore thumb on an hourly rate price breakdown sheet. If you quote a job 25% lower than what customers can find elsewhere, you can incorporate a price increase while still giving the impression that they are getting your services for "peanuts."

Some shops charge "by the line" for alterations and corrections rather than at an hourly rate. When customers insist on an hourly rate, you can offer a lower hourly rate for handling alterations and corrections. This gives your customer a feeling that they're getting a bargain (even though you still earn a good profit).

How Much Can You Raise Your Price?

Finding the customer's point of acceptance/resistance is a challenge. It involves knowing your market, your competitors, and your customer base price elasticity.

An increase of $5 an hour may be palatable. Raising rates by $10 an hour may be too much.

If you're new and your business is evolving rapidly, shift immediately to a well-researched solid rate regardless what increment you determine is appropriate. Just be certain that your customers still perceive sufficient value in your services.

If your analysis and calculations indicate a $15 an hour increase is appropriate, take the steps to move immediately to this price. Most people recommend that you avoid the step increases because these can cause confusion and word will spread rapidly that one client got a similar job done for a better price. If you can justify the increase and give your customer base advance warning, boldly move forward and increase your hourly rate. Be sure to replace your signs and price sheets.

Some shop owners say that the price is right when 20% of your customers complain that you're too expensive. Typically an average price increase is 5-10 percent.

Subtle Ways to Raise Your Prices

You can effectively raise prices by eliminating discounts and by reducing credit terms. Just reducing the payment terms from 30 days to two weeks will cause a noticeable increase in your cash flow position.

Handling Objections to a Price Increase

As you discuss a price increase with your team, you'll encounter some interesting objections from your own people.

Here are some common objections.

"We'll lose customers."

"The customer buys on price alone, not quality."

"Our quality isn't high enough, so we need to discount our price."

"We'll lose long term business."

"The competition will eat us alive."

To help your staff understand why a price increase is necessary, hold a company meeting in which you openly and honestly explain your pricing strategy.

Then conduct an "objection clinic" with your employees. Using role playing, have them counter objections that a customer might make. Often the employees can create objection scenarios that your customers haven't thought of. This role playing experience is helpful in getting both your staff and your customers comfortable with any price increase that has occurred. The banking and financial services profession uses this technique when adding products, eliminating products, or changing fees. If it works for them, it just may work for you, too.

Choosing a Final Price

Determining final prices for your products and services takes time and work. Perform the analysis. Develop a draft set of prices. Compare these against the objectives and strategic and tactical pricing plan that you've developed. Work up a break-even analysis, and a margin curve analysis for each product or service. Obtain market intelligence on potential customers and existing competitors. Determine the likely reactions that your existing customers and competitors will take when you make your prices known. Include in your analysis the expected impact each price change will have on your other products and services. Be certain that you adhere to local, state, and federal regulations so you don't run into legal trouble.

Once you feel that you have a good price list, develop a contingency plan on how to handle potential adverse consequences. If you know that a price increase will upset certain customers, develop a strategy to carefully work the increase into your operation.

Don't lock yourself into a price. Cast your pricing strategy in "Jello™"—a semi-rigid plan. There are always circumstances that require a slightly different approach to pricing—an opportunity, a threat, etc. When you bid jobs, price your work based on how much it will cost to perform on that particular job. Often the cost to perform on one job is greatly different than the cost to perform on another similar job.

Finally, develop a policy of periodically reviewing your pricing strategy. Don't be afraid to modify your prices as market conditions change. Pricing is an on-going process. It doesn't end the moment you publish your counter price list.

Street Smart Pricing

Having a pricing strategy is a major part of your battle to gain market share and increase bottom line profits. You must still deal with the insistent telephone price-shopper. And you must build and maintain your company image in any economic climate. To do this, you'll need all the "street smart" guerilla tactics that life and business has to offer. Here are some helpful tips.

Quoting a Price

You'll always have those telephone shoppers who want to know what you'll charge to design and print a certain form, flyer, or document. For them, you'll need quick access to your counter price list.

Telephone shoppers are price shoppers. They're searching for the lowest priced for a job. Quality comes second. But price is king. They look for this first.

When they call, get as much information on the job as you can. Put bounds on the amount of effort you'll need to apply. Then, be prepared to respond quickly in quoting a "ball park" price for the job. Not being willing or able to quote an approximate price can signal a potential "rip off" or suggest that you're unsure of your own abilities and resources.

On Donating Your Services

Most shop owners occasionally donate time and services to charitable or religious organizations. There is a risk to being generous when people get professional services at little or no cost. Some people develop a perception that the value of your time and service equals the price they pay. Some also expect the same rapid response that you give to your "paying" customers.

Another risk is present when you do something without charge for one group. Other groups may show up expecting similar free support.

You can easily spread the word about your business by doing volunteer work in community groups. But

often, when you later try to charge for additional services, many turn away because they want your professional services at no cost and are not interested in paying
for your support (even when the project is outside the
interests of the nonprofit group).

A good strategy is to limit what you contribute freely,
and make it very clear from the outset that you are
donating your time for services that you normally charge
a customer. Explain that you are in business to earn a
living, and you cannot provide free services without
detracting from your income. If people balk, ask them if
they would ask an attorney or doctor for free advice.
You may be amazed at how some people see nothing
wrong with doing this. However, just asking the question
helps to educate them that you are a professional and are
not there as a free commodity.

Some DTPers submit an invoice with each completed
job, specifying what the work should cost. At the bottom
of the invoice, they mark "Complimentary" or "No
Charge to Non-Profit Organization."

But every job has a cost, and at the least, you should
be reimbursed for the cost of materials.

Adding Loss Leader Jobs

Don't accept unprofitable business just to get more
exposure in the market place. You need profit, not
exposure. If you take a job at a loss, you dedicate
valuable resources that would be better used supporting
a profit-making job.

There are better ways to reach the market.

Analyze Your Customer Base by Profit

Most of us categorize customers based on sales
volume. But, there's much more to customer analysis
than this.

Customers generally fall into one of two categories—
price sensitive customers or service-sensitive customers.
You need to determine which they are. Price-sensitive

customers still want service. In fact they often demand much more than they are willing to pay for.

As you analyze your customer base, note how much profit each client generates. You could discover that small customers are more profitable than the larger clients. In fact, the small jobs could be subsidizing those large contracts. This is why many shops don't go after the school and government markets. Hard negotiations and extended payments can make profiting in these markets tough and stressful.

For those customers who place service as top priority, make extra effort to develop a good relationship with these businesses. These are the customers who will bring repeat business. They will also be excellent referrals for long term business growth.

Another consideration involves resource utilization and spreading the source of your sales income. It may be better to have 100 customers producing $500 each than five customers generating $10,000 each. Most of us prefer to spread our sales income over as many sources as possible to account for varying market conditions and to maximize resource utilization.

In this way, the loss of one major account won't put part of your staff out of work.

Pricing Assumptions by Your Competition

If your pricing information is based on inadequate sample sizes, or bad information, you could put your faith in, and make pricing decisions on data that may be grossly in error.

If your competitors are reacting to each other's pricing moves, they may follow each other down to consistent losses. Don't mirror the competition. Do your own analysis; develop your own desired prices; then compare these with the competition to see how they vary. Closely evaluate prices that differ widely from the price that your competition charges. Modify as necessary until you achieve a price list based on sound cost analysis and savvy market research.

Adding Products and Services

Quick printers, who are members of the National Association of Quick Printers (NAQP), are rapidly adopting and offering DTP services. The number of printers introducing DTP as part of their business is dramatically increasing. This represents solid competition for the independent DTP owner-operators.

Quick print and copy shops are also renting DTP system time to their customers. The average charge for DTP system use is $40 an hour. Most shops charge additional for each page of output produced and for each clip art graphic used.

DTP services and support is becoming a lucrative side-line business. Typical charges are $1/page for laser printer output, $13/page for high-res output (1,000 dpi or better) and $1.50 for use of each illustration or graphic clip art. See the green pricing tables for more details on "standard prices."

You can establish an hourly DTP system rental price by developing a profile of an average desktop publishing job. What equipment and software are required? How many hours are spent typesetting? How many hours are spent performing layout and design? How many pages are in the typical design job? How many pages are typically printed out on a laser printer? What supplies are consumed?

When you rent your hardware and software, bill more for the labor intensive activities than you do for those that consume machine time, because some users will expend more time using the hardware and software than others. Then, base your final price on costs and desired profit.

Check the products and services being sold by other DTP and prepress shops and the quick print stores for ideas on new things that you can add to your business offerings.

Don't Give Away the Store

I say again. Don't give away the store! At this point, you have the information necessary to get paid what you're worth. You have the information to reap larger profits. All that's needed is for you to build the courage to ask the prices that you deserve to earn.

One of the startling findings of our surveys, and of the hundreds of interviews that we conducted, is that a large number of DTPers simply don't value their own skills high enough to command the salaries that they should earn. In fact, statistically women pay themselves over 20% less than their male counterparts—even when they own and operate the business!

A careful study of the survey results presented in the last half of this reference should convince you. You CAN (and SHOULD) charge fees that are more in line with the education, skills, and experience that you have. But you must believe this statement before you will earn what you deserve.

Rather than giving free scanning and clip art use to customers who buy design support, unbundle these services and establish a price for each. Then charge for these "freebies." You bought them to generate income. You should receive a return on each business investment.

Rather than giving unlimited hand-holding and consulting to your customers (who won't complain at the free service), recognize that this information has value. Consider a consulting fee with a minimum charge based on 10 minutes of time. Not only will you make money for your knowledge, but you'll also reduce the repeated requests for free advice. This will let you put more time and energy into other activities that earn income.

How to Break Out Top Profits

Thousands of small shops are struggling with plunging profits. The triple whammy—recession, diminishing margins, and tougher competition—is hitting everyone hard. Yet, some shops are not just holding their own in this economic climate, they are realizing profit margins of 30 and 40 percent! Why? How? What do they know that many others don't?

Interestingly, what they know works best, both in good times and in bad, is to focus on the basics. This means that they apply common sense to their business practices. They develop close customer relationships. They form partnerships with their customers, their vendors, and even their competitors, and they offer flexible products and services. But more important, they understand that they are in business to make money. They charge for their time and their equipment and materials.

. These people succeed regardless of what niche they are in, regardless of their size or location in North America. They can operate independently out of a shop-barn on the plains of Kansas and still generate a six figure income. And they can operate out of an 800 square foot condo in a metropolitan area and do the same.

Meanwhile, other shops offer products and services based solely on what they think everyone else is charging. They lose money on their service because they underestimate the time and energy required. They fail to use the business expertise and contact base of their suppliers. And they leave dollars on the table each time they negotiate a job.

High-margin shops implement good business methods. They charge separately for each service, or they bundle all the tasks into a composite job with a keen eye toward break-even and maximum profit. The successful shops offer different packages, hourly rates, and support services to their customer base. When the economy slows, they don't change their service. They just change how it's packaged. They make pay schedules and contracts flexible and work to ease the cash flow problems of their customers.

Other highly successful shops achieve a 30% margin by staying within a small business niche, adding performance, and carefully watching their checking account. They regularly talk themselves out of taking on certain jobs if the work will spread them too thin. They won't promise the quality or schedules that they can't deliver. Thus, they keep customers coming back.

Some hire part time professionals and work hard to develop a cadre of experts who have the broad overall knowledge and business skills needed. By forming partnerships with their customers, their vendors, and other shops, they keep their own personnel costs down and maximize their individual profit potential.

The consistent advice from high-profit shop owners is to be a business person first and then work to make your customers successful. View profit, return on investment, and margins as more important than having the latest equipment and the newest version of software.

Instead of getting caught up in the technology of DTP and prepress, get caught up in business planning and sound implementation. Become business and profit oriented. Everything else follows.

Successful shop owners suggest that you work to reduce your fixed costs. Forecast cash flow; find better ways to manage your variable costs, and take the time to do a better job defining the market.

Focus on the kind of business that you want to be, and then gear all of your time and energy toward that focus. Yet, you should be sensitive to change. Know your limits, and don't be afraid to adapt as conditions change. Recognize that your business is constantly evolving. In this information age, you cannot afford to remain static. To do so will cause your shop to be left behind in the dust of competition.

Instead of pricing at what the market will bear, high margin people price using cost plus techniques and build in plenty of profit. Rather than chasing volume, these shops control their growth. They walk away from deals that don't offer the profit they want. They are convinced that they can't make lost profit up in volume.

And they cultivate customer relationships like horticulturists cultivate fine roses. They learn their customer's needs and maintain an attitude that the customer is always right. They also work hard to learn the business issues of potential customers. The more they know, the more value they offer to their customer base.

These entrepreneurs realize that once they get a client, they can substantially increase their profit by getting repeat business. Once the marketing and advertising has brought in the business, all repeat jobs generate residual income to the shop. The net profit is higher on repeat and referral jobs.

Rather than taking a short term view of their business, they look and plan long term. They are willing to invest money now to build their business so they can earn more later.

They also go out of their way to build lasting relationships. For example, one shop redesigns flyers that arrive in the "junk" mail. The owner-operator corrects the warts and moles, and then sends a copyrighted re-designed flyer to the company that originally sent the advertisement. This shop doesn't initially make money on the re-design, but it often gets substantial follow-on jobs for its efforts. Their strategy is simple. Give more value than the customer expects. View each customer as a 20-year client. Expect follow-on jobs, and consistently work as part of a customer-vendor team. This is a key strategy for success.

Countering Cutthroat Pricing

As expressed by Nathan Morton writing in *Computer Reseller News*: "We are today in a 'take no prisoners' phase of weeding out the weak, the mundane, the imitators and the opportunist from the marketplace."

" We are going through maturation and the purification that comes from soul searching and a heavy dose of cutthroat competition for market share both occurring at the same time."

" We are pushing, thinking, shoving, cutting, focusing, listening, and inventing like we have never done before."

Morton was describing the computer revolution. He may as well have been describing desktop publishing and prepress today. We truly are in the initial stages of an Information Age revolution that will forever change the way we live and work.

Massive workplace restructuring is placing hundreds of thousands of jobs at risk. Over two million middle level managers are now out of work with the odds of someone over 40 finding a job and regaining equal pay work getting slimmer all the time. Many are opting to start new companies.

People from all walks of life are setting up side jobs and starting part time businesses to give them some form of security as they continue to worry about their primary employment. Many of these people are opening desktop publishing shops.

This has made desktop publishing one of the fastest growing home businesses. The number of DTP shops continues to grow at an exponential rate. Just examine the telephone yellow pages so see the rapid rise in shops providing these services.

Most of these entrepreneurs are complete novices at operating and managing a business. Yet they jump into business with both feet. Often they sink in a quicksand of business mistakes.

This is our third year of conducting a national survey on pricing. When the first edition of this book came out, we noted wide price ranges in our survey data for almost every service associated with desktop publishing. We expected this broad range to decrease as the industry matured and professionals became more experienced in the true costs of doing DTP. This has not happened. Instead, we've seen the price ranges widening. Of most concern is the trend toward lower prices.

I believe there are three primary reasons for this phenomenon. First, there is a huge influx of new startups. With corporate-level jobs dissolving like snow on a hot day, many people are starting home businesses as primary or secondary sources of income. Many of these businesses are in DTP.

Most of these shop owners understand the concepts of desktop publishing. Some have only the rudiments of DTP training. But many individuals in both of these groups fail to understand the realities of running a business.

Second, there is a relatively low entrance fee to starting a DTP business. Many people already have a computer and a laser printer. This means that almost anyone can hang out a shingle and claim to operate a desktop publishing business.

Third, DTP shops can operate anywhere. Many of them are located in the home. Home business entrepreneurs often fail to perceive many of their operating costs. Whether a shop is operating out of a home office or out of a rented strip center storefront, rent and insurance still apply. This means that prices must be based on sound business basics. Novice DTP shop owners often fail to have the big picture. They also often start from a position of not knowing the value of their skills.

Whatever the cause, their primary mistake is in poor pricing. Since they don't have a handle on their personal value, their shop's break even or true costs, they look at their competitors to determine what to charge for their work. Then they simply undercut every price they see.

This puts tremendous pressure on successful shop owners who perceive these cutthroat shops as sharks — willing to do any job at any price. The result is a reduction in the average price for DTP work. Often shops underbid everyone and walk away with a dollar drain hole that actually takes money out of the business as they perform the work. Yet the job has still slipped through the fingers of the price- and cost-conscious professional. To compete they retaliate by lowering their prices. They stress service to the point that they often give away valuable information.

Jim Latham of Ink Spot Printing Services states that the printing industry is in a "lamentable state of competition." He may as well have been describing desktop publishing and prepress. We seem to add value, but we don't charge for it. To be a DTP professional requires a tremendous investment in gaining technical knowledge and skills. Why then do we spend so much time telling our customers how we do our job? This information represents trade secrets for our profession.

As we educate our clients and customers on the DTP process, the hardware and software that we use to produce quality work, these people listen and learn. Sometimes they become competitors against us. Often they learn enough to brow-beat us into price concessions on jobs that we should be paid much more to perform. By our intellectual indiscretion, we place our shops in the customer's vise and then help them turn down the screws to our own business survival.

This behavior cheapens a proud and noble art. By not setting and holding to fair prices, the rest of us make ourselves participants in this tragedy. We go along with the crowd and lower our own prices leading each other into Chapter 11 bankruptcy.

Savvy buyers know how to sniff out and exploit weakness within the ranks. They suck the financial energy out of a low-price cutthroater until that shop sinks into oblivion. Then these "leeches" move on to the next unsuspecting cutthroater and begin the process all over.

As prices fall, many desktop publishing products and services become mere commodities. The price of 300 dpi laser print output has fallen from over a dollar a page to less than 10¢ a page in some areas. This puts laser printing at the level of desktop copying.

So how do we counter cutthroat pricing? Jeff Hayzlett, former owner of several printing shops and now a public relations expert, suggests that we jostle lowballers by inundating them with jobs.

According to Hayzlett, "If a competitor bids well below cost, I'd sell them as many jobs as possible." "That increases my profit margin since they're doing the job for less money than I can."

Hayzlett feels that subcontracting more business to the low-price competitor eventually crushes them in their own losses. As you'll see in Chapter 5, there is a way to evaluate project bids to estimate how much profit a competing shop will realize if they win a job. Sometimes by winning a project award, a shop can lose thousands of dollars just by performing the work. Thus, passing work to them while they consistently sell below their costs eventually sinks them. Hayzlett suggests that you become their worst nightmare.

I feel that the way out of the price-only situation is to build value in the customer's eyes. As cutthroat prices produce razor-thin margins, keep a tight lid on your costs and specialize. As a business banker once shared: "Stick to the basics. Stick to what you do well, and the money will follow." She was right. By keeping a focus on a specialized product (or a specialized industry) you heighten your efficiency and increase your ability to respond positively to price pressures. Become known as the best that there is in your area of expertise. Then price accordingly.

Don't get discouraged. As creative DTP business names come and go, rays of brilliant sunlight will shine on your business and your bank account. Focus on value and keep costs constantly in mind. Then price for whatever the market will bear. Don't become known as the "cheapest price in town." Become known s the "highest quality shop in town."

Ethics and the DTP Professional

Ethics. The very term means different things to each of us. When I use the term ethics, I'm referring to "fair play." There is an eternal order to life. This likely caused the adage: "What goes around, comes around." If we want to be treated fairly in business as well as in other relationships, we must treat others the same way.

If your intent is to jump into business, make a quick buck and then jump out with the cash, you may be tempted to operate in the gray area of right and wrong and as close to the legal limits as possible. You may make money, but you'll not make a business.

As professionals, most of us are not in this business solely for the money. Most of us are in it because we like our work. And if we want to continue doing work that we enjoy, we must perform in certain ways. Most of us have decided that our business behavior must be that of fairness, honesty, and integrity.

Although the line between right and wrong is not always clear—often fostered by government regulations and complex tax laws —we must define the guide-rails of society and of our profession. When you meet a customer who will pay whatever you ask—who really doesn't understand the "going rate," hold to your published price standards. Don't gouge an unsuspecting customer. That customer may tell someone else— someone who knows what they should have paid. They may even tell law enforcement officials.

But, more importantly, we will know in our mind that what we considered was actually "unethical." We must accept the premise that doing "right" is far superior to "doing them in."

As professionals, we must do all we can to prevent the "bait-and-switch" tactics that gave a black eye to appliance and car dealers. We should educate each other that it's illegal to offer one price and then suggest that no more of that product is in stock or that the advertised offer expired, so we can push the customer into some other more expensive purchase. This is not only illegal, it's unethical—and to me, that's far worse.

In every country, ethical behavior is defined by the norms of that society. Ethics can be an exercise in gamesmanship. Even in North America, ethical behavior has certain accepted limits. Years ago, we as a society defined what was ethical in our conduct and the conduct of others. Some hold that right is right, and wrong is wrong. They don't accept a gray area where right may be partly wrong and visa versa.

Ethical conduct is particularly difficult when a small shop owner-operator is both the check and the balance for proper business behavior. As business reversals occur, small shops are tempted to cut ethical corners because they have minimal risk of detection. Their structure makes them extremely vulnerable to ethics violations. Without an attorney on their staff to explain legality, many can be swayed into performance that borders on the unethical.

My philosophy is simple— if we want to be treated fairly by those from whom we buy, then we should be an example and provide that same treatment to our own customers.

Some people feel like Diogenes wandering through the streets of ancient Greece, holding up a lighted lantern in the bright sunlight and seeking an honest man. He couldn't find one. Perhaps we need to consider his cynical philosophy and decide if we should be the example of what is right in business.

Take the Rosco Syndrome. Rosco was a small Midwest printer who offered a limited set of products and services. Each time a customer came in, Rosco would re-define the customer's job so it fit the operational constraints of his shop. He never turned away a job.

Many customers couldn't tell that he had altered their projects. Often, Rosco led them to believe that his solution was the best one possible given their requirements. Customers initially believed Rosco and paid him handsomely for their perceived value in his actions.

However, over time, the customers became more sophisticated. They learned that Rosco had been leading them into accepting his limited shop capability. They learned that he had changed their jobs and forced their requirements to fit his standard products and services. This awareness translated into a negative perception of Rosco and of his printing shop.

Word spread quickly. His business activity fell off, and soon Rosco was no longer in business. Perception and ethics run deep in the waters of business.

The early Roman sculpturers called their work "sine cera" when no cracks in the marble had been filled with a wax imitation of the stone. The words "sine cera" evolved into "sincere"—meaning honest and genuine In dealing with our employees and our customers, we should at all times demonstrate conduct that is sincere—without wax. Ethics and sincerity are synonymous.

Even though you'll encounter competitors who are at best unethical, someone needs to be the example of honest and professional conduct. Let's face it. When we look around for a leader, an example to follow, we're it. Be the leader. Others will follow.

Summary

A chapter on strategy is a book unto itself. However, strategy is only made good when implemented in a professional environment. In Chapter 3, you'll learn how to charge for your services. You'll see that there are many ways to price your work and some ways are more suited for a job than others depending of the characteristics of the work.

How to Charge for Service

*"Intuitive pricing is a fool's folly
in today's highly competitive world."*

There are many ways to price a product or service. We can charge by the piece, by the job, by the hour, by whatever unit we can imagine. The challenge is to determine which method of pricing is appropriate for the job. This chapter deals with how shop owners charge for their services.

Terms to Remember

Alterations - Customer-directed changes to a design.

Budgeted Hourly Rate - The dollar amount that covers the costs to perform a specific service. A price associated with a particular functional area in a shop.

Corrections - Typically these are design or printout changes made necessary because of errors made by shop personnel or shop equipment.

Shop Hourly Rate - An overall hourly billing price for services. This price assumes a standard fee is applied to every service. Materials costs are extra..

Different Ways to Charge for Services

The functions of desktop publishing and prepress are merging. And commercial and quick printers are rapidly incorporating desktop publishing into their service offering. Even secretarial services and word processing businesses are moving into desktop publishing following improvements in word processing software and demand by customers for more graphics integration into their documents. Yet, these businesses typically implement varying methods to charge for products and services.

Designers typically charge by the hour, by the project, or by the page, while typesetters and typing services typically charge by the number of lines or keystrokes. DTPers and typesetters typically estimate a job based on the number of expected pages, the amount of conceptual, layout, the design needed, and the costs for photography, illustrations, and actual printing. Laser printer and imagesetter output can be billed by resolution required, the output material, or by the page. Scanning can be billed by the scan or by the hour if touch-up is included.

Today, word processing software forms the basis for the text in most DTP documents. Therefore, page costs should be based on the time it takes to format the text, design the page, and then import the text into the layout program to produce the final document. Both design and typesetting functions are involved.

With so many diverse ways to figure composition, design and production costs, the specific method of charging depends on the work, the volume, the customer, your resources, and the marketplace.

Pricing by the Character and by the Line

In our survey data, we were interested in how many shops priced their keyboarding and typography work by the character. Of those that used this method, most quoted prices by the thousand characters (1,000 keystrokes). They used their software to calculate the total character count in a document. Or they counted the characters in 10 lines of text and took this as a basis for counting the number of lines of text. By multiplying the average number of characters in a line by the total number of lines typeset, they achieved a value representing the total number of characters in the document.

This method works well with text material. It works better when the software can count the characters. You get a more accurate count. The software will also account for condensed or expanded fonts and varying typefaces.

We've heard about, but didn't note any shop owners billing by square inch for composition services. The square inch method is fast, but it doesn't compensate for the time it takes to set special typefaces or varying type widths.

Pricing by the Page

Pricing a job by the page can be tricky. The time and energy spent on each customer can vary significantly. Per-page pricing requires that you know exactly how each page will be designed. Changing the style can affect the total page count and cause significant re-design.

Without a page layout and a good count of each type of page, you must estimate a job based on many possible design configurations. You could establish a "base page" price and then adjust this price depending on job complexity, the customer, the turnaround time desired, the amount of skill required, and special conditions related to the job (e.g., comparable costs of mechanical art production, competitor pricing for similar work, and the hardware and software resources required). The idea is to know your costs, then add in profit and ROI to get an idea of what to charge per page.

There is a simply way to track average page costs for desktop publishing. Make notes on the job folder associated with each project that you complete. Your notes should include page count, page complexity, the units of time spent and the total costs involved.

Develop a running record of all of your projects over a period of time. Then perform a cumulative analysis on this information. A computer spreadsheet program is an invaluable tool for this.

In your analysis, make a list of each multiple page job, the number of pages, the total costs (less out-of-pocket expenses), and any special things that should be considered. Delete the charges for alterations and corrections to normalize on just the basic project cost. Also note special shortcuts that you found and used.

Divide the costs for each project by the number of pages to get a basic cost per page value. You'll find that larger projects typically have a lower cost per page, and you'll find that alterations and corrections can dramatically affect the final cost to the client.

Some people group pages and go for an average page complexity. They look primarily at projects involving 16 pages or more and exclude small projects involving fewer than 16 pages. They feel that the effort varies substantially with short projects and can skew the data for larger projects such as books and manuals. In addition, complex jobs with multiple columns, lots of graphics and wrap-around text can increase the time spent on each page.

The costs will probably vary from $20 to $125 for each page in the project. David Doty, Editor and Publisher of *ThePage* found that his costs averaged just over $50 per page. Be certain that your price incorporates all of your pro-rated costs — labor, materials, and overhead.

Knowing your typical per page cost can be extremely helpful when you bid on future jobs.

Quoting From a Form

A tighter analysis for per page pricing can be achieved by establishing a complexity standard defining the amount of text and graphic image on each page. Then every page in a project is assigned a complexity rating and priced accordingly. This pricing system works regardless of page count.

David Hornung, owner of The Graphic Center in Fond du Lac, Wisconsin described in an *Instant Printer* article how he uses a Composition Class Job Pricing sheet to quickly price a job.

He made a counter sample composition form by dividing an 8.5" x 11" sheet into five areas. Each area represents a page composition category (very light, light, medium, heavy, or extra heavy). A sample of each composition category appears on his form so he can quickly determine how much a job will price out at and how long it should take to complete.

On the reverse side of his form, Hornung designed six columns—the first listing the paper size dimensions (in square inches of copy), and then a column for each of the five composition categories. Each category column is labelled and then lists a price for each paper size identified in the first column. By matching the paper size and print composition, he can quickly quote a price and close a sale.

You may want to implement some version of this idea in your own business. Figure 3-1 describes a form you can consider. It was designed based on the description Hornung provided in the article.

VERY LIGHT	LIGHT	MEDIUM	HEAVY	EXTRA HEAVY
ekc hfjdjsk eid eid ee id idi diek dhehdi dk did eivi	wlwidjdkfkej id e iel diel did dhid dhdh diei dd didi di deidndid eid ei	w iwi slsheueif idel diexi die die id dield ei die di ed dkdi eie didid dk dieos nsid diblo doe sum	hwl isleide ld;d dieldieh dield id die did didkd ei dleo dod do do dod od di sunbiscumdi	eid ielgi eithd dieldie edi die deoldoe doe d dd idi ekdi cd catjprod doe

SIZE	VERY LIGHT	LIGHT	MEDIUM	HEAVY	EXTRA HEAVY
4x6	$xx/pg	$xx/pg	$xx/pg	$xx/pg	$xx/pg
5x7	$xx/pg	$xx/pg	$xx/pg	$xx/pg	$xx/pg
5.5x8.5	$xx/pg	$xx/pg	$xx/pg	$xx/pg	$xx/pg
7x9	$xx/pg	$xx/pg	$xx/pg	$xx/pg	$xx/pg
8x10	$xx/pg	$xx/pg	$xx/pg	$xx/pg	$xx/pg
8.5x11	$xx/pg	$xx/pg	$xx/pg	$xx/pg	$xx/pg
8.5x14	$xx/pg	$xx/pg	$xx/pg	$xx/pg	$xx/pg
A4 size	$xx/pg	$xx/pg	$xx/pg	$xx/pg	$xx/pg
B4 size	$xx/pg	$xx/pg	$xx/pg	$xx/pg	$xx/pg
Tabloid	$xx/pg	$xx/pg	$xx/pg	$xx/pg	$xx/pg
(special)	$xx/pg	$xx/pg	$xx/pg	$xx/pg	$xx/pg
(special)	$xx/pg	$xx/pg	$xx/pg	$xx/pg	$xx/pg
(special)	$xx/pg	$xx/pg	$xx/pg	$xx/pg	$xx/pg
(special)	$xx/pg	$xx/pg	$xx/pg	$xx/pg	$xx/pg

Figure 3-1. Quick Quote pricing form.

For customers new to DTP and prepress, don't offer per-page billing. Instead, opt for an hourly rate. Inexperienced customers often require significant hand-holding and make many design changes before a final product emerges. Every time you think you're done, you're probably not. Changes in the layout, text, graphics, or output form will occur, so plan extra time to handle these. And plan to charge for all of the work that is actually performed.

Pricing Based On Shop's Hourly Rate

The hourly rate that you use to develop your bids and that you use as a basis for your pricing considerations can be based on costs and return information for the shop as a whole or on individual functions within the shop.

Your *shop's hourly rate* is calculated using the total wages paid each hour, your overhead costs per hour, and the amount of return on investment and profit you need to earn each hour to achieve the results that you expect. This is an overall shop hourly rate. It does not allocate a separate hourly rate to unique services.

Typically, profit is calculated using the sum of hourly pay plus hourly overhead costs. Your profit planning is based on these two costs outlays.

Let's assume that you operate a sole proprietorship with a single employee—you. You put $10,000 into your business and find your overhead running at 50% of what you make each month — your gross income. Your income has been running $6,000 a month, but overhead will eat up $3,000 of it. Based on $6,000 per month of income, your shop should bring in $72,000 a year. You pay yourself $15 an hour and work 52 weeks (2080 hours) a year. (You defer vacations during these startup years). You'd like to earn 10% return on your investment and another 10% profit on expenses. What should you charge?

First, realize that a one-person shop will likely be 30% productive at best. This means that you will bill out for only 30% of the time that you work. Also, even though you are alone, you have certain overhead costs that must be covered. Your overhead costs are around 50% of income. Your profit is based on how much you spend for wages and overhead.

Table 3-1 shows how to calculate your hourly shop billing rate.

<table>
<tr><td>Hourly Wage
(one person, $15/hr))</td><td>$15.00</td></tr>
<tr><td>Hours worked per year
(40 hrs/wk x 52 wks = 2080 hrs)</td><td></td></tr>
<tr><td>Hourly Overhead expense
[(72,000*.5) / 2,080]</td><td>17.31</td></tr>
<tr><td>Hourly Return on investment
(10,000 * .1) / 2,080</td><td>0.48</td></tr>
<tr><td>Hourly Business Profit Desired
[(15 + 17.31) * .1]</td><td>3.23</td></tr>
<tr><td>Total hourly income needed
each week (one employee)
(100% productivity)</td><td>$36.02</td></tr>
<tr><td>Total hourly income needed
if 30% productive</td><td>$120.07
SHOP BILLING RATE</td></tr>
</table>

**Table 3-1. Hourly rate calculation
for a representative one-person DTP shop.**

You should be charging a shocking $120.07 an hour for your work just to make this operation profitable! What can you do? You decide to modify your spreadsheet to show that you work 60 hours a week and calculate costs and profit based on working 40 hours. (You go on salary.) This makes each day appear more productive. By working more hours, you double your effective productivity. You redo your calculations. (See Table 3-2.)

Hourly Wage
($15 - effectively $10/hr @60 hrs) $15.00

Hours shop operated each year
(60 hrs/wk x 52 wks = 3120 hrs)

Hourly Overhead expense
[(72,000*.5) / 3120   11.54

Hourly Return on investment
(10,000 * .1) / 3120   0.32

Hourly Business Profit Desired
[(15 + 11.54) * .1]   2.65

Total hourly income needed
each week
(100% productivity) $29.51

Total hourly income needed
if 60% productive $49.19
                                    SHOP BILLING RATE

**Table 3-2. Hourly rate calculation for a
1-person DTP shop operating 60 hours each week.**

Well this is better. But $49.19 an hour still exceeds the average $43/hr fee in North America Backing into the numbers, it turns out that you need to earn over $92,000 just to pay your costs. What else can you do?

You could work 80 or more hours a week, but what would happen if you simply added staff? Adding just one more employee means that you share the shop's non-earning tasks such as answering the telephone, mailing, and certain administrative functions. Naturally, there must be enough work to keep both of you fully occupied (at maximum productivity).

If you pay this person $7 an hour, you both work 40 hours a week, and neither of you take paid vacations, you can achieve a better hourly rate. This is shown in Table 3-3 below.

Hourly Wage $7 +15)	$22.00
Hours shop operated each year (40 hrs/wk x 52 wks = 2080 hrs)	
Hourly Overhead expense [(72,000*.5) /2080	17.30
Hourly Return on investment (10,000 * .1) / 2080	0.48
Hourly Business Profit Desired [(22+ 17.30) * .1]	3.93
Total hourly income needed each week (100% productivity)	$43.73
Total hourly income needed per employee (100% productive)	$21.86
Total hourly income needed if each are 45% productive	$48.58
	SHOP BILLING RATE

**Table 3-3. Hourly rate calculation for a
2-person DTP shop open 40 hours each week.**

By adding another employee and by both working 40 hours each week, you can achieve 45% productivity for the shop. Now you can reduce your hourly rate to $48.58 from the $49.19 you would need to charge if you ran your shop by yourself and worked 60 hours a week. Not much difference, but now you're working a reasonable 40 hour week.

Next, let's see what happens if you increase your staff by hiring two 40-hour employees. Each employee will work 40 hours a week. More workers means that you can handle more jobs. Hopefully, you'll also earn more income for the shop.

Assume that you expect to earn over $130,000 next year. Your overhead has been running about 40 percent of gross income. You want to determine the actual hourly rate that you should charge to earn a desired profit and return on investment. Employee 1 is paid $6 an hour. Employee 2 is paid $7 an hour, and you (employee 3) get paid $15 an hour. Your annual overhead costs are $52,000 ($130,000 times 40% typical overhead = 52,000). Each employee will work 40 hours a week and take two weeks vacation. This yields 2,000 hours of work each year from each employee (40 hours/week x 50 weeks/year = 2,000 hours/year). Therefore, three workers will put in 2,000 each or 6,000 total hours annually.

Dividing the $52,000/year overhead costs by the 2080 actual shop operating hours (40 hrs/wk x 52 wks = 2080 hrs) yields $25 an hour as the amount charged to overhead each hour. Suppose that you want to earn a profit of 10% on overhead and wages. Adding labor costs of $28 (6 + 7 + 15 = $28/hr) and overhead of $25 results in $53/ hour overhead and wage costs. The contribution to profit is 10 percent of $53 is $5.30 an hour.

Then, let's say that you want to realize a 10% return on your $10,000 start-up investment. The return on investment equals the investment times the desired return divided by the hours worked times the number of workers. This equals [(10,000 * 0.1) / (2,000 * 3)] or $0.17 an hour of billable fee that must contribute to ROI.

Adding the hourly labor costs ($28), overhead costs ($25), profit ($5.30), and ROI ($0.17) and then dividing by the number of employees, you get a total income required from each employee each hour of $19.49 ($58.47/3 = $19.49). This is the hourly rate that you must bill out if everyone is 100% productive as shown in Table 3-4. But, remember that a shop with only three workers will likely be 50% productive at best. If you don't put in extra (uncharged) hours to handle administrative functions, your billable hourly rate will shift to $38.98 per hour. This is what you need to budget and charge if you want to realize the 10% ROI and 10% profit on wages and overhead.

Hourly Wages (6 + 7 + 15)	$28.00
Hours shop operated each year (40 hrs/wk x 52 wks = 2080 hrs)	
Overhead expense (52,000/2080)	25.00
Return on investment (10,000 * .1) / (2000 x 3)	0.17
Business Profit Desired [(28 + 25) * .1]	5.30
Total hourly income needed at 40 billable hours a week (100% productivity)	$58.47
Hourly income needed per shop employee (100% productivity)	$19.49
Total hourly income needed per employee if 50% productivity	$38.98
	SHOP BILLING RATE

Table 3-4. Service rate calculation for a three-person shop.

This brings your rates within the national average. The hourly fees for desktop publishing services in North America vary from $15 to $100 an hour. The median is about $42 an hour—most shops charge $42 an hour. This means that many small shops with one or two workers are absorbing part of their overhead costs and are charging too little for their work. They are likely working more than 40 hours a week (even if they calculate on a 40-hour basis).

By analyzing these tables you can see that you can operate a successful shop if you keep your costs low and your productivity high. Since your shop will be less productive with fewer employees, you must carefully analyze your costs and output if you want to bring your required hourly rate in line with what the current market (and your pocket book) will bear. Labor is your single biggest expense. This is why many shops hire freelance part time help and hold the full time employee load at a minimum.

A small shop simply will not reach the 50% productivity level without additional employees and added income, so most operators work more than a 40-hour week. They shoot for 45-50% shop productivity. And they also try to reduce their overhead to 35% or less.

Typically, wages are 60% of your costs. General and administrative expenses can average 32% of your expenses. Rent costs can eat up 5-9% of your total costs. You can keep rent low by operating out of smaller spaces, sharing a shop, or operating out of a home office.

The home office option has its own set of problems and challenges. While many DTPers still operate out of their home, the space and electricity needs, as they approach service bureau size, often forces them into outside office spaces.

Most owner-operators of DTP shops and service bureaus charge too little for their products and services. These professionals must increase their hourly rates if they expect to earn a decent living and get a suitable return on their investment of time and money.

The median price for DTP design is around $40 an hour. The advantage of pricing by the hour is that you get paid for all of the time involved. The downside is that it's sometimes difficult to know how long a job will take so you can't give your customer a flat rate. However, if you have enough historical data, you can estimate a project based on similar jobs and be close enough to warrant the effort. Particularly in this case, experience pays. But there is a better way — budgeted hourly rates.

Pricing Based On Budgeted Hourly Rates

Every service that your shop performs is comprised of unique operations or tasks, each with a related set of costs. By breaking out the individual costs associated with labor and materials, you can calculate a *budgeted hourly rate* for each of these operations. This can be used to determine a selling price for a particular service.

You start by partitioning all of your shop's services into individual operations. For example, producing a newsletter could involve receiving text on a disk and converting the file into a usable form (file conversion), correcting typographical or grammar mistakes in the text (editing), designing a style sheet (design), importing graphics and text into an electronic page (layout), and generating a laser printout (print out). Each of these operations can have an associated budgeted hourly rate.

Once all of your operations are identified — keyboarding, file conversion, typography, scanning,, design, layout, print output, and so on, you specify the labor skills and equipment required for each operation. Consider every resource in your business — people, equipment, software, facility, and investment capital. Then identify the annual costs of these resources as allocated to each operation. These costs will be fixed or variable.

Dividing the total annual costs for each operation by an estimate of the annual billable hours for that operation gives you a set of budgeted hourly cost rates. Using these, you can price a job based on the combination of the individual hourly rates for each operation.

So how do you use a budgeted hourly rate to establish selling price? Several organizations have developed production standards for the various functions involved in desktop publishing and prepress. These "industry production standards" establish how long it takes an average person to perform a specific task. Thus, performing typography on a single column 8.5" x 11" page using 12 point type may have an "industry standard" rating of 0.22. This means that it takes 0.22 of an hour (13.2 minutes) for an average employee to change the typeface, font, point size, leading, or kerning of a page of text. The 0.22 value was established based on surveys and monitoring actual employees performing this task.

To determine your selling price for this service, multiply the industry standard by the budgeted hourly rate for this function. Add the costs of materials and some profit. Add any costs for outside services. The sum of these factors yields a total cost plus profit factor to use as the selling price.

[(BHR x Prod Std x units) + Material Cost + Other Costs + Profit] = Selling Price

Suppose you have a job typesetting 10 pages of text in 12 point type, and you're to produce 300 dpi laser printed sheets for the customer. If your budgeted hourly rate for this function is $40 an hour, multiply 40 times the production standard 0.22 times the 10 pages to get $88. Then add the costs for 10 pages of 300 dpi laser output — 10 times $1.64 = $16.40 and a profit (say 10%) of 0.1 times 88 (40 x 0.22 x 10) or $8.80 to yield $113.20 (88 + 16.40 + 8.80 = 113.20) for the job. Assuming there are no other costs to recover, this is what you would charge your customer.

The best production standards are those that you develop yourself . These are described as "baseline standards" in Chapter 4. By having an accurate understanding of the time it takes to perform on each function, you can easily use the budgeted hourly rate method to calculate selling price.

But be aware that changes in hardware, software, or production procedures can significantly alter your budgeted hourly baseline. You must keep on top of your standard times. (A spreadsheet program works well for this.) As you upgrade your systems — both hardware and software — you will find certain jobs take less time to perform. An upgrade to OCR scanning software can enable scanning and interpretation of text in less than half the original time. This can translate into cost benefits for both yourself and your customers.

Keep a list or record of the average times to perform each task. Use these to update your baseline production standard. Don't forget "system start-up" and "modified start-up" (re-start) times. Many shops call this "set up" time. They often charge a flat rate for setting a system up to perform a specific service.

Incorporate start-up and re-start in your final bill. It can take about three minutes for your computer system to initialize, run an application program and open in the job that you will be working. The first effort on a job includes page setup time. Once the page format is established, then each time that you go back to the job, you must re-start the system—boot up the application program and open the job that were working on. The total job time should incorporate these re-start actions.

With budgeted hourly cost rates, you can factor in productivity, return on investment, profit, expected sales, the marketplace and your competition to generate a budgeted price basis for each task. Then when you price a job, you can separate out the activities and quote a job by tasks with unique rates for each task. Budgeted hourly rates vary from $15 to $75.

If all the functions in a shop are called individual profit centers, then the budgeted hourly rate concept can successfully be used to allocate specific hourly rates to each center. This is approach is covered quite nicely in *Desktop Dividends: Managing Electronic Prepress for Profit* by Philip K. Ruggles.

An important factor to understand is that both fixed and variable costs are used in determining your budgeted hourly rate for a particular service or profit center. If you vary the number of hours each day that the service is provided or the profit center is active, fixed costs can have a major impact on the budgeted hourly rate that you calculate. Essentially this means that the more utilization you have, the lower the budgeted hourly rate because you spread the fixed costs out over more hours. Likewise an underutilized function or profit center can have a higher budgeted hourly rate. This can cause your shop to be no longer competitive in certain areas.

Budgeted hourly rates don't incorporate all costs such as employee benefit expenses, but they are an accepted way for pricing out a job. Because they depend on an industry or custom production standard,s the budgeted hourly rate method can provide an easy way to quickly price a job.

Pricing by the Job - Flat Rate Pricing

Clients, who are uncomfortable paying an hourly rate, will often accept a flat-fee price. Some people dislike working with professionals who charge by the hour. For these customers, it's better to express job cost as a total package price.

With flat rate job pricing, you can incorporate fees and charges that would stand out like a sore thumb on a price breakdown sheet. If you quote a price that's 25% lower than what a customer can find elsewhere, you can incorporate a price increase while still giving your customer the impression that they're getting your services for "peanuts."

On flat rate jobs, analyze the total number of pages involved, the complexity of each page, the volume of work this client brings to you, and the type of tasks that you will perform (data editing, grammar checking, spell-checking, illustrations, etc.). Then establish a price for the overall job. This is much like the budgeted hourly rate technique described earlier.

Charging for Alterations and Corrections

A customer often only hears the first price quoted. Some grumble and argue when extra charges are added for changes—even when THEY are the reason that changes are made. You must be certain that your customers clearly understand that they will be charged for customer-directed (or caused) changes. Then let them decide if what they are considering is really worth the added cost.

If your proof copy has errors, you should correct typographical or image errors without cost to the customer. But changes that vary from the original job specifications should be paid for by the customer. Once you perform to the original specs, if the customer decides to alter the design, you charge for the additional work.

Alterations and corrections can be billed in various ways including by the word, by the line, by the correction, by the page or even by the job. If a customer insists on an hourly rate for handling alterations and corrections, offer an hourly fee that is lower than your standard shop rate. This gives the customer a feeling that they're getting a bargain (even though you still earn a suitable profit).

Establish a shop policy for handling revisions and alterations. Many successful shops use a Design Acceptance form that they have their customers sign. This form establishes how changes or alterations will be handled. It becomes a basis of acceptance between buyer and seller. À sample design acceptance form is shown in Figure 3-2

ACCEPTANCE ACKNOWLEDGEMENT FORM

NOTICE: PLEASE READ CAREFULLY
If you O.K. errors shown on this proof without indicating corrections required, we cannot be held responsible.

If we make a mistake, and you indicate such on this proof, we will make the correction without charge to you.

But any changes or alterations that you make to your original specification will be charged to you at the rate of $_________ per _______.

A minimum of $________ applies for any alterations or revisions.

Please acknowledge understanding of this policy by sign-ing and dating this form.

I have carefully examined the attached proof and authorize you to proceed after making corrections and changes as noted on the proof.

Signed ______________________________ Date ____________

Figure 3-2. Changes and Alternation acceptance form.

When it comes to making changes in the design, a rule of thumb is to charge $2 to $5 for each change or correction that is directly caused by customer action (or inaction). This includes changing typefaces and fonts, moving text, and shifting illustrations.

Pricing is a fascinating process. You can become successful and grow a thriving business by making certain that you are paid for each service that you provide. Don't let dollars fall between the cracks in a job. Get the most return for your efforts. Price with precision.

Summary

There are many ways to price desktop publishing and prepress services. Each has its advantage. Each has some limitation. Knowing which method to employ takes time, experience and courage.

In the next chapter, you'll learn how to bid and negotiate a job.

Chapter 4

Estimating, Bidding And Negotiating

"Prices do not merely reflect information — they convey it."
- Andrea Terzi in letter to *Business Europe*

Terms to Remember

Bid - To offer a price at which you'll provide a product or service.

Estimating - The act of appraising or placing a value on a job.

Job-Out - A portion of a job that has been subcontracted out to another business. Also called "farm out" and "buy-out."

Machine Standard - A reference time associated with the performance of equipment. It defines the fastest time to complete a specified task.

Negotiate - To confer with another business person in expectation of arriving at a compromise settlement price for products or services.

Quote - A current price, or bid offer.

Production Standard - A time reference based on the configuration of the equipment being used and on the experience of the employee using the equipment.

RFB (Request for Bid) - A formal document asking you to bid on a particular job. An RFB is synonymous with Invitation for Bid (IFB), and Request for Quote (RFQ).

Introduction to Estimating

Estimating combines art with science and business skills to produce a document that clearly describes project costs and provides sufficient funds for profit and return on investment.

In the world of estimating, there's no such thing as having too much information. The more information you have, the better your estimate. In DTP shops and service bureaus, good estimating requires great discipline and integrity. You must clearly understand your own staff and their capabilities before you can make a good forecast on time to perform and at what price you are willing to trade energy and expertise for customer need. It's critical to know how much time and material each operation actually requires. Estimating helps you find your true cost basis. Estimating lets you determine the minimum price at which you can sell your services and still make some profit.

When a customer calls, asking for a verbal quote, many business managers can toss out a ballpark figure based on the customer's response to a series of questions and a detailed knowledge of the shop's capability. They use the cost per page or cost per piece concept. This doesn't make them accurate. It makes them responsive. It works on simple jobs. But for those real "money-makers," we need to accurately estimate the true costs to perform.

Three factors drive accurate estimating: job decomposition, team productivity, and estimating experience. The finer you partition a job into tasks—a process called *"functional decomposition"*—the easier it is to assign a difficulty weight and cost to each digestible piece. Breaking a large job down into simpler tasks is a form of "normalization." Every job is composed of a series of small tasks, and identifying each task makes project estimating much easier.

With each task functionally identified, you can then assign a difficulty weight to each of them. Some tasks will be complex, some difficult, some standard, and some easy. This step gets easier with experience and observation, but you must determine the rate at which a person should be able to complete each task. Then you can assign a time estimate and dollar value to the task.

Then factor in productivity. You should be tracking both shop productivity and the productivity of each employee. Shop productivity will be about 30-50%. The productivity of direct labor employees can be as high as 90% depending on the number of people on the staff and a myriad of motivational and attitudinal factors.

The final factor behind good estimating is experience. You get this by learning and by applying. As an estimator, you must clearly understand every task in each production center. You must also know the complexity of each software package that will be used—word processing, graphics, scan, OCR, layout and design, image manipulation, retouch, and even format conversion software. You should also understand how customer-generated files interface with your DTP and prepress software, how desktop publishing, mechanical art production, stats, and other prepress functions such as stripping all relate to the final product.

Homework Before Estimate-Work

Before you can begin estimating a job, you must first get a clear understanding of all the costs associated with performing on the project. You should have a good idea how long it takes to perform each task in your shop. Cost should be budgeted to an hourly figure. You should develop baseline standards and be able to track your costs on a page-by-page and task-by-task basis. Then you can begin estimating in earnest.

Identifying Project Costs

It's a good idea to first identify the specific production times associated with each of your shop operations. Then these times are multiplied by your budgeted hourly costs. Material costs such as film and special paper are added to produce the baseline cost to which profit, return on investment, and intangibles such as job turn-around time, design skill, and competitive advantage are added to achieve the final bid price. It begins with clearly knowing the tasks associated with a job.

Each of these tasks are income-generation sources. They also generate a cost to your shop. Sometimes understanding and defining these costs can be one of the toughest jobs that you'll tackle. Your estimate can only be as accurate as the information used to generate it. Not only do you need a good understanding of how much each task costs to perform, but be sure that you don't forget some. Be careful to include every action and activity associated with performing on a job. These include the time spent on indirect cost activities:

- meeting with a client
- corresponding
- answering questions
- communicating on the telephone
- communicating by fax or modem
- scheduling work
- recording actions and times

And they include the time spent on direct cost activities:

- system power up
- program execution

- converting files to a useable form
- converting data for importing
- job preparation and setup
- downloading project data
- proofreading and spell checking
- editing
- text generation
- other keyboarding
- typography
- innovating a design concept
- developing a style sheet
- designing illustrations and artwork
- designing a logo
- designing clip art
- scanning art and photographs
- image manipulation and retouch
- developing a thumbnail layout
- creating a design
- implementing a design
- importing text and graphics
- importing clip art
- importing CD-ROM photographs
- more keyboarding
- dropping illustrations into the design
- adjusting the layout
- revising the draft design
- paste-up
- producing color proofs
- producing color separations
- typesetting/imagesetting
- generating camera ready output
- printing
- post printing
- etc.

Anything that takes you away from income-generating activities becomes an indirect costs or overhead. When you meet with illustrators or photographers, or when you meet with a client to present draft copies or to deliver the final output, you are taking time away from other potential earnings. Thus, you should include a block of time to cover these activities while estimating the total hours and minutes that a job will take.

When you break out your machine and labor costs, remember the overhead allocated to the costs of your equipment. If you're making payments on hardware, you should allocate this cost over the hours that the hardware will be used. (Historical use is helpful in making this estimation.)

And it's wise to include a cost factor for future replacement at the end of the equipment's life cycle. Replacement cost can be determined by taking the total cost of the current hardware (including finance charges), factoring in inflation over its useful life, subtracting the expected trade-in value, and then dividing by the estimated life of the machine to get an annual replacement rate. Dividing again by 12 months and then again by approximately 168 hours a month will give you an estimated hourly replacement cost factor.

Let's say you want to lease an imagesetter. It costs $100,000 and has a 5-year useful life. You can lease it for $1,274.82 a month on a 5-year contract at 10%. Inflation is expected to average 3% for the next five years. Your total costs is equal to the $100,000 purchase price, plus $1,274.82 times 60 months ($16,489), plus 3% inflation on $100,000 over five years ($15,930) less the residual trade in of $40,000. Total cost is $92,419. Dividing by 5 years useful life, dividing by 12 months per year and dividing by 168 hours per month, you calculate $9.17 as the hourly replacement cost for having this system. By estimating how many copies of RC paper or film you can output each hour, you can incorporate a portion of the $9.17 hourly replacement cost into your per copy charge.

Since both time and costs are critical in making an accurate estimate for bidding, it helps to develop an activity-time worksheet for each job that you do. On this form you can estimate the time spent on indirect project activities. You can estimate the creative time you believe you will need. And you can estimate the production time required.

Next, you should estimate your "out-of-pocket" expenses to do the job. These include raw materials and various actions necessary to perform the job. Consider:

- laser printer paper
- toner
- file conversion costs
- special typefaces and fonts
- stats
- illustrations
- film
- resin-coated paper
- telephone calls
- travel
- postage
- facsimile

Within your materials costs are hidden charges that you should also consider. It takes time (and hence costs your shop money) to order, receive, and pay for materials. Credit card purchases mean possible interest payments. Don't forget waste and spoilage. Not all of the paper that you buy will be converted into a final product. You'll use paper producing drafts; you'll find some damaged when you open the packages, and some will be used in setting up the machine to produce acceptable output pages.

About 5% of your materials costs should be added to handle accounting functions. Another 20% in expenses should be added to cover waste and spoilage.

Some of the tasks involved in completing a job will not be within the scope of your capabilities. These will be subcontracted out as *"buy-outs" or "job-outs."* If you farm portions of a job out to an outside vendor, the costs to you should be marked up to cover working through them, and to cover your accounting and transportation costs. Many shops mark up subcontractor charges by 50% to arrive at the selling price to quote their customers.

With time and costs understood, decide how you want to price the job—by the page, by the hour or as one flat rate. Your billing baseline depends on the type of job and the customer. Many new owner-operators start with a fixed hourly rate on everything (e.g., $35/hr). As they get more experience, some DTPers develop a unique hourly rate for each service that they provide. Then they fine tune these hourly rates and establish page or word count baselines for pricing.

How Do I Measure Time to Perform?

This is a function of discipline and habit. Ask each person to log the time that they spend performing each task. This will take about 10 minutes a day—an acceptable investment in time to get useful data. Not only will one person take less time to perform the same task than another, but you yourself will take more time one day to do a task than you will on another day. This is a reality when people are involved in the process. Each of us has a talent, and each of us can perform certain tasks faster and with less error. By tracking time-to-perform over a period such as a month, a pattern will develop that shows the best, worst, and most likely time for each direct labor employee to complete each functional task. Develop and use your own project time tracking form. Figure 4-1 shows a form that you could adopt for your business.

Time Tracking Sheet				
NAME: _________________________			DATE_________	
PROJECT	TIME IN	TIME OUT	ACTIVITY	TOTAL MINUTES

Figure 4-1. Sample project time tracking form.

When you bid a flat rate on a job, use the worst time scenario to form your cost basis. Then, if you can assign employees to their best tasks, you should complete the job in less time (closer to the best measured). This increases the profit potential for your shop. However, sometimes the best person for a job is already committed. In this case, a slower worker can be assigned the task and still be able to complete the job with acceptable profitability to the business.

Be cautious. Never reveal the individual time data to your staff. Keep this to yourself or your estimator.

Employees get concerned that you'll use this information alone to evaluate performance for a salary review. Show by example that you use it to assign workers to their best tasks. And also use the information to plan training and skill sessions for workers.

If you intend to apply pay for performance, recognize that if you tell them that they will be paid on their productivity, most will focus on the easy jobs to keep their productivity figure high. The detail to which you partition jobs into functional tasks will help keep the evaluation even. Just be certain to consider ALL work associated with a task. Productivity should include direct labor and the rework resulting from pushing so hard that errors occur. Corrections can take as long as doing it right the first time.

Developing Budgeted Costs

Each time you do a job, keep a detailed log of the activities and time spent on each task. A range of times-per-task will develop. From these you can determine the average time it takes to perform. Assuming that you are at least as motivated as the most productive person in your shop, you can use your results to compare with those of your other workers. This process lets you generate average performance times for your shop. These times can be converted to costs that you budget or allocate to each task. They then become your budgeted costs before profit and return on investment are added.

A budgeted cost can be assigned to every function that is performed in the DTP and prepress process. Here's a simple way to determine your cost basis:

1. Partition the operations in your shop into cost categories (e.g., keyboarding, layout and design, graphics, typesetting, prepress, bindery, etc.)

2. Develop specifications for the employees and equipment associated with each cost category.

3. Determine the specific annual operating costs associated with each major piece of equipment.

4. Determine an hourly overhead cost for the shop.
5. Determine the number of chargeable hours that each cost category generates.
6. Divide the total annual costs for each category by the annual chargeable hours for that category to achieve a budgeted hourly cost rate that can be used for estimating.

The more detailed you make your cost breakdown, the easier it is to define tasks and build an estimate. The idea is to have the total shop's operating costs partitioned into chargeable activities. A job will be comprised of several specific activities. Each activity has an associated cost category and a budgeted hourly cost rate.

A cost rate is not the actual rate that you quote your customer. Once you have your budgeted hourly cost rates, you should factor in productivity, ROI, and markup to generate a "straw-man" price that you can quote. Then look at your marketplace and your competition to establish hourly billing rates for each functional activity. These are the rates that you publish on your counter price sheets.

A recent International Prepress Association survey concluded that the best approach for pricing desktop publishing is to establish a budgeted hourly rate for each piece or group of equipment worked on. This allocates or budgets pricing to the hardware and software used to perform a job. Good time assessments on each type of project can then help you apply proper markup and establish budgeted hourly prices that work.

Building Your Own Standards

To simplify the bidding process, create a standard framework within which to estimate time. How long does it take to scan 20 illustrations into a computer? How long will it take to design an average 4-page newsletter? How long will it take to print 500 flyers on a laser printer?

There are three "standards" on which you can base your bid decision—a machine standard, a production standard, and a baseline standard.

The *machine standard* is based on the capability of your equipment. It takes a finite time for a computer to import a document file into a layout program during design. It takes a finite time for a scanner to move the lamp over the page (or the page past the lamp). And, it takes a finite time for a laser printer to print a sheet. These times are directly related to the performance capability of the equipment that you are using.

Whether you can print six, eight, or more pages each minute with a particular laser printer depends on the printer. The best use for a machine standard is to establish a limit on how long it takes to do a particular task using specific equipment. It becomes the top end of the time boundary for estimating a task. You can't push a machine faster than it's design capability. The slowest device in a computer establishes the maximum speed that the computer can run. Having a "screamer" PC with minimum RAM and a slow hard disk drive causes the computer performance to be limited by the number of hard disk accesses that occur during a task. Adding RAM can significantly improve performance — particularly when working with graphics.

The *production standard* describes how long it takes to complete a task or to produce a document (or other output product) using the equipment that you have installed and the experience level of your people. This standard incorporates how you use your equipment. It helps you determine the typical times to perform shop activities.

Production speed depends on the type of computers and peripherals that you are using, the organization of the hard disk resources (fragmented files take longer to access) and the clock speed of each system. The slowest device determines the best speed possible in your electronic factory.

A production standard is established by conducting actual time studies, applying rules of thumb, studying historical records of past jobs, and by focusing on improving the skills of your staff. Your own judgement is critical in setting production standards unique to your shop.

Some professional groups such as the National Association of Quick Printers and the National Association of Secretarial Services have developed production standards that you can obtain. These should be used as a guide—only as a guide. Each job depends on many variables, and you must learn to incorporate every possible variable into your analysis. Production standards represent the typical, and they are a good place to start. They are useful for evaluating the performance output of individual employees, and they provide a marketing advantage when you advertise that your prices are based on "published industry standards."

Industry standards can be used as indicators to help you recognize deficiencies in your own pricing structure. Most standards organizations are careful to point out that your shop's cost rates and production speeds may be higher or lower than their "standard" published rates. Many variables are involved including hours of operation, wages, overhead, business volume, equipment, and the type of work.

At this point you can define a *baseline standard* that combines the machine and production standards. Using cost analysis, define how long it should take to complete each task so all the associated costs can be passed through within the billable time allocated to the job. Your baseline standard is based on your own shop, your personnel and your historical job records. It compensates for differences between an industry standard and your particular shop. It is the best source for estimating project costs.

For example, you get a request to provide 600 dpi printouts of several different manuals. Your production standard says that you need to power up and prepare the computer and the laser printer. Then you must execute the application program from which the manuals will be printed, go into the print mode, command a printout—possibly wait for PostScript conversion—and then wait for the output printer to produce each page of the manual. Your baseline standards (incorporating the machine and production standards) establish a time basis for the job. The machine standard says your printer can output eight sheets a minute. However, your system has a print spooler and multitasking capability. Thus you can command the computer to print this job in the background while you work on another job in the foreground.

Rather than charging each job for a portion of the time to warm-up, checkout, and execute the layout print actions, you bill out each job at the baseline standard full production rate. It's important to present consistent pricing to your customers.

Often shops will create and display a statement near the work input counter indicating that prices are based on published industry standards. Figure 4-2 is an example of such a statement.

FOR YOUR PROTECTION

(Company Name) uses a common pricing system based on industry production standards published by (name the source) for desktop publishing and prepress services.

These standards are based on the average time required to perform specific duties related to project production by professional DTP and prepress operators.

As such, they protect you from being overcharged for work by a slower operator. Through consistent and equal task billing all customers are charged the same price for the same service performed.

Figure 4-2. Sample production standard pricing statement.

A nice feature of baseline standards is that they establish all work at an average level. This means that efficient workers who finish faster and actually spend less time on a job don't cause a project to bill less revenue. The billing is based on the standard time, not the actual performance time of the worker.

Suppose a designer-operator has several jobs to perform. When the first job is designed, the operator commands a print output. Printing takes about 20 minutes, so while the printer is chugging out the first job, the operator begins work on the next job. This time-leveraging lets one person perform several tasks simultaneously. Yet you bill each job as if each were unique and had a dedicated person attending to the job during the full time of performance. This provides a cushion for rework caused by inadvertent errors or system breakdown.

At some point, you decide to upgrade your hardware and software. You had been charging $30 an hour based on your cost using the old hardware and software. When you install and place the new system into operation, you recalculate your costs basis and determine that you must charge $45 an hour. This looks good until you realize that you are now able to perform the same job in half the time. Should the customer be charged only $67.50 for a job that previously they were paying $90 for you to do? Perhaps.

You raised your rates, but could bring in less income for the same job. If you charge by the hour, rather than by the job, you will pass a production efficiency to your customer and earn less in the process. Owning the best equipment and current software is good, but shops owners invariably pass the time savings of these capabilities on to the client. The good side is that your bid price can now be lower making you more competitive, and you can handle more jobs each work day.

In another scenario, you get an order to print camera ready copy of a 20-page catalog. You have several different computers and printers available for the job.

Each machine operates at a different clock speed so the actual time to perform depends on the configuration that you use. The actual production time using the slower equipment can be significantly longer than the time to do the job with the newest and fastest hardware. If you base your estimate on production standards alone, you will end up with two different prices for the same job. You choose the longer time basis for your estimate to ensure that you will cover costs and earn a profit regardless which machine configuration you use. The risk here is that your equipment may be so old that bidding on its slowest performance time could put your estimates outside the ballpark of customer acceptance. A competitor with new hardware and current software could out-produce and under-bid you.

Using historical data to estimate a job is useful, but be careful that production inefficiencies aren't reflected in the older data. You may have developed your old standard using slower equipment and slower operators. Also, you may have developed your historical data using a very skilled employee. Each time you consider historical data, clearly understand how it was developed. It helps if you convert historical data into baseline standards and compare them to published production information.

By saving historical baseline standards you can identify trends and monitor shop efficiency and productivity based on actual averages custom to your business.

Use a Time in Tenths Chart

Many larger shops bill service by portions of an hour. Of these, some use the tenth of an hour increment. This means that they partition actual performance into hours and tenths-of-an-hour. Others build a twelfth-of-an-hour chart and bill out in 5 minute increments. They also round up to the nearest tenth of an hour when time-to-perform exceeds a tenth-of-an-hour increment.

Once you've established budgeted hourly rates for each service, you can develop an incremental time chart that breaks down your hourly rates. This quickly shows a customer what is owed on a job. As shown in Figure 4-3, basing your chart on industry standards (incorporated in your baseline standard) helps add credibility to your pricing structure.

Incremental Pricing Chart
(based on Industry Production Standards)

Time		Hourly Rate						
Tenths	Minutes	$30	$36	$39	$42	$45	$48	$52
0.1	6	3.00	3.60	3.90	4.20	4.50	4.80	5.20
0.2	12	6.00	7.20	7.80	8.40	9.00	9.60	10.40
0.3	18	9.00	10.80	11.70	12.60	13.50	14.40	15.60
0.4	24	12.00	14.40	154.60	16.80	18.00	19.20	20.80
0.5	30	15.00	18.00	19.50	21.00	22.50	24.00	26.00
0.6	36	18.00	21.60	23.40	25.20	27.00	28.80	31.20
0.7	42	21.00	25.20	27.30	29.40	31.50	33.60	36.40
0.8	48	24.00	28.80	31.20	33.60	36.00	38.40	41.60
0.9	54	27.00	32.40	35.10	37.80	40.50	43.20	46.80
1.0	60	30.00	36.00	39.00	42.00	45.00	48.00	52.00

Figure 4-3. Sample incremental time -pricing chart.

If you have only a few budgeted hourly rates, then you can generate a simpler chart. The important thing is to have this in your counter price book so customers can quickly see what they'll pay.

Estimating In Earnest

With costs clearly defined and understood, you're ready to tackle the estimating process. You'll begin by clearly specifying a job. This means that you must get all the information from the customer that is possible to identify each specific task that will be involved in completing the job. Then you'll develop a cost estimate using a worksheet form. There are various estimating programs on the market to help in this process.

Specifying a Job

Many factors must be considered when estimating a job—style sheets, additional support personnel, special equipment, materials, required output, and how to handle additions and corrections,.

Every time you have an opportunity to quote on a job, it's important to clearly specify what is being requested. Job specifications provide details on each task to be performed—the number of text characters in the document, the estimated number of pages, the typefaces and fonts to be used, the graphics and photographs to be stripped in, the expected amount of graphic and image manipulation, the layout grid, and the type of output desired (laser paper, RC paper, film, etc.).

Some customers won't know what is possible in DTP design and production, so you may be educating and guiding your clients during the development of job specs. You'll have customers come in who have done little preliminary planning. Usually the graphic image or photo that they want to use is unrealistic or requires re-work or re-touching. It's critical that both you and your customer understand what job is being discussed and what final product to expect.

After gaining experience, you'll develop an ability to quickly ballpark the price for a job based on its characteristics.

Creating an Estimating Form

Most DTP shops and service bureaus develop their own estimating worksheet. This custom form describes the job, the client and provides start and finish dates. Then it breaks the complete project into specific tasks. You should design a worksheet that is unique to your business. Figure 4-4 (pages 150 and 151) shows how a simple form can be constructed.

List all the tasks associated with a job in a column on the left side of your form. In a column to the right of each task list the hours estimated and the price to charge for each hour or page. Usually, indirect and innovative times are billed at an hourly rate. Production times are often billed out on a per page basis.

On the far right make a column to list the subtotal charge for each task. At the lower portion of the form, list each "out-of-pocket" expense. Add 10-20% to each of these expenses to cover administrative costs. Total all of the individual costs, and place this value in the lower right corner of your form. Remember that this is an estimate of what it will cost to do the job. If your hourly rates don't incorporate profit and ROI, you'll need to add a percentage for profit, and a percentage for return on investment to get a price on which you can base a quote.

Once your estimating form is complete, save your estimates of times and costs so you can compare these with actuals after project performance. This helps you refine your estimating skill. A spreadsheet program works well for performing this analysis.

PROJECT COST ESTIMATING FORM

PROJECT: _________________________ DATE: __________

CLIENT: _______________________________________

Indirect Costs

Hours x $/hour = Total/Task

Proposal preparation
Client kickoff meeting
Follow-up meeting 1
Follow-up meeting 2
Draft submission meeting
Final submission meeting
Telephone calls with client
Travel time
Close-out project

Creative Costs

Hours x $/hour = Total/Task

Conceptual development
Style template
Manuscript preparation
Writing copy
Designing charts
Designing graphs
Designing tables
Designing illustrations

Production Costs

Qty x $/per ea = Total/Task

Disk file conversion
Manuscript download
Spelling/Grammar checking
Prepare/Format text
Import text into layout program
Typography
Place graphics
Layout document
First draft
Corrections/Alterations
Paste-up
Final proof

Out-of-Pocket Expenses

	Total
File conversion support (____ files @ $___ ea)	
Laser proofs (____ @ $___ ea)	
Typeset output (____ @ $ ___ ea)	
Photographs (____ @ $ ___ ea)	
Illustrations (____ @ $ ___ ea)	
Stats (____ @ $ ___ ea)	
Color processing (____ @ $ ___ ea)	
Paste-up support	
Printing (____ cys @ $ ___ ea)	
Collating (____ shts @ $ ___ ea)	
Binding (____ pgs @ $ ___ ea)	
Travel (____ trips @ $ ___ ea)	
Delivery (____ trips @ $ ___ ea)	
Other	

Total Indirect Costs: ___________

Total Creative Costs: ___________

Total Production Costs: ___________

Total Out-of-Pocket Expenses: ___________

Shop Overhead Costs: ___________

TOTAL PROJECT COST: ___________

Fig. 4-4. Sample Project Cost Estimating Form

ALPHAQUOTE Estimating and Copyfitting Program

Available as a complimentary gift with your *Pricing Guide* is ALPHAQUOTE, a typesetting and copyfitting program developed by Bruce Roby of AlphaBytes in Washington, D.C. This program provides a fast and consistent way to price a job or to compare the cost of desktop publishing with traditional typesetting/ imagesetting. ALPHAQUOTE includes the ability to print reports, save estimates to disk, instantly preview estimates, and calculate costs based on page or character count.

It's greatest strength is its ability to show a desktop publisher or non-traditional typesetter what a job is worth.

ALPHAQUOTE can be used to estimate both consistent layouts such as books and manuals, and inconsistent layouts such as magazines and newsletters with varying graphic areas and column widths.

The user manual and ALPHAQUOTE program disk will be shipped to you at no additional cost when you return the card found at the back of this reference book.

Follow Up On Your Estimates

Following up to determine how an estimate fared with reality is one of the most profitable things an estimator can do. Good follow-up produces a methodical comparison between initial cost figures and actual costs accrued during performance.

Careful follow-up will highlight deficiencies in your estimating strategy. It helps you spot holes and errors. It is also a way to confirm that all jobs have been estimated accurately. This process fine-tunes your estimating process and helps you avoid errors in future efforts.

By comparing the actual costs with the expected costs, you are forcing yourself to apply critical reasoning and careful analysis to the process. You can't affect jobs that have been awarded, but you can certainly adjust your numbers and improve your win ratio on future opportunities.

Some professional estimators set performance goals for themselves. They try to get their cost estimates to come is within 5% of actual costs. A good ballpark range is 3-5% accuracy.

As with most aspects of business, a computer spreadsheet is a valuable tool to use in performing post-production analysis.

When Estimating Your Next Job

DTPers sometimes overlook important factors when preparing their estimate and quote package. Here are some things to remember when you prepare your next estimate.

Style Sheet. Establish a separate price for developing the style sheet. This part of the process can be time-consuming and involve a detailed understanding of layout and style sheet development.

Additions, Alterations and Corrections. Know in advance how you will handle the customer's alterations, printer's alterations, and customer-directed changes. Both you and your customer should know when additional charges will occur?

Job Characteristic. Pricing design work depends on the complexity of the job. A document with consistent layout can be priced at a different dollar amount than one with lots of design elements.

Copyright. Usually when a DTPer is hired to design a document, or some other form of product, the final product belongs to the client. They pay you for a service. You are essentially operating as "work for hire." If you are involved in a unique design with potential for multi-applications, make a conscious decision to discuss copyright ownership of the design and "other future use" rights regarding your work. You may be able to negotiate future residual rights (hence additional income) should the design be used in other products..

Art & Graphics. Try to determine the percent of art that will be included. By knowing the number of figures, illustrations and photographs you can get an idea of the complexity and the size of the job. This lets you quote based on how much work you'll expect in the job. You can also estimate final page count based on a standard art size and amount of artwork to be included.

Bidding

A bid is an offer of price. It defines the dollar amount at which you are willing to exchange a product or service.

An Estimate is Not a Bid

In the optimum situation, an expert generates an estimate specifying all of the costs associated with a particular job. This cost estimator has no responsibility for setting the bid price or establishing profit. Instead, another person, probably a marketing type, independently establishes a rough bid price based on the competition, what the customer was charged last time, the work load, and the pricing strategy.

It is at this point, that the cost estimate and the rough bid price are compared. If the spread between the costs and the "could charge" is large, there is room to negotiate. If the spread is too narrow, the company may decide to pass on this job—or decide to live with the low margin for a strategic business-related reason.

Given the small staff in most DTP and service bureau operations, one person likely completes the cost estimate AND determines the price to bid.

However, the key point is that estimating and bidding are separate actions. An estimate is based on historical fact—actual performance averages and industry production standards. The bid price is based on judgement—interpretation of the external competition and the needs of the customer. Each process should be performed independently—not simultaneously— and then compared.

Getting Bid Opportunities

Bid opportunities can be found everywhere. But you must be there when the opportunities arise, or you must make your prospective customers know that your support is available when their need arises. To do this, you must keep prospects aware of who you are and what you can do. This can be accomplished by making cold calls in person, telemarketing, networking at trade shows and meetings of professional associations, advertising in magazines, newspapers, flyers, inserts, and door hangers, and by having your current customers, vendors, or colleagues tell others about your business.

The appendix to this guide provides valuable insights into what lead-generation method worked best for the businesses that participated in our recent survey.

For those interested in doing business with the government, get on a Qualified Bidders List. Contact the purchasing offices for each government organization that you want to serve. Once you get on a list, you may have to update your qualification each year to remain listed.

Be aware that government jobs may be plentiful, but their payment schedule is typically complex and slow. More than just a few businesses have folded after putting too many eggs (jobs) into the government basket and having extended payments restrict their cash flow too long to survive. You should spread your work over as many customer types as possible.

Once you're on a qualified bidders list, you'll occasionally receive a request for quote (RFQ) or request for bid (RFB) from one of your prospective government customers. Large corporations and educational institutions also go out for bid on large jobs.

A request for bid (RFB) can come at any time— especially if you keep your company's name on a qualified bidders list. Typically the RFB will include a written statement of the requirements of the job and an indication of how long you have to respond. A good RFB provides a basis for understanding and on which you can make contractual commitments.

The request package should establish a competitive environment between proposed vendors. It's used by the client to develop a legally binding contract. Responding to an RFB places you in a competitive position where the price that you quote is usually less than the price you can give to individual prospects coming in off the street.

Responding to a Request for Bid

You can't make a commitment on response time and the form of output product or service without a detailed description of the complete job. Each aspect of the job must be itemized. All required specifications should be included in the bid request package that you receive. If they aren't, then ask.

Each task in the Statement of Work should be clear and concise. Each deliverable must be defined and described. If the customer didn't provide it in their RFB, include in your response your terms and conditions that tie payments to the acceptance of deliverables. Therefore, acceptance criteria must also be clearly cited.

In addition, the RFB should clearly explain what actions or conditions could void the agreement and any criteria for accepting one bid over another based on some factor other than price.

Some RFBs ask you to submit samples of past work. This is a good reason to make extra copies of those "really nice jobs" that have been very successful.

If the RFB asks for references, be sure to check with your clients before you put their name and telephone number on your bid response. You want strong supporters and very satisfied customers on your reference list.

The RFB should include a procedure for getting answers to questions, and it should identify the cutoff date and time, and where to return the bid.

Developing a bid response is time consuming, but once you master the process, you should be able to generate a bid quickly and professionally. Your word processor and spreadsheet programs are valuable tools in this process.

Your proposal should be clear and concise. Don't assume that your client understands any specification that was omitted in their RFB. Cover each aspect of the job and cover all the contingencies that you can imagine. Remember: Murphy is alive and well in the world of contract performance.

A final comment concerns the look and feel of your bid package. A professional look can impact its acceptance. Your bid package is often a prospective customer's first look at you and your work. Sloppy bid packages make for infrequent contract awards. Spend the time and money to give it the look of quality.

Symptoms of a Poor Bid Response

There are six things that can get you labelled non-responsive on a bid request.
1. You can fail to meet the terms specified in the RFB.
2. You may not be able to back up what you claim.
3. Your references may not be suitable.
4. You may be recommending a sub-optimum solution.
5. You may fail to consider the complete job,.
6. You may fail to consider a customer's actual needs.

When submitting your bid package, be certain that you have covered each of these factors.

Bidding Strategies

Estimating gives you a good feel for the potential net profit in a job. It's based on fact. Estimating is a science. Bidding is how you use your estimate. Bidding is based on diplomacy, tack, and skill. Bidding is an art.

There are many ways to bid a job. Just be certain that you don't bid too low. New desktop publishers tend to undercharge. They risk ending up with clients who feel that they don't have to pay much for your work. When these entrepreneurs become aware, they find that they must reeducate these clients or drop them and find new ones.

How Should I Bid a Job?

Desktop publishing and prepress mean different things to different customers. The wide range of talent and available skills makes comparing apples-to-apples difficult. You may bid based on logical analysis and clear understanding of what a job requires. A competitor may be just starting out—be completely naive, be business illiterate, or be after every customer that comes along. So they may bid aggressively and LOW. You're shocked at what they quote to do a job. You're sure that they're not earning a living from their cutthroat pricing. You know that they'll be out of business within a year. Yet these types of competitors keep coming out of the woodwork.

The primary reason that they bid so low is that they haven't the foggiest idea what they should be charging. They look around at their competition and then set their rates at half or less than everyone else.

As they wonder why they can't seem to make money in this business, you shake your head and move on to the next proposal. But should you? Perhaps you could help everyone in our profession by speaking with the low bidder. They may appreciate your words of wisdom. If not, call the customer to assure them of your support in case the shop that they selected fails to perform satisfactorily. It may be that the IRS will shut that competitor's doors long before delivery is made on the contract. This could be an opportunity for you.

Although DTP is maturing, there are still enough alligators in the swamp to make estimating part magic. Hard disk drives still crash (usually at the most inopportune times) and incompatibility still rears its ugly head when we try to "improve" our system software.

If you've never performed cost analysis and have never met the alligators, you can make some disastrous bids. The "new kids on the street" often learn by failing. There is a better way—careful cost analysis and street-smart pricing.

Bidding By The Page

Pricing a job by the page can be tricky because the time and energy spent on each customer can vary significantly. The per-page pricing method requires that you know exactly how each page will be designed. It depends on the total number of pages in the job, the complexity of each page, the volume of work this client brings to you, and the type of tasks that you'll be performing (data editing, grammar checking, spell-checking, illustrations, etc.). Changing the style can affect the total page count and cause significant re-design.

Without a page layout template and a good count of the number of pages of each layout complexity (simple, standard, and complex), you must estimate a job based on many possible design configurations.

You could establish a "base page" price and then adjust this price depending on job complexity, the customer, the turnaround time desired, the amount of DTP skill required, and special conditions related to the job (e.g., comparable costs of mechanical art production, competitor pricing for similar work, and the hardware and software resources required).

Some estimators partition a page layout into simple, moderate, or complex. A simple page has a single column and simple headings. They establish a base rate for this simple page layout. As the design becomes increasingly complex, they add a percentage to the base price.

For example, two columns adds 50% more to the base rate. Three columns adds another 50% to the base rate. Thus, a three column design would have an estimate of 100% base rate plus 50% for a second column, plus 50% for the third column or an estimate that is 200% of the base page rate. A $12 base charge and a three column design would equate to a $24 charge for each three-column page ($12 + $6 + $6 = $24).

These estimators charge another 25% of the base rate for each special feature such as drop caps, pull quotes, photos, etc., and 10% more for each instance of kerning, drop ins, large type, and graphic sizing required.

This means that a page with two columns, a drop cap, a graphic illustration, and a photo would price out at $12 base, plus $6 for the second column, plus $3 for the drop cap, plus $1.20 for sizing the graphic, plus $3 for adding a photograph. The total bill comes to $25.20 for this page. Charts or graphs can add additional charges to the job.

Add up all the costs for each page and total the package. Then factor in the cost to stat (or scan) photographs, imageset the pages, and deliver the final product. This becomes the cost basis for the project. Then add overhead and the other associated expenses and profit to derive your final quote.

Before you establish a per-page rate, do some testing. Develop a style sheet and lay out some pages. This will give you a feel for the size of the project.

Bidding by the Job

While most shops charge for document design by the page or by the hour., on larger jobs they bid by the project. Hourly shop rates help establish a basis from which to work. They are good for providing on-site support to a client. And they are good for building a bid package.

As you learned in the last section, some shops charge by the page starting with a base rate and then add an adjustment surcharge for complexity. The base figure incorporates cost analysis for the shop, comparable rates from competitors, and the skills available to work on the job.

The best approach is to ask to see the work. Take time to really study the job, ask questions, and get all the clarity possible. A snap bid can appear unprofessional and make a customer think that you run a simple "job shop" and not a professional graphics and document design organization. However, if you feel comfortable with the description of the job, you can give them a conservative "ballpark" bid based on your worst-case conditions. Tell them the job could cost less if everything runs smoothly. And tell them that you can give them a final bid once you look over the material.

When a new customer with little or no DTP or prepress experience comes in to discuss a job, you should incorporate several factors into the price that you quote. If you don't bid an hourly rate with a minimum fee, you may waste time "educating" and "hand-holding" that customer. New customers may have no concept of how much work is involved, or how a final document will look. They could start changing the design the moment you begin working on the project. This could impact your schedule and substantially increase your costs.

When you get a call asking how much a "simple" job will cost, avoid a snap answer. Instead, ask a series of questions. Is the design complete? How many pages? How many columns? How many heads and subheads? How many tables, charts, and diagrams? Will columns need to follow a certain design form (e.g., line up at the bottom as well as top)? How much art? How many photographs? Is all the art and graphics camera ready? The way the caller answers these questions will usually tell you how much of your resources will be required to complete that job.

Both parties must know how the job will be delivered to you—in hard copy, on film, or on disk. If on disk, what is the application program and operating system format? Will conversion be required? Are proofreading and spell-checking needed?

Also, determine how the finished job will be delivered—the print resolution, the output form (paper or film), and how many copies of the galleys or camera-ready mechanicals are desired.

Be certain to clarify ownership for the disks, artwork, and film associated with a job. You may assume that you own these, but your customer may feel that they paid for these in their fee. Specify ownership rights in the agreement or job order that your customer signs. Be sure that they understand what they will receive upon payment for a job.

During the discussion process with a prospective customer, keep notes on how you calculate time and costs. Also note what you say to the customer and what the customer indicates they want. What they think they want and what they actually want are often two different products. If there will be original artwork that you will create, bid by the hour. Avoid a fixed fee. In giving them a ballpark figure, allow time for an initial design plus several hours of alterations. If they decide not to select your shop for the job, you may be lucky. Sometimes the winner of a bid ends up being the loser in income earned compared with the cost to perform and deliver.

For original artwork creation, you could bid a ballpark figure that incorporates time for an initial design plus several hours of alterations. A good strategy is to quote a ballpark figure, but bill by the hour. You could negotiate minimum and maximum price boundaries.

Steve Morris of Signal Graphics Printing Franchises described front counter tips in a recent *Instant Printer* article. When a customer asks for a "ballpark" figure, he gives them several. He uses a "good, better, best" principle. He gives them the "better" price first based on his experience of an in-between cost to do the job. Then he gives them a lower price alternative based on using different, or lower quality materials. Finally he gives them a premium or "best" price based on using the best materials. This tactic removes the perceived need to shop around. And Steve has less need to negotiate a discounted price from those he quotes. Effectively the customer has completed all of the comparison shopping at Steve's front counter. No matter which option they choose, Steve gets the job.

Bidding by the Hour

In this technique, an owner calculates all the labor and materials costs associated with a particular job. Each piece of hardware and software that will be used is included in the cost basis. Even software and hardware maintenance contracts are amortized over each job. (Software maintenance usually costs between $300 and $1,000 a year.) Then overhead, profit, and return on any investments are added to reach the final number to quote.

The quote that you make can be one figure that includes each task and all hardware and software components required, or it can be partitioned into separate rates for each task and each piece of hardware or software used on a job. The budgeted hourly rate method described in Chapter 3 is useful when bidding by the hour or by the job.

Depending on who is doing the work and how alert they are each time they approach the job, you can average the time to perform a task—check a document file for spelling and format, import a file, layout and typeset a certain number of characters each minute, etc.. You can also establish an average time for handling graphics and photographs. Include the time to input each graphic, manipulate and re-size images, re-touch photos and proof and print the final job.

Add up all the associated times for each task and multiply by your budgeted hourly rate. This results in a job estimate price bid. You can determine the cost per page by dividing the estimated price by the number of pages. This can be used to estimate future jobs that are similar and based on the same budgeted hourly rate.

The Case for Market-Based Bidding

Many DTP shops and service bureaus price products and services as though they operate in a regulated economy. Each owner will add a mark-up to the costs and then price a job. These cost-driven owner-operators often multiply production standards by industry or custom cost rates to establish a baseline. Then they add mark-up to achieve the price to quote. Some industry standard tables already incorporate mark-up into each suggested price.

Quoting a job based on standard rates is relatively easy, but quoting a job based on market conditions may be more profitable. In a market-driven approach, you bid based on what the market will bear. You are constrained by what your competition is doing, but markup has little affect on your price.

The cost-driven entrepreneur establishes a quote using internal expenses. These costs are accepted as a given in this formula. Job prices are driven primarily by the expenses involved.

The market-driven approach uses the market place as the driving factor in price. Market driven estimators focus on knowing the competition and being sensitive to the perceived value of their work. By performing competitive pricing and customer value analysis, profitability can rise even while general prices decrease.

Successful DTPers work hard to increase productivity and efficiency. They consistently try to cut costs and reduce overhead. They seek ways to gain an edge over their competition by making their products or services unique. And they price jobs to optimize the use of all of their resources (people, equipment, software, facilities, and time). The productivity of both the shop and of the employees becomes critical in this formula. Market price variations are countered by accommodating them internally in capital equipment and in business operation.

Most shops use both job cost estimating and market analysis to help determine price. Job cost estimating is one of the tools that you'll use in business. Some of these tools are better than others. Estimating a job based on cost predictions can provide a rough idea of potential profit, but it doesn't show how much you could be charging for the same job. Job cost estimating is best used to help weed out unprofitable jobs—know when to decline (no-bid) work. It's a good marketing analysis tool for making rejection judgements. Cost estimating helps you determine your "rock-bottom" price.

The best approach is to let market forces establish your top end bid. Use cost estimating tools to determine your break-even and to guide your bid decisions. But make your bid based on the maximum price that you can get in the current market condition.

In a recent *MSM* magazine article, Dan Evans, founder of a sales training and marketing development company, described a strong correlation between the actions to match the specific needs of a customer to your shop's capability and a successful sale. He says that the more specific you get about how your products or services will benefit a customer, the stronger this correlation becomes. Evans also points out that large contracts are lost or won during the probing of fact finding and the need-satisfaction process that occurs before your client has a chance to order. Therefore, ask questions, evaluate, match your products and services to the customer's needs, and then, if what you offer matches their needs, ask for the business.

If your market analysis suggests that you can succeed with much higher price, go slow. Don't change your prices radically or you'll send shock waves through your customer base. Even if you improve your operation, continue to use the old base estimating standard to give you negotiating room during the bid process. You can back off on your quote without having to lower it to near break-even. Remember that your cost basis determines the minimum price at which you can accept a job and still make money. It does not define the maximum price at which you'd like to quote and be awarded a job. This is relegated to market-driven pricing.

Price is determined using external information. What you estimate and choose to quote is determined using external analysis. By comparing price against estimated costs you can quickly determine the margin that is available.

If market-driven pricing consistently produces margins that are unattractive, you should analyze your operation to find ways to improve efficiency. Perhaps you're using obsolete equipment or out-dated software. Perhaps you need to reorganize your shop according to process flow so the work moves through your business in an optimal path. It could be that your overhead is too high and must be pared down. And it could be that you are simply expecting too much profit from a low margin world.

As printing productivity specialist, Roger Dickeson puts it: "You'd be ahead to dump the cost tables and load a price laundry list in your Macintosh and use the keyboard like they do at Burger King to pump out a quote. Be a quick pricer. But you'd better competitive-shop Hardee's and MacDonald's to keep your computer price list updated for a quarter-pounder."

Submitting a Formal Quote

When a client asks for a formal bid, provide your response in writing. Usually this is done on office letterhead. Your bid should partition the job into broad categories and provide a bottom line price.

Figure 4-5 is an example of a quotation form that you can adopt for your own business.

YOUR BUSINESS NAME
Quotation

(Good for 30 days)

To: ABC Company   **Date:** _________
1177 Happiness Lane
Pleasant Valley, NY 11011

For:

(describe project)

1. $

2. $

(describe tasks)

3. $

4. $

5. $

Total: $

Accepted: ______________________   Date: ____________

This estimate is based on current labor and materials costs for the work described. Final prices are subject to revision if costs or specifications change. Alterations, and customer-directed changes will incur extra charges.

Fig. 4-5. A sample formal quotation form.

Be sure to include a description of what the client will do and what the shop will do. Include a caveat that your price quote is based on typical performance schedules. If your client wants faster response, you can put a RUSH on the job. Usually, this expedite action results in a 25-50% increase in the invoice billing.

Negotiating Techniques

When negotiations begin, the desktop publisher get "seasoned by fire"—you learn by occasionally "getting burned." Each side wants to maximize its own position. However, negotiations should not be perceived as a form of mutual sacrifice. In this activity, buying and selling become opposite sides of the same coin. Negotiations produce the formula that helps both sides maximize their own interests. This process should result in everyone leaving the table a winner.

Your challenge is to find an arrangement that lets everyone win. The customer knows that you must make a profit in order to stay in business — although they don't like to admit this. And you know that each customer has a finite budget within which to operate.

Negotiation is a continuing process. No issues are irrevocable—even after agreements are reached and signatures are placed on paper. Both the buyer and the seller should understand and accept the business needs of the other party. And each should be flexible and willing to look at alternatives.

Cooperation creates harmony, and competition creates efficiency. The best negotiators don't try to manipulate. They try to understand and work out a mutual solution.

The problems occur when you discover that you are negotiating with a party that doesn't have the business ethics that you believe in and demonstrate. They push, cajole, persuade, and do their best to manipulate you to accept their rigid views and demands. Their actions stimulate the street smarts that you learned by being "burned" before (or by reading about and accepting what others have experienced).

How can you successfully negotiate a job so both you and your customer come out on top? First, do your homework. You not only need to know your job, but you also must know about the business that your customer is in. You must know what importance (and priority) your customer places on quality, form, substance, delivery, and price.

Then you need to understand what issues can be negotiated. These include:

- price
- terms
- delivery
- tasks
- materials
- time schedule
- level of service
- output form
- output quality
- warranty
- follow-on jobs

Identify your goals. What is it you want to accomplish? What is the minimum price at which you will accept the job? What is the highest price you think you can charge? Understanding and timing can be everything in this process.

If you can get a client to reveal the budget that they have for a job, you can use this as a yardstick for how far you can go with your bid. Try not to come in too low or too high relative to their budget.

From the moment you and your customer first communicate, you are in negotiations. This means that you must be prepared to discuss service and support from the start. A chance encounter at an airport, in the line at the post office, or even during a business association meeting can become the beginning stage in the negotiation process.

From this point on, you move in a complex maze of tactics, strategies, and discussions. It helps to have previewed the issues that could be introduced during the process. You can do this by developing a question map to help you think out and structure answers to each question that might be posed.

The next time you meet, be sure the right party is present. Negotiate with the decision maker, not the messenger.

Whether follow-on meetings occur at your shop or at the office of your customer, you should identify the issues that both sides accept and those issues that must be negotiated. Ask questions and keep an open mind. Your questions should establish need, concern, and resistance. Your attitude should reflect a willingness to find a workable formula.

Listening is critical in this process. You need to learn where your prospect is and where they want to go with the project. You can't learn when you're talking. You must listen. Listen and observe first. Then talk.

Much of the message that your customer conveys will come in the form of nonverbal communication—in the gestures and body language that they use, in the tone of their voice, in the way they move, and in the direction they look when you ask certain pointed questions. Buy a book or take a course on nonverbal communication techniques. It'll be worth the investment.

Through dialogue and attentive listening, you can establish issues and create alternatives for your prospective customer. Neutral issues are usually handled quickly. For those issues that must be negotiated, have available alternative solutions—designs, terms, package deals, quality, quantity, and prices.

There are many formulas defining how a job can be performed and delivered. You should be open to discussing different alternatives. Just be certain that both of you are speaking the same language. You should quickly overcome semantic and technical language difficulties. If you each have a different perception of a camera ready proof, clarity and agreement must be achieved before you can proceed. Produce a sample proof that is acceptable to both sides. This then becomes the criteria for suitability.

You should never begin negotiations unless you are willing to walk away. You need emotional detachment and a tough mental attitude to achieve your own negotiating objectives. The party who wants to deal the most, must deal from a disadvantage. So even if you desperately want that job, don't let the other party sense this. Be patient, but hold to a high standard of value for yourself and your shop's capability and performance.

The idea is not to close doors or limit what each will do based on the negotiation, but to clearly convey that you are providing quality service. You want open and friendly discourse. Therefore, try to clearly understand what they want and need. Then help them understand what you want and what you can provide.

Use gestures and speak with a confident voice consistent with the meeting topic. Many negotiators adopt a "matter-of-fact" tone of voice. They use neutral terms that don't incorporate value judgements. Yet they're still open to explore many alternative solutions.

Ask for more than you expect to get. This lets you give up less important issues while retaining the larger issues. If they want you to concede on some issues, give in slowly and reluctantly. But get something in return for each issue that you give on.

Be certain what issues you are willing to concede. Also know when you will be willing to make these concessions. You don't want to be the first to make a major concession because this puts you in an inferior position. Instead, give on small concessions slowly. A small concession that you give reluctantly can seem like a greater win for the other side than it really is.

Try to keep the quote at a "whole job" level. If they want to break up each task into cost elements, they may "nickel and dime" you out of significant profit by negotiating each issue separately.

If they change the scope of the job, and increase the volume of work, be open to offering a volume discount. Many shop owners reduce their prices between five and 15 percent for quantity buys. If they don't ask for it, don't offer it, unless you are trading for something else during the negotiation.

Remain reasonable and stick to facts. This can encourage your prospect to accept the reality of the costs involved in providing the service or support that they seek. By getting them to understand your position, you can often get them to support your case and accept a price closer to what you want.

If they ask a question, be certain that you understand what they are asking. Have them repeat the question if you aren't sure what they really asked. Then only answer the question asked. A sharp negotiator will try to get you to talk more because it strokes your ego while it provides them information that they might use against you later in the negotiation process.

Instead, do the opposite. Listen more. Play dumb. Ask them to explain points and issues. Appeal to their knowledge of the subject matter. Build their ego so you can build a bridge to early agreement.

When they make their first offer, don't accept it—even if it is a great deal. When you feel like saying "yes," say "no." This serves as a sanity check for the actual bottom line of the other party.

Several important elements affect the final price that you reach—the payment terms and schedule, maintaining a lead over your competition, maintaining your work load near capacity, full employment for you and your staff, future business, and market timing.

The final price should not be unilateral. It should represent the consideration of both sides in the negotiation. It should be a win-win compromise where both parties come away satisfied, not a splitting of differences in which someone may remain dissatisfied.

Usually, a realistic price is realized long before the subject is directly addressed. At that point, asking your price becomes almost a ritual. You should never give your prospect the feeling that they have asked too little or demanded too much. Always treat them (and their package) with respect. No matter how great a win you achieved, always protect their ego. Help them save face. Treat the agreement as a true win-win for both parties.

When you do present your bid, show confidence and pride that you are agreeing to do the job at a price that is best for both parties.

If your bid just cannot come in below their budget, see if they can do some of the work themselves. Perhaps they can do their own collating, or comb binding. Perhaps they can provide paper, bindings, disks, boards, or other required materials.

If these things won't work, firmly, but gracefully announce an impasse and close the negotiations. Keep the options open to negotiate on other business opportunities in the days and weeks ahead. They just might call tomorrow and give you a better final offer on this job. Don't burn your bridges.

Getting Help on the Negotiation Process

You can significantly increase your success in the negotiation process by reading, studying, and practicing. One of the best teachers of negotiation has been Gerard Nierenberg. His book *The Art of Negotiation* and corresponding audio tape series are available through Nightingale-Conant Corporation, 7300 North Lehigh Ave., Chicago, IL 60648, (800) 323-5552.

His son, Roy Nierenberg recently developed a PC program with the same title as his father's book. Roy's software package works on MS-DOS computers. It helps you prepare for a negotiating session by presenting questions that force you to define and plan a strategy. The questions and answers can be ordered the way you want and printed out as a checklist that you can use during negotiations.

The program is available from Experience in Software, 2039 Shattuck Ave., Ste. 401, Berkeley, CA 94704, (415) 644-0694.

Put It in Writing

When you both agree on performance and price, get your agreement in writing. The document you use can be an Agreement, a Contract, or even a Purchase Order. Just be certain that you are both signing to what you agreed during formal negotiations.

Be sure that each issue that you discussed and worked out is clearly described in the document. Be certain that it covers all aspects of the job.

List the specific tasks that will be performed under that contract. With each task listed, identify who is responsible. Some tasks will be the responsibility of your customer (e.g., provide art and photos by a certain date and time). The majority of tasks will be performed by you and your staff. However, late delivery of the initial disks, art, or rough documents by your customer can affect the quality and schedule of your own performance.

Indicate when you will make delivery of a draft copy, the number of edit revisions allowed without added charges, how graphics will be received and handled, and when alteration charges will occur.

Allow flexibility for the customer to make changes (chargeable, of course) during the design process. Impromptu changes by a vacillating customer can create havoc when you don't have a clear understanding of change versus complete re-design alteration and the number and scope of change allowed before extra charges apply. Design changes by a waffling customer can be a lucrative way to increase job profits, but be sure they are aware that their indecision and tendency to change are adding to the total job cost.

If any point is not listed on the agreement document, write it in. Each party should initial acceptance of the addition on both copies of the original agreement. The same goes for incorrect statements. Mark your changes on the original agreement forms. Then, both of you initial your acceptance. This eventually results in a document-pair that represents everything that the two parties agreed should occur.

The agreement should list each company's name, address and telephone number, and a point of contact for each party. For large companies, include their purchase order number (if provided). At this point, both parties should sign and keep a copy.

With your copy of the agreement in hand, begin work and do all you can to perform exactly as agreed or better. Remember the advice on early delivery. You want repeat business, and here's your chance to build a lasting relationship. Just don't inconvenience the customer by delivering too early.

Omissions in Many "Standard" Contracts

Potential problems can occur when critical factors are not included in a work agreement or contract for services. These omissions are like holes in "Swiss cheese." They become loopholes through which misunderstanding and poor perceived performance can flow out of a relationship. To avoid problems, be careful to:

1. Clearly specify the deliverables.

2. Tie payments to the acceptance of deliverables. (It's normal to get a 10-33% deposit on large jobs)

3. Use wording that adequately covers defects and correction procedures.

4. Specify what actions a customer could take that would void warranties.

5. Incorporate specifics on task descriptions, responsibilities, and schedule dates in the proposal and subsequent contract.

6. Provide fail-safe dates and provisions to cancel the contract if either party is unable to perform for an extended period of time.

7. Specify whether additional materials are being provided or will be charged extra.

8. Specify legal remedies if your customer "goes south" on you and refuses to pay. You'll appreciate having a clause in your "contract" that specifies that if you take legal action against them, whoever wins the case can recover the legal costs involved.

Forgetting any of these factors can set you on a risky course through rock-strewn waters. You may be able to navigate through, but it's much easier when the course is well established.

Tracking Bids and Buyer Decisions

When you bid on a job and the bid goes to someone else, contact the buyer and ask for feedback on your quote. Even if you win the job, ask for feedback.

Explain that you consistently strive to improve and you would like to find out where your bid stood among the competing bids. If a competitor beat you out and their winning bid was half of your bid, probe to determine the experience level of the buyer. Sometimes a buyer has little understanding of what is really involved in a job. And sometimes a competitor is trying to "get their foot in the door" with the customer and plans to "recover" by charging a high fee for changes and alterations after the contract is awarded.

Try to track all the bids on a particular job. If you can, find out how the buyer decided the winning bid.

By taking these steps for every job that you bid, you'll develop a historical database on both your customers and your competitors. This information can help you make even better bid decisions in the future.

If you decide to bid lower, keep your break-even point in mind. Recognize that, as the economy passes through a down cycle, your customers will take extra effort to cut a tighter deal for themselves.

Getting Paid

The agreement that you and your customer sign should clearly describe how and when payment will be made. There are many possible payment schedules—cash upon delivery of the final work, net due in two weeks, net due in 30 days, etc. Just be certain that the term "payment" means "payment received by" and not "payment requested from their own Accounts Payable Department by." This is particularly appropriate when doing business with government organizations, schools, and most large companies.

Never, NEVER take on a large job without getting "earnest" money up front. I like to work on a three-step basis—one-third of the agreed price is paid up front, one-third is paid upon submission of the first draft, and the last third is paid upon delivery of the final product. If a customer doesn't produce payment in full when you're ready to deliver, have them wait until they have the money before you turn over any work.

For those customers that pay on a net-<days> basis, be sure to invoice them immediately to start the clock. And be sure to provide the invoice to the correct department (e.g., Accounting Department). Some government organizations don't believe in starting their clock until their accounting department receives the actual invoice. If you go through the department for which you performed the work, they may take several weeks to "approve" payment, and then it may take several more days to get the invoice routed to the Accounts Payable desk in their Accounting Department.

On most net-pay jobs, I place a statement on the invoice that makes interest accrue and the whole amount due and payable on a day-by-day basis after the net-due date is passed.

Summary

Estimating and bidding is a complex process, and many people do nothing else. However, most DTP shops and service bureaus can't afford a dedicated person to handle these functions. The owner-manager is usually the person who takes on these jobs (with a myriad of other tasks).

Nevertheless, estimating and bidding can provide a substantial boost to your sales income. The better you are at these functions, the better your bottom line will look at the end of the business year.

After addressing strategy, bidding and negotiation, you're armed with some powerful tools for success. In the next chapter you'll find street smart ideas for maximizing your success potential. Chapter 5 covers operational ideas based on the best tricks in the trade.

Street Smart Operations

"The only acceptable profit is the maximum profit."

This chapter is about tactics. It provides ideas for implementing the strategy that you developed in earlier chapters. Through the use of street smart techniques and various management tools, you can successfully set price and recognize when to pursue or decline a project. In this chapter you'll also find forms and worksheets that can help streamline your operation. And you'll learn how to design your own counter price sheet. Case studies will provide concrete examples of how to put strategy into action.

The successful shops are able to change rapidly and provide fast service. They appear capable and perform professionally. Chapter 5 shows you how to make every day an opportunity for extended success.

Terms to Remember

Counter Price Book - A collection of sheets describing your pricing structure. This is what you show a customer who wants to know how much you charge.

FTE - A full-time equivalent employee. The average number of 8-hour employees in your shop.

Tactics - Where the the "rubber meets the road" — when you put strategy into action. The operational result of strategic planning. Strategy describes what. Tactics describes how.

Do It By The Numbers

Financial illiteracy has cost small business both growth and income,. In some cases, it cost dearly —a future for an aspiring owner-operator. Poor financial understanding is the Achilles heel of the entrepreneur. It is the bane of the DTP professional. An old axiom suggests that a dumb competitor is the worst kind. There are many "dumb" competitors in the DTP and prepress profession.

Success is not just knowing what to do. It's also in knowing how to do it. Let's improve your odds by tackling some economic and financial issues that directly relate to price.

Return on Investment

Return on investment can be a tricky animal to harness. Of the many accounting and economics books that I researched, a number of ways to calculate ROI came to light. Accountants seem to enjoy complicated formulas. The formula that they use depends on if they are generating numbers for the stockholders or for upper management. I prefer the "keep it simple" principle.

Therefore I view return on investment as the bang you get for the buck you spend. What financial gain will you realize by your monetary investment in your business?

In this way, the formula becomes simpler.

$$ROI = \frac{net\ profit}{investment}$$

If you put $10,000 into your business to get it started, you deserve a return on this investment just as if you had invested this money in mutual funds or treasury bonds. Today, you should be able to earn 5-10% on your money. This means that you factor a ROI into your pricing.

Take the investment and decide on an acceptable return. Then as we did in Chapter 2, integrate this return directly into your hourly rates. For a $10,000 investment, an expected return of 10%, and a 2080 hour working year, you should allocate 48¢ to each hour that is billed out. (See Table 2-1)

If you use the $10,000 to purchase equipment and software, the return then becomes a return on assets.

Return on Assets

In the world of financial analysis, people often use subjective decisions to make objective conclusions. They assume a given result and then base dollar investment numbers on the assumption. Although this seems silly, sometimes it's the best shot we can make at evaluating a business approach.

The concept of *return on assets* (ROA) is such a case. ROA is like return on investment. We want to realize a percentage of monetary good for an investment in something tangible like computer equipment or better software. In this case, we attempt to anticipate a revenue gain given we make a certain hardware or software investment. Our formula goes like this:

$$C = \frac{ER}{1 + r}$$

where C is cost, ER is expected revenue, and r is the expected rate of return (a percentage expressed as a decimal).

$$\text{Cost of Equip/Software} = \frac{\text{Expected Revenue}}{1 + \text{Expected Rate of Return}}$$

We're calculating the expected revenue value, so we rearrange the formula.

$$ER = C (1 + r)$$

If we spend $10,000 for a new computer workstation with all the latest and greatest features, and we want to get a return on this hardware investment of at least 20%, we drop these numbers into our formula and solve for what we must earn to achieve this return. (A spreadsheet program works great for this.)

$$ER = 10,000 (1 + r)$$

$$ER = 10,000 (1 + 0.2)$$

$$ER = \$12,000$$

Thus, we must earn $12,000 in each year of ownership to realize the 20% return that we feel is necessary to cost-justify the purchase.

Conversely, we can anticipate an income from making an asset purchase and then calculate the expected rate of return on this business decision. Again we rearrange the formula. Replace r, expected rate of return with ROA, Return on Assets.

$$C = \frac{ER}{1 + ROA}$$

$$C (1 + ROA) = ER$$

$$1 + ROA = \frac{ER}{C}$$

$$ROA = \frac{ER}{C} - 1$$

To illustrate this point, suppose that we are considering the purchase of a new color scanner. The purchase price is $6,000. We feel that we can sell $7,000 worth of scans in a year. What is our ROA?

$$ROA = \frac{7,000}{6,000} - 1$$

$$ROA = 0.166667$$

Expressed as a percent, our ROA is 16.7%. By making purchase decisions based on an expected ROA, we can optimize our asset investments. Remember that we are assuming how much additional annual revenue we'll earn using this new scanner.

An important factor to keep in mind is that technology and customer needs can change rapidly. To keep up, you should base your calculations on a 2-year replacement life. This means that you plan to buy new equipment in two years, so you must be able to resell the old equipment for enough (residual value) that you can make the replacement purchase while realizing a return on the initial investment. Some owners try to garner enough business so they can run two shifts. This gives them a better chance of increasing the return on their equipment investment.

In accounting books, you can find the same formula being used for both ROI and ROA. Small DTP shops and service bureaus are unique. We apply our own application of these concepts. Thus the ROI and ROA formulas described above are for us.

Analyzing Financial Numbers

There is a certain symmetry to income statements. After you've looked at a hundred or so, you see that the revenue that a shop earns can be partitioned into various factors such as costs, taxes, and profit. In fact, these typical expenses can be partitioned out by percentage as shown in Table 5-1.

	Percent	
Revenue	100%	
Materials Costs		10%
Manufacturing Costs		70%
Gross Margin	20%	
Sales Cost		10%
G&A		6%
Operating Profit	4%	
Interest Expense		2%
Pretax Profit	2%	
Tax (based on 40%)		0.8%
Net Profit		1.2%

Table 5-1.. Breaking down an income statement.

Given a total income for a year, it turns out that desktop publishing shops have a relatively low materials cost (toner, paper, film, etc.), but a relatively high manufacturing cost (labor intensive). Subtracting materials and manufacturing costs from our income yields the shop's gross margin. From this gross margin or gross profit, we must take out sales and general and administrative costs.

Sales costs for a shop typically comprise between 8 and 12 percent of total sales revenue. In the DTP and prepress industry G&A costs take up 5 - 8 percent of every sales dollar. General and administrative includes all the indirect costs, the administrative expenses to do business.

Depending on debt load, interest expense can be 1 - 5 percent. Then if we subtract our sales costs and G&A from the gross margin, we can determine our operating profit. From the operating profit, we deduct interest expense to get our pretax profit. Most shops face a tax rate (federal and state) of about 40 percent on the pretax profit. We apply the shop's tax rate to this pretax profit to realize a net profit on the bottom line. Does 1.2% look low? In most industry groups (including printing, prepress, and desktop publishing), the bottom line profit is typically between 0.2 and 3 percent.

The government and several research groups monitor the breakdown of financial data for all of the major industry groups. The percentage for each category depends a lot on the type and size of the business. For example, in the world of the software developer, small software companies spend around 25% of their sales dollar on general and administrative costs. The larger software houses such as Microsoft spend as little as 8% on G&A.

This means that a small DTP shop with one or two employees will likely spend much more on G&A than a larger shop employing over 10 employees. This is also why there's such a push to control operating expenses — in particular, general and administrative. Cutting down expenses is crucial to optimizing profitability. And operating expenses can be what separates the high- and low-profit performers.

Once we establish the financial profile for our own business, we can use this information to make some interesting comparisons. For example, we can use these percent ranges to analyze each job that our shop per-forms to see where the wheat is from the chaff. You'll probably discover that 80% of your profit comes from 20% of your customer base.

Evaluate Competition
Using Financial Numbers

We can also use these percentage breakdowns to compare bids on various jobs. This is a quick way to see who's losing their shirt by underbidding on a job. For example, assume that we bid $10,000 on a DTP design project but were beat out by a competitor who submitted a winning $7,000 bid.

If we assume that the competitor uses similar equipment (hardware and software) and has the same or similar costs that we do, then we can enter his winning bid into our spreadsheet and discover approximately how much that shop won (or lost) on the bid.

Look at Table 5-2. This breaks down the $10K and $7K bids just as we saw in Table 5-1. The competitor has a lower revenue level but the same outlay for materials and manufacturing (shop labor). This means that after the cost to produce are handled, this shop is already $1,000 in the hole, and it gets worse as we look down the column. By the time we factor in the cost of sales, G&A, and interest, they're losing over two-thousand dollars just by accepting the job.

	Our Bid		Competitor	
Price	10,000	100%	7,000	100.0%
Materials	1,000	10%	1,000	14.3%
Mfg Cost	7,000	70%	7,000	100.0%
Gross Margin	2,000	20%	(1,000)	(14.3%)
Sales Cost	1,000	10%	700	10%
G&A	600	6%	420	6%
Oper Profit	400	4%	(2,120)	(30.3%)
Interest	200	2%	140	2%
Pretax Profit	200	2%	(2,260)	(32.3%)
Tax (40%)	80	.8%	0	0%
Net Profit	140	1.2%	(2,260)	(32.3%)

Table 5-2. Breaking down DTP project award prices.

What a startling revelation! By taking a single data point (their winning bid) and dropping the bid value into your price breakdown spreadsheet, you can readily see that this competitor is losing $2,260 by taking on that job. Perhaps it's time to send cards to all of that competitor's customers telling them that your shop will still be open six months from now should they need another source for support — when the IRS closes the door on this failing competitor.

The sad truth is that there are many shops operating today who low-ball price and consistently operate on the razor's edge of survival simply because they do not understand these principles. No matter how you cut the pie, you still must pay for hardware, software, and professionals to make a project happen. For most shops, the numbers will pencil out remarkably similar.

Bidding below break-even only speeds your shop's eventual demise. Unfortunately, many shops are doing this without even knowing it. Knowledge is power. Knowledge can also be profit.

Measuring Profitability

It's important that shop owners fine tune their intelligence gathering skills. Every employee in your shop must become sensitive to customer and competitor information. As the economy changes and as skill concentration increases, so does competition for existing business.

This means that owners must consistently evaluate their operations and financial results to determine where they stand relative to their competitors and then adjust their business strategies as necessary. As shown in Figure 5-1, the gross income of businesses providing desktop publishing services varies widely. Gross income is one way to compare businesses. But there's a better way. This one measures profitability per employee.

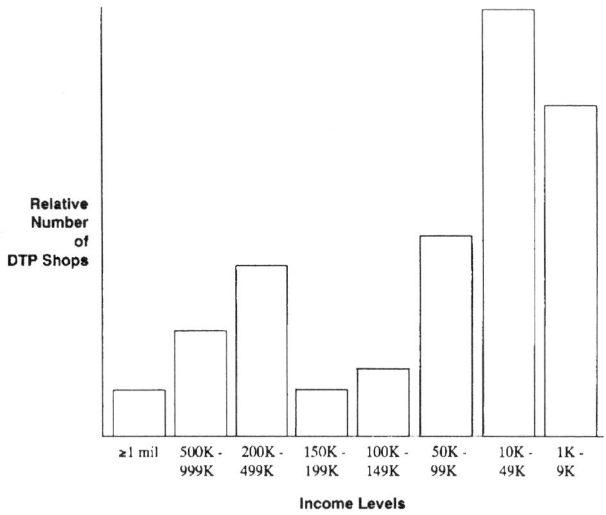

Figure 5-1. Relative number of desktop publishing businesses at various income levels.

An interesting way to evaluate a business is by using a barometer called the *economic model of business profitability*. This model measures profitability in terms of services sold rather than goods produced per employee. It's also a measure of productivity, so you may find it referred to as an *economic model of productivity*.

The model is normalized to what is called a "full time equivalent" (FTE) employee. By comparing the average income generated by a full time equivalent employee with the income revenue per FTE of competitors, you can determine if your shop has a profitability advantage or disadvantage. This can be equated to productivity per employee. This takes the total income out of the picture and lets you focus on how much an equivalent person in your shop earns. Looking at individual equivalent employee worth (profitability) can be a fascinating way to evaluate business success.

If your shop has six full time employees and earns $300,000 a year, it has a gross average income per employee of $50,000 (300,000 / 6 = 50,000). This gross measure can be applied against your competitor's earnings to develop an economic model for comparison. If a competitor is earning $750,000 annually with 10 full time employees, their sales per employee is $75,000. When compared with your $50,000 income per employee, your competitor has a 50 percent profitability advantage over your shop based on an apples-to-apples revenue-dollars-per-FTE basis.

We used our survey data to evaluate the desktop publishing industry. Since the survey asked for income data and the number of full time, part time, and freelance employees, we could use this data to calculate an average revenue per FTE for the profession.

First, we investigated the economic model of sales per employee for other industries and companies. As shown in Table 5-3, the revenue per employee varies widely.

Company	Income/Employee
Worthington Industries,	$445,000
Microsoft	$289,000
Novell	$288,000
Corel	$269,000
Sony	$230,000
Lotus Development	$206,000
Image Graphics, Inc.	$130,000
Local bank	$120,000
Thompson Consumer Electronics,	$115,000
Digital Equipment Corporation	$108,000
George Lithograph	$100,000
Copier dealers	$100,000
National Graphics	$62,400

Table 5-3. Income per Full Time Equivalent Employee

Most $/FTE economic model data is calculated on larger companies. Bull Customer Service Operations, has 32,500 employees. Obviously, Microsoft, Lotus, and the others are also larger companies. Over 75% of all the companies in the U.S. have less than 10 employees. The $/FTE norm for the U.S. has been established at $100,000. This suggests that staff additions may be necessary when income per FTE exceeds the $100,000 threshold.

Where do we in the DTP profession stand when it comes to revenue per employee? The key to evaluation is to know where you are in relation to your competition. To find out, you must ferret out revenue and employee information on competing shops. Look for comparables. Watch for comments in news articles and business profiles printed in trade publications. Listen to industry speakers. Check the library and government labor department for industry norms. Since our company collects business information on desktop publishing and prepress, we analyzed our own data to see if we could define an average revenue per FTE for our industry.

Desktop publishing is a relatively new profession. We began in the middle of the last decade. Most of our shops started in the last five years. We operate out of condos, houses, garages, light industrial office spaces, and store fronts. Our cost basis and earnings vary widely.

Since we are a new industry, our average revenue per FTE employee should be below $100,000. The wide variance in the profiles of DTP shops can seem confusing, yet, taken as a whole, an analysis of the data from our pricing and salary survey yields fascinating insight into where we stand as a collection of entrepreneurs. The results described next are unique to the business profiles used to generate this reference book. A different sample size would produce different specific values but should produce relatively similar results since our tables are developed from actual numbers.

The range of income and number of employees in desktop publishing varies widely. New shop owners tend to undercharge for most services. Women owner-operators tend to pay themselves less than their male counterparts. They also tend to charge their customers less for DTP services. And counter prices tend to increase as a business matures.

We are primarily sole proprietorships with many of us operating out of the home. More women than men or couples are owner-operators. Our income varies from less than $3,000 a year freelance to over several million dollars a year in established full-time businesses.

Define a full time equivalent employee as someone working 40 hours a week. Then a 20-hour part time worker can be classified at 0.5 FTE and a 4-hour freelancer becomes 0.1 FTE (4 hrs / 40 hrs = 0.1). This provides a weighted scoring method for determining the total number of equivalent full time employees in your business.

By multiplying the number of full timers by 1, the number of part timers by 0.5 and the number of freelancers by 0.1, you can calculate the total number of FTE employees for any business. A shop earning $500,000 a year with 5 full time, 1 part time, and 3 freelance employees will have a 5.8 FTE rating (5 x 1.0 + 1 x 0.5 + 3 x 0.1 = 5.8) and a revenue per FTE of $86,207 (500,000 / 5.8 = 86,207).

If a full time worker brings in $10,000 per month in sales and a part time worker earns $7,500 a month, dividing the income by the FTE basis means that the part time worker is actually 50 percent more profitable to your business (7,500 / 0.5 = 15,000) relative to a full time employee. This assumes that each expends a proportional amount of overhead budget and has the same earning opportunity. In addition, if a shop owner works 60 hours a week, this represents 1.5 FTE and this becomes that person's basis for calculation and comparison.

The FTE concept can be useful. We can evaluate revenue per FTE against various factors—overall shop earnings, design projects completed, scans performed and charged, typeset pages billed, etc.

In your economic model it is also useful to know the average revenue per FTE, the range of revenue dollars per FTE, and the average number of employees in a typical shop. In our survey, the average FTE in a DTP shop is 1.7, the average FTE for a prepress shops is 7.1.

Next we analyzed the revenue per FTE by income category. We partitioned the income data into categories as shown in Table 5-4. Then we determined the range of FTE employees in each category. Based on this, we had the computer remove outlier data (data outside a normal distribution curve) and calculate the average FTE for each income category.

FTE ECONOMIC MODEL by Overall Shop Earnings				
INCOME RANGE	FTE RANGE	AVG FTE	RELATIVE $/FTE RANGE	AVG $/FTE
$1 - $5 million	12 - 90	39.8	$55,556 - $83,333	$74,847
500K - 999K	5.3 - 12	7.7	56,818 - 133,929	87,732
100K - 499K	1.3 - 7.1	3.7	26,829 - 115,385	69,140
50K - 99K	1.0 - 3.6	1.7	16,556 - 100,000	45,348
25K - 49K	0.5 - 3.0	1.5	10,000 - 175,000	48,517
10K - 24K	0.1 - 2.2	0.9	5,682 - 50,000	26,841
1K - 9K	0.1 - 6.0	1.3	588 - 60,000	9,258

Table 5-4. The FTE economic model for desktop publishing businesses.

We determined the range of relative revenue per FTE and had the computer calculate the average relative income per FTE. If a moonlighter works on a 0.1 FTE employee basis and earns $5,000 in a year, this represents $50,000 on a 1.0 FTE basis. Thus, in the $10,000 - $24,999 category, the average relative $/FTE came out to be $26,841 indicating that many of these owner-operators are working part time or just starting their business. The lowest income category is presented for information only. These shops are new or are maintained as freelance or second-job businesses.

As shown in the table, the top earning businesses averaged 39.76 FTE and averaged $74,847 per employee. In the $500K - $999K category, these shops averaged 7.73 employees earning $87,732 each. Between $100K and $499K, shops averaged 3.66 workers earning $69,140. As the total income revenue decreases, notice the resulting decrease in FTE employees. Except for the $25K to $49K category, the average relative FTE also decreases from the preceding value.

Since our data base was really humming at this point, we turned our analytical focus to the FTE and $/FTE based on the primary computer platform used in the business. This time, the data came out as shown in Table 5-5.

FTE ECONOMIC MODEL by Computer Platform					
COMPUTER PLATFORM	Average All Shops	$500K - 5 million	$100K - 499K	$50K - 99K	$10K - 49K
MACINTOSH					
FTE	5.64	10.4	3.4	1.4	1.2
$/FTE	$57,382	$68,138	$63,082	$48,564	$26,895
PC					
FTE	1.47	12.0	2.9	1.7	1.1
$/FTE	$32,858	$83,333	$76,348	$52,257	$39,600
BOTH					
FTE	10.1	18.8	4.3	2.2	0.7
$/FTE	$91,410	$89,124	$56,316	$30,332	$8,058

Table 5-5. FTE and $/FTE based on computer platform used.

As you can see in this table, the PC-based shops fared better than the Mac-only shops. At the high income end, using both PC and Mac machines is an advantage. Notice how the average FTE and average $/FTE track from one income category to the next.

Naturally, a different partitioning will yield different values, but the message from this data is clear. Most DTP shops (45%) have incomes between $10K and $100K. The PC-based shops seem to fare better than their Mac-based counterparts.

Back to Table 5-4. Discounting the lowest income category as representing new start-ups, this makes the $25K - $49K and $50K - $99K categories important. The average revenue per FTE of these two categories is $46,933. If we take this as a comparison basis, any shop that produces more than this value in revenue per FTE is more profitable (hence more productive) than the average shop. Likewise, a shop with less than $46,933 revenue per FTE is less profitable compared with this suggested standard. Thus this value can be used as a benchmark to evaluate your own business and that of competitors.

In its own way, the FTE economic model can provide the small DTP shop a way to compare profitability, productivity and competitive advantage with similar shops. It can show you that your business formula still needs tweaking.

However, in a general sense, our lower revenue per FTE — lower than the $100,000 per FTE for the U.S. in general — suggests a more disturbing problem. Perhaps our pricing strategy is out of line with mainline American business. Perhaps we are only hurting ourselves when we accept jobs paying lower prices than we could (or should) get.

In our cut-throat world, we sometimes deal with razor-thin margins, and struggle to remain profitable. Larger companies keep a tight lid on costs and use a common profit-boosting strategy — they hire fewer workers and focus on highly profitable projects. We can do more to make our projects more profitable. Pricing is key to our profit picture.

Making Your Own Profitability Model

Once you have had an opportunity to let the revenue per full time equivalent concept sink in, you'll want to monitor your own shop to see how you stand relative to the rest of the industry.

Table 5-6 is a sample production summary form that you can adapt to your own profitability/productivity monitoring program. It partitions each month into working days. Then there is a column for each employee in your shop or in a profit center. The form is used to record the dollars billed and the hours worked.

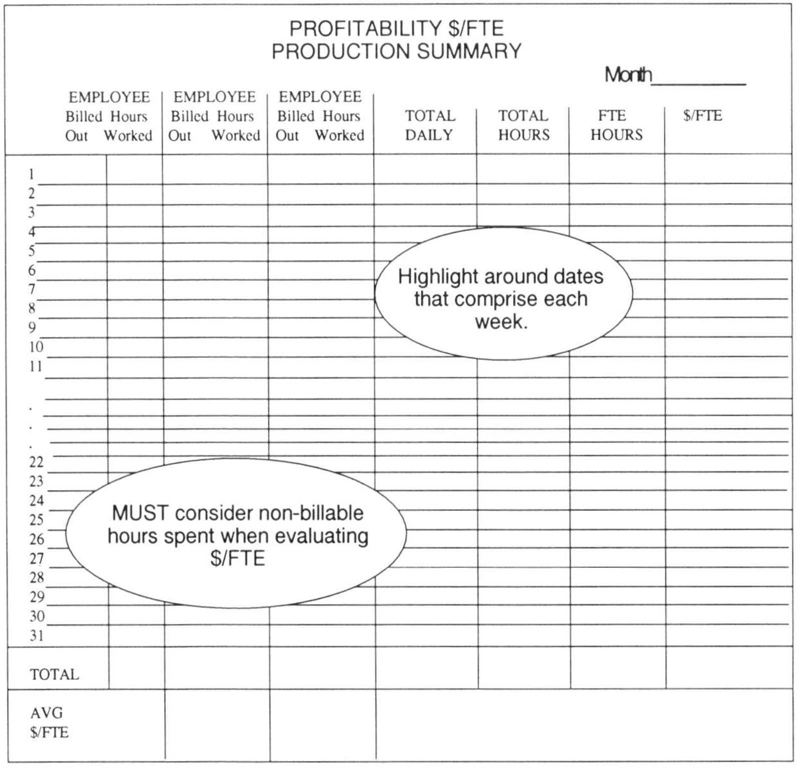

Table 5-6. Production summary form.

Each month a "highlighter" pen is used to outline the dates that constitute each working week. Then data is filled in for the days that work occurs.

On the right are columns that summarize the activity for each day. One column lists the total daily income, another lists the total hours worked, another lists the total number of 8-hour FTE equivalent hours worked, and the last column records the dollars of income per hours FTE worked ratio.

You could add a third column for each employee to normalize their output to a standard 8-hour full time equivalent.

At the bottom of form, the total dollars billed and hours worked for each employee are summarized. Then the hours are divided by the number of possible 8-hour work days in the month to get an equivalent FTE hour rating for each worker. This is divided into the total dollars earned to get a dollars per FTE value for each employee.

You could design this form to record weekly subtotals during the month with a final tally at the end of the month.

By associating the columns recording dollars billed and hours worked with the dollars earned per hour worked, you force your attention on the income that each employee earns for the shop.

At the end of the year, the total income per employee is added and the total hours worked per year per employee are added to get annual values. The total hours worked are divided by a value representing the total hours possible to get an equivalent FTE rating for the year. For example, if Employee 1 worked 1,040 hours of 2,080 hours possible for an 8-hour worker, the ratio of 0.5 represents one half an FTE. If they billed $30,000 for the shop during the year they represent $60,000/1.0 FTE for your business. This is good.

On the other hand, if they generate only $10,000 in billable income, they represent a $20,000/FTE worker to the shop.

If all workers perform non-billable work relatively equally, then all the employees can be compared with each other, and the shop in general can be compared with other shops to determine who is more productive, who is more profitable to the company.

Making a Counter Price Book

When customers ask to see your prices, some shop owners can reach for a sheet or set of sheets describing the services that they offer and the rates that they charge. If these price sheets are kept in a binder, the package is called a *"counter price book."*

There are many ways to structure the services described in your counter price book. Some shops use a simple one-page form. Others put the time into developing a detail listing of services with volume discounts and various prices based on operation, complexity, and output desired.

There are several key things to include on your price sheets. First, the name of your business (telephone number included). Second, the date that a sheet was last revised. This helps you know how long it's been since you last updated your prices, and it lets the customer know that you probably DO occasionally update your rates.

Make your price sheets as functional as you can. Organize the information so related services are collected in the same area of the forms. For example, place design, conversion, input, and output services in their own areas on the forms.

Take the time to make your price sheets look as readable as you can. Use columns, rows, and bold typefaces on headings. And use boxes to separate and border various areas of your service. Some counter books include a time-increment hourly-rate breakdown chart on one of the sheets.

If you provide file conversion, chart out the type of conversion by file size and price. Since we're dealing with hardware, software and time, work up your billing rates and then charge by the amount of time the system is busy on that service — often time is represented by file size (10K, 100K, 500K, etc.). You can determine how long it takes to convert various block sizes of text, spreadsheet or graphics information. Then prorate your base billing rate and present your prices based on the size of file being converted. Make a note on the form how odd-number file sizes will be treated. And consider using a minimum fee for selected services that you perform.

Remember that it takes time to setup a job for a customer. It also takes time to close a job down after the work has been completed. You should consider charging setup fees for various types of jobs. The more successful shops use the setup charge and minimum fee concept sparingly—but firmly. Your shop should be paid for all the time and resources that are applied to a service.

If you're describing scanning or print output, show your prices for various resolutions and sizes. For example, laser printing can be described in a boxed row-and-column area with resolutions at the top of the columns and page sizes at the beginning of each row. This matrix gives a professional look to your form. If you also price print output based on the amount of toner on a sheet, provide small sample complexity drawings to help the customer recognize that everything has been considered and you will be charging a unique rate for those sheets that need more toner coverage.

If you provide imagesetter output, generate a chart like that for laser printer output based on dpi and output size — one for RC paper and another for film.

If you price your design based on budgeted hourly rates, you can list each service with its corresponding billable hourly rate. Various design services and rates can also be presented in chart form.

Every document that you produce for customer view is like a billboard for your business. Therefore, it's important to make each pricing sheet look as "professional" as possible. The idea is to let your price sheets advertise all of the services that your shop can provide. It does little good to have a unique capability and not let your customers know. Your price sheets should mentally seed ideas in the minds of your customers for other things that they may want your shop to do for them later. Knowing that your shop can do OCR scanning or PC-to-Mac and Mac-to-PC conversion can be valuable information for your customer. They not only will remember these facts the next time they perceive a need, they could also tell others about you and your services.

Sometimes little jobs can lead to large projects. If your customer knows for example that you can convert word processing and graphics file formats, they may bring some of their work to you. They could also include you in a major project that they are tackling because they know from your counter price book that your shop has the resources and ability to make their own job easier.

Case Study: Use Break-Even Analysis to Decide What to Charge

John had reviewed his strategic plan and completed a tactical plan for operating his business for the upcoming year. His shop was located in a strip shopping mall, a few doors away from a post office store. There was a steady stream of customers using the services of the private post office. His strategy is to draw these customers to his shop for services that compliment those of the post office store. One service that seemed appropriate is to offer color copying and printing. He already offered black and white copying service.

After analyzing the available technology, John decided to install a color laser copier/printer. The machine that John selected can produce 7 copies each minute and can interface to a desktop computer. It can accept originals in the form of computer graphics, still video images, black and white originals, original art, photos, and slides and negatives. The copier/printer he selected has a suggested retail price of $42,000. John can obtain a three-year lease at 0.0175. This means that he pays 1.75¢ for each dollar of cost — a total of $735 a month. Foot traffic for his desktop publishing and black and white copy business is running 50 customers a day. The critical question is what to charge for each color copy produced.

He has a good handle on his shop overhead costs. And John has an average operational cost breakdown for the copier/printer provided by the vendor. His challenge is to find the point at which his costs are covered and profit can begin to accrue. The relationship between cost, sales and profit is called *break-even analysis*. John decides to perform a break-even analysis on his color copier/printer investment.

He has two ways to approach break-even analysis. He can compare his total expected sales volume with the associated costs or he can compare the total expected items (units) produced and sold with this same cost. In both methods, John must clearly understand his operating expenses.

Part of his expenses are fixed—they don't change as sales volume fluctuates. These fixed costs include rent, utilities, salaries, and insurance. Other costs vary with the job. These variable costs include hourly wages, the costs of paper, toner, developer, drum or photoreceptor, fusing oil, preventive maintenance, and additional utility expenses to produce the color output that he sells. To make a profit, John must pay both his fixed and variable expenses and then have some income left over. The residual income represents before-tax profit and return-on-investment (he loaned money to his company on start-up). John will analyze his color output business potential based on sales volume and on total copies sold.

First John must determine his total fixed costs. The machine will cost John $8,820 a year (735 X 12). He plans to use the copier/printer 1200 hours a year. About half the time, he will use the machine as a copier; the other half of the time, he'll use it as a printer connected to his computer. The hourly fixed cost contribution of the copier/printer is $7.35 ($8,820/1200 = $7.35). This cost becomes part of his shop overhead expense.

The computer that John will use with the copier/printer costs $5,000 and has a useful life of five years. This represents $1,000 depreciated cost each year. The computer is used continually during the work day — 2,080 hours a year. The hourly fixed cost contribution of the computer is 48¢ ($1,000 / 2,080 hrs = $0.48/hr). Of the 2,080 hours of computer use, 600 hours will be for color printing. The depreciated annual costs of the computer as used for color printing is $288 (600 hours times 48¢/hr). This costs also becomes part of his shop overhead expense.

Thus, to operate and use the color copier/printer, John pays $9,108 ($8,820 + $288 = $9,108) annually. Every hour of copier/printer operation costs John $7.83 ($7.35 + $0.48 = $7.83).

Now, John's overhead costs are running $17 an hour so the overhead contribution attributable to the color service is $20,400 ($17/hr x 1200 hrs). This makes the fixed part of his cost $20,688 a year. Now he analyzes his variable costs.

The average operational cost for the color copier/printer (including utilities) is 50¢ an hour—$600 per year. John's $6-an-hour employee will cost $7,200 a year for the time spent making color copies. This makes John's variable cost $7,600. His fixed and variable costs come to $28,288 a year.

At 1200 hours of operation, his color copier/printer is available 72,000 minutes a year. At seven copies per minute, John can get a maximum of 504,000 printouts in each year. This is if the equipment were in continuous use. It won't be, but this provides a best-case situation. In continuous use, John could break even on costs by charging 5.6¢ a copy ($28,288 / 504,000). However, John expects to use the machine only 10% of the available time — 50,400 copies.

This suggests that John needs to charge 56¢ for each copy to cover his costs (28,288 / 50,400 = 0.56). From a survey of local competitors, John found that color copy prices ranged from 60¢ to $3 each. The average selling price is $1.26. He tentatively selects $1.25 as his price. He also found that color laser printer prices range from $1.75 to $20 per page. It takes longer for his employee to set up the computer to print a color copy. He tentatively selects $5 per page as his color printing selling price.

His variable cost contribution is $7,600 divided by 50,400 or $0.15 per copy. John wonders how many copies he must sell to reach the copier/printer's break even point.

He subtracts his $1.25 selling price from the $0.15 unit variable cost and then divides the $1.10 result into his $20,688 fixed cost. This indicates that he will break even at 18,807 copies ($23,509 in sales).

This is shown graphically in Figure 5-2. If John sells color printer output at $5 a page, he can break even in one-fourth the volume (4,702 pages).

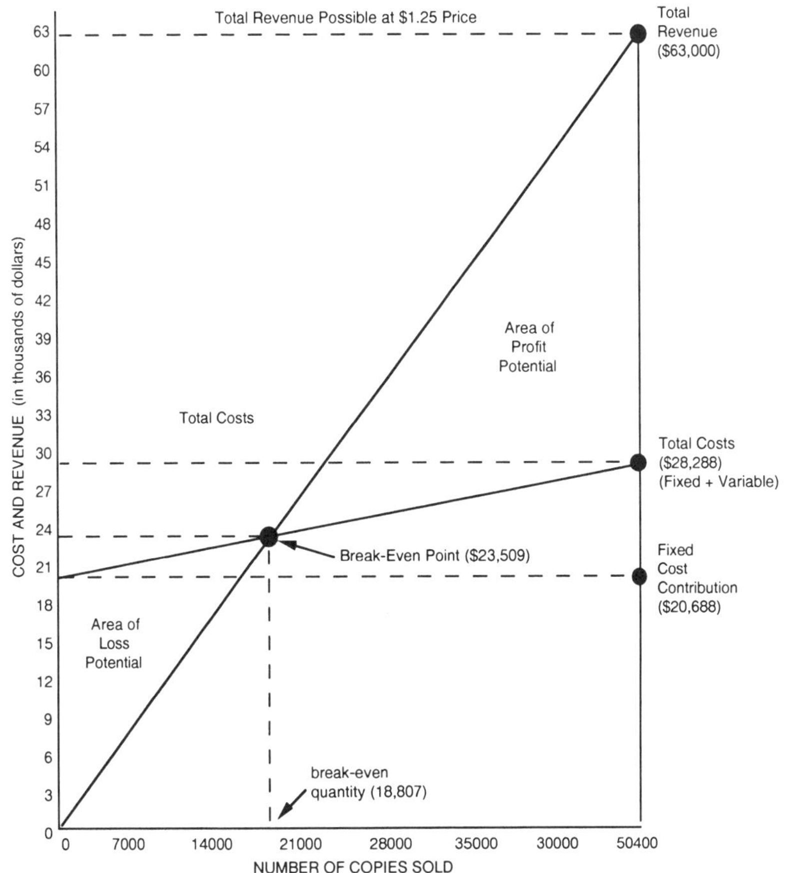

Figure 5-2. Break-even analysis for color copier/printer.

To check his math, John divides his average variable cost of $0.15 by the $1.25 average selling price and then subtracts this from 1 to get .88. Then he divides his fixed costs ($20,688) by .88 to get $23,509 as his break-even sales volume.

Therefore, at $1.25 a copy, John's copier/printer service will break even when his shop prints its 18,807th copy and earns a cumulative $23,509 in sales. For every computer-generated laser color printer output, John earns $5 instead of $1.25. If he sells scanned copies of photographs and transparencies, he can further increase his "per-output" price. Each higher-priced product reduces his required sales before break-even. Nevertheless, John bases his calculations on the worst-case, lower income sale. Can he sell at least 18,897 copies a year? That's approximately 73 color copies each of the 260 days a year that his shop is open for business.

John changes the variables in his computer spreadsheet B-E model and determines new break-even points based on different selling prices and costs. He finds the computer model particularly helpful when performing "what if" per-copy price-change analysis.

Break-even analysis helps him decide the viability of his copier/printer and at what price it becomes too costly to produce and sell copier/printer services. To increase the income generated, John raises the price in his computer model. He recognizes that this is not always possible in the sometimes cold trenches of business. Competition may hold market prices too low to make this product or service worth selling. John's costs can also vary. And John realizes that break-even analysis doesn't consider discounting, customer demand (elasticity) and the pricing reactions by competitors. Nevertheless, it does help John quickly see the impact of various pricing strategies. And that in itself makes the analysis worth the effort.

Break-even is one of the analysis tools that John uses to manage his business. By knowing each break-even point, he can determine which products or services to offer. It also helps John decide if making an unprofitable sale to gain a long term customer is really worth the sacrifice. If John lowers his sales price, each sale contributes less toward paying his fixed and variable costs, and less remains for profit and investment return. In effect, a lower sales price pushes the break-even point further out along the horizontal axis in Figure 1.

Typically, the smallest 20% of John's orders will account for less than 5% of his sales income. It may not be worth making these sales at all. There's a point at which John's fixed costs exceed his income and he should decline the sale. John's break-even analysis shows him mathematically and graphically why some sales just don't make financial sense. A bushel of low quantity sales may generate revenue consistently below his fixed costs with a small variable cost added. This would suggest that John should decline these sales, or add a surcharge (charge a higher price) for low dollar sales. Based on this, John selects a sliding scale of prices for copier/printer output. A lower price will be charged for larger volume jobs. He develops his pricing strategy to encourage an average sale of $25 or more. Thus, he wants customers to buy 20 or more color copies, or five or more color printouts with each order. Break-even analysis helps him determine this desired sales amount. He also seeks other business models that may be useful.

To succeed, John will consider every analysis tool that can help him make better pricing decisions. No stone remains unturned in his search for maximum profit. Only the novice will attempt to operate a shop without analysis, planning, and business-based pricing.

Case Study: Job Estimating in the Trenches

Mary had just completed her weekly review of cash flow when she received a call from a prospect she met at a recent business networking meeting. The caller was the president of a local alumni club for a university in the East. The club wanted to produce a directory of members. Having learned that Mary was a desktop publisher, the caller had decided to ask Mary to bid on the job. Mary was elated, but this would be her first directory. She needed to understand the job thoroughly before she could offer a price to do the work. She scheduled a meeting with the club president.

During the meeting, Mary wrote down the specifications for the job. The club had just under 300 members—graduates of a university in Pennsylvania. The president of the club wanted a mailing list generated that could be maintained and updated. This mailing list would form the basis for the membership directory. During the meeting, the club president decided that the directory should have a coated cover, a title page followed by a list of club officers and the by-laws of the club, and then a listing of each member with graduation date and degree(s) earned. Both the home address and business address of each member would be included in the directory. The page size and binding weren't critical with this first directory, and the club president would rely on Mary to recommend what she felt is appropriate. The university logo would appear on the cover and first page of the document. The club president asked Mary to base her quote on producing 300 copies of the directory.

Upon learning that Mary had a bulk mail permit, the club president also asked Mary to include in her bid, the cost to mail the printed directory to club members. Mary was to provide all mailing envelopes and handle the complete process. The club president told Mary that $1,000 had been budgeted by the club. Mary returned to her shop, sharpened her calculating pencil and went to work on her estimate.

She broke the project down into functions. These included data entry, scanning of the university logo and by-laws provided by the club president, directory design, cover design, page layout, camera-ready printout, directory printing, binding, shipping and mailing. First, she would have to enter partially typed, partially hand-written membership information into the computer. From this, Mary would generate a mailing list so she could print labels for mailing. From the same database records, she would print complete member information for the directory. Selected fields in her membership database would be printed to a separate file for importing into a word processing program where the data would be typeset for a two-column page. Mary would scan the club by-laws and save these in her word processing format. Then she would merge the by-laws with the membership data. Next she would scan the university logo and save it as a graphic file. She would design the cover and title page in her page layout program and then import the word processing directory file. But what size page should she design to?

Mary placed two columns of address labels over an 8.5" x 11" sheet of paper. Leaving room for top and bottom margins, she could fit 10 addresses in each column. She could also use font sizing and leading to make the information fit within the design footprint. If she designed to a 5.5" x 8.5" page, she could get eight addresses in each column. The club currently has 284 members. If it takes two addresses to list each member (home and work addresses), she would need 29 pages at 8.5" x 11" and 36 pages at 5.5" x 8.5" size. She can reduce the type size and leading to fit the data on each page.

If she designed at full size, she could mail each directory as a non-letter flat for 23.3¢ each. First class mailing would be 98¢ each. If Mary designed the directory for the smaller size and kept the document thinner than 0.25 inches, she can mail each directory as a bulk mail letter for between 16.5¢ and 19.8¢ each. Mailing 125 or more to the same ZIP code three-digit prefix would qualify the mailing for the lower rate. Since postage costs represent a significant part of the project, Mary decided to design to the smaller size.

She would use 10-point coated-one-side stock (10ptC1S) for the cover. It would be folded and saddle stitched to the directory sheets. The inside sheets would be 60# book stock. The entire job would be printed in black ink. She would generate camera ready sheets at 600 dpi and use a local quick printer to produce 300 copies of the directory. To cut printing costs, Mary would provide the cover and sheet paper stock to the printer avoiding the printer's markup and getting the lowest trade rate.

For the mailing, Mary would purchase blank 6" x 9" envelopes and print a return address and mailing address label for each. She made a list of each function with a time estimate for completion. The labor tasks and time estimates are shown in Table 4-8:

Client meetings	-	2 hours
Database design	-	1 hour
Database data entry	-	2 hours
OCR scanning	-	0.25 hours
Logo scanning	-	0.25 hours
File transfer	-	0.5 hours
Document design	-	2 hours
Cover and title page design	-	0.5 hours
Importing text	-	0.5 hours
Page layout	-	11 hours
Draft directory printout	-	1 hour
Changes & alterations	-	1 hour
Printing shop interface	-	1 hour
Label printing (return address)	-	1 hour
Label printing (mailing address)	-	1 hour
Applying labels to envelopes	-	2 hours
Stuffing mailing envelopes	-	2 hours
Bulk mail preps	-	2 hours
Post office mailing	-	1 hour
Customer follow-up	-	1 hour

TOTAL TIME ESTIMATED = 33 hours

Table 5-7. Total time estimate.

Next Mary places a budgeted cost next to each function. She uses both standard rates for her area and actual prices for her own and the work of others. She plans to hire help at $5 per hour for the simpler jobs. She will hire a $12 freelancer to help desktop publish the project. Mary's budgeted labor rates are $20 an hour with a 40% productivity assumed and shop overhead incorporated. This results in a $50/hour billing rate for her shop. Mary applies the shop's $50 per hour billing rate to her own portion of the job. Her labor costs are as shown in Table 5-8.

FUNCTION	TIME (hours)	RATES ($/hr)	COSTS ($/hr)	TOTAL COSTS
Client meetings	2		$50	$100
Database design	1		12	12
Database data entry	2	$25	12	24
OCR scanning	0.25	35	12	4
Logo scanning	0.25	36	12	4
File transfer	0.5	40	12	6
Document design	2	35	12	24
Cover design	0.5	45	12	6
Importing text	0.5	45	12	6
Page layout	11	45	12	132
Draft printout	1	25	12	12
Chgs & alterations	1	40	50	50
Print shop interface	1	35	12	12
Label printing	2		12	12
Envelope stuffing	2	5	5	10
Applying labels	2	5	5	10
Bulk mail preps	2	5	5	10
Bulk mailing	1	5	50	50
Customer follow-up	1	50	50	50

TOTAL TIME: 33 hours = $546 estimated

Table 5-8. Budgeted labor costs.

Next, Mary analyzes the actual costs of materials that will be used during the project. Her materials costs were calculated as shown in Table 5-9.

Laser printout - 100 shts @ 5¢ each
   (incorporates toner and paper costs)   = $5
Envelopes - 300 @ 3¢ each   = $9
Cover stock - 1 pkg, 250 sheets 10ptC1S   = $22
Offset paper stock - 3,500 sheets 60# white offset   = $23
Labels - 568 @ 2¢ each   = $11

TOTAL MATERIALS COSTS = $61 actual

Table 5-9. Actual costs of materials.

She will subcontract out for the printing, collating and saddle stitch binding at trade rates. Her printing cost estimate is shown in Table 5-10.

Printing, collating and saddle stitching   = $235
   (Does not include sales tax)

TOTAL PRINTING COSTS = $235 actual

Table 5-10. Actual trade printing costs.

Mary will mail the directories using her bulk mail permit. Her postage estimate is shown in Table 5-11.

Bulk mailing 284 pcs @ 19.8¢ ea   = $56

TOTAL BULK MAILING COSTS = $56 actual

Table 5-11. Actual bulk mailing postage costs.

If she can collect the bulk mail into 125 or more pieces with the same three-digit ZIP code prefix, she can reduce her bulk mailing costs to $46.86, but Mary will estimate based on the higher cost.

Thus Mary's total cost estimate came to \$898 (\$546 + \$61 + \$235 + \$56 = \$898). Next she had to determine what she could charge and make a fair profit and return on her investment in hardware and software.

Mary marked each material cost up by 100%. And she priced each hour of work at her \$50 billing rate. The project quote builds as shown in Table 5-12.

LABOR
All 33 hours of work performed at \$50/hr shop rates
LABOR CHARGES = <u>\$1,650</u>

MATERIALS & SERVICES
Database data entry - 20¢ per record, 284 records = \$57
OCR scanning - 1 scan @ \$6/scan = \$6
Logo scanning - 1 scan @ \$6/scan = \$6
Label printing (return address) - 284 @ 5¢ ea = \$14.20
Label printing (mailing address) - 284 @ 5¢ ea = \$14.20
Camera ready 600 dpi - 20 sheets @ \$1.50 ea = \$30
Laser paper - 100 sheets @ 10¢ each = \$10
Envelopes - 300 @ 6¢ each = \$18
Cover stock - 1 ream, 500 sheets 10ptC1S = \$44
Offset paper stock - 3,500 sheets 60# white offset = \$46
MATERIALS CHARGES = <u>\$245.40</u>
(marked up as appropriate)

PRINTING
Print 300 directories, 2-sided, black ink, cover 1-side black ink, collate, fold and saddle stitch.
PRINTING CHARGES: <u>\$282</u>
(marked up 20%)

MAILING
284 pieces @ 19.8¢ each
BULK MAILING CHARGES = <u>\$56</u>

TOTAL PROJECT PRICE = \$2,233.40 (plus sales tax)
(Bottom End Price = \$1,077.60 plus sales tax)

Table 5-12. Project quote (top and bottom end prices).

This is the top end of her quote range. This price does not include sales tax which is added to services and materials provided the customer. The bottom end quote assuming 10% profit and return on investment is $1,077.60 ($898 plus 10% profit and 10% ROI). By accepting a 5% profit and 5% return on investment, Mary can quote the job at $987.80.

By using part time help, Mary is able to bring her quote in below the $1,000 budgeted by the university club. She has some options that could also increase her profit. She could use remainder label stock that had already been purchased for an earlier project. And she could use the lowest-paid part time employee to do data entry, scanning, label printing, print shop delivery and pickup, and post office mailing. This will add another $85.50 to the bottom line. By lowing the costs to $812.50 and receiving $987.80 for the job, Mary can realize a 22% profit on this project.

Mary bids $987.80 for the job. She is awarded the contract. Her actual mailing costs are $46.86 (an additional $9.14 falls through to her bottom line). Label printing actually takes only one hour (another $12 in profit). And actual page layout takes two hours less ($24 more in profit). Thus, Mary gets the job for $987.80. Her actual costs are $767.50. Mary's achieves a 29% gross profit over her costs. Assuming a small cost for administrative handling of the part time workers, Mary still realizes a comfortable gross profit on the job. If the client wants the job completed on a rush schedule, Mary will add 100% more to her bid. Either way, Mary has a good understanding of her costs and her potential profit and return on investment.

The job went well. Mary provided a quality product to a new client. Bulk mailing within the county took only one to two days. Her client was happy. Mary enabled three people to earn money for their work. And she has the mailing list firmly saved on her own hard disk, ensuring Mary of future jobs from this client.

Case Study: Trade Rate Ripoff

A DTP colleague shared this one with me in hopes that you don't experience the same treatment. A photographer got an opportunity to design a catalog for a national race car organization. He asked my colleague if she would quote a price to design and layout the catalog.

She quoted an hourly rate of $30, which she felt was fair given that the standard rate in the area was closer to $40 an hour.

The publisher called her back and told her that he was awarded the job. He explained that he told the organization that he would charge them $30 and hour. Then he told my friend that he would pay her $18 an hour for her services and pocket the $12 an hour difference as his share. Naturally, she told him to fly a kite.

What could she have done?

Trade rate services are typically 20-25% of full retail. This weasel was planning to establish a 45% discount (in his favor). Based on a 20% trade discount, the photographer should been charged $32 an hour ($40/hr x 0.8 = $32/hr).

Before you ever agree to support on someone else's contract, state your full rate in writing and then show the discount that you will offer. Make your proposal in writing. On the bottom of your proposal have a line for an acceptance signature and another for your agreement signature.

Sign and date two copies. Send the two copies to the buyer asking that the buyer sign off on one copy and return to you.

Be very specific about what you will and what you will not do in support of the agreement. Also be very clear about how many "proof" copies you will provide and how alterations and revisions will be handled.

This process does two things. It drives away ripoff artists, and it establishes position for any small claims court action that may result.

Case Study: What Billing Rate Should I Use?

Your company downloads graphic images from a modem, cleans them up and produces a 600 dpi laser printer printout of each image. These printouts are picked up daily by a local architectural company. You are paid by the printout for your work. You have two employees and estimate that you and these two support people can clean up and print out 20 images a day. It takes an average of 30 minutes to download, clean up and print each image. You take a flat weekly paycheck of $600 gross and pay your support people $15 an hour each. The support staff works 40 hours a week. You also have a bookkeeper who works for you 10 hours a week.

Determine how much you should charge each hour for the service described. To make it easy, assume there are no holidays and no vacation days to take you away from this work. Also assume a shop productivity factor of 50 percent.

QUESTIONS:
1. What figure should you use to determine the annual number of hours used in your billing?
2. Should you include the $10 an hour that you pay your bookkeeper in your billing-rate calculation?
3. You rent your computer, modem and laser printer for $900 a month. Should this be included in the cost portion to determine your billing rate?
4. You pay $500 a month for your small storefront office. You also pay $130 a month for utilities and $65 a month for cleaning the office. What annualized amount should be included in your billing rate calculations?
5. Health insurance for each full-time employee costs you $300 a month. However, one of your staff is already covered under her husband's policy. How much should you include at part of the billing-rate calculations?
6. Besides recovering all of your costs, you also want to make a profit this year of $18,000. Should this be included in the billing rate calculations?

7. Your company belongs to the National Association of Desktop Publishers. Annual dues are $95. Is this figure part of the billing-rate calculations?

8. All of your staff wear special lab jackets that you provide. These jackets have your company logo embroidered on them to provide a team appearance in your shop. Your company pays $1,050 annually for the cleaning these jackets. Should you include the cleaning costs in your billing rate calculations?

9. You send your employees to training classes to maintain their technical competence. This cost $1,500 a year. Should this be included in the calculations?

10. Assume that you pay $8,678 annually in payroll taxes and given all of the above, what is your billing rate per hour?

ANSWERS:

1. 7,800 hours — [(20 images x 30 minute/image) / 60 minutes/hour x 5 days/week x 3 people x 52 weeks/year = 7,800 hours/year]

2. Yes

3. Yes

4. $8,340 — [(500 x 12) + (130 x 12) + (65 x 12) = 8,340]

5. $7,200 — [$600 for you and $600 for one of your employees]

6. [600 + (15 x 8 x 5) + (15 x 8 x 5) = $1,800/week x 52 weeks = $93,600/year] [93,600 x 0.0765) + (93,600 x 0.0082) + (93,600 x 0.026)]

7. Yes

8. Yes

9. Yes

10. — [93,600 employees + 5,200 bookkeeper + 10,800 auto + 8,340 office + 7,200 health insurance + 18,000 profit + 95 dues + 1,050 cleaning + 1,500 training + 8,678 payroll taxes] / 7800 hours = $19.79/hr. Based on 50% productivity, your billing rate should be $39.58/hour.

Guerilla Operations for Business Survival

Business profitability runs in cycles depending on the agenda of the politicians in office, the mood of the country, and the conditions in the rest of the world. Cycles are natural. When the economic cycle is at the top, we're all happily busy depositing our sales success in the bank. But when the cycle turns down, things get scary. Business professionals become increasingly concerned when ominous black clouds form over our economy. When, each day we notice more "For Lease" signs posted in front of empty stores and tiny notes in local newspaper reporting increases in business bankruptcies our intuition tells us that the economy is heading into deeper trouble. We must act immediately to develop a survival strategy for our businesses.

In a down economy, survival can occur only by sticking to the basics and capitalizing on the strengths fundamental to your business. You should concentrate on those services that have the best potential for growth. You should also reduce expenses wherever possible. An analysis of your operation will identify areas where you can still lower costs, increase productivity, increase cash flow, and maintain or improve profit.

Your largest costs involve salary and benefits. Shop around for a better benefit package and shift to an employee cost-shared plan. Fewer medical claims directly translate into reduced health costs, so offer a cash bonus to those who keep healthy during the year. Pay a cash incentive to employees who improve their physical health — lose 10 pounds, reduce body fat by some percentage, or who stop smoking. Give them another bonus for maintaining their achievement for at least a year. Also pay a bonus to those who get an annual physical checkup. A healthier staff means healthier profit potential.

Adopt a "pay for performance" policy based on output quality, timeliness, and acceptance. Partition each employee's compensation into three parts—base pay, a performance bonus, and a customer evaluation bonus. Let an employee earn between 5% and 45% of their base pay by performing at optimum and making their customer happy with the service that the shop offers.

Consistently strive for maximum shop and individual productivity. To achieve this, establish weekly goals for yourself and your staff. Cross-trained each employee on the services that your business performs. Everyone should be given an opportunity to make suggestions, learn, and increase their skills and abilities. Loan manuals out overnight so employees can study at home. Inform each worker that survival of the business depends on teamwork and "elbow grease."

Carefully monitor the output and performance of your team. Release less productive workers. Farm out energy-intensive jobs to freelancers to reduce salary-benefit expenses and cut utility costs. Set standards for job performance and then encourage workers to telecommute and work from home. By paying a set rate for a given job, you can transfer utility costs and work break delays to these home workers. Your employees gain by the convenience of working at home without the stress caused by freeway commutes. When you need more help, hire part-time hourly workers to avoid the additional salary and benefit package costs. Wherever possible, hire your own children to shift income to your kids while teaching them the value of thrift and hard work.

Became an expert at combining tasks. Batch, or combine jobs. Batch telephone calls, and batch errand trips. Make your errands on off times so you won't get caught in traffic jams. Became an expert at discount buying. After developing a list of expected prices, monitor office supply sales and watch for business-failure auctions. Be aware that some "sale" prices are only reductions from an inflated level. Also realize that some "auction" prices are often at or above retail. Became a smart shopper. Look for good deals on everything. Ask your suppliers for better payment terms and deeper discounts. Offer to pay cash for a "substantial" discount.

For the duration of the economic downturn, hold a tight rein on major purchases. Carefully analyze the cost versus benefit for each hardware and software product being considered. Require a substantial gain in earnings potential to justify any purchase. Consider renting during short-term hardware needs. And avoid buying "toys." A 14,400 bps modem is of little use if your clients are only using 2400 baud devices. Include the cost for consumables in your evaluation of hardware purchases.

If you want a software upgrade, try to wait until near the end of an upgrade offer before making the purchase. Call tech support and read magazine reviews to identify bugs in the software and to let corrective actions be made to the earlier version of the program.

Actively seek to reduce debt load. Convert high interest loans to lower interest options. Double-pay on the high-interest debt. And set a goal to reduce expenses by at least 10 percent within the first year. Eliminate things that are unnecessary. Before improving any activity, question if it should be done at all. Eliminate unprofitable products and services. If overhead expenses don't show a demonstrated return, try to minimize or eliminate them too. Only add products and services that relate to you basic business. And do this carefully. In each case, expect a return on your investment for every dollar that you spend.

To improve productivity, replace parts before they began to waste energy. Lighting accounted for much of your electrical costs. You may realize a 20% savings on your utility bill by installing task lighting and periodically cleaning the bulbs. By adjusting indoor light levels to the amount of daylight available, you can turn off overhead lighting. Also turn incandescent lights off when not in use.

Clean out your files to gain storage space and speed information processing. Organize your shop according to work flow to minimize bottlenecks and unnecessary steps.

Offer cash incentives to employees who make cost-saving suggestions in areas not directly related to their tasks. Pay them up to 25 percent of the first year's actual savings based on a four-year effective life of a suggestion.

When your vehicle needs replacement, buy a two-year-old model and save 25-30% on the total cost of vehicle ownership. Increase the deductibles on you vehicle's collision insurance coverage to lower ownership costs even more. And increase your gas mileage up to 30% by scheduling oil and filter changes and lubrication jobs based on the miles driven. Change the oil in your vehicle every 3,000 miles. Every 6,000 miles change both the air and oil filters and have a lube job performed on the vehicle.

To enhance cash flow, pay bills at the last minute. File them by date and paid them only when due. Take advantage of credit card grace periods and then pay your expenses in full. Increase your personal tax exemption to minimize the refund and provide more disposable income. Then help your employees do the same.

Change your billing and receiving procedure to make it easy for your customers to make payments. On large projects, bill more often so you collect more often. Keep the balances small so customers will be more prone to pay you first when they experience cash problems. Shorten payment due dates from net 30 to net 10 days. Offer a 2% discount for payments made before a due date.

Negotiate progress payments on jobs that extend for several months. Then invoice twice a month. Convince clients to pay up front for work in exchange for a discount.

Besides tightening your credit policy, also quickly begin collection actions on overdue accounts receivable. Work on a cash-basis with all new customers and be slow to approve credit terms. If you discover that a customer is about to "go under," operate on a cash-first basis with them. And be prepared for potential "price wars" by assessing how much you can cut your fees and still break even. By knowing how much profit you have in each job, you can negotiate with confidence.

Every week, call 10 old customers and attempt to revive business. Ask what you can do to get their business back, and then act on their comments.

Recycle printed computer paper to use the reverse side. Design and used a stamp for the upper right-hand corner of the first page of each fax. It should identify the sender and receiver and eliminate the need for a separate cover page. Send more information by modem than by the U.S. Post Office to reduce mailing costs.

Analyze the use of paper, toner, envelopes and other office consumables. Establish a monthly average and then set a re-order point so you can buy during sales. Buy only what will be used within three months. By watching for announcements of product shortages or pending price increases, try to save 50% by volume purchasing from companies that are shutting down a line of things that you use.

Learn how to recharge your own laser printer toner cartridges and use these cartridges for standard office printing. Use commercial cartridges for client printing jobs.

To fill idle time, initiate staff training and increase preventive maintenance on your own equipment. Contact local businesses with similar hardware and software to offer your shop's support to them when they experience temporary work overload.

Increase your marketing and sales efforts. Keep in touch with your customers through postcards, phone calls, or personal visits. Query them on how you can serve them better. And act quickly on complaints. By visiting clients, you can reinforce your determination to maintain a high level of customer satisfaction.

To foster mutual support, refer leads to non-competing businesses who could return the favors. Join a support group and begin attending meetings of a local multi-discipline professional association. Encourage your staff to do the same.

To get recognition by local businesses, begin giving free presentations on how to reduce costs on DTP projects. Distribute fliers and donate services to local community activities. In every case, bring a large sign showing your business name and an ample quantity of promotional material.

Also encourage your staff to write short "What I Heard" notes that identify potential community business problems and opportunities. Follow-up and make these additional action items for your marketing efforts.

Fine tuned your listening skills and become sensitive to the needs and desires of potential business customers. Make you and your team experts in marketplace intelligence collection. By recognizing problems in other businesses, you can research the subject and then quickly offer a solution. By building on these opportunities, you can increase your business activity and keep your staff working through the valley of a business cycle.

Homework, hard work, and good business sense can make you and your staff immune to the ravages of a down business cycle. By becoming a street smart guerilla, your business can not only survive, it can gain a significant share of the market.

Summary

This chapter covered the street smart tactics of successful owner-operators. As you read, there are ways to maximize the probability of your business success.

In the next chapter, you'll find specifics on what DTP

shops and service bureaus are actually charging for their products and services. This information is based on an extensive survey involving over 20,000 desktop publishing and prepress shops across North America. It is provided to help you compare your own calculated hourly rates and product output prices with those of shops run by other professionals in the business.

Chapter 6

Pricing Tables

To develop the following tables, magazines, newsletters, books, journals, newspapers, and on-line bulletin boards and databases were searched to collect pricing information covering desktop publishing and DTP-related services in North America. In addition, an extensive survey was conducted through direct contact with over 20,000 DTP shops and service bureaus. The 8-page confidential survey requested information on ownership, business form, income, number of employees, compensation, services provided, billing rates, hardware and software used, publications read, associations joined, and sources for the best business leads.

Thirty-six percent of the respondents returned completed survey forms. Although this survey was more extensive than that conducted a year ago, a number of interesting comparisons have been made. Just as we found through surveys over the past two years, many small business owners still struggle with pricing products and services. Many fail to strategically plan and to carefully develop sound pricing policies. We found a wide range between the lowest and highest billing rate in almost every category–even within the same towns and cities. This wide price distribution occurs throughout North America.

To present the survey results, North America was partitioned into eight regions as described in Table 6-1. Pricing information for each region is provided in this chapter. A ninth section contains data that represents national results.

NEW ENGLAND	NORTH CENTRAL	MOUNTAIN
Connecticut	Illinois	Arizona
Maine	Indiana	Colorado
Massachusetts	Iowa	Idaho
New Hampshire	Kansas	Montana
Rhode Island	Michigan	Nevada
Vermont	Minnesota	New Mexico
	Missouri	Utah
MID ATLANTIC	Nebraska	Wyoming
New Jersey	North Dakota	
New York	Ohio	PACIFIC
Pennsylvania	South Dakota	Alaska
	Wisconsin	California
SOUTH ATLANTIC		Hawaii
Delaware	SOUTH CENTRAL	Oregon
District of Columbia	Alabama	Washington
Florida	Arkansas	
Georgia	Kentucky	CANADA
Maryland	Louisiana	Alberta
North Carolina	Mississippi	British Columbia
South Carolina	Oklahoma	Manitoba
Virginia	Tennessee	New Brunswick
West Virginia	Texas	Ontario
		Quebec
		Saskatchewan

Table 6-1. Regional breakdown by state plus Canada

The composite information described in Table 6-2 on the next page provides a fascinating overview of desktop publishing as a profession.

Organizational Structure of Businesses

Corporation	11.9%
Subchapter S Corporation	9.5%
Sole Proprietorship	67.7%
General Partnership	5.3%
Limited Partnership	1.1%

Year Business Began

1985 and earlier	26.1%
1986	4.6%
1987	3.8%
1988	7.5%
1989	11.1%
1990	9.7%
1991	9.7%
1992	14.6%
1993	9.5%

Gender of Owner

Female	51.8%
Male	46.5%
Couple	2.7%

Operating Out Of

Home Office	62.4%
Rented Office	22.8%
Rented Store Front	8.4%
Own Building	5.3%

Gross Sales by Organization Structure

Corporation	$1,000 - $5,000,000
Subchapter S	$1,000 - $3,000,000
General Partnership	$5,500 - $400,000
Limited Partnership	$1,600 - $10,800,000
Sole Proprietorship	$1,000 - $875,000

Gross Sales by Operating Location

Home Office	$1,000 - $10,800,000*
Own Building	$8,000 - $3,400,000
Store Front	$17,000 - $1,300,000
Other Rented Office	$1,000 - $2,500,000

*in Connecticut

Table 6-2. Desktop publishing in North America.

The responses returned by survey participants provided an interesting lesson in the attitudes and emotions of desktop publishers around the country. Many low-income shop owners were reluctant to provide income data on their response. This prompted many surveys being sent back for incompleteness. When these forms were returned, they indicated a meager income from the business. These participants were uncomfortable admitting that their formula was far from optimum.

Our data-entry team don't focus on who is earning what or who is doing what or providing what. They only focus on transferring information from the survey forms into our growing database.

High income shops had little or no reluctance in sharing their income and business profile data. After three years collecting proprietary data, we've earned a reputation for keeping private information just that — private.

Information is anchored in our database program by ZIP Code. This means that even our own people can only pull pricing, salary, income and other data out by ZIP code—not by company name. And this is as it should be.

The surveys confirmed that is still a new and evolving profession. Sixty-three percent of you began your business after 1987. Over half of you (62%) operate out of a home office, and 68% of you operate your business as a sole proprietorship. Your income varies from $1,000 a year freelance to over $10 million a year full-time. Almost 40% of you operate alone. Even as an independent owner-operator, some of you earn over $95,000 a year. More than half of you (50.4%) are women owner-operators.

Many of you take no pay out of your business. And a large number of you have no medical or health benefit protection provided by your business. Most of you (77.9%) operate full time (40+ hours a week). Just under 22% work part time and some even work freelance.

There are slightly more "PC-only" than "Mac-only" users (42.7% PC versus 38.3% Mac) with over 16% of you using both computer platforms in your work. A small number of Mac-only shops are using Apple Quadras. Many PC-only shops are migrating up to systems using the 80486 microprocessor.

A majority of Mac users prefer Microsoft Word, SuperPaint, FreeHand, PhotoShop, PageMaker and QuarkXpress. Most PC users prefer WordPerfect, CorelDraw, FreeHand, Photostyler, and PageMaker.

Many owner-operators don't know the difference between draw, paint and graphics software, although some of you use software for a variety of functions (e.g., PageMaker for word processing).

Many of you don't use modems yet and of those that do, many use freeware or shareware communications programs and operate at 2400 baud. We did notice a small, but growing number of shops using fax-boards.

Confusion exists about prepress and its place in desktop publishing. The distinction between service bureau prepress and DTP continues to blend. Commercial and quick print shops are integrating desktop publishing into their operations.

Many of you don't charge for all that you could. You tend to leave money on the negotiating table, and many of you don't place a high value on your knowledge and expertise. The price ranges found in this survey are wider than that of the survey a year ago. This suggests that many new DTPers are opening shops without adequate knowledge of the business side of the profession. Some seem to be attempting to create a sideline business from a hobby.

Yet there are others who appear to approach DTP in a professional business manner. They earn comfortable salaries, provide suitable benefits, and even work a 40-hour week.

As expected, higher prices were found in the larger metropolitan areas. And design fees are higher in

California, Florida, and New York, although a wide range exists between the highest and lowest fees in every location. In almost every category, we noted a billing rate spread of at least $50/hour. This suggests that many small business operators are not sophisticated in establishing pricing strategy. Seat-of-the-pants pricing doesn't help your bottom line or that of your professional colleagues.

We were also interested in determining the additional services that some shops provide such as collating, folding, labelling, binding and stapling. While we didn't receive many responses in these categories, we did include the results in this edition.

Comparison of Low and High End Desktop Publishers

A comparison of the low-end and high-end DTP shops provides profound insights into the mindset of the professionals operating these businesses. Although the size of their staff varies, the hardware and software support tools are similar. The major differences between the more successful shops and the "still growing" shops is in the pricing structure and how each group generates customer leads.

The low-end group charges between $20 and $40 an hour for document design. The high-end group charges between $75 and $100 for the same service. The same holds for scanning and laser printer output. Even clip art is charged at a different rate.

The survey responses that fell between these two data grouping extremes showed a gradual trend toward the high end as DTP shop owners grew in experience and in their ability to set price. Typically, as shop owners gain confidence and experience, they increase their prices accordingly.

At the low end, shop owners believe that advertising in a telephone directory is the best way to get leads. Of secondary importance is newspaper advertising and cold calls.

The owners of high-end shops feel that word of mouth is by far the best way to get new business. Their focus is on customer service. They want people to talk about them.

The low-end shops usually focus on attracting new business (via advertising). High-end shops focus on keeping customers and causing satisfied clients to advertise for them (word-of-mouth referrals).

These two ends of the DTP business spectrum focus in different directions for new business. It's obvious which group has the most successful strategy.

Incidentally, the reported incomes of the middle group of shops seems to increase as these shops adopt more of the pricing and business attitudes of the high-end group.

How to Use the Pricing Tables

The next nine sections (green sheets) provide in-depth information on current prices in the U.S. and Canada. There were few survey participants from Canada, so responses from all of the Canadian provinces are combined into a single composite-Canada group. Owner-operators from Canada should consider the data listed for Canadian shops and then compare this data with that for shops in the U.S. region immediately below their particular province.

To make this guide easy-to-use, the regional data for each category was processed and then summarized as an average, and typical (most common) price. All of the regional data for the U.S. was then combined and processed to generate composite-U.S. information on the average, and typical prices for each category.

Both regional and composite (national) information are listed in the same category table. This lets you look up a particular function, such as Brochure Design and quickly read the average, and typical price being charged by others in your region. On the same page and to the right of these prices you'll find composite information covering the U.S. and Canada. (We labelled the headings of the composite columns "U.S." because there were too few Canadian responses to bias the results.

Besides hourly rates, many categories include price per page, price per job, or price per activity. Where noteworthy, we also included minimum charge and cost-plus percent information.

The values in these tables represent actual survey data. Because the table values are driven by survey responses and not all owner-operators offer the same type of service, occasionally the average and typical price for a higher capability will be lower than the preceding tabulated price. For those categories in which "no data" was returned, use the composite data for U.S. and Canada, and check the prices being charged in adjoining regions.

A number of survey participants offer services that they personally don't own. Instead, they "job-out" or sub-contract for those services that their clients require. In these cases, the owner-operator filling in the survey form typically specified a percentage markup above cost. The typical cost is marked up by between 15 and 40 percent. This approach is typical when DTP shops offer imagesetting, collating, and binding services without owning the equipment to do these functions.

Pricing information on finishing services such as binding, collating, cutting, trimming, drilling, folding, and stapling, and other special services such as mailing and fax support are included in this edition. Of course, this contributed to the greatly expanded size of this reference.

We also included statistical information on what percent of survey participants offer a particular service. This will help you identify marketing and sales opportunities in your own region.

As you use these tables, keep these facts in mind. The average is the mean value within the set of responses to a particular category. The typical price is the most common price near the mid-point of the data. It represents the data point with the most occurrences. If no mode value was available, we used the median. If there were more than one collection of "typical" prices, what statisticians call "bimodal," we used the mode value closest to the average.

As you will notice by analyzing the tables, there were sometimes wide variations in the per piece, per each, prices. This was due to assumptions made by the survey respondents. To one person, a page may mean something slightly different that what a page means to another in a different business (e.g., new desktop publisher and advertising/marketing graphics directory). The best and most reliable information is contained in the hourly data.

Most experienced shops have adopted the budgeted hourly rate basis for calculating prices. These are amply reflected in the data to follow.

As you use these table to compare with your own calculated prices, let us know if there are better ways to represent the information contained in these regional tables.

This *Pricing Guide* is intended to "get you up to the next level" and to optimize your own profit margin. Use this reference book. Study the strategies and the tips from the experts. Then price for profit. May the fonts be with you.

Price Distribution
NEW ENGLAND
CT, NH, MA, ME, RI, VT

FILE CONVERSION

GENERAL NOTE: Survey responses listed as $/minute were converted to $/hr.

BOOKS ON DISK

$/per	Survey %	Average	Typical	U.S. Avg.	U.S. Typ	U.S. Max
Disk	0.0%			10.57	10.00	25.00
Page	2.9%	10.00	10.00	6.00	5.50	10.00
Hour	0.0%			40.11	35.00	95.00
Minimum	0.0%			15.00	15.00	15.00

CD-ROM

$/per	Survey %	Average	Typical	U.S. Avg.	U.S. Typ	U.S. Max
Page	0.0%			8.00	8.00	8.00
Disk	0.0%			25.00	25.00	25.00
Hour	0.0%			48.00	43.00	85.00
Minimum	0.0%			70.00	70.00	125.00

CROSS PLATFORM

$/per	Survey %	Average	Typical	U.S. Avg.	U.S. Typ	U.S. Max
Page	2.9%	2.00	2.00	3.83	2.88	8.00
File	2.9%	8.00	8.00	7.85	9.00	20.00
Disk	8.8%	10.33	8.00	11.85	10.00	50.00
Hour	14.7%	57.00	60.00	46.31	45.00	100.00
Minimum	5.9%	15.00	15.00	14.25	12.50	35.00

DATABASE FILES

$/per	Survey %	Average	Typical	U.S. Avg.	U.S. Typ	U.S. Max
Record	0.0%			0.16	0.15	0.25
File	0.0%			7.02	10.00	20.00
Disk	2.9%	15.00	15.00	21.67	15.00	50.00
Hour	2.9%	25.00	25.00	42.46	40.50	100.00
Minimum	0.0%			22.50	20.00	35.00

DOCUMENT FILES

$/per	Survey %	Average	Typical	U.S. Avg.	U.S. Typ	U.S. Max
K byte	0.0%			5.25	5.25	5.25
Page	0.0%			2.71	2.75	3.50
File	0.0%			8.38	10.00	15.00
Disk	5.9%	12.61	12.50	15.73	15.00	50.00
Hour	14.7%	48.00	35.00	41.23	35.00	100.00
Minimum	2.9%	15.00	15.00	21.00	15.00	35.00

DOCUMENTS ON DISK

$/per	Survey %	Average	Typical	U.S. Avg.	U.S. Typ	U.S. Max
Page	5.9%	6.00	6.00	6.17	7.00	15.00
File	0.0%			12.00	15.00	15.00
Disk	5.9%	9.07	9.00	14.00	10.00	50.00
Hour	5.9%	25.26	25.00	38.77	35.00	75.00
Minimum	0.0%			12.50	13.00	15.00

FORMS CONVERSION

$/per	Survey %	Average	Typical	U.S. Avg.	U.S. Typ	U.S. Max
Page	0.0%			187.18	190.00	200.00
File	0.0%			26.00	10.00	50.00
Disk	0.0%			15.00	10.00	25.00
Hour	0.0%			47.68	40.00	100.00
Minimum	0.0%			12.50	15.00	15.00

GRAPHIC FORMAT FILES

$/per	Survey %	Average	Typical	U.S. Avg.	U.S. Typ	U.S. Max
K byte	0.0%			5.25	5.25	5.25
Page	0.0%			18.32	20.00	20.00
File	0.0%			8.50	5.88	20.00
Disk	5.9%	12.50	13.00	15.36	15.00	50.00
Hour	11.7%	45.00	35.00	44.32	40.00	100.00
Minimum	2.9%	15.00	15.00	19.17	15.00	35.00

MEDIA CONVERSION

$/per	Survey %	Average	Typical	U.S. Avg.	U.S. Typ	U.S. Max
File	0.0%			15.00	12.50	25.00
Disk	2.9%	15.00	15.00	13.05	10.00	50.00
Hour	5.9%	62.37	62.50	48.64	45.00	100.00
Minimum	2.9%	15.00	15.00	13.75	15.00	15.00

PAGE LAYOUT FILES

$/per	Survey %	Average	Typical	U.S. Avg.	U.S. Typ	U.S. Max
500 K byte	0.0%			15.00	15.00	15.00
Page	0.0%			37.50	37.50	60.00
File	0.0%			12.70	12.50	25.00
Disk	5.9%	13.50	14.00	19.25	15.00	50.00
Hour	5.9%	22.50	22.50	42.91	40.00	100.00
Minimum	0.0%			20.00	15.00	35.00

SPREADSHEET FILES

$/per	Survey %	Average	Typical	U.S. Avg	U.S. Typ	U.S. Max
25 K byte	0.0%			7.50	7.50	7.50
Page	0.0%			2.88	2.88	2.00
File	0.0%			12.30	10.88	25.00
Disk	2.9%	15.00	15.00	26.25	20.00	50.00
Hour	5.9%	22.50	24.00	40.98	40.00	100.00
Minimum	0.0%			22.50	20.00	35.00

VIDEO TAPE TRANSFER

$/per	Survey %	Average	Typical	U.S. Avg	U.S. Typ	U.S. Max
Disk	0.0%			25.00	25.00	25.00
Per Hour	0.0%			48.33	45.00	75.00
Minimum	0.0%			15.00	15.00	15.00

WORD PROCESSOR FILE TO SGML

$/per	Survey %	Average	Typical	U.S. Avg	U.S. Typ	U.S. Max
Disk	0.0%			25.00	25.00	25.00
Hour	0.0%			45.00	40.00	75.00
Minimum	0.0%			15.00	15.00	15.00

TEXT CREATION

GENERAL COPY WRITING

$/per	Survey %	Average	Typical	U.S. Avg	U.S. Typ	U.S. Max
Line	2.9%	0.20	0.20	0.20	0.20	0.20
Page	11.4%	22.50	20.00	30.38	20.00	87.50
Hour	34.3%	40.21	42.50	41.43	35.00	300.00
Minimum	0.0%			19.00	15.00	35.00

NEWSLETTER COPY

$/per	Survey %	Average	Typical	U.S. Avg	U.S. Typ	U.S. Max
Column	0.0%			10.48	10.50	11.00
Page	14.3%	33.80	40.00	40.96	40.00	125.00
Hour	31.4%	40.68	42.50	39.31	35.00	300.00
Minimum	0.0%			283.33	125.00	800.00

PUBLICITY / ADVERTISING COPY

$/per	Survey %	Average	Typical	U.S. Avg	U.S. Typ	U.S. Max
Page	8.6%	63.33	50.00	40.31	40.00	100.00
Piece	0.0%			260.00	300.00	425.00
Hour	25.7%	39.94	42.50	43.56	38.00	300.00
Minimum	0.0%			19.00	15.00	35.00

RESUME WRITING

$/per	Survey %	Average	Typical	U.S. Avg.	U.S. Typ	U.S. Max
Page	20.0%	33.43	30.00	32.43	25.00	100.00
Hour	31.4%	36.45	33.00	38.11	35.00	300.00
Minimum	0.0%			110.00	65.00	300.00

TECHNICAL WRITING

$/per	Survey %	Average	Typical	U.S. Avg.	U.S. Typ	U.S. Max
Page	11.4%	66.25	50.00	53.54	35.00	300.00
Hour	20.0%	42.43	50.00	45.99	35.00	300.00
Minimum	0.0%			35.00	35.00	55.00

DATA INPUT / EDITING

DATA ENTRY / KEYBOARDING

$/per	Survey %	Average	Typical	U.S. Avg.	U.S. Typ	U.S. Max
Character	0.0%			0.02	0.02	0.02
Page	5.9%	22.00	22.00	11.32	10.00	50.00
Hour	55.9%	33.39	25.00	32.64	28.00	100.00
Minimum	0.0%			20.00	15.00	35.00

COPY EDITING

$/per	Survey %	Average	Typical	U.S. Avg.	U.S. Typ	U.S. Max
Word	0.0%			0.06	0.06	0.11
Page	8.8%	10.00	5.00	9.47	7.00	50.00
Hour	52.9%	35.33	30.00	36.58	30.00	100.00
Minimum	0.0%			20.00	15.00	35.00

CONTENT EDITING

$/per	Survey %	Average	Typical	U.S. Avg.	U.S. Typ	U.S. Max
Word	0.0%			0.11	0.11	0.11
Page	5.9%	1.00	1.00	5.33	5.00	50.00
Hour	44.1%	33.93	35.00	37.44	36.00	100.00
Minimum	0.0%			33.50	35.00	35.00

PROOF READING

$/per	Survey %	Average	Typical	U.S. Avg.	U.S. Typ	U.S. Max
Page	11.8%	9.50	8.00	6.71	5.00	50.00
Hour	52.9%	35.28	30.00	35.63	30.00	100.00
Minimum	0.0%			33.50	35.00	35.00

REWRITING

$/per	Survey %	Average	Typical	U.S. Avg.	U.S. Typ	U.S. Max
Word	0.0%			0.07	0.03	0.11
Line	0.0%			0.25	0.20	1.00
Page	8.8%	25.67	15.00	22.67	13.50	50.00
Hour	35.3%	34.92	36.00	38.81	35.00	100.00
Minimum	0.0%			35.00	35.00	35.00

INDEXING

$/per	Survey %	Average	Typical	U.S. Avg.	U.S. Typ	U.S. Max
Page	0.0%			2.80	2.00	5.00
Hour	17.7%	26.00	24.00	38.60	35.00	100.00
Minimum	0.0%			87.50	87.50	140.00

MODEM INPUT

$/per	Survey %	Average	Typical	U.S. Avg.	U.S. Typ	U.S. Max
Page	0.0%			3.33	3.00	5.00
File	0.0%			10.00	10.00	10.00
K bytes	0.0%			1.32	1.40	1.50
Disk	0.0%			8.33	5.00	25.00
Minute	0.1%	10.57	10.57	1.50	1.50	2.00
Hour	23.5%	39.63	33.00	41.62	38.00	100.00
Minimum	0.0%			12.50	12.50	15.00

TEXT FILE IMPORTING

$/per	Survey %	Average	Typical	U.S. Avg.	U.S. Typ	U.S. Max
Page	2.9%	9.97	10.00	14.60	5.00	50.00
File	1.8%			11.00	10.00	25.00
K bytes	0.0%			1.32	1.40	1.50
Disk	2.9%	5.00	5.00	10.00	10.00	15.00
Minute	0.0%			1.50	1.50	2.00
Hour	29.4%	46.70	50.00	39.10	35.00	100.00
Minimum	0.0%			21.25	22.00	35.00

TRANSCRIPTION

$/per	Survey %	Average	Typical	U.S. Avg.	U.S. Typ	U.S. Max
Line	2.9%	0.24	0.25	0.17	0.17	0.25
Page	0.0%			4.79	4.25	8.00
File	0.0%			10.57	10.57	25.00
Disk	0.0%			25.00	25.00	25.00
Hour	26.5%	28.78	25.00	31.64	30.00	75.00
Minimum	0.0%			25.00	25.00	35.00

TRANSLATION

$/per	Survey %	Average	Typical	U.S. Avg	U.S. Typ	U.S. Max
Word	0.0%			0.17	0.17	0.20
Page	2.9%	49.50	50.00	24.17	22.50	50.00
Hour	14.7%	34.80	25.00	44.49	40.00	150.00
Minimum	0.0%			35.00	35..00	35.00

TYPOGRAPHY (General)

$/per	Survey %	Average	Typical	U.S. Avg	U.S. Typ	U.S. Max
Line	0.0%			0.25	0.25	0.25
Page	2.9%	33.24	33.00	21.48	15.00	75.00
Hour	55.9%	40.11	35.00	39.27	35.00	100.00
Minimum	0.0%			18.83	15.00	35.00

TYPOGRAPHY (Spreadsheet)

$/per	Survey %	Average	Typical	U.S. Avg	U.S. Typ	U.S. Max
Line	0.0%			0.25	0.25	0.25
Page	2.9%	14.97	15.00	24.06	17.00	75.00
Hour	47.1%	42.31	40.00	41.47	36.00	150.00
Minimum	0.0%			35.00	35.00	35.00

WORD PROCESSSING

$/per	Survey %	Average	Typical	U.S. Avg	U.S. Typ	U.S. Max
Line	2.9%	0.19	0.20	0.13	0.10	0.20
Page	0.0%			8.67	8.25	25.00
Hour	58.8%	31.65	28.00	32.90	25.00	100.00
Minimum	0.0%			21.67	15.00	35.00

DATA MANAGEMENT

GENERAL NOTES:
1. Assume customer pays for cost of media extra.
2. On $/word, assume 2K words per page.
3. Per file cost assumed to be for 1 year.
4. Assume $/file same as $/image.

ARCHIVING SERVICE

$/per	Survey %	Average	Typical	U.S. Avg	U.S. Typ	U.S. Max
Page	0.0%			7.50	7.50	7.50
File	0.0%			9.63	15.00	25.00
Tape	0.0%			37.50	20.00	150.00
Hour	5.9%	67.67	67.50	46.05	40.00	95.00
Minimum	0.0%			14.17	10.00	25.00

IMAGE MANAGEMENT

$/per	Survey %	Average	Typical	U.S. Avg.	U.S. Typ	U.S. Max
Page	0.6%	16.67	16.67	6.50	5.50	10.00
File	2.9%	6.00	6.00	16.67	15.00	50.00
Disk	0.0%			30.00	30.00	50.00
Hour	8.8%	65.00	50.00	44.81	40.00	110.00
Minimum	0.0%			14.17	10.00	25.00

NOTE: Assume $/.file same as $/image.

TEXT MANAGEMENT

$/per	Survey %	Average	Typical	U.S. Avg.	U.S. Typ	U.S. Max
Page	0.0%			8.67	6.00	15.00
File	2.9%	6.00	6.00	16.67	15.00	50.00
Disk	0.0%			23.33	15.00	50.00
Hour	8.8%	56.67	50.00	44.51	35.00	95.00
Minimum	0.0%			14.17	10.00	25.00

IMAGING SERVICES

DOCUMENT CAPTURE

$/per	Survey %	Average	Typical	U.S. Avg.	U.S. Typ	U.S. Max
Page	0.0%			3.65	3.00	7.50
File	0.0%			6.50	5.00	10.00
Hour	2.9%	85.00	85.00	39.41	35.00	95.00
Minimum	2.9%	7.50	7.50	16.25	16.25	25.00

DOCUMENT RETRIEVAL

$/per	Survey %	Average	Typical	U.S. Avg.	U.S. Typ	U.S. Max
Page	0.0%			1.50	1.50	2.00
File	2.9%	5.00	5.00	5.03	5.00	10.00
Hour	2.9%	85.00	85.00	38.82	39.00	85.00
Minimum	2.9%	7.50	7.50	16.25	16.25	25.00

GRAPHICS FILE IMPORTING

$/per	Survey %	Average	Typical	U.S. Avg.	U.S. Typ	U.S. Max
File	8.8%	10.67	12.00	6.98	5.00	15.00
Disk	2.9%	5.00	5.00	5.00	5.00	5.00
Hour	11.8%	52.50	50.00	43.35	36.00	100.00
Minimum	2.9%	7.50	7.50	14.17	14.17	35.00

PHOTO CD-ROM IMPORTING

$/per	Survey %	Average	Typical	U.S. Avg.	U.S. Typ	U.S. Max
Image	2.9%	5.00	5.00	10.02	7.25	45.00
Stock Fee	2.9%	75.00	75.00	75.00	75.00	75.00
Hour	8.8%	55.00	50.00	48.60	45.00	100.00
Minimum	2.9%	7.50	7.50	16.25	15.00	25.00

SCANNING (B&W Grey Scale)

$/per	Survey %	Average	Typical	U.S. Avg.	U.S. Typ	U.S. Max
Hour	2.9%	40.00	40.00	42.82	40.00	100.00
75-200 dpi	0.0%			10.10	9.00	75.00
300-400 dpi	20.6%	7.43	9.00	11.93	10.00	75.00
600-800 dpi	8.8%	21.67	10.00	13.51	11.00	75.00
1200 dpi	0.00%			20.20	12.00	75.00
2400 dpi	0.00%			36.86	30.00	75.00

SCANNING (B&W Line Art)

$/per	Survey %	Average	Typical	U.S. Avg.	U.S. Typ	U.S. Max
Hour	8.8%	43.33	40.00	40.94	40.00	100.00
75-200 dpi	5.9%	6.50	6.50	10.59	9.00	75.00
300-400 dpi	26.5%	8.78	8.00	11.92	10.00	75.00
600-800 dpi	11.8%	10.25	10.00	12.51	10.00	75.00
1200 dpi	2.9%	12.00	12.00	15.59	11.00	75.00
2400 dpi	0.0%			35.75	27.50	75.00
Per K	5.9%	40.00	40.00	51.67	50.00	75.00

SCANNING (B&W Photo)

$/per	Survey %	Average	Typical	U.S. Avg.	U.S. Typ	U.S. Max
Hour	11.8%	43.75	40.00	45.16	40.00	100.00
75-200 dpi	5.9%	9.00	9.00	12.28	10.00	75.00
300-400 dpi	20.6%	18.57	9.00	13.92	12.40	75.00
600-800 dpi	8.8%	7.67	8.00	14.79	12.60	75.00
1200 dpi	2.9%	50.00	50.00	19.88	17.50	75.00
2400 dpi	2.9%	50.00	50.00	35.56	31.00	75.00
Per K	2.9%	50.00	50.00	62.50	62.50	75.00

SCANNING (Color Illustration)

$/per	Survey %	Average	Typical	U.S. Avg.	U.S. Typ	U.S. Max
Hour	2.9%	30.00	30.00	49.23	50.00	125.00
75-200 dpi	0.0%			19.08	15.00	75.00
300-400 dpi	5.9%	9.50	9.50	21.03	19.00	82.00
600-800 dpi	5.9%	42.50	42.50	22.36	21.50	75.00
1200 dpi	0.0%			26.47	23.00	75.00
2400 dpi	0.0%			46.22	50.00	75.00

SCANNING (Color Photo)

$/per	Survey %	Average	Typical	U.S. Avg.	U.S. Typ	U.S. Max
Hour	0.0%			49.23	50.00	125.00
75-200 dpi	0.0%			20.44	15.00	75.00
300-400 dpi	5.9%	9.50	9.50	20.97	17.75	82.00
600-800 dpi	2.9%	10.00	10.00	19.75	15.00	75.00
1200 dpi	0.0%			30.13	30.00	75.00
2400 dpi	2.9%	137.00	137.00	61.54	60.00	137.00

SCANNING (HIGH END)
(Loose Scan)

$/per	Survey %	U.S. Avg.	U.S. Typ	U.S. Max
2 x 3	0.1%	13.33	10.00	25.00
3 x 5	0.1%	11.25	10.00	20.00
4 x 5	0.1%	16.00	10.00	33.00
5 x 7	0.1%	18.00	10.00	37.00
5.5 x 8.5	0.1%	17.33	10.00	39.00
6 x 9	0.1%	24.67	15.00	49.00
8 x 10	0.1%	41.60	50.00	70.00
10 x 12	0.1%	47.80	60.00	84.00
11 x 14	0.1%	81.67	70.00	105.00
12 x 18	0.1%	90.67	80.00	122.00
16 x 20	0.1%	162.00	162.00	162.00
20 x 24	0.1%	199.00	199.00	199.00
Hour	0.1%	47.00	45.00	60.00

SCANNING (HIGH END)
(Drum Scan)

$/per	Survey %	U.S. Avg.	U.S. Typ	U.S. Max
2 x 3	0.1%	56..92	54.25	71.50
4 x 5	0.1%	57.21	55.00	94.50
5 x 7	0.1%	65.75	70.00	106.00
6 x 8	0.1%	103.13	102.50	117.50
6 x 9	0.1%	57.00	45.00	85.00
8 x 10	0.1%	51.25	50.00	60.00
10 x 12	0.1%	58.33	60.00	60.00
11 x 14	0.1%	71.25	72.50	75.00
12 x 18	0.1%	86.67	85.00	100.00
24 x 27	0.1%	600.00	600.00	600.00

SCANNING (HIGH END)
(High Res Scan to Disk)

$/per	Survey %	U.S. Avg.	U.S. Typ	U.S. Max
2 x 3	0.1%	20..50	19.50	25.00
4 x 5	0.1%	26.17	27.50	30.00
5 x 7	0.1%	34.00	35.00	41.00
6 x 9	0.1%	39.80	39.00	50.00

SCANNING (HIGH END)
(High Res Scan to Disk)

$/per	Survey %	U.S. Avg.	U.S. Typ	U.S. Max
8 x 10	0.1%	45.50	45.00	60.00
10 x 12	0.1%	56.83	59.00	70.00
11 x 14	0.1%	65.08	64.00	89.00
12 x 18	0.1%	78.90	75.00	100.00
16 x 20	0.1%	96.33	99.00	130.00
20 x 24	0.1%	128.00	134.00	160.00
24 x 27	0.1%	156.25	156.25	200.00

SCANNING (Transparency)

$/per	Survey %	Average	Typical	U.S. Avg.	U.S. Typ	U.S. Max
Each	0.0%			18.70	16.00	45.00
Hour	2.9%	137.00	60.00	65.29	55.00	137.00

SCANNING (Slide)

$/per	Survey %	Average	Typical	U.S. Avg.	U.S. Typ	U.S. Max
Each	0.0%			23.00	16.99	65.00
Hour	2.9%	137.00	60.00	68.42	55.00	137.00

COLOR CORRECTION

$/per	Survey %	Average	Typical	U.S. Avg.	U.S. Typ	U.S. Max
Hour	5.9%	80.00	80.00	65.80	50.00	300.00

IMAGE EDITING

$/per	Survey %	Average	Typical	U.S. Avg.	U.S. Typ	U.S. Max
Each	5.9%	15.00	15.00	20.75	15.00	50.00
Hour	5.9%	40.00	40.00	55.47	45.00	300.00

IMAGE ENHANCEMENT

$/per	Survey %	Average	Typical	U.S. Avg.	U.S. Typ	U.S. Max
Hour	8.8%	63.33	50.00	57.60	50.00	300.00

RETOUCHING

$/per	Survey %	Average	Typical	U.S. Avg.	U.S. Typ	U.S. Max
Each	0.0%			27.67	40.00	50.00
Hour	23.5%	67.38	70.00	58.60	50.00	300.00
Minimum	0.0%			26.08	25.00	35.00

TEXT SCAN (OCR)

$/per	Survey %	Average	Typical	U.S. Avg.	U.S. Typ	U.S. Max
Page	14.7%	3.60	4.00	7.82	5.00	95.00

TEXT SCAN (OCR)

$/per	Survey %	Average	Typical	U.S. Avg.	U.S. Typ	U.S. Max
Hour	14.7%	37.00	25.00	36.33	30.00	75.00
Minimum	0.0%			19.08	16.90	35.00

NOTE:

1. Prices assume spell check conducted on scanned text.

2. Assumes 2 Kb per page, so $1/Kb response incorporated as $2/page.

NEGATIVE CREATION

$/per	Survey %	Average	Typical	U.S. Avg.	U.S. Typ	U.S. Max
Each	0.0%			22.00	22.00	40.00
Hour	0.0%			56.71	56.71	100.00
Minimum	0.0%			16.67	16.67	25.00

DESIGN SERVICES

ANNOUNCEMENTS

$/per	Survey %	Average	Typical	U.S. Avg.	U.S. Typ	U.S. Max
Text Page	11.8%	22.00	25.00	37.05	24.00	250.00
w/Graphics	8.8%	21.67	25.00	65.36	36.50	500.00
Hour	32.4%	36.09	35.00	42.21	40.00	100.00

ANNUAL REPORTS
(1C, 2C, Up To Letter Size Pages)

$/per	Survey %	Average	Typical	U.S. Avg.	U.S. Typ	U.S. Max
Text	5.9%	27.50	27.50	114.75	62.50	1000.00
w/Graphics	5.9%	27.50	27.50	222.00	100.00	7680.00
Hour	32.4%	44.91	50.00	46.58	45.00	100.00

ANNUAL REPORTS
(3C, 4C, Larger Size Pages)

$/per	Survey %	Average	Typical	U.S. Avg.	U.S. Typ	U.S. Max
Text	0.0%			214.55	100.00	1500.00
w/Graphics	0.0%			422.50	175.00	11520.00
Hour	26.5%	47.67	50.00	46.34	45.00	100.00

BAR CODING

$/per	Survey %	Average	Typical	U.S. Avg.	U.S. Typ	U.S. Max
Each	0.0%			13.25	11.00	150.00
Page	0.0%			29.00	29.00	50.00
Hour	8.8%	41.67	25.00	47.83	45.00	100.00

BOOKLETS

$/per	Survey %	Average	Typical	U.S. Avg.	U.S. Typ	U.S. Max
Text Page	11.8%	38.50	40.00	48.40	30.00	500.00
w/Graphics	2.9%	50.00	50.00	110.53	50.00	650.00
Hour	58.8%	40.90	50.00	43.87	25.00	100.00

BOOK COVERS

$/per	Survey %	Average	Typical	U.S. Avg.	U.S. Typ	U.S. Max
Text	2.9%	30.00	30.00	143.10	75.00	500.00
w/Graphics	0.0%			403.36	300.00	1800.00
Hour	23.5%	42,50	35.00	47.83	45.00	120.00

BOOK BODY

$/per	Survey %	Average	Typical	U.S. Avg.	U.S. Typ	U.S. Max
Text Page	0.0%			26.65	20.00	75.00
w/Graphics	0.0%			41.11	25.00	85.00
Hour	23.5%	41.75	44.00	44.26	40.00	100.00

BOOK JACKETS

$/per	Survey %	Average	Typical	U.S. Avg.	U.S. Typ	U.S. Max
Text	2.9%	30.00	30.00	161.54	175.00	500.00
w/Graphics	0.0%			491.00	325.00	1000.00
Hour	14.7%	47.00	35.00	48.63	45.00	120.00

BROCHURE
(1C, 2C, Up To Letter Size Sheet)

$/per	Survey %	Average	Typical	U.S. Avg.	U.S. Typ	U.S. Max
Text Page	11.8%	47.25	44.00	72.59	47.50	500.00
w/Graphics	2.9%	85.00	85.00	156.74	82.50	750.00
Hour	61.8%	41.10	44.00	42.85	40.00	125.00

BROCHURE
(3C, 4C, Larger Size Sheet)

$/per	Survey %	Average	Typical	U.S. Avg.	U.S. Typ	U.S. Max
Text Page	2.9%	85.00	85.00	123.79	60.00	1000.00
w/Graphics	2.9%	95.00	95.00	227.71	100.00	1500.00
Hour	55.9%	41.00	50.00	44.17	40.00	125.00

BULLETIN

$/per	Survey %	Average	Typical	U.S. Avg.	U.S. Typ	U.S. Max
Text Page	2.9%	40.00	40.00	32.75	25.00	150.00
w/Graphics	2.9%	45.00	45.00	47.81	35.00	200.00
Hour	35.3%	39.08	50.00	42.36	40.00	100.00

BUSINESS CARDS

$/per	Survey %	Average	Typical	U.S. Avg.	U.S. Typ	U.S. Max
Text Card	14.7%	21.70	20.00	38.81	25.00	500.00
w/Graphics	5.9%	265.00	265.00	91.70	40.00	1000.00
Hour	61.8%	39.38	40.00	43.19	40.00	150.00

BUSINESS REPLY CARDS

$/per	Survey %	Average	Typical	U.S. Avg.	U.S. Typ	U.S. Max
Text Card	5.9%	26.50	26.50	34.32	31.50	150.00
w/Graphics	0.0%			67.50	35.00	250.00
Hour	26.5%	39.11	35.00	43.79	40.00	100.00

BUSINESS LETTERS

$/per	Survey %	Average	Typical	U.S. Avg.	U.S. Typ	U.S. Max
Text Page	8.8%	6.83	5.00	17.23	12.25	90.00
w/Graphics	5.9%	9.50	9.50	27.08	18.75	100.00
Hour	38.2%	36.77	35.00	39.38	35.00	100.00

CALENDARS

$/per	Survey %	Average	Typical	U.S. Avg.	U.S. Typ	U.S. Max
Text Page	2.9%	30.00	30.00	82.50	50.00	500.00
w/Graphics	0.0%			53.18	45.00	150.00
Hour	17.7%	34.80	25.00	43.77	40.00	100.00

CALLIGRAPHY

$/per	Survey %	Average	Typical	U.S. Avg.	U.S. Typ	U.S. Max
Line	2.9%	1.00	1.00	1.00	1.00	60.00
Page	0.0%			40.00	35.00	100.00
Hour	14.7%	28.80	25.00	45.50	40.00	175.00

CARDS (FOLD-OVER)

$/per	Survey %	Average	Typical	U.S. Avg.	U.S. Typ	U.S. Max
Text Card	0.0%			31.45	25.00	60.00
w/Graphics	0.0%			65.47	46.40	250.00
Hour	14.7%	37.80	30.00	43.63	40.00	100.00

CARDS (ROLODEX)

$/per	Survey %	Average	Typical	U.S. Avg.	U.S. Typ	U.S. Max
Text Card	0.0%			37.34	25.00	150.00
w/Graphics	0.0%			63.00	48.00	250.00
Hour	11.7%	41.25	50.00	44.94	41.00	100.00

CARTOONS

$/per	Survey %	Average	Typical	U.S. Avg.	U.S. Typ	U.S. Max
Each	0.0%			119.29	60.00	400.00
Page	0.0%			163.33	65.00	400.00
Hour	8.8%	55.00	65.00	48.15	45.00	90.00

CATALOGS

$/per	Survey %	Average	Typical	U.S. Avg.	U.S. Typ	U.S. Max
Text Page	8.8%	38.00	40.00	69.03	40.00	500.00
w/Graphics	2.9%	40.00	40.00	129.05	67.50	1000.00
Hour	41.2%	43.21	50.00	45.68	45.00	125.00

CERTIFICATES

$/per	Survey %	Average	Typical	U.S. Avg.	U.S. Typ	U.S. Max
Text	14.7%	15.30	10.00	23.56	16.25	125.00
w/Graphics	5.9%	35.00	35.00	35.07	25.00	150.00
Hour	17.7%	33.17	25.00	42.15	40.00	100.00

CHARTS / DIAGRAMS

$/per	Survey %	Average	Typical	U.S. Avg.	U.S. Typ	U.S. Max
Text	8.8%	33.00	30.00	36.19	32.50	150.00
w/Graphics	5.9%	37.50	37.50	53.14	47.50	150.00
Hour	41.2%	42.86	50.00	44.29	40.00	100.00

COMIC BOOKS

$/per	Survey %	Average	Typical	U.S. Avg.	U.S. Typ	U.S. Max
Each Page	0.0%			65.00	60.00	100.00
Hour	2.9%	25.00	25.00	47.12	50.00	80.00

COMIC STRIPS

$/per	Survey %	Average	Typical	U.S. Avg.	U.S. Typ	U.S. Max
Each Strip	0.0%			38.33	30.00	60.00
Hour	2.9%	25.00	25.00	46.78	50.00	80.00

COMPUTER GENERATED ART

$/per	Survey %	Average	Typical	U.S. Avg.	U.S. Typ	U.S. Max
Page	5.9%	287.50	287.50	121.40	50.00	500.00
Hour	35.3%	45.42	50.00	46.70	42.00	175.00

CUSTOM DISPLAYS

$/per	Survey %	Average	Typical	U.S. Avg.	U.S. Typ	U.S. Max
Text	0.0%			192.14	60.00	1000.00
w/Graphics	2.9%	500.00	500.00	265.71	100.00	1000.00
Hour	17.7%	43.33	50.00	48.95	45.00	100.00

DATABASE DESIGN

$/per	Survey %	Average	Typical	U.S. Avg.	U.S. Typ	U.S. Max
Text	0.0%			38.33	30.00	60.00
w/Graphics	0.0%			43.33	40.00	60.00
Hour	11.8%	31.25	25.00	42.45	41.00	80.00

DIGITAL SLIDE PRESENTATIONS

$/per	Survey %	Average	Typical	U.S. Avg.	U.S. Typ	U.S. Max
Text	2.9%	30.00	30.000	27.13	27.50	60.00
w/Graphics	2.9%	30.00	30.00	35.00	32.50	60.00
Hour	11.8%	41.25	50.00	45.81	45.00	100.00

DIRECT MAIL PACKAGES

$/per	Survey %	Average	Typical	U.S. Avg.	U.S. Typ	U.S. Max
Text	5.9%	30.00	30.00	298.46	60.00	1500.00
w/Graphics	2.9%	30.00	30.00	413.50	65.00	2000.00
Hour	32.4%	46.36	50.00	47.05	45.00	100.00

DIRECTORY

$/per	Survey %	Average	Typical	U.S. Avg.	U.S. Typ	U.S. Max
Text	5.9%	37.00	35.00	38.72	30.00	150.00
w/Graphics	2.9%	30.00	30.00	73.53	40.00	500.00
Hour	26.5%	38.78	30.00	43.08	40.00	125.00

DISPLAY ADVERTISING

$/per	Survey %	Average	Typical	U.S. Avg.	U.S. Typ	U.S. Max
Text	5.9%	35.00	35.00	109.28	30.00	1000.00
w/Graphics	8.8%	190.00	40.00	304.64	45.00	2500.00
Hour	41.2%	43.14	50.00	48.23	45.00	115.00

DISPLAY EXHIBITS

$/per	Survey %	Average	Typical	U.S. Avg.	U.S. Typ	U.S. Max
Text Panel	0.0%			858.57	90.00	5000.00
w/Graphics	2.9%	500.00	500.00	896.67	100.00	5000.00
Hour	14.7%	39.00	35.00	51.43	50.00	115.00

DOOR HANGERS

$/per	Survey %	Average	Typical	U.S. Avg.	U.S. Typ	U.S. Max
Text	0.0%			42.46	25.00	250.00
w/Graphics	0.0%			87.50	35.00	500.00
Hour	2.9%	25.00	25.00	47.19	45.00	100.00

DRAFTING

$/per	Survey %	Average	Typical	U.S. Avg.	U.S. Typ	U.S. Max
Page	0.0%			45.00	45.00	60.00
Hour	8.8%	40.00	35.00	46.62	45.00	100.00

FINANCIAL DOCUMENTS

$/per	Survey %	Average	Typical	U.S. Avg.	U.S. Typ	U.S. Max
Text Page	2.9%	33.00	33.00	45.33	33.00	150.00
w/Graphics	0.0%			92.00	60.00	150.00
Hour	14.7%	44.00	35.00	47.20	45.00	125.00

FLYERS

$/per	Survey %	Average	Typical	U.S. Avg.	U.S. Typ	U.S. Max
Text Page	17.7%	39.83	40.00	39.21	25.00	325.00
w/Graphics	11.8%	83.75	40.00	66.84	35.00	325.00
Hour	58.8%	42.70	50.00	42.22	40.00	100.00

FORMS

$/per	Survey %	Average	Typical	U.S. Avg.	U.S. Typ	U.S. Max
Text Page	17.7%	29.67	33.00	52.60	30.00	750.00
w/Graphics	11.8%	46.25	40.00	81.67	37.50	10000.00
Hour	52.9%	37.17	35.00	41.75	40.00	125.00

HANDBOOKS

$/per	Survey %	Average	Typical	U.S. Avg.	U.S. Typ	U.S. Max
Text Page	5.9%	35.00	35.00	38.22	25.00	150.00
w/Graphics	5.9%	37.50	37.50	62.46	35.00	250.00
Hour	47.1%	39.63	50.00	43.53	40.00	100.00

INSERTS

$/per	Survey %	Average	Typical	U.S. Avg.	U.S. Typ	U.S. Max
Text Page	8.8%	24.33	20.00	70.58	27.50	1000.00
w/Graphics	2.9%	25.00	25.00	193.50	35.00	2500.00
Hour	38.2%	40.69	40.00	43.99	40.00	100.00

INVITATIONS

$/per	Survey %	Average	Typical	U.S. Avg.	U.S. Typ	U.S. Max
Text	11.8%	25.63	30.00	35.01	25.00	250.00
w/Graphics	5.9%	23.50	25.00	73.16	35.00	750.00
Hour	47.1%	38.88	35.00	41.85	40.00	100.00

LABELS (Custom)

$/per	Survey %	Average	Typical	U.S. Avg.	U.S. Typ	U.S. Max
Text	0.0%			40.06	20.00	250.00
w/Graphics	0.0%			121.16	55.00	600.00
Hour	32.4%	42.09	50.00	43.55	40.00	100.00

LARGE FORMAT GRAPHICS

$/per	Survey %	Average	Typical	U.S. Avg.	U.S. Typ	U.S. Max
Text Page	0.0			40.00	37.50	45.00
w/Graphics	0.0%			71.00	70.00	85.00
Hour	8.2%	51.67	50.00	47.95	45.00	90.00

LETTERHEAD & ENVELOPES

$/per	Survey %	Average	Typical	U.S. Avg.	U.S. Typ	U.S. Max
Text	11.8%	73.75	20.00	59.65	25.00	750.00
w/Graphics	5.9%	197.50	195.00	136.48	40.00	1000.00
Hour	67.7%	38.96	40.00	43.60	40.00	150.00

LINE ART & GENERAL ILLUSTRATIONS

$/per	Survey %	Average	Typical	U.S. Avg.	U.S. Typ	U.S. Max
Text Page	0.0%			64.17	47.50	135.00
w/Graphics	0.0%			221.89	100.00	1000.00
Hour	41.2%	43.93	40.00	46.24	43.50	115.00

LITIGATION GRAPHICS

$/per	Survey %	Average	Typical	U.S. Avg.	U.S. Typ	U.S. Max
Text Page	0.0%			75.00	75.00	75.00
w/Graphics	0.0%			100.00	100.00	100.00
Hour	5.9%	52.50	52.50	50.13	45.00	200.00

LOGOS

$/per	Survey %	Average	Typical	U.S. Avg.	U.S. Typ	U.S. Max
Each	5.9%	257.50	250.00	281.23	200.00	2000.00
Hour	47.1%	43.00	50.00	46.02	45.00	125.00

LOGOTYPE

$/per	Survey %	Average	Typical	U.S. Avg.	U.S. Typ	U.S. Max
Page	2.9%	500.00	500.00	304.36	300.00	1000.00
Hour	14.7%	51.00	50.00	48.68	45.00	125.00

MAGAZINES

$/per	Survey %	Average	Typical	U.S. Avg.	U.S. Typ	U.S. Max
Text Page	0.0%			60.49	35.00	250.00
w/Graphics	0.0%			90.89	40.00	500.00
Hour	14.7%	43.00	35.00	45.91	45.00	125.00

NOTES:
1. Multiple page prices converted to $/page.
2. Other prices noted for magazine design: $500 setup; $1,000 ea.

MAILERS

$/per	Survey %	Average	Typical	U.S. Avg.	U.S. Typ	U.S. Max
Text Page	0.0%			64.08	25.00	500.00
w/Graphics	0.0%			82.36	40.00	500.00
Hour	32.4%	44.82	50.00	46.11	42.00	100.00

MANUALS

$/per	Survey %	Average	Typical	U.S. Avg.	U.S. Typ	U.S. Max
Text Page	5.9%	7.25	7.25	42.06	17.50	500.00
w/Graphics	5.9%	10.25	10.00	58.10	30.00	500.00
Hour	50.00%	40.35	50.00	42.63	40.00	100.00

MAPS
(1C, 2C, Letter Size)

$/per	Survey %	Average	Typical	U.S. Avg.	U.S. Typ	U.S. Max
Simple	0.0%			76.25	70.00	250.00
Complex	0.0%			206.14	75.00	600.00
Hour	14.7%	38.00	30.00	46.90	45.00	100.00

MAPS
(4C, Larger Than Letter Size)

$/per	Survey %	Average	Typical	U.S. Avg.	U.S. Typ	U.S. Max
Simple	0.0%			168.75	72.50	500.00
Complex	0.0%			490.71	300.00	1600.00
Hour	11.8%	40.00	35.00	48.08	45.00	100.00

MARKETING PLANS

$/per	Survey %	Average	Typical	U.S. Avg.	U.S. Typ	U.S. Max
Text Page	0.0%			59.00	10.00	250.00
w/Graphics	0.0%			182.67	40.00	500.00
Hour	17.7%	43.83	50.00	47.80	45.00	100.00

MEMO PADS

$/per	Survey %	Average	Typical	U.S. Avg.	U.S. Typ	U.S. Max
Text	0.0%			20.14	14.50	100.00
w/Graphics	0.0%			31.79	17.50	150.00
Hour	14.7%	47.00	50.00	43.94	40.00	100.00

MENUS

$/per	Survey %	Average	Typical	U.S. Avg.	U.S. Typ	U.S. Max
Text Page	5.9%	40.00	40.00	75.65	35.00	500.00
w/Graphics	2.9%	45.00	45.00	125.25	45.00	1000.00
Hour	41.2%	37.29	35.00	44.35	40.00	150.00
Minimum	0.6%	500.00	500.00	233.75	200.00	500.00

NEWSLETTERS

$/per	Survey %	Average	Typical	U.S. Avg.	U.S. Typ	U.S. Max
Text Page	8.8%	38.00	40.00	62.86	45.00	200.00
w/Graphics	8.8%	39.67	40.00	76.16	50.00	200.00
Hour	67.7%	41.61	44.00	42.97	40.00	160.00

NOTEPADS

$/per	Survey %	Average	Typical	U.S. Avg.	U.S. Typ	U.S. Max
Text	5.9%	17.50	18.00	32.28	25.00	100.00
w/Graphics	2.9%	20.00	20.00	41.37	35.00	150.00
Hour	32.4%	39.91	35.00	43.72	40.00	100.00

PACKAGING

$/per	Survey %	Average	Typical	U.S. Avg.	U.S. Typ	U.S. Max
Text	0.0%			276.00	100.00	1000.00
w/Graphics	0.0%			478.18	250.00	2500.00
Hour	32.4%	46.36	50.00	51.64	50.00	150.00

PEN RULER

$/per	Survey %	Average	Typical	U.S. Avg.	U.S. Typ	U.S. Max
Page	0.0%			45.00	45.00	45.00
Hour	5.9%	52.50	50.00	48.81	50.00	85.00

PERIODICAL (OTHER)

$/per	Survey %	Average	Typical	U.S. Avg.	U.S. Typ	U.S. Max
Text Page	0.0%			36.00	25.00	150.00
w/Graphics	0.0%			58.00	35.00	250.00
Hour	11.8%	41.25	35.00	46.86	45.00	125.00

POINT-OF-PURCHASE DISPLAYS

$/per	Survey %	Average	Typical	U.S. Avg.	U.S. Typ	U.S. Max
Text Page	0.0%			650.00	600.00	1000.00
w/Graphics	0.0%			800.00	800.00	1000.00
Hour	11.8%	53.75	60.00	50.15	50.00	100.00

POST CARDS

$/per	Survey %	Average	Typical	U.S. Avg.	U.S. Typ	U.S. Max
Text Page	2.9%	20.00	20.00	45.18	20.00	400.00
w/Graphics	2.9%	20.00	20.00	64.31	30.00	500.00
Hour	29.4%	41.80	50.00	42.38	40.00	100.00

POSTERS

$/per	Survey %	Average	Typical	U.S. Avg.	U.S. Typ	U.S. Max
Text Page	0.0%			123.67	50.00	500.00
w/Graphics	0.0%			259.71	250.00	1000.00
Hour	32.4%	41.64	35.00	45.60	45.00	100.00

PRESENTATION MATERIALS

$/per	Survey %	Average	Typical	U.S. Avg.	U.S. Typ	U.S. Max
Text Page	2.9%	15.00	15.00	27.65	20.00	100.00
w/Graphics	2.9%	20.00	20.00	44.38	25.00	180.00
Hour	35.3%	44.83	50.00	45.04	45.00	100.00

PRICE LISTS

$/per	Survey %	Average	Typical	U.S. Avg.	U.S. Typ	U.S. Max
Text Page	2.9%	40.00	40.00	40.63	35.00	150.00
w/Graphics	2.9%	40.00	40.00	51.79	40.00	160.00
Hour	38.2%	38.54	33.00	42.68	40.00	100.00

PRINT ADS

$/per	Survey %	Average	Typical	U.S. Avg.	U.S. Typ	U.S. Max
Text	0.0%			107.09	45.00	1000.00
w/Graphics	0.0%			179.74	80.00	1100.00
Hour	38.2%	42.31	50.00	44.84	40.00	100.00

PROCEDURE GUIDES

$/per	Survey %	Average	Typical	U.S. Avg.	U.S. Typ	U.S. Max
Text Page	0.0%			60.00	15.00	300.00
w/Graphics	0.0%			93.21	25.00	500.00
Hour	8.8%	41.67	25.00	45.67	45.00	100.00

PRODUCT LITERATURE

$/per	Survey %	Average	Typical	U.S. Avg.	U.S. Typ	U.S. Max
Text Page	2.9%	20.00	20.00	67.97	30.00	500.00
w/Graphics	2.9%	40.00	40.00	118.81	40.00	1000.00
Hour	35.3%	41.33	45.00	45.43	42.00	100.00

PRODUCT SPECIFICATION SHEETS

$/per	Survey %	Average	Typical	U.S. Avg.	U.S. Typ	U.S. Max
Text Page	2.9%	30.00	30.00	70.95	25.00	500.00
w/Graphics	2.9%	35.00	35.00	168.89	35.00	1000.00
Hour	20.6%	50.71	50.00	46.44	45.00	100.00

PROGRAMS

$/per	Survey %	Average	Typical	U.S. Avg.	U.S. Typ	U.S. Max
Text Page	2.9%	25.00	25.00	43.92	25.00	200.00
w/Graphics	2.9%	30.00	30.00	95.94	35.00	500.00
Hour	23.5%	40.25	40.00	46.61	45.00	150.00

PUBLICATIONS (OTHER)

$/per	Survey %	Average	Typical	U.S. Avg.	U.S. Typ	U.S. Max
Text Page	2.9%	30.00	30.00	46.00	30.00	150.00
w/Graphics	2.9%	30.00	30.00	87.73	35.00	500.00
Hour	38.2%	38.62	33.00	44.63	40.00	125.00

RECORD BOOKS

$/per	Survey %	Average	Typical	U.S. Avg.	U.S. Typ	U.S. Max
Text Page	0.0%			20.67	15.00	45.00
w/Graphics	0.0%			35.00	35.00	45.00
Hour	8.8%	46.67	35.00	46.63	45.00	80.00

RESUMES

$/per	Survey %	Average	Typical	U.S. Avg.	U.S. Typ	U.S. Max
Each	8.8%	29.33	25.00	31.21	25.00	150.00
Page	11.8%	31.38	25.00	31.52	30.00	150.00
Hour	47.1%	35.44	33.00	40.96	40.00	150.00

RULERS

$/per	Survey %	Average	Typical	U.S. Avg.	U.S. Typ	U.S. Max
Each	0.0%			250.00	375.00	500.00
Hour	5.9%	52.50	50.00	49.08	50.00	100.00

SALES PRESENTATIONS

$/per	Survey %	Average	Typical	U.S. Avg.	U.S. Typ	U.S. Max
Text Page	0.0%			23.14	20.00	45.00
w/Graphics	0.0%			29.50	25.00	45.00
Hour	23.5%	41.00	35.00	46.13	45.00	100.00

SIGNAGE

$/per	Survey %	Average	Typical	U.S. Avg.	U.S. Typ	U.S. Max
Text	0.0%			27.50	35.00	55.00
w/Graphics	0.0%			159.06	35.00	575.00
Hour	20.6%	35.00	35.00	45.60	45.00	100.00

SLIDE DESIGN

$/per	Survey %	Average	Typical	U.S. Avg.	U.S. Typ	U.S. Max
Text	0.0%			25.00	20.00	75.00
w/Graphics	0.0%			30.11	25.00	100.00
Hour	17.7%	47.50	50.00	46.17	45.00	100.00

SLIDE SHOW DESIGN

$/per	Survey %	Average	Typical	U.S. Avg.	U.S. Typ	U.S. Max
Text Page	0.0%			30.00	25.00	75.00
w/Graphics	0.0%			40.00	30.00	100.00
Hour	14.7%	47.00	50.00	47.98	50.00	100.00

SPREADSHEET DESIGN

$/per	Survey %	Average	Typical	U.S. Avg.	U.S. Typ	U.S. Max
Text Page	0.0%			35.00	35.00	45.00
w/Graphics	0.0%			45.50	45.00	45.00
Hour	20.6%	43.29	35.00	45.82	45.00	125.00

TABLOIDS

$/per	Survey %	Average	Typical	U.S. Avg.	U.S. Typ	U.S. Max
Text Page	0.0%			70.71	45.00	200.00
w/Graphics	0.0%			67.50	50.00	120.00
Hour	17.7%	38.33	35.00	46.32	45.00	125.00

TABS

$/per	Survey %	Average	Typical	U.S. Avg.	U.S. Typ	U.S. Max
Text	0.0%			20.00	20.00	20.00
w/Graphics	0.0%			20.00	20.00	20.00
Hour	11.8%	53.75	60.00	47.58	45.00	100.00

TAGS

$/per	Survey %	Average	Typical	U.S. Avg.	U.S. Typ	U.S. Max
Each	2.9%	8.50	10.00	17.83	10.00	35.00
Hour	11.8%	42.00	33.00	44.69	42.00	80.00

TECHNICAL DOCUMENTS

$/per	Survey %	Average	Typical	U.S. Avg.	U.S. Typ	U.S. Max
Text Page	5.9%	25.00	25.00	72.69	40.00	250.00
w/Graphics	5.9%	37.50	38.00	87.50	45.00	500.00
Hour	32.4%	38.73	35.00	44.05	40.00	125.00

TECHNICAL ILLUSTRATIONS

$/per	Survey %	Average	Typical	U.S. Avg.	U.S. Typ	U.S. Max
Page	0.0%			70.45	75.00	200.00
Hour	17.7%	46.67	50.00	47.28	45.00	200.00

TICKETS

$/per	Survey %	Average	Typical	U.S. Avg.	U.S. Typ	U.S. Max
Text	5.9%	9.25	9.50	24.72	20.00	50.00
w/Graphics	2.9%	15.00	15.00	30.25	30.00	50.00
Hour	17.7%	38.67	33.00	42.53	40.00	100.00

TRANSPARENCY DESIGN (B&W)

$/per	Survey %	Average	Typical	U.S. Avg.	U.S. Typ	U.S. Max
Text Page	2.9%	25.00	25.00	34.00	25.00	130.00
w/Graphics	0.0%			92.50	45.00	250.00
Hour	17.7%	41.00	40.00	42.68	40.00	100.00

TRANSPARENCY DESIGN (COLOR)

$/per	Survey %	Average	Typical	U.S. Avg.	U.S. Typ	U.S. Max
Text Page	0.0%			27.50	30.00	45.00
w/Graphics	0.0%			32.50	40.00	45.00
Hour	14.7%	47.00	50.00	44.69	45.00	100.00

OTHER DESIGN

$/per	Survey %	Average	Typical	U.S. Avg.	U.S. Typ	U.S. Max
Hour	11.8%	42.50	50.00	48.76	45.00	100.00

LASER PRINTER OUTPUT

GENERAL NOTES:
1. Some shops bill as $ set-up fee plus price per page.
2. Some shops bill as $/hr plus $/page.
3. A few shops price at $/hr (typically same price as other services).
4. Some laser printer output priced as $/job plus $/pg.

LASER PRINTING
(Up to 300 dpi)

$/per	Survey %	Average	Typical	U.S. Avg.	U.S. Typ	U.S. Max
8.5 x 11	26.5%	0.87	1.00	1.64	1.00	15.00
8.5 x 14	5.9%	2.25	3.00	1.95	3.00	10.00
11 x 17	0.0%			3.13	2.25	6.00
Cost Plus	2.9%	15.00	15.00	31.25	30.00	50.00
Minimum	2.7%	15.00	15.00	15.00	5.00	25.00

LASER PRINTING
(400 dpi)

$/per	Survey %	Average	Typical	U.S. Avg.	U.S. Typ	U.S. Max
8.5 x 11	0.0%			3.03	1.93	15.50
8.5 x 14	0.0%			2.71	2.00	6.00
11 x 17	0.0%			6.75	4.50	20.00
Cost Plus	2.9%	15.00	15.00	28.00	20.00	50.00
Minimum	2.7%	15.00	15.00	15.00	5.00	25.00

LASER PRINTING
(600 dpi)

$/per	Survey %	Average	Typical	U.S. Avg.	U.S. Typ	U.S. Max
8.5 x 11	2.9%	1.75	1.75	1.88	1.00	15.00
8.5 x 14	2.9%	2.25	2.25	1.88	1.95	4.46
11 x 17	0.0%			4.12	5.16	6.00
Cost Plus	2.9%	15.00	15.00	28.00	20.00	50.00

LASER PRINTING
(800dpi)

$/per	Survey %	Average	Typical	U.S. Avg.	U.S. Typ	U.S. Max
8.5 x 11	2.9%	0.30	2.00	2.75	2.00	12.00
8.5 x 14	2.9%	0.50	3.00	2.94	4.00	5.00
11 x 17	0.0%			6.00	6.00	6.00
Cost Plus	2.9%	15.00	15.00	28.00	20.00	50.00
Minimum	2.7%	15.00	15.00	15.00	5.00	25.00

LASER PRINTING
(1000 dpi)

$/per	Survey %	Average	Typical	U.S. Avg.	U.S. Typ	U.S. Max
8.5 x 11	0.0%			3.10	3.00	7.00
8.5 x 14	0.0%			4.06	4.00	7.00
11 x 17	0.0%			6.00	6.00	6.00
Cost Plus	2.9%	15.00	15.00	28.00	20.00	50.00
Minimum	2.7%	15.00	15.00	15.00	10.00	25.00

LASER PRINTING
(1200 dpi)

$/per	Survey %	Average	Typical	U.S. Avg.	U.S. Typ	U.S. Max
8.5 x 11	0.0%			2.89	3.00	6.00
8.5 x 14	0.0%			4.82	6.00	6.43
11 x 17	0.0%			7.18	6.00	13.25
Cost Plus	2.9%	15.00	15.00	28.00	20.00	50.00
Minimum	2.7%	15.00	15.00	15.00	10.00	25.00

FOR PREPRESS AND OTHER SERVICES (INCLUDING IMAGESETTING OUTPUT), REFER TO THE SECTION MARKED "NATIONAL."

Price Distribution
MID ATLANTIC
NJ, NY, PA

FILE CONVERSION

GENERAL NOTE: Survey responses listed as $/minute were converted to $/hr.

BOOKS ON DISK

$/per	Survey %	Average	Typical	U.S. Avg.	U.S. Typ	U.S. Max
Disk	0.0%			10.57	10.00	25.00
Page	4.3%	6.50	6.75	6.00	5.50	10.00
Hour	4.3%	37.50	38.00	40.11	35.00	95.00
Minimum	10.0%			15.00	15.00	15.00

TO CD-ROM

$/per	Survey %	Average	Typical	U.S. Avg.	U.S. Typ	U.S. Max
Page	2.1%	8.00	8.00	8.00	8.00	8.00
Disk	0.0%			25.00	25.00	25.00
Hour	4.3%	72.50	70.00	48.00	43.00	85.00
Minimum	0.0%			70.00	70.00	125.00

CROSS PLATFORM

$/per	Survey %	Average	Typical	U.S. Avg.	U.S. Typ	U.S. Max
Page	2.1%	8.00	8.00	3.83	2.88	8.00
File	6.4%	7.41	5.00	7.85	9.00	20.00
Disk	2.1%	11.47	10.00	11.85	10.00	50.00
Hour	12.8%	46.54	60.00	46.31	45.00	100.00
Minimum	0.0%			14.25	12.50	35.00

DATABASE FILES

$/per	Survey %	Average	Typical	U.S. Avg.	U.S. Typ	U.S. Max
Record	0.0%			0.16	0.15	0.25
File	2.1%	10.00	10.00	7.02	10.00	20.00
Disk	4.3%	12.50	13.00	21.67	15.00	50.00
Hour	8.5%	52.50	60.00	42.46	40.50	100.00
Minimum	0.0%			22.50	20.00	35.00

DOCUMENT FILES

$/per	Survey %	Average	Typical	U.S. Avg.	U.S. Typ	U.S. Max
K byte	0.0%			5.25	5.25	5.25
Page	0.0%			2.71	2.75	3.50
File	2.1%	10.00	10.00	8.38	10.00	15.00
Disk	4.3%	10.00	10.00	15.73	15.00	50.00
Hour	14.9%	52.14	50.00	41.23	35.00	100.00
Minimum	0.0%			21.00	15.00	35.00

DOCUMENTS ON DISK

$/per	Survey %	Average	Typical	U.S. Avg.	U.S. Typ	U.S. Max
Page	4.3%	9.00	8.50	6.17	7.00	15.00
File	0.0%			12.00	15.00	15.00
Disk	2.1%	50.00	48.00	14.00	10.00	50.00
Hour	8.5%	33.75	40.00	38.77	35.00	75.00
Minimum	0.0%			12.50	13.00	15.00

FORMS CONVERSION

$/per	Survey %	Average	Typical	U.S. Avg.	U.S. Typ	U.S. Max
Page	0.0%			187.18	190.00	200.00
File	2.1%	10.00	10.00	26.00	10.00	50.00
Disk	2.1%	10.00	10.00	15.00	10.00	25.00
Hour	4.3%	47.50	45.00	47.68	40.00	100.00
Minimum	0.0%			12.50	15.00	15.00

GRAPHIC FORMAT FILES

$/per	Survey %	Average	Typical	U.S. Avg.	U.S. Typ	U.S. Max
K byte	2.1%	5.25	5.25	5.25	5.25	5.25
Page	2.1%	20.00	20.00	18.32	20.00	20.00
File	6.4%	5.00	5.00	8.50	5.88	20.00
Disk	4.3%	10.00	10.00	15.36	15.00	50.00
Hour	19.2%	56.11	60.00	44.32	40.00	100.00
Minimum	0.0%			19.17	15.00	35.00

MEDIA CONVERSION

$/per	Survey %	Average	Typical	U.S. Avg.	U.S. Typ	U.S. Max
File	2.1%	19.00	10.00	15.00	12.50	25.00
Disk	6.4%	18.33	10.00	13.05	10.00	50.00
Hour	4.3%	60.00	60.00	48.64	45.00	100.00
Minimum	0.0%			13.75	15.00	15.00

PAGE LAYOUT FILES

$/per	Survey %	Average	Typical	U.S. Avg.	U.S. Typ	U.S. Max
500 K byte	0.0%			15.00	15.00	15.00
Page	2.1%	60.00	60.00	37.50	37.50	60.00
File	0.0%			12.70	12.50	25.00
Disk	2.1%	15.00	15.00	19.25	15.00	50.00
Hour	14.9%	55.71	60.00	42.91	40.00	100.00
Minimum	0.0%			20.00	15.00	35.00

SPREADSHEET FILES

$/per	Survey %	Average	Typical	U.S. Avg.	U.S. Typ	U.S. Max
25 K byte	0.0%			7.50	7.50	7.50
Page	0.0%			2.88	2.88	2.00
File	0.0%			12.30	10.88	25.00
Disk	2.1%	15.00	15.00	26.25	20.00	50.00
Hour	4.3%	57.50	55.00	40.98	40.00	100.00
Minimum	0.0%			22.50	20.00	35.00

VIDEO TAPE TRANSFER

$/per	Survey %	Average	Typical	U.S. Avg.	U.S. Typ	U.S. Max
Disk	0.0%			25.00	25.00	25.00
Per Hour	0.0%			48.33	45.00	75.00
Minimum	0.0%			15.00	15.00	15.00

WORD PROCESSOR FILE TO SGML

$/per	Survey %	Average	Typical	U.S. Avg.	U.S. Typ	U.S. Max
Disk	0.0%			25.00	25.00	25.00
Hour	0.0%			45.00	40.00	75.00
Minimum	0.0%			15.00	15.00	15.00

TEXT CREATION

GENERAL COPY WRITING

$/per	Survey %	Average	Typical	U.S. Avg.	U.S. Typ	U.S. Max
Line	0.0%			0.20	0.20	0.20
Page	6.4%	53.33	50.00	30.38	20.00	87.50
Hour	48.9%	45.87	40.00	41.43	35.00	300.00
Minimum	0.0%			19.00	15.00	35.00

NEWSLETTER COPY

$/per	Survey %	Average	Typical	U.S. Avg.	U.S. Typ	U.S. Max
Column	0.0%			10.48	10.50	11.00
Page	4.3%	45.00	45.00	40.96	40.00	125.00
Hour	34.0%	45.94	40.00	39.31	35.00	300.00
Minimum	0.0%			283.33	125.00	800.00

PUBLICITY / ADVERTISING COPY

$/per	Survey %	Average	Typical	U.S. Avg.	U.S. Typ	U.S. Max
Page	0.0%			40.31	40.00	100.00
Piece	0.0%			260.00	300.00	425.00
Hour	21.3%	45.50	40.00	43.56	38.00	300.00
Minimum	0.0%			19.00	15.00	35.00

RESUME WRITING

$/per	Survey %	Average	Typical	U.S. Avg.	U.S. Typ	U.S. Max
Page	19.2%	49.44	35.00	32.43	25.00	100.00
Hour	25.5%	42.50	40.00	38.11	35.00	300.00
Minimum	0.0%			110.00	65.00	300.00

TECHNICAL WRITING

$/per	Survey %	Average	Typical	U.S. Avg.	U.S. Typ	U.S. Max
Page	0.0%			53.54	35.00	300.00
Hour	17.0%	55.63	45.00	45.99	35.00	300.00
Minimum	0.0%			35.00	35.00	55.00

DATA INPUT / EDITING

DATA ENTRY / KEYBOARDING

$/per	Survey %	Average	Typical	U.S. Avg.	U.S. Typ	U.S. Max
Character	0.0%			0.02	0.02	0.02
Page	4.3%	26.80	25.00	11.32	10.00	50.00
Hour	59.6%	36.36	35.00	32.64	28.00	100.00
Minimum	0.0%			20.00	15.00	35.00

COPY EDITING

$/per	Survey %	Average	Typical	U.S. Avg.	U.S. Typ	U.S. Max
Word	0.0%			0.06	0.06	0.11
Page	6.4%	23.00	10.00	9.47	7.00	50.00
Hour	40.4%	40.42	35.00	36.58	30.00	100.00
Minimum	0.0%			20.00	15.00	35.00

CONTENT EDITING

$/per	Survey %	Average	Typical	U.S. Avg.	U.S. Typ	U.S. Max
Word	0.0%			0.11	0.11	0.11
Page	2.1%	50.00	50.00	5.33	5.00	50.00
Hour	31.9%	37.53	38.00	37.44	36.00	100.00
Minimum	0.0%			33.50	35.00	35.00

PROOF READING

$/per	Survey %	Average	Typical	U.S. Avg.	U.S. Typ	U.S. Max
Page	6.4%	23.00	10.00	6.71	5.00	50.00
Hour	51.1%	38.88	40.00	35.63	30.00	100.00
Minimum	0.0%			33.50	35.00	35.00

REWRITING

$/per	Survey %	Average	Typical	U.S. Avg.	U.S. Typ	U.S. Max
Word	0.0%			0.07	0.03	0.11
Line	0.0%			0.25	0.20	1.00
Page	2.1%	50.00	50.00	22.67	13.50	50.00
Hour	38.3%	38.50	40.00	38.81	35.00	100.00
Minimum	0.0%			35.00	35.00	35.00

INDEXING

$/per	Survey %	Average	Typical	U.S. Avg.	U.S. Typ	U.S. Max
Page	0.0%			2.80	2.00	5.00
Hour	21.3%	48.50	50.00	38.60	35.00	100.00
Minimum	0.0%			87.50	87.50	140.00

MODEM INPUT

$/per	Survey %	Average	Typical	U.S. Avg.	U.S. Typ	U.S. Max
Page	0.0%			3.33	3.00	5.00
File	0.0%			10.00	10.00	10.00
K bytes	0.0%			1.32	1.40	1.50
Disk	0.0%			8.33	5.00	25.00
Minute	0.0%			1.50	1.50	2.00
Hour	17.0%	50.63	50.00	41.62	38.00	100.00
Minimum	0.0%			12.50	12.50	15.00

TEXT FILE IMPORTING

$/per	Survey %	Average	Typical	U.S. Avg.	U.S. Typ	U.S. Max
Page	2.1%	59.00	50.00	14.60	5.00	50.00
File	4.3%	5.00	5.00	11.00	10.00	25.00
K bytes	0.0%			1.32	1.40	1.50
Disk	0.0%			10.00	10.00	15.00
Minute	0.0%			1.50	1.50	2.00
Hour	25.5%	48.33	50.00	39.10	35.00	100.00
Minimum	0.0%			21.25	22.00	35.00

TRANSCRIPTION

$/per	Survey %	Average	Typical	U.S. Avg.	U.S. Typ	U.S. Max
Line	0.0%			0.17	0.17	0.25
Page	2.1%	8.00	8.00	4.79	4.25	8.00
File	0.0%			10.57	10.57	25.00
Disk	2.1%	25.00	25.00	25.00	25.00	25.00
Hour	12.8%	41.67	40.00	31.64	30.00	75.00
Minimum	0.0%			25.00	25.00	35.00

TRANSLATION

$/per	Survey %	Average	Typical	U.S. Avg.	U.S. Typ	U.S. Max
Word	2.1%	0.16	0.17	0.17	0.17	0.20
Page	0.0%			24.17	22.50	50.00
Hour	0.0%			44.49	40.00	150.00
Minimum	0.0%			35.00	35..00	35.00

TYPOGRAPHY (General)

$/per	Survey %	Average	Typical	U.S. Avg.	U.S. Typ	U.S. Max
Line	0.0%			0.25	0.25	0.25
Page	6.4%	46.67	60.00	21.48	15.00	75.00
Hour	51.1%	42.71	40.00	39.27	35.00	100.00
Minimum	0.0%			18.83	15.00	35.00

TYPOGRAPHY (Spreadsheet)

$/per	Survey %	Average	Typical	U.S. Avg.	U.S. Typ	U.S. Max
Line	0.0%			0.25	0.25	0.25
Page	0.0%			24.06	17.00	75.00
Hour	36.2%	46.18	50.00	41.47	36.00	150.00
Minimum	0.0%			35.00	35.00	35.00

WORD PROCESSSING

$/per	Survey %	Average	Typical	U.S. Avg.	U.S. Typ	U.S. Max
Line	0.0%			0.13	0.10	0.20
Page	2.1%	4.00	4.00	8.67	8.25	25.00
Hour	48.9%	33.35	30.00	32.90	25.00	100.00
Minimum	0.0%			21.67	15.00	35.00

DATA MANAGEMENT

GENERAL NOTES:
1. Assume customer pays for cost of media extra.
2. On $/word, assume 2K words per page.
3. Per file cost assumed to be for 1 year.
4. Assume $/file same as $/image.

ARCHIVING SERVICE

$/per	Survey %	Average	Typical	U.S. Avg.	U.S. Typ	U.S. Max
Page	0.0%			7.50	7.50	7.50
File	0.0%			9.63	15.00	25.00
Tape	2.1%	19.97	20.00	37.50	20.00	150.00
Hour	2.1%	85.00	85.00	46.05	40.00	95.00
Minimum	0.0%			14.17	10.00	25.00

IMAGE MANAGEMENT

$/per	Survey %	Average	Typical	U.S. Avg.	U.S. Typ	U.S. Max
Page	2.1%	50.00	50.00	6.50	5.50	10.00
File	0.0%			16.67	15.00	50.00
Disk	0.0%			30.00	30.00	50.00
Hour	2.1%	85.00	85.00	44.81	40.00	110.00
Minimum	0.0%			14.17	10.00	25.00

NOTE: Assume $/.file same as $/image.

TEXT MANAGEMENT

$/per	Survey %	Average	Typical	U.S. Avg.	U.S. Typ	U.S. Max
Page	2.1%	50.00	50.00	8.67	6.00	15.00
File	0.0%			16.67	15.00	50.00
Disk	0.0%			23.33	15.00	50.00
Hour	2.1%	85.00	85.00	44.51	35.00	95.00
Minimum	0.0%			14.17	10.00	25.00

IMAGING SERVICES

DOCUMENT CAPTURE

$/per	Survey %	Average	Typical	U.S. Avg.	U.S. Typ	U.S. Max
Page	0.0%			3.65	3.00	7.50
File	0.0%			6.50	5.00	10.00
Hour	6.3%	51.00	50.00	39.41	35.00	95.00
Minimum	0.0%			16.25	16.25	25.00

DOCUMENT RETRIEVAL

$/per	Survey %	Average	Typical	U.S. Avg.	U.S. Typ	U.S. Max
Page	0.0%			1.50	1.50	2.00
File	0.0%			5.03	5.00	10.00
Hour	4.2%	51.50	51.50	38.82	39.00	85.00
Minimum	0.0%			16.25	16.25	25.00

GRAPHICS FILE IMPORTING

$/per	Survey %	Average	Typical	U.S. Avg.	U.S. Typ	U.S. Max
File	8.3%	5.63	5.00	6.98	5.00	15.00
Disk	0.0%			5.00	5.00	5.00
Hour	14.6%	51.86	50.00	43.35	36.00	100.00
Minimum	0.0%			14.17	14.17	35.00

PHOTO CD-ROM IMPORTING

$/per	Survey %	Average	Typical	U.S. Avg.	U.S. Typ	U.S. Max
Image	4.2%	17.50	17.50	10.02	7.25	45.00
Stock Fee	0.0%			75.00	75.00	75.00
Hour	8.3%	50.75	60.00	48.60	45.00	100.00
Minimum	0.0%			16.25	15.00	25.00

SCANNING (B&W Grey Scale)

$/per	Survey %	Average	Typical	U.S. Avg.	U.S. Typ	U.S. Max
Hour	4.2%	37.50	37.50	42.82	40.00	100.00
75-200 dpi	8.3%	9.00	10.00	10.10	9.00	75.00
300-400 dpi	37.5%	13.54	10.00	11.93	10.00	75.00
600-800 dpi	10.4%	13.40	10.00	13.51	11.00	75.00
1200 dpi	6.3%	21.67	20.00	20.20	12.00	75.00
2400 dpi	0.0%			36.86	30.00	75.00

SCANNING (B&W Line Art)

$/per	Survey %	Average	Typical	U.S. Avg.	U.S. Typ	U.S. Max
Hour	8.3%	35.00	40.00	40.94	40.00	100.00
75-200 dpi	8.3%	12.50	10.00	10.59	9.00	75.00
300-400 dpi	35.4%	10.99	10.00	11.92	10.00	75.00
600-800 dpi	10.4%	13.40	10.00	12.51	10.00	75.00
1200 dpi	6.3%	20.00	20.00	15.59	11.00	75.00
2400 dpi	0.0%			35.75	27.50	75.00
Per K	0.0%			51.67	50.00	75.00

SCANNING (B&W Photo)

$/per	Survey %	Average	Typical	U.S. Avg.	U.S. Typ	U.S. Max
Hour	6.3%	38.33	40.00	45.16	40.00	100.00
75-200 dpi	8.3%	9.00	10.00	12.28	10.00	75.00
300-400 dpi	25.0%	11.21	10.00	13.92	12.40	75.00
600-800 dpi	6.3%	12.33	10.00	14.79	12.60	75.00
1200 dpi	6.3%	21.67	20.00	19.88	17.50	75.00
2400 dpi	0.0%			35.56	31.00	75.00
Per K	0.0%			62.50	62.50	75.00

SCANNING (Color Illustration)

$/per	Survey %	Average	Typical	U.S. Avg.	U.S. Typ	U.S. Max
Hour	4.2%	37.50	37.50	49.23	50.00	125.00
75-200 dpi	4.2%	19.50	19.50	19.08	15.00	75.00
300-400 dpi	12.5%	24.67	30.00	21.03	19.00	82.00
600-800 dpi	6.3%	28.33	30.00	22.36	21.50	75.00
1200 dpi	6.3%	33.33	30.00	26.47	23.00	75.00
2400 dpi	0.0%			46.22	50.00	75.00

SCANNING (Color Photo)						
$/per	Survey %	Average	Typical	U.S. Avg.	U.S. Typ	U.S. Max
Hour	6.3%	38.33	40.00	49.23	50.00	125.00
75-200 dpi	4.2%	19.50	19.50	20.44	15.00	75.00
300-400 dpi	12.5%	24.67	30.00	20.97	17.75	82.00
600-800 dpi	6.3%	25.00	30.00	19.75	15.00	75.00
1200 dpi	6.3%	33.33	30.00	30.13	30.00	75.00
2400 dpi	2.1%	60.00	60.00	61.54	60.00	137.00

SCANNING (HIGH END) (Loose Scan)				
$/per	Survey %	U.S. Avg.	U.S. Typ	U.S. Max
2 x 3	0.1%	13.33	10.00	25.00
3 x 5	0.1%	11.25	10.00	20.00
4 x 5	0.1%	16.00	10.00	33.00
5 x 7	0.1%	18.00	10.00	37.00
5.5 x 8.5	0.1%	17.33	10.00	39.00
6 x 9	0.1%	24.67	15.00	49.00
8 x 10	0.1%	41.60	50.00	70.00
10 x 12	0.1%	47.80	60.00	84.00
11 x 14	0.1%	81.67	70.00	105.00
12 x 18	0.1%	90.67	80.00	122.00
16 x 20	0.1%	162.00	162.00	162.00
20 x 24	0.1%	199.00	199.00	199.00
Hour	0.1%	47.00	45.00	60.00

SCANNING (HIGH END) (Drum Scan)				
$/per	Survey %	U.S. Avg.	U.S. Typ	U.S. Max
2 x 3	0.1%	56..92	54.25	71.50
4 x 5	0.1%	57.21	55.00	94.50
5 x 7	0.1%	65.75	70.00	106.00
6 x 8	0.1%	103.13	102.50	117.50
6 x 9	0.1%	57.00	45.00	85.00
8 x 10	0.1%	51.25	50.00	60.00
10 x 12	0.1%	58.33	60.00	60.00
11 x 14	0.1%	71.25	72.50	75.00
12 x 18	0.1%	86.67	85.00	100.00
24 x 27	0.1%	600.00	600.00	600.00

SCANNING (HIGH END) (High Res Scan to Disk)				
$/per	Survey %	U.S. Avg.	U.S. Typ	U.S. Max
2 x 3	0.1%	20..50	19.50	25.00
4 x 5	0.1%	26.17	27.50	30.00
5 x 7	0.1%	34.00	35.00	41.00
6 x 9	0.1%	39.80	39.00	50.00

SCANNING (HIGH END)
(High Res Scan to Disk)

$/per	Survey %	U.S. Avg.	U.S. Typ	U.S. Max
8 x 10	0.1%	45.50	45.00	60.00
10 x 12	0.1%	56.83	59.00	70.00
11 x 14	0.1%	65.08	64.00	89.00
12 x 18	0.1%	78.90	75.00	100.00
16 x 20	0.1%	96.33	99.00	130.00
20 x 24	0.1%	128.00	134.00	160.00
24 x 27	0.1%	156.25	156.25	200.00

SCANNING (Transparency)

$/per	Survey %	Average	Typical	U.S. Avg.	U.S. Typ	U.S. Max
Each	0.0%			18.70	16.00	45.00
Hour	0.0%			65.29	55.00	137.00

SCANNING (Slide)

$/per	Survey %	Average	Typical	U.S. Avg.	U.S. Typ	U.S. Max
Each	0.0%			23.00	16.99	65.00
Hour	0.0%			68.42	55.00	137.00

COLOR CORRECTION

$/per	Survey %	Average	Typical	U.S. Avg.	U.S. Typ	U.S. Max
Hour	10.4%	52.00	50.00	65.80	50.00	300.00

IMAGE EDITING

$/per	Survey %	Average	Typical	U.S. Avg.	U.S. Typ	U.S. Max
Each	0.0%			20.75	15.00	50.00
Hour	22.9%	53.64	50.00	55.47	45.00	300.00

IMAGE ENHANCEMENT

$/per	Survey %	Average	Typical	U.S. Avg.	U.S. Typ	U.S. Max
Hour	16.7%	49.38	50.00	57.60	50.00	300.00

RETOUCHING

$/per	Survey %	Average	Typical	U.S. Avg.	U.S. Typ	U.S. Max
Each	0.0%			27.67	40.00	50.00
Hour	31.3%	70.00	60.00	58.60	50.00	300.00
Minimum	2.1%	18.00	18.00	26.08	25.00	35.00

TEXT SCAN (OCR)

$/per	Survey %	Average	Typical	U.S. Avg.	U.S. Typ	U.S. Max
Page	14.6%	11.86	6.00	7.82	5.00	95.00

TEXT SCAN (OCR)

$/per	Survey %	Average	Typical	U.S. Avg.	U.S. Typ	U.S. Max
Hour	14.6%	42.86	45.00	36.33	30.00	75.00
Minimum	4.2%	9.00	9.00	19.08	16.90	35.00

NOTE:

1. Prices assume spell check conducted on scanned text.
2. Assumes 2 Kb per page, so $1/Kb response incorporated as $2/page.

NEGATIVE CREATION

$/per	Survey %	Average	Typical	U.S. Avg.	U.S. Typ	U.S. Max
Each	2.1%	40.00	40.00	22.00	22.00	40.00
Hour	4.2%	32.50	32.50	56.71	56.71	100.00
Minimum	2.1%	18.00	18.18	16.67	16.67	25.00

DESIGN SERVICES

ANNOUNCEMENTS

$/per	Survey %	Average	Typical	U.S. Avg.	U.S. Typ	U.S. Max
Text Page	8.3%	27.50	12.50	37.05	24.00	250.00
w/Graphics	6.3%	62.50	18.75	65.36	36.50	500.00
Hour	37.5%	39.67	40.00	42.21	40.00	100.00

ANNUAL REPORTS
(1C, 2C, Up To Letter Size Pages)

$/per	Survey %	Average	Typical	U.S. Avg.	U.S. Typ	U.S. Max
Text	4.2%	25.00	25.00	114.75	62.50	1000.00
w/Graphics	0.0%			222.00	100.00	7680.00
Hour	31.3%	47.33	50.00	46.58	45.00	100.00

ANNUAL REPORTS
(3C, 4C, Larger Size Pages)

$/per	Survey %	Average	Typical	U.S. Avg.	U.S. Typ	U.S. Max
Text	2.1%	25.00	25.00	214.55	100.00	1500.00
w/Graphics	0.0%			422.50	175.00	11520.00
Hour	27.1%	45.38	45.00	46.34	45.00	100.00

BAR CODING

$/per	Survey %	Average	Typical	U.S. Avg.	U.S. Typ	U.S. Max
Each	4.2%	13.50	13.00	13.25	11.00	150.00
Page	0.0%			29.00	29.00	50.00
Hour	14.6%	45.50	45.00	47.83	45.00	100.00

BOOKLETS

$/per	Survey %	Average	Typical	U.S. Avg.	U.S. Typ	U.S. Max
Text Page	12.5%	50.42	70.00	48.40	30.00	500.00
w/Graphics	8.3%	87.50	150.00	110.53	50.00	650.00
Hour	66.7%	43.48	40.00	43.87	25.00	100.00

BOOK COVERS

$/per	Survey %	Average	Typical	U.S. Avg.	U.S. Typ	U.S. Max
Text	4.2%	12.50	12.50	143.10	75.00	500.00
w/Graphics	6.3%	112.50	18.75	403.36	300.00	1800.00
Hour	35.42%	42.85	40.00	47.83	45.00	120.00

BOOK BODY

$/per	Survey %	Average	Typical	U.S. Avg.	U.S. Typ	U.S. Max
Text Page	2.1%	20.00	20.00	26.65	20.00	75.00
w/Graphics	4.2%	17.50	20.00	41.11	25.00	85.00
Hour	37.5%	44.53	45.00	44.26	40.00	100.00

BOOK JACKETS

$/per	Survey %	Average	Typical	U.S. Avg.	U.S. Typ	U.S. Max
Text	0.0%			161.54	175.00	500.00
w/Graphics	2.1%	300.00	300.00	491.00	325.00	1000.00
Hour	25.0%	44.88	45.00	48.63	45.00	120.00

BROCHURE
(1C, 2C, Up To Letter Size Sheet)

$/per	Survey %	Average	Typical	U.S. Avg.	U.S. Typ	U.S. Max
Text Page	10.4%	81.50	70.00	72.59	47.50	500.00
w/Graphics	10.4%	120.00	125.00	156.74	82.50	750.00
Hour	64.6%	44.16	40.00	42.85	40.00	125.00

BROCHURE
(3C, 4C, Larger Size Sheet)

$/per	Survey %	Average	Typical	U.S. Avg.	U.S. Typ	U.S. Max
Text Page	8.3%	115.63	150.00	123.79	60.00	1000.00
w/Graphics	6.3%	133.33	125.00	227.71	100.00	1500.00
Hour	50.0%	44.54	45.00	44.17	40.00	125.00

BULLETIN

$/per	Survey %	Average	Typical	U.S. Avg.	U.S. Typ	U.S. Max
Text Page	8.3%	51.88	20.00	32.75	25.00	150.00
w/Graphics	4.2%	25.00	25.00	47.81	35.00	200.00
Hour	31.3%	35.73	40.00	42.36	40.00	100.00

BUSINESS CARDS

$/per	Survey %	Average	Typical	U.S. Avg.	U.S. Typ	U.S. Max
Text Card	20.8%	23.00	20.00	38.81	25.00	500.00
w/Graphics	12.5%	52.08	60.00	91.70	40.00	1000.00
Hour	56.2%	42.46	40.00	43.19	40.00	150.00

BUSINESS REPLY CARDS

$/per	Survey %	Average	Typical	U.S. Avg.	U.S. Typ	U.S. Max
Text Card	12.5%	21.67	12.50	34.32	31.50	150.00
w/Graphics	6.3%	24.17	18.75	67.50	35.00	250.00
Hour	37.5%	41.44	42.50	43.79	40.00	100.00

BUSINESS LETTERS

$/per	Survey %	Average	Typical	U.S. Avg.	U.S. Typ	U.S. Max
Text Page	14.6%	13.21	12.50	17.23	12.25	90.00
w/Graphics	6.3%	14.17	18.75	27.08	18.75	100.00
Hour	41.7%	40.80	42.50	39.38	35.00	100.00

CALENDARS

$/per	Survey %	Average	Typical	U.S. Avg.	U.S. Typ	U.S. Max
Text Page	8.3%	15.83	18.75	82.50	50.00	500.00
w/Graphics	4.2%	25.00	25.00	53.18	45.00	150.00
Hour	37.5%	44.22	45.00	43.77	40.00	100.00

CALLIGRAPHY

$/per	Survey %	Average	Typical	U.S. Avg.	U.S. Typ	U.S. Max
Line	4.2%	1.00	1.00	1.00	1.00	60.00
Page	0.0%			40.00	35.00	100.00
Hour	22.9%	52.18	40.00	45.50	40.00	175.00

CARDS (FOLD-OVER)

$/per	Survey %	Average	Typical	U.S. Avg.	U.S. Typ	U.S. Max
Text Card	8.3%	33.88	35.50	31.45	25.00	60.00
w/Graphics	6.3%	56.67	47.50	65.47	46.40	250.00
Hour	29.2%	41.18	40.00	43.63	40.00	100.00

CARDS (ROLODEX)

$/per	Survey %	Average	Typical	U.S. Avg.	U.S. Typ	U.S. Max
Text Card	6.3%	45.00	55.00	37.34	25.00	150.00
w/Graphics	2.1%	75.00	75.00	63.00	48.00	250.00
Hour	18.8%	45.67	42.50	44.94	41.00	100.00

CARTOONS

$/per	Survey %	Average	Typical	U.S. Avg.	U.S. Typ	U.S. Max
Each	0.0%			119.29	60.00	400.00
Page	0.0%			163.33	65.00	400.00
Hour	14.6%	41.21	40.00	48.15	45.00	90.00

CATALOGS

$/per	Survey %	Average	Typical	U.S. Avg.	U.S. Typ	U.S. Max
Text Page	8.3%	43.75	60.00	69.03	40.00	500.00
w/Graphics	6.3%	133.33	125.00	129.05	67.50	1000.00
Hour	48.0%	46.35	50.00	45.68	45.00	125.00

CERTIFICATES

$/per	Survey %	Average	Typical	U.S. Avg.	U.S. Typ	U.S. Max
Text	6.3%	6.00	5.50	23.56	16.25	125.00
w/Graphics	4.2%	175.00	175.00	35.07	25.00	150.00
Hour	37.5%	39.39	40.00	42.15	40.00	100.00

CHARTS / DIAGRAMS

$/per	Survey %	Average	Typical	U.S. Avg.	U.S. Typ	U.S. Max
Text	2.1%	20.00	20.000	36.19	32.50	150.00
w/Graphics	2.1%	25.00	25.00	53.14	47.50	150.00
Hour	39.6%	45.45	50.00	44.29	40.00	100.00

COMIC BOOKS

$/per	Survey %	Average	Typical	U.S. Avg.	U.S. Typ	U.S. Max
Each Page	0.0%			65.00	60.00	100.00
Hour	6.3%	39.50	40.00	47.12	50.00	80.00

COMIC STRIPS

$/per	Survey %	Average	Typical	U.S. Avg.	U.S. Typ	U.S. Max
Each Strip	0.0%			38.33	30.00	60.00
Hour	6.3%	39.50	40.00	46.78	50.00	80.00

COMPUTER GENERATED ART

$/per	Survey %	Average	Typical	U.S. Avg.	U.S. Typ	U.S. Max
Page	0.0%			121.40	50.00	500.00
Hour	37.5%	48.42	40.00	46.70	42.00	175.00

CUSTOM DISPLAYS

$/per	Survey %	Average	Typical	U.S. Avg.	U.S. Typ	U.S. Max
Text	0.0%			192.14	60.00	1000.00
w/Graphics	0.0%			265.71	100.00	1000.00
Hour	25.0%	47.21	45.00	48.95	45.00	100.00

DATABASE DESIGN

$/per	Survey %	Average	Typical	U.S. Avg.	U.S. Typ	U.S. Max
Text	0.0%			38.33	30.00	60.00
w/Graphics	0.0%			43.33	40.00	60.00
Hour	14.6%	41.21	45.00	42.45	41.00	80.00

DIGITAL SLIDE PRESENTATIONS

$/per	Survey %	Average	Typical	U.S. Avg.	U.S. Typ	U.S. Max
Text	0.0%			27.13	27.50	60.00
w/Graphics	0.0%			35.00	32.50	60.00
Hour	12.5%	39.75	45.00	45.81	45.00	100.00

DIRECT MAIL PACKAGES

$/per	Survey %	Average	Typical	U.S. Avg.	U.S. Typ	U.S. Max
Text	2.1%	60.00	60.00	298.46	60.00	1500.00
w/Graphics	0.0%			413.50	65.00	2000.00
Hour	33.3%	47.88	45.00	47.05	45.00	100.00

DIRECTORY

$/per	Survey %	Average	Typical	U.S. Avg.	U.S. Typ	U.S. Max
Text	4.2%	30.00	30.00	38.72	30.00	150.00
w/Graphics	0.0%			73.53	40.00	500.00
Hour	35.4%	45.50	45.00	43.08	40.00	125.00

DISPLAY ADVERTISING

$/per	Survey %	Average	Typical	U.S. Avg.	U.S. Typ	U.S. Max
Text	0.0%			109.28	30.00	1000.00
w/Graphics	0.0%			304.64	45.00	2500.00
Hour	29.2%	50.25	50.00	48.23	45.00	115.00

DISPLAY EXHIBITS

$/per	Survey %	Average	Typical	U.S. Avg.	U.S. Typ	U.S. Max
Text Panel	0.0%			858.57	90.00	5000.00
w/Graphics	0.0%			896.67	100.00	5000.00
Hour	18.8%	49.83	45.00	51.43	50.00	115.00

DOOR HANGERS

$/per	Survey %	Average	Typical	U.S. Avg.	U.S. Typ	U.S. Max
Text	2.1%	20.00	20.00	42.46	25.00	250.00
w/Graphics	0.0%			87.50	35.00	500.00
Hour	16.7%	46.69	45.00	47.19	45.00	100.00

DRAFTING

$/per	Survey %	Average	Typical	U.S. Avg.	U.S. Typ	U.S. Max
Page	0.0%			45.00	45.00	60.00
Hour	14.6%	45.50	45.00	46.62	45.00	100.00

FINANCIAL DOCUMENTS

$/per	Survey %	Average	Typical	U.S. Avg.	U.S. Typ	U.S. Max
Text Page	0.0%			45.33	33.00	150.00
w/Graphics	0.0%			92.00	60.00	150.00
Hour	25.0%	52.38	45.00	47.20	45.00	125.00

FLYERS

$/per	Survey %	Average	Typical	U.S. Avg.	U.S. Typ	U.S. Max
Text Page	16.7%	50.63	60.00	39.21	25.00	325.00
w/Graphics	8.3%	36.88	35.00	66.84	35.00	325.00
Hour	62.5%	40.97	40.00	42.22	40.00	100.00

FORMS

$/per	Survey %	Average	Typical	U.S. Avg.	U.S. Typ	U.S. Max
Text Page	8.3%	40.63	25.00	52.60	30.00	750.00
w/Graphics	4.2%	25.00	25.00	81.67	37.50	10000.00
Hour	54.2%	41.50	40.00	41.75	40.00	125.00

HANDBOOKS

$/per	Survey %	Average	Typical	U.S. Avg.	U.S. Typ	U.S. Max
Text Page	4.2%	22.50	22.00	38.22	25.00	150.00
w/Graphics	2.1%	25.00	25.00	62.46	35.00	250.00
Hour	45.8%	44.16	40.00	43.53	40.00	100.00

INSERTS

$/per	Survey %	Average	Typical	U.S. Avg.	U.S. Typ	U.S. Max
Text Page	6.3%	11.67	12.50	70.58	27.50	1000.00
w/Graphics	4.2%	18.75	18.75	193.50	35.00	2500.00
Hour	41.7%	41.55	40.00	43.99	40.00	100.00

INVITATIONS

$/per	Survey %	Average	Typical	U.S. Avg.	U.S. Typ	U.S. Max
Text	10.4%	41.10	35.50	35.01	25.00	250.00
w/Graphics	8.3%	70.75	50.00	73.16	35.00	750.00
Hour	48.0%	41.26	40.00	41.85	40.00	100.00

LABELS (Custom)

$/per	Survey %	Average	Typical	U.S. Avg.	U.S. Typ	U.S. Max
Text	6.3%	30.83	18.75	40.06	20.00	250.00
w/Graphics	6.3%	38.33	25.00	121.16	55.00	600.00
Hour	39.6%	42.42	45.00	43.55	40.00	100.00

LARGE FORMAT GRAPHICS

$/per	Survey %	Average	Typical	U.S. Avg.	U.S. Typ	U.S. Max
Text Page	0.0%			40.00	37.50	45.00
w/Graphics	0.0%			71.00	70.00	85.00
Hour	18.8%	47,61	45.00	47.95	45.00	90.00

LETTERHEAD & ENVELOPES

$/per	Survey %	Average	Typical	U.S. Avg.	U.S. Typ	U.S. Max
Text	16.7%	53.75	25.00	59.65	25.00	750.00
w/Graphics	12.5%	92.08	50.00	136.48	40.00	1000.00
Hour	66.7%	41.81	40.00	43.60	40.00	150.00

LINE ART & GENERAL ILLUSTRATIONS

$/per	Survey %	Average	Typical	U.S. Avg.	U.S. Typ	U.S. Max
Text Page	2.1%	40.00	40.00	64.17	47.50	135.00
w/Graphics	4.2%	200.00	200.00	221.89	100.00	1000.00
Hour	54.2%	43.10	40.00	46.24	43.50	115.00

LITIGATION GRAPHICS

$/per	Survey %	Average	Typical	U.S. Avg.	U.S. Typ	U.S. Max
Text Page	0.0%			75.00	75.00	75.00
w/Graphics	0.0%			100.00	100.00	100.00
Hour	14.6%	45.50	45.00	50.13	45.00	200.00

LOGOS

$/per	Survey %	Average	Typical	U.S. Avg.	U.S. Typ	U.S. Max
Each	18.8%	273.89	300.00	281.23	200.00	2000.00
Hour	75.0%	43.28	45.00	46.02	45.00	125.00

LOGOTYPE

$/per	Survey %	Average	Typical	U.S. Avg.	U.S. Typ	U.S. Max
Page	4.2%	200.00	200.00	304.36	300.00	1000.00
Hour	43.8%	44.93	40.00	48.68	45.00	125.00

MAGAZINES

$/per	Survey %	Average	Typical	U.S. Avg.	U.S. Typ	U.S. Max
Text Page	0.0%			60.49	35.00	250.00
w/Graphics	0.0%			90.89	40.00	500.00
Hour	22.9%	47.14	45.00	45.91	45.00	125.00

NOTES:
1. Multiple page prices converted to $/page.
2. Other prices noted for magazine design: $500 setup; $1,000 ea.

MAILERS

$/per	Survey %	Average	Typical	U.S. Avg.	U.S. Typ	U.S. Max
Text Page	2.1%	25.00	25.00	64.08	25.00	500.00
w/Graphics	2.1%	25.00	25.00	82.36	40.00	500.00
Hour	31.3%	44.23	45.00	46.11	42.00	100.00

MANUALS

$/per	Survey %	Average	Typical	U.S. Avg.	U.S. Typ	U.S. Max
Text Page	6.3%	22.50	25.00	42.06	17.50	500.00
w/Graphics	2.3%	24.00	25.00	58.10	30.00	500.00
Hour	45.8%	43.80	40.00	42.63	40.00	100.00

MAPS
(1C, 2C, Letter Size)

$/per	Survey %	Average	Typical	U.S. Avg.	U.S. Typ	U.S. Max
Simple	0.0%			76.25	70.00	250.00
Complex	0.0%			206.14	75.00	600.00
Hour	22.9%	50.32	45.00	46.90	45.00	100.00

MAPS
(4C, Larger Than Letter Size)

$/per	Survey %	Average	Typical	U.S. Avg.	U.S. Typ	U.S. Max
Simple	0.0%			168.75	72.50	500.00
Complex	0.0%			490.71	300.00	1600.00
Hour	22.9%	50.32	45.00	48.08	45.00	100.00

MARKETING PLANS

$/per	Survey %	Average	Typical	U.S. Avg.	U.S. Typ	U.S. Max
Text Page	0.0%			59.00	10.00	250.00
w/Graphics	0.0%			182.67	40.00	500.00
Hour	20.8%	47.35	45.00	47.80	45.00	100.00

MEMO PADS

$/per	Survey %	Average	Typical	U.S. Avg.	U.S. Typ	U.S. Max
Text	4.2%	6.25	6.50	20.14	14.50	100.00
w/Graphics	4.2%	12.50	13.00	31.79	17.50	150.00
Hour	39.6%	42.82	40.00	43.94	40.00	100.00

MENUS

$/per	Survey %	Average	Typical	U.S. Avg.	U.S. Typ	U.S. Max
Text Page	10.4%	117.50	50.00	75.65	35.00	500.00
w/Graphics	8.3%	125.00	50.00	125.25	45.00	1000.00
Hour	52.1%	44.64	40.00	44.35	40.00	150.00
Minimum	0.6%	50.00	50.00	233.75	200.00	500.00

NEWSLETTERS

$/per	Survey %	Average	Typical	U.S. Avg.	U.S. Typ	U.S. Max
Text Page	16.7%	50.56	35.00	62.86	45.00	200.00
w/Graphics	14.6%	68.43	50.00	76.16	50.00	200.00
Hour	75.0%	43.28	42.50	42.97	40.00	160.00

NOTEPADS

$/per	Survey %	Average	Typical	U.S. Avg.	U.S. Typ	U.S. Max
Text	0.0%			32.28	25.00	100.00
w/Graphics	0.0%			41.37	35.00	150.00
Hour	37.5%	44.36	40.00	43.72	40.00	100.00

PACKAGING

$/per	Survey %	Average	Typical	U.S. Avg.	U.S. Typ	U.S. Max
Text	2.1%	25.00	25.00	276.00	100.00	1000.00
w/Graphics	2.1%	25.00	25.00	478.18	250.00	2500.00
Hour	27.2%	49.18	60.00	51.64	50.00	150.00

PEN RULER

$/per	Survey %	Average	Typical	U.S. Avg.	U.S. Typ	U.S. Max
Page	0.0%			45.00	45.00	45.00
Hour	18.8%	47.06	45.00	48.81	50.00	85.00

PERIODICAL (OTHER)

$/per	Survey %	Average	Typical	U.S. Avg.	U.S. Typ	U.S. Max
Text Page	2.1%	10.00	10.00	36.00	25.00	150.00
w/Graphics	0.0%			58.00	35.00	250.00
Hour	18.8%	45.94	45.00	46.86	45.00	125.00

POINT-OF-PURCHASE DISPLAYS

$/per	Survey %	Average	Typical	U.S. Avg.	U.S. Typ	U.S. Max
Text Page	0.0%			650.00	600.00	1000.00
w/Graphics	0.0%			800.00	800.00	1000.00
Hour	25.0%	49.04	45.00	50.15	50.00	100.00

POST CARDS

$/per	Survey %	Average	Typical	U.S. Avg.	U.S. Typ	U.S. Max
Text Page	6.3%	33.33	15.00	45.18	20.00	400.00
w/Graphics	6.3%	74.17	18.75	64.31	30.00	500.00
Hour	50.0%	43.06	40.00	42.38	40.00	100.00

POSTERS

$/per	Survey %	Average	Typical	U.S. Avg.	U.S. Typ	U.S. Max
Text Page	0.0%			123.67	50.00	500.00
w/Graphics	0.0%			259.71	250.00	1000.00
Hour	37.5%	46.58	45.00	45.60	45.00	100.00

PRESENTATION MATERIALS

$/per	Survey %	Average	Typical	U.S. Avg.	U.S. Typ	U.S. Max
Text Page	6.3%	12.50	6.25	27.65	20.00	100.00
w/Graphics	6.3%	16.67	12.50	44.38	25.00	180.00
Hour	37.5%	44.50	40.00	45.04	45.00	100.00

PRICE LISTS

$/per	Survey %	Average	Typical	U.S. Avg.	U.S. Typ	U.S. Max
Text Page	6.3%	30.00	25.00	40.63	35.00	150.00
w/Graphics	4.2%	42.40	42.00	51.79	40.00	160.00
Hour	47.9%	44.17	42.50	42.68	40.00	100.00

PRINT ADS

$/per	Survey %	Average	Typical	U.S. Avg.	U.S. Typ	U.S. Max
Text	10.4%	124.00	70.00	107.09	45.00	1000.00
w/Graphics	12.5%	242.92	150.00	179.74	80.00	1100.00
Hour	52.1%	44.34	45.00	44.84	40.00	100.00

PROCEDURE GUIDES

$/per	Survey %	Average	Typical	U.S. Avg.	U.S. Typ	U.S. Max
Text Page	4.2%	12.50	12.50	60.00	15.00	300.00
w/Graphics	4.2%	18.75	18.50	93.21	25.00	500.00
Hour	27.1%	42.96	40.00	45.67	45.00	100.00

PRODUCT LITERATURE

$/per	Survey %	Average	Typical	U.S. Avg.	U.S. Typ	U.S. Max
Text Page	4.2%	18.75	18.75	67.97	30.00	500.00
w/Graphics	4.2%	25.00	25.00	118.81	40.00	1000.00
Hour	39.6%	42.03	40.00	45.43	42.00	100.00

PRODUCT SPECIFICATION SHEETS

$/per	Survey %	Average	Typical	U.S. Avg.	U.S. Typ	U.S. Max
Text Page	4.2%	18.75	18.75	70.95	25.00	500.00
w/Graphics	4.2%	25.00	25.00	168.89	35.00	1000.00
Hour	37.5%	43.25	40.00	46.44	45.00	100.00

PROGRAMS

$/per	Survey %	Average	Typical	U.S. Avg.	U.S. Typ	U.S. Max
Text Page	4.2%	12.50	12.50	43.92	25.00	200.00
w/Graphics	4.2%	18.75	18.50	95.94	35.00	500.00
Hour	37.5%	42.42	40.00	46.61	45.00	150.00

PUBLICATIONS (OTHER)

$/per	Survey %	Average	Typical	U.S. Avg.	U.S. Typ	U.S. Max
Text Page	2.1%	25.00	25.00	46.00	30.00	150.00
w/Graphics	2.1%	25.00	25.00	87.73	35.00	500.00
Hour	33.3%	45.22	45.00	44.63	40.00	125.00

RECORD BOOKS

$/per	Survey %	Average	Typical	U.S. Avg.	U.S. Typ	U.S. Max
Text Page	0.0%			20.67	15.00	45.00
w/Graphics	0.0%			35.00	35.00	45.00
Hour	14.6%	45.50	45.00	46.63	45.00	80.00

RESUMES

$/per	Survey %	Average	Typical	U.S. Avg.	U.S. Typ	U.S. Max
Each	14.6%	25.44	25.10	31.21	25.00	150.00
Page	16.7%	31.28	35.00	31.52	30.00	150.00
Hour	60.4%	41.59	40.00	40.96	40.00	150.00

RULERS

$/per	Survey %	Average	Typical	U.S. Avg.	U.S. Typ	U.S. Max
Each	0.0%			250.00	375.00	500.00
Hour	14.6%	45.50	45.00	49.08	50.00	100.00

SALES PRESENTATIONS

$/per	Survey %	Average	Typical	U.S. Avg.	U.S. Typ	U.S. Max
Text Page	6.3%	15.00	12.50	23.14	20.00	45.00
w/Graphics	6.3%	19.17	18.75	29.50	25.00	45.00
Hour	31.3%	43.73	45.00	46.13	45.00	100.00

SIGNAGE

$/per	Survey %	Average	Typical	U.S. Avg.	U.S. Typ	U.S. Max
Text	4.2%	12.50	15.00	27.50	35.00	55.00
w/Graphics	4.2%	18.75	20.00	159.06	35.00	575.00
Hour	39.6%	42.55	40.00	45.60	45.00	100.00

SLIDE DESIGN

$/per	Survey %	Average	Typical	U.S. Avg.	U.S. Typ	U.S. Max
Text	2.1%	15.00	15.00	25.00	20.00	75.00
w/Graphics	2.1%	30.00	30.00	30.11	25.00	100.00
Hour	22.9%	47.59	45.00	46.17	45.00	100.00

SLIDE SHOW DESIGN

$/per	Survey %	Average	Typical	U.S. Avg.	U.S. Typ	U.S. Max
Text Page	0.0%			30.00	25.00	75.00
w/Graphics	0.0%			40.00	30.00	100.00
Hour	20.8%	45.85	45.00	47.98	50.00	100.00

SPREADSHEET DESIGN

$/per	Survey %	Average	Typical	U.S. Avg.	U.S. Typ	U.S. Max
Text Page	0.0%			35.00	35.00	45.00
w/Graphics	0.0%			45.50	45.00	45.00
Hour	20.8%	46.35	45.00	45.82	45.00	125.00

TABLOIDS

$/per	Survey %	Average	Typical	U.S. Avg.	U.S. Typ	U.S. Max
Text Page	0.0%			70.71	45.00	200.00
w/Graphics	2.1%	120.00	120.00	67.50	50.00	120.00
Hour	20.8%	49.35	50.00	46.32	45.00	125.00

TABS

$/per	Survey %	Average	Typical	U.S. Avg.	U.S. Typ	U.S. Max
Text	0.0%			20.00	20.00	20.00
w/Graphics	0.0%			20.00	20.00	20.00
Hour	20.8%	48.35	45.00	47.58	45.00	100.00

TAGS

$/per	Survey %	Average	Typical	U.S. Avg.	U.S. Typ	U.S. Max
Each	0.0%			17.83	10.00	35.00
Hour	22.9%	43.05	40.00	44.69	42.00	80.00

TECHNICAL DOCUMENTS

$/per	Survey %	Average	Typical	U.S. Avg.	U.S. Typ	U.S. Max
Text Page	2.1%	25.00	25.00	72.69	40.00	250.00
w/Graphics	2.1%	25.00	25.00	87.50	45.00	500.00
Hour	31.3%	44.23	45.00	44.05	40.00	125.00

TECHNICAL ILLUSTRATIONS

$/per	Survey %	Average	Typical	U.S. Avg.	U.S. Typ	U.S. Max
Page	0.0%			70.45	75.00	200.00
Hour	31.3%	53.23	45.00	47.28	45.00	200.00

TICKETS

$/per	Survey %	Average	Typical	U.S. Avg.	U.S. Typ	U.S. Max
Text	4.2%	12.50	12.50	24.72	20.00	50.00
w/Graphics	4.2%	18.75	18.75	30.25	30.00	50.00
Hour	37.5%	41.58	40.00	42.53	40.00	100.00

TRANSPARENCY DESIGN (B&W)

$/per	Survey %	Average	Typical	U.S. Avg.	U.S. Typ	U.S. Max
Text Page	0.0%			34.00	25.00	130.00
w/Graphics	0.0%			92.50	45.00	250.00
Hour	33.3%	41.00	40.00	42.68	40.00	100.00

TRANSPARENCY DESIGN (COLOR)						
$/per	Survey %	Average	Typical	U.S. Avg.	U.S. Typ	U.S. Max
Text Page	0.0%			27.50	30.00	45.00
w/Graphics	0.0%			32.50	40.00	45.00
Hour	27.1%	41.62	40.00	44.69	45.00	100.00

OTHER DESIGN						
$/per	Survey %	Average	Typical	U.S. Avg.	U.S. Typ	U.S. Max
Hour	14.6%	51.43	45.00	48.76	45.00	100.00

LASER PRINTER OUTPUT

GENERAL NOTES:
1. Some shops bill as $ set-up fee plus price per page.
2. Some shops bill as $/hr plus $/page.
3. A few shops price at $/hr (typically same price as other services).
4. Some laser printer output priced as $/job plus $/pg.

LASER PRINTING (Up to 300 dpi)						
$/per	Survey %	Average	Typical	U.S. Avg.	U.S. Typ	U.S. Max
8.5 x 11	36.7%	2.14	1.00	1.64	1.00	15.00
8.5 x 14	10.2%	2.96	3.00	1.95	3.00	10.00
11 x 17	4.1%	3.50	4.00	3.13	2.25	6.00
Cost Plus	0.0%			31.25	30.00	50.00
Minimum	2.7%	15.00	15.00	15.00	5.00	25.00

LASER PRINTING (400 dpi)						
$/per	Survey %	Average	Typical	U.S. Avg.	U.S. Typ	U.S. Max
8.5 x 11	6.1%	1.92	2.00	3.03	1.93	15.50
8.5 x 14	2.0%	1.95	2.00	2.71	2.00	6.00
11 x 17	6.1%	4.67	5.00	6.75	4.50	20.00
Cost Plus	0.0%			28.00	20.00	50.00
Minimum	2.7%	15.00	15.00	15.00	5.00	25.00

LASER PRINTING (600 dpi)						
$/per	Survey %	Average	Typical	U.S. Avg.	U.S. Typ	U.S. Max
8.5 x 11	10.2%	1.37	2.25	1.88	1.00	15.00
8.5 x 14	4.1%	1.48	1.95	1.88	1.95	4.46
11 x 17	2.0%	5.00	5.00	4.12	5.16	6.00
Cost Plus	0.0%			28.00	20.00	50.00

LASER PRINTING
(800dpi)

$/per	Survey %	Average	Typical	U.S. Avg.	U.S. Typ	U.S. Max
8.5 x 11	8.2%	3.00	3.00	2.75	2.00	12.00
8.5 x 14	4.1%	4.50	4.50	2.94	4.00	5.00
11 x 17	2.0%	6.00	6.00	6.00	6.00	6.00
Cost Plus	0.0%			28.00	20.00	50.00
Minimum	2.7%	15.00	15.00	15.00	5.00	25.00

LASER PRINTING
(1000 dpi)

$/per	Survey %	Average	Typical	U.S. Avg.	U.S. Typ	U.S. Max
8.5 x 11	4.1%	3.00	3.00	3.10	3.00	7.00
8.5 x 14	2.0%	4.00	4.00	4.06	4.00	7.00
11 x 17	2.1%	6.00	6.00	6.00	6.00	6.00
Cost Plus	0.0%			28.00	20.00	50.00
Minimum	2.7%	15.00	15.00	15.00	10.00	25.00

LASER PRINTING
(1200 dpi)

$/per	Survey %	Average	Typical	U.S. Avg.	U.S. Typ	U.S. Max
8.5 x 11	4.1%	3.00	3.00	2.89	3.00	6.00
8.5 x 14	2.0%	4.00	4.00	4.82	6.00	6.43
11 x 17	2.1%	6.00	6.00	7.18	6.00	13.25
Cost Plus	0.0%			28.00	20.00	50.00
Minimum	2.7%	15.00	15.00	15.00	10.00	25.00

FOR PREPRESS AND OTHER SERVICES (INCLUDING IMAGESETTING OUTPUT), REFER TO THE SECTION MARKED "NATIONAL."

MID ATLANTIC

Price Distribution
SOUTH ATLANTIC
DC DE FL GA MD NC SC VA WV

FILE CONVERSION

GENERAL NOTE: Survey responses listed as $/minute were converted to $/hr.

BOOKS ON DISK

$/per	Survey %	Average	Typical	U.S. Avg.	U.S. Typ	U.S. Max
Disk	0.0%			10.57	10.00	25.00
Page	0.0%			6.50	5.50	10.00
Hour	6.1%	30.18	30.00	40.11	35.00	95.00
Minimum	3.0%	15.00	15.00	15.00	15.00	15.00

CD-ROM

$/per	Survey %	Average	Typical	U.S. Avg.	U.S. Typ	U.S. Max
Page	0.0%			8.00	8.00	8.00
Disk	0.0%			25.00	25.00	25.00
Hour	3.0%	36.00	36.00	48.00	43.00	85.00
Minimum	3.0%	15.00	15.00	70.00	70.00	125.00

CROSS PLATFORM

$/per	Survey %	Average	Typical	U.S. Avg.	U.S. Typ	U.S. Max
Page	0.0%			3.83	2.88	8.00
File	9.1%	11.33	10.00	7.85	9.00	20.00
Disk	3.0%	16.00	15.00	11.85	10.00	50.00
Hour	18.2%	32.00	36.00	46.31	45.00	100.00
Minimum	6.1%	12.50	12.50	14.25	12.50	35.00

DATABASE FILES

$/per	Survey %	Average	Typical	U.S. Avg.	U.S. Typ	U.S. Max
Record	3.0%	0.15	0.15	0.16	0.15	0.25
File	0.0%			7.02	10.00	20.00
Disk	0.0%			21.67	15.00	50.00
Hour	9.1%	27.00	25.00	42.46	40.50	100.00
Minimum	3.0%	15.00	15.00	22.50	20.00	35.00

DOCUMENT FILES

$/per	Survey %	Average	Typical	U.S. Avg.	U.S. Typ	U.S. Max
K byte	0.0%			5.25	5.25	5.25
Page	3.0%	3.50	3.50	2.71	2.75	3.50
File	3.0%	4.00	4.00	8.38	10.00	15.00
Disk	3.0%	10.00	10.00	15.73	15.00	50.00
Hour	15.2%	24.27	20.50	41.23	35.00	100.00
Minimum	3.0%	15.00	15.00	21.00	15.00	35.00

DOCUMENTS ON DISK

$/per	Survey %	Average	Typical	U.S. Avg.	U.S. Typ	U.S. Max
Page	3.0%	15.00	15.00	6.17	7.00	15.00
File	0.0%			12.00	15.00	15.00
Disk	3.1%	10.00	10.00	14.00	10.00	50.00
Hour	18.2%	29.56	36.00	38.77	35.00	75.00
Minimum	6.1%	12.50	12.50	12.50	13.00	15.00

FORMS CONVERSION

$/per	Survey %	Average	Typical	U.S. Avg.	U.S. Typ	U.S. Max
Page	0.0%			187.18	190.00	200.00
File	0.0%			26.00	10.00	50.00
Disk	0.0%			15.00	10.00	25.00
Hour	3.0%	36.00	36.00	47.68	40.00	100.00
Minimum	3.0%	15.00	15.00	12.50	15.00	15.00

GRAPHIC FORMAT FILES

$/per	Survey %	Average	Typical	U.S. Avg.	U.S. Typ	U.S. Max
K byte	0.0%			5.25	5.25	5.25
Page	0.0%			18.32	20.00	20.00
File	0.0%			8.50	5.88	20.00
Disk	3.0%	10.00	10.00	15.36	15.00	50.00
Hour	6.1%	28.00	28.00	44.32	40.00	100.00
Minimum	3.0%	15.00	15.00	19.17	15.00	35.00

MEDIA CONVERSION

$/per	Survey %	Average	Typical	U.S. Avg.	U.S. Typ	U.S. Max
File	0.0%			15.00	12.50	25.00
Disk	0.0%			13.05	10.00	50.00
Hour	3.0%	36.00	35.00	48.64	45.00	100.00
Minimum	3.0%	15.00	15.00	13.75	15.00	15.00

PAGE LAYOUT FILES

$/per	Survey %	Average	Typical	U.S. Avg.	U.S. Typ	U.S. Max
500 K byte	0.0%			15.00	15.00	15.00
Page	0.0%			37.50	37.50	60.00
File	0.0%			12.70	12.50	25.00
Disk	0.0%			19.25	15.00	50.00
Hour	6.1%	35.50	35.00	42.91	40.00	100.00
Minimum	3.0%	15.00	15.00	20.00	15.00	35.00

SPREADSHEET FILES

$/per	Survey %	Average	Typical	U.S. Avg	U.S. Typ	U.S. Max
25 K byte	0.0%			7.50	7.50	7.50
Page	0.0%			2.88	2.88	2.00
File	3.0%	4.00	4.00	12.30	10.88	25.00
Disk	0.0%			26.25	20.00	50.00
Hour	9.1%	28.67	25.00	40.98	40.00	100.00
Minimum	3.0%	15.00	15.00	22.50	20.00	35.00

VIDEO TAPE TRANSFER

$/per	Survey %	Average	Typical	U.S. Avg	U.S. Typ	U.S. Max
Disk	0.0%			25.00	25.00	25.00
Per Hour	0.0%			48.33	45.00	75.00
Minimum	3.0%	15.00	15.00	15.00	15.00	15.00

WORD PROCESSOR FILE TO SGML

$/per	Survey %	Average	Typical	U.S. Avg	U.S. Typ	U.S. Max
Disk	0.0%			25.00	25.00	25.00
Hour	0.0%			45.00	40.00	75.00
Minimum	3.0%	15.00	15.00	15.00	15.00	15.00

TEXT CREATION

GENERAL COPY WRITING

$/per	Survey %	Average	Typical	U.S. Avg	U.S. Typ	U.S. Max
Line	0.0%			0.20	0.20	0.20
Page	3.0%	20.00	20.00	30.38	20.00	87.50
Hour	66.7%	35.59	35.00	41.43	35.00	300.00
Minimum	3.0%	15.00	15.00	19.00	15.00	35.00

NEWSLETTER COPY

$/per	Survey %	Average	Typical	U.S. Avg	U.S. Typ	U.S. Max
Column	3.0%	10.00	10.00	10.48	10.50	11.00
Page	3.0%	62.50	60.00	40.96	40.00	125.00
Hour	66.7%	33.56	25.00	39.31	35.00	300.00
Minimum	3.0%	15.00	15.00	283.33	125.00	800.00

PUBLICITY / ADVERTISING COPY

$/per	Survey %	Average	Typical	U.S. Avg	U.S. Typ	U.S. Max
Page	3.0%	15.00	15.00	40.31	40.00	100.00
Piece	0.0%			260.00	300.00	425.00
Hour	45.5%	39.00	35.00	43.56	38.00	300.00
Minimum	3.0%	15.00	15.00	19.00	15.00	35.00

RESUME WRITING

$/per	Survey %	Average	Typical	U.S. Avg.	U.S. Typ	U.S. Max
Page	9.1%	18.33	20.00	32.43	25.00	100.00
Hour	39.4%	39.08	35.00	38.11	35.00	300.00
Minimum	9.1%	48.33	55.00	110.00	65.00	300.00

TECHNICAL WRITING

$/per	Survey %	Average	Typical	U.S. Avg.	U.S. Typ	U.S. Max
Page	3.0%	30.00	30.00	53.54	35.00	300.00
Hour	21.2%	40.71	35.00	45.99	35.00	300.00
Minimum	6.1%	35.00	35.00	35.00	35.00	55.00

DATA INPUT / EDITING

DATA ENTRY / KEYBOARDING

$/per	Survey %	Average	Typical	U.S. Avg.	U.S. Typ	U.S. Max
Character	0.0%			0.02	0.02	0.02
Page	3.0%	4.00	4.00	11.32	10.00	50.00
Hour	45.5%	34.66	40.00	32.64	28.00	100.00
Minimum	3.0%	15.00	15.00	20.00	15.00	35.00

COPY EDITING

$/per	Survey %	Average	Typical	U.S. Avg.	U.S. Typ	U.S. Max
Word	0.0%			0.06	0.06	0.11
Page	3.0%	10.00	10.00	9.47	7.00	50.00
Hour	54.6%	36.44	35.00	36.58	30.00	100.00
Minimum	0.0%			20.00	15.00	35.00

CONTENT EDITING

$/per	Survey %	Average	Typical	U.S. Avg.	U.S. Typ	U.S. Max
Word	0.0%			0.11	0.11	0.11
Page	3.0%	8.00	8.00	5.33	5.00	50.00
Hour	45.5%	38.53	25.00	37.44	36.00	100.00
Minimum	0.0%			33.50	35.00	35.00

PROOF READING

$/per	Survey %	Average	Typical	U.S. Avg.	U.S. Typ	U.S. Max
Page	3.0%	5.00	5.00	6.71	5.00	50.00
Hour	66.7%	33.97	35.00	35.63	30.00	100.00
Minimum	0.0%			33.50	35.00	35.00

REWRITING

$/per	Survey %	Average	Typical	U.S. Avg.	U.S. Typ	U.S. Max
Word	0.0%			0.07	0.03	0.11
Line	0.0%			0.25	0.20	1.00
Page	0.0%			22.67	13.50	50.00
Hour	39.4%	39.08	20.00	38.81	35.00	100.00
Minimum	0.0%			35.00	35.00	35.00

INDEXING

$/per	Survey %	Average	Typical	U.S. Avg.	U.S. Typ	U.S. Max
Page	0.0%			2.80	2.00	5.00
Hour	15.2%	35.60	25.00	38.60	35.00	100.00
Minimum	0.0%			87.50	87.50	140.00

MODEM INPUT

$/per	Survey %	Average	Typical	U.S. Avg.	U.S. Typ	U.S. Max
Page	0.0%			3.33	3.00	5.00
File	0.0%			10.00	10.00	10.00
K bytes	0.0%			1.32	1.40	1.50
Disk	0.0%			8.33	5.00	25.00
Minute	0.0%			1.50	1.50	2.00
Hour	15.2%	35.47	32.00	41.62	38.00	100.00
Minimum	0.0%			12.50	12.50	15.00

TEXT FILE IMPORTING

$/per	Survey %	Average	Typical	U.S. Avg.	U.S. Typ	U.S. Max
Page	0.0%			14.60	5.00	50.00
File	0.0%			11.00	10.00	25.00
K bytes	0.0%			1.32	1.40	1.50
Disk	0.0%			10.00	10.00	15.00
Minute	0.0%			1.50	1.50	2.00
Hour	30.3%	36.44	40.00	39.10	35.00	100.00
Minimum	0.0%			21.25	22.00	35.00

TRANSCRIPTION

$/per	Survey %	Average	Typical	U.S. Avg.	U.S. Typ	U.S. Max
Line	0.0%			0.17	0.17	0.25
Page	3.0%	3.50	3.50	4.79	4.25	8.00
File	0.0%			10.57	10.57	25.00
Disk	0.0%			25.00	25.00	25.00
Hour	18.2%	26.92	21.00	31.64	30.00	75.00
Minimum	0.0%			25.00	25.00	35.00

TRANSLATION

$/per	Survey %	Average	Typical	U.S. Avg.	U.S. Typ	U.S. Max
Word	0.0%			0.17	0.17	0.20
Page	3.0%	20.00	20.00	24.17	22.50	50.00
Hour	3.0%	60.00	60.00	44.49	40.00	150.00
Minimum	0.0%			35.00	35..00	35.00

TYPOGRAPHY (General)

$/per	Survey %	Average	Typical	U.S. Avg.	U.S. Typ	U.S. Max
Line	0.0%			0.25	0.25	0.25
Page	9.1%	10.33	7.00	21.48	15.00	75.00
Hour	51.5%	39.64	40.00	39.27	35.00	100.00
Minimum	3.0%	15.00	15.00	18.83	15.00	35.00

TYPOGRAPHY (Spreadsheet)

$/per	Survey %	Average	Typical	U.S. Avg.	U.S. Typ	U.S. Max
Line	0.0%			0.25	0.25	0.25
Page	6.1%	18.50	19.00	24.06	17.00	75.00
Hour	45.5%	35.59	40.00	41.47	36.00	150.00
Minimum	0.0%			35.00	35.00	35.00

WORD PROCESSSING

$/per	Survey %	Average	Typical	U.S. Avg.	U.S. Typ	U.S. Max
Line	0.0%			0.13	0.10	0.20
Page	6.1%	3.00	3.00	8.67	8.25	25.00
Hour	57.6%	49.23	40.00	32.90	25.00	100.00
Minimum	3.0%	15.00	15.00	21.67	15.00	35.00

DATA MANAGEMENT

GENERAL NOTES:
1. Assume customer pays for cost of media extra.
2. On $/word, assume 2K words per page.
3. Per file cost assumed to be for 1 year.
4. Assume $/file same as $/image.

ARCHIVING SERVICE

$/per	Survey %	Average	Typical	U.S. Avg.	U.S. Typ	U.S. Max
Page	0.0%			7.50	7.50	7.50
File	0.0%			9.63	15.00	25.00
Tape	0.0%			37.50	20.00	150.00
Hour	3.0%	20.35	21.00	46.05	40.00	95.00
Minimum	0.0%			14.17	10.00	25.00

IMAGE MANAGEMENT

$/per	Survey %	Average	Typical	U.S. Avg.	U.S. Typ	U.S. Max
Page	0.0%			6.50	5.50	10.00
File	0.0%			16.67	15.00	50.00
Disk	0.0%			30.00	30.00	50.00
Hour	3.0%	20.35	21.00	44.81	40.00	110.00
Minimum	0.0%			14.17	10.00	25.00

NOTE: Assume $/.file same as $/image.

TEXT MANAGEMENT

$/per	Survey %	Average	Typical	U.S. Avg.	U.S. Typ	U.S. Max
Page	0.0%			8.67	6.00	15.00
File	0.0%			16.67	15.00	50.00
Disk	0.0%			23.33	15.00	50.00
Hour	3.0%	420.35	21.00	44.51	35.00	95.00
Minimum	0.0%			14.17	10.00	25.00

IMAGING SERVICES

DOCUMENT CAPTURE

$/per	Survey %	Average	Typical	U.S. Avg.	U.S. Typ	U.S. Max
Page	0.0%			3.65	3.00	7.50
File	0.0%			6.50	5.00	10.00
Hour	6.1%	30.18	30.00	39.41	35.00	95.00
Minimum	0.0%			16.25	16.25	25.00

DOCUMENT RETRIEVAL

$/per	Survey %	Average	Typical	U.S. Avg.	U.S. Typ	U.S. Max
Page	0.0%			1.50	1.50	2.00
File	0.0%			5.03	5.00	10.00
Hour	3.0%	20.35	20.00	38.82	39.00	85.00
Minimum	0.0%			16.25	16.25	25.00

GRAPHICS FILE IMPORTING

$/per	Survey %	Average	Typical	U.S. Avg.	U.S. Typ	U.S. Max
File	0.0%			6.98	5.00	15.00
Disk	0.0%			5.00	5.00	5.00
Hour	15.2%	45.25	36.00	43.35	36.00	100.00
Minimum	0.0%			14.17	14.17	35.00

PHOTO CD-ROM IMPORTING

$/per	Survey %	Average	Typical	U.S. Avg.	U.S. Typ	U.S. Max
Image	3.0%	45.00	45.00	10.02	7.25	45.00
Stock Fee	0.0%			75.00	75.00	75.00
Hour	9.1%	43.78	36.00	48.60	45.00	100.00
Minimum	0.0%			16.25	15.00	25.00

SCANNING (B&W Grey Scale)

$/per	Survey %	Average	Typical	U.S. Avg.	U.S. Typ	U.S. Max
Hour	27.3%	46.26	40.00	42.82	40.00	100.00
75-200 dpi	9.1%	30.00	10.00	10.10	9.00	75.00
300-400 dpi	27.3%	18.00	10.00	11.93	10.00	75.00
600-800 dpi	6.1%	47.50	47.50	13.51	11.00	75.00
1200 dpi	3.0%	75.00	25.00	20.20	12.00	75.00
2400 dpi	3.0%	75.00	30.50	36.86	30.00	75.00

SCANNING (B&W Line Art)

$/per	Survey %	Average	Typical	U.S. Avg.	U.S. Typ	U.S. Max
Hour	24.2%	47.67	45.00	40.94	40.00	100.00
75-200 dpi	6.1%	42.50	10.00	10.59	9.00	75.00
300-400 dpi	30.3%	15.70	10.00	11.92	10.00	75.00
600-800 dpi	6.1%	45.00	11.00	12.51	10.00	75.00
1200 dpi	3.1%	75.00	12.00	15.59	11.00	75.00
2400 dpi	3.0%	74.50	25.00	35.75	27.50	75.00
Per K	3.0%	75.00	50.00	51.67	50.00	75.00

SCANNING (B&W Photo)

$/per	Survey %	Average	Typical	U.S. Avg.	U.S. Typ	U.S. Max
Hour	21.2%	48.76	45.00	45.16	40.00	100.00
75-200 dpi	9.1%	30.00	10.00	12.28	10.00	75.00
300-400 dpi	15.2%	25.20	15.00	13.92	12.40	75.00
600-800 dpi	9.1%	35.33	25.00	14.79	12.60	75.00
1200 dpi	3.0%	75.00	20.00	19.88	17.50	75.00
2400 dpi	3.0%	75.00	30.00	35.56	31.00	75.00
Per K	3.0%	75.00	60.00	62.50	62.50	75.00

SCANNING (Color Illustration)

$/per	Survey %	Average	Typical	U.S. Avg.	U.S. Typ	U.S. Max
Hour	15.2%	45.27	45.00	49.23	50.00	125.00
75-200 dpi	3.0%	75.00	15.00	19.08	15.00	75.00
300-400 dpi	6.1%	52.50	30.00	21.03	19.00	82.00
600-800 dpi	9.1%	42.33	40.00	22.36	21.50	75.00
1200 dpi	3.0%	75.00	30.00	26.47	23.00	75.00
2400 dpi	3.0%	75.00	50.00	46.22	50.00	75.00

SCANNING (Color Photo)

$/per	Survey %	Average	Typical	U.S. Avg.	U.S. Typ	U.S. Max
Hour	12.1%	45.34	50.00	49.23	50.00	125.00
75-200 dpi	6.1%	47.50	45.00	20.44	15.00	75.00
300-400 dpi	6.1%	52.50	52.00	20.97	17.75	82.00
600-800 dpi	9.1%	42.33	40.00	19.75	15.00	75.00
1200 dpi	6.1%	60.00	60.00	30.13	30.00	75.00
2400 dpi	3.0%	75.00	75.00	61.54	60.00	137.00

SCANNING (HIGH END)
(Loose Scan)

$/per	Survey %	U.S. Avg.	U.S. Typ	U.S. Max
2 x 3	0.1%	13.33	10.00	25.00
3 x 5	0.1%	11.25	10.00	20.00
4 x 5	0.1%	16.00	10.00	33.00
5 x 7	0.1%	18.00	10.00	37.00
5.5 x 8.5	0.1%	17.33	10.00	39.00
6 x 9	0.1%	24.67	15.00	49.00
8 x 10	0.1%	41.60	50.00	70.00
10 x 12	0.1%	47.80	60.00	84.00
11 x 14	0.1%	81.67	70.00	105.00
12 x 18	0.1%	90.67	80.00	122.00
16 x 20	0.1%	162.00	162.00	162.00
20 x 24	0.1%	199.00	199.00	199.00
Hour	0.1%	47.00	45.00	60.00

SCANNING (HIGH END)
(Drum Scan)

$/per	Survey %	U.S. Avg.	U.S. Typ	U.S. Max
2 x 3	0.1%	56..92	54.25	71.50
4 x 5	0.1%	57.21	55.00	94.50
5 x 7	0.1%	65.75	70.00	106.00
6 x 8	0.1%	103.13	102.50	117.50
6 x 9	0.1%	57.00	45.00	85.00
8 x 10	0.1%	51.25	50.00	60.00
10 x 12	0.1%	58.33	60.00	60.00
11 x 14	0.1%	71.25	72.50	75.00
12 x 18	0.1%	86.67	85.00	100.00
24 x 27	0.1%	600.00	600.00	600.00

SCANNING (HIGH END)
(High Res Scan to Disk)

$/per	Survey %	U.S. Avg.	U.S. Typ	U.S. Max
2 x 3	0.1%	20..50	19.50	25.00
4 x 5	0.1%	26.17	27.50	30.00
5 x 7	0.1%	34.00	35.00	41.00
6 x 9	0.1%	39.80	39.00	50.00

SCANNING (HIGH END)
(High Res Scan to Disk)

$/per	Survey %	U.S. Avg.	U.S. Typ	U.S. Max
8 x 10	0.1%	45.50	45.00	60.00
10 x 12	0.1%	56.83	59.00	70.00
11 x 14	0.1%	65.08	64.00	89.00
12 x 18	0.1%	78.90	75.00	100.00
16 x 20	0.1%	96.33	99.00	130.00
20 x 24	0.1%	128.00	134.00	160.00
24 x 27	0.1%	156.25	156.25	200.00

SCANNING (Transparency)

$/per	Survey %	Average	Typical	U.S. Avg.	U.S. Typ	U.S. Max
Each	0.0%			18.70	16.00	45.00
Hour	6.1%	47.68	45.00	65.29	55.00	137.00

SCANNING (Slide)

$/per	Survey %	Average	Typical	U.S. Avg.	U.S. Typ	U.S. Max
Each	0.0%			23.00	16.99	65.00
Hour	6.1%	47.68	45.00	68.42	55.00	137.00

COLOR CORRECTION

$/per	Survey %	Average	Typical	U.S. Avg.	U.S. Typ	U.S. Max
Hour	12.1%	47.50	50.00	65.80	50.00	300.00

IMAGE EDITING

$/per	Survey %	Average	Typical	U.S. Avg.	U.S. Typ	U.S. Max
Each	0.0%			20.75	15.00	50.00
Hour	18.2%	44.23	45.00	55.47	45.00	300.00

IMAGE ENHANCEMENT

$/per	Survey %	Average	Typical	U.S. Avg.	U.S. Typ	U.S. Max
Hour	12.1%	57.50	60.00	57.60	50.00	300.00

RETOUCHING

$/per	Survey %	Average	Typical	U.S. Avg.	U.S. Typ	U.S. Max
Each	0.0%			27.67	40.00	50.00
Hour	18.2%	49.33	45.00	58.60	50.00	300.00
Minimum	0.0%			26.08	25.00	35.00

TEXT SCAN (OCR)

$/per	Survey %	Average	Typical	U.S. Avg.	U.S. Typ	U.S. Max
Page	12.1%	4.75	5.00	7.82	5.00	95.00

TEXT SCAN (OCR)

$/per	Survey %	Average	Typical	U.S. Avg.	U.S. Typ	U.S. Max
Hour	24.2%	45.79	40.00	36.33	30.00	75.00
Minimum	0.0%			19.08	16.90	35.00

NOTE:

1. Prices assume spell check conducted on scanned text.

2. Assumes 2 Kb per page, so $1/Kb response incorporated as $2/page.

NEGATIVE CREATION

$/per	Survey %	Average	Typical	U.S. Avg.	U.S. Typ	U.S. Max
Each	0.0%			22.00	22.00	40.00
Hour	6.1%	47.68	45.00	56.71	56.71	100.00
Minimum	0.0%			16.67	16.67	25.00

DESIGN SERVICES

ANNOUNCEMENTS

$/per	Survey %	Average	Typical	U.S. Avg.	U.S. Typ	U.S. Max
Text Page	0.0%			37.05	24.00	250.00
w/Graphics	0.0%			65.36	36.50	500.00
Hour	42.4%	39.67	40.00	42.21	40.00	100.00

ANNUAL REPORTS
(1C, 2C, Up To Letter Size Pages)

$/per	Survey %	Average	Typical	U.S. Avg.	U.S. Typ	U.S. Max
Text	3.0%	125.00	125.00	114.75	62.50	1000.00
w/Graphics	0.0%			222.00	100.00	7680.00
Hour	48.5%	43.83	36.00	46.58	45.00	100.00

ANNUAL REPORTS
(3C, 4C, Larger Size Pages)

$/per	Survey %	Average	Typical	U.S. Avg.	U.S. Typ	U.S. Max
Text	3.0%	125.00	125.00	214.55	100.00	1500.00
w/Graphics	0.0%			422.50	175.00	11520.00
Hour	39.4%	42.41	36.00	46.34	45.00	100.00

BAR CODING

$/per	Survey %	Average	Typical	U.S. Avg.	U.S. Typ	U.S. Max
Each	0.0%			13.25	11.00	150.00
Page	0.0%			29.00	29.00	50.00
Hour	12.1%	57.75	75.00	47.83	45.00	100.00

BOOKLETS

$/per	Survey %	Average	Typical	U.S. Avg.	U.S. Typ	U.S. Max
Text Page	3.0%	125.00	125.00	48.40	30.00	500.00
w/Graphics	0.0%			110.53	50.00	650.00
Hour	72.7%	39.51	40.000	43.87	25.00	100.00

BOOK COVERS

$/per	Survey %	Average	Typical	U.S. Avg.	U.S. Typ	U.S. Max
Text	3.0%	300.00	300.00	143.10	75.00	500.00
w/Graphics	3.0%	500.00	500.00	403.36	300.00	1800.00
Hour	33.3%	47.85	45.00	47.83	45.00	120.00

BOOK BODY

$/per	Survey %	Average	Typical	U.S. Avg.	U.S. Typ	U.S. Max
Text Page	0.0%			26.65	20.00	75.00
w/Graphics	0.0%			41.11	25.00	85.00
Hour	30.3%	41.00	35.00	44.26	40.00	100.00

BOOK JACKETS

$/per	Survey %	Average	Typical	U.S. Avg.	U.S. Typ	U.S. Max
Text	0.0%			161.54	175.00	500.00
w/Graphics	0.0%			491.00	325.00	1000.00
Hour	21.2%	48.62	40.00	48.63	45.00	120.00

BROCHURE
(1C, 2C, Up To Letter Size Sheet)

$/per	Survey %	Average	Typical	U.S. Avg.	U.S. Typ	U.S. Max
Text Page	6.1%	25.00	30.00	72.59	47.50	500.00
w/Graphics	3.0%	87.50	87.50	156.74	82.50	750.00
Hour	72.7%	37.76	40.00	42.85	40.00	125.00

BROCHURE
(3C, 4C, Larger Size Sheet)

$/per	Survey %	Average	Typical	U.S. Avg.	U.S. Typ	U.S. Max
Text Page	3.0%	150.00	150.00	123.79	60.00	1000.00
w/Graphics	0.0%			227.71	100.00	1500.00
Hour	60.6%	39.82	36.00	44.17	40.00	125.00

BULLETIN

$/per	Survey %	Average	Typical	U.S. Avg.	U.S. Typ	U.S. Max
Text Page	3.0%	40.00	40.00	32.75	25.00	150.00
w/Graphics	3.0%	40.00	40.00	47.81	35.00	200.00
Hour	24.2%	45.67	40.00	42.36	40.00	100.00

BUSINESS CARDS

$/per	Survey %	Average	Typical	U.S. Avg.	U.S. Typ	U.S. Max
Text Card	12.1%	38.75	40.00	38.81	25.00	500.00
w/Graphics	3.0%	40.00	40.00	91.70	40.00	1000.00
Hour	72.7%	39.19	36.00	43.19	40.00	150.00

BUSINESS REPLY CARDS

$/per	Survey %	Average	Typical	U.S. Avg.	U.S. Typ	U.S. Max
Text Card	0.0%			34.32	31.50	150.00
w/Graphics	0.0%			67.50	35.00	250.00
Hour	45.5%	38.40	35.00	43.79	40.00	100.00

BUSINESS LETTERS

$/per	Survey %	Average	Typical	U.S. Avg.	U.S. Typ	U.S. Max
Text Page	3.0%	5.00	5.00	17.23	12.25	90.00
w/Graphics	3.0%	5.00	5.00	27.08	18.75	100.00
Hour	51.5%	36.52	35.00	39.38	35.00	100.00

CALENDARS

$/per	Survey %	Average	Typical	U.S. Avg.	U.S. Typ	U.S. Max
Text Page	3.0%	10.00	10.00	82.50	50.00	500.00
w/Graphics	3.0%	10.00	10.00	53.18	45.00	150.00
Hour	42.4%	41.81	35.00	43.77	40.00	100.00

CALLIGRAPHY

$/per	Survey %	Average	Typical	U.S. Avg.	U.S. Typ	U.S. Max
Line	0.0%			1.00	1.00	60.00
Page	3.0%	5.00	5.00	40.00	35.00	100.00
Hour	18.2%	55.06	75.00	45.50	40.00	175.00

CARDS (FOLD-OVER)

$/per	Survey %	Average	Typical	U.S. Avg.	U.S. Typ	U.S. Max
Text Card	0.0%			31.45	25.00	60.00
w/Graphics	0.0%			65.47	46.40	250.00
Hour	24.2%	38.79	35.00	43.63	40.00	100.00

CARDS (ROLODEX)

$/per	Survey %	Average	Typical	U.S. Avg.	U.S. Typ	U.S. Max
Text Card	0.0%			37.34	25.00	150.00
w/Graphics	0.0%			63.00	48.00	250.00
Hour	24.2%	41.29	40.00	44.94	41.00	100.00

CARTOONS

$/per	Survey %	Average	Typical	U.S. Avg.	U.S. Typ	U.S. Max
Each	0.0%			119.29	60.00	400.00
Page	0.0%			163.33	65.00	400.00
Hour	15.2%	47.67	36.00	48.15	45.00	90.00

CATALOGS

$/per	Survey %	Average	Typical	U.S. Avg.	U.S. Typ	U.S. Max
Text Page	3.0%	150.00	150.00	69.03	40.00	500.00
w/Graphics	3.0%	150.00	150.00	129.05	67.50	1000.00
Hour	48.5%	41.65	36.00	45.68	45.00	125.00

CERTIFICATES

$/per	Survey %	Average	Typical	U.S. Avg.	U.S. Typ	U.S. Max
Text	0.0%			23.56	16.25	125.00
w/Graphics	0.0%			35.07	25.00	150.00
Hour	27.3%	38.37	35.00	42.15	40.00	100.00

CHARTS / DIAGRAMS

$/per	Survey %	Average	Typical	U.S. Avg.	U.S. Typ	U.S. Max
Text	6.1%	80.00	80.00	36.19	32.50	150.00
w/Graphics	6.1%	90.00	90.00	53.14	47.50	150.00
Hour	54.6%	42.35	40.00	44.29	40.00	100.00

COMIC BOOKS

$/per	Survey %	Average	Typical	U.S. Avg.	U.S. Typ	U.S. Max
Each Page	0.0%			65.00	60.00	100.00
Hour	3.0%	75.00	75.00	47.12	50.00	80.00

COMIC STRIPS

$/per	Survey %	Average	Typical	U.S. Avg.	U.S. Typ	U.S. Max
Each Strip	0.0%			38.33	30.00	60.00
Hour	3.0%	75.00	75.00	46.78	50.00	80.00

COMPUTER GENERATED ART

$/per	Survey %	Average	Typical	U.S. Avg.	U.S. Typ	U.S. Max
Page	0.0%			121.40	50.00	500.00
Hour	51.5%	42.02	35.00	46.70	42.00	175.00

CUSTOM DISPLAYS

$/per	Survey %	Average	Typical	U.S. Avg.	U.S. Typ	U.S. Max
Text	0.0%			192.14	60.00	1000.00
w/Graphics	0.0%			265.71	100.00	1000.00
Hour	42.4%	48.03	40.00	48.95	45.00	100.00

DATABASE DESIGN

$/per	Survey %	Average	Typical	U.S. Avg.	U.S. Typ	U.S. Max
Text	0.0%			38.33	30.00	60.00
w/Graphics	0.0%			43.33	40.00	60.00
Hour	9.1%	51,67	40.00	42.45	41.00	80.00

DIGITAL SLIDE PRESENTATIONS

$/per	Survey %	Average	Typical	U.S. Avg.	U.S. Typ	U.S. Max
Text	0.0%			27.13	27.50	60.00
w/Graphics	0.0%			35.00	32.50	60.00
Hour	18.2%	47.50	50.00	45.81	45.00	100.00

DIRECT MAIL PACKAGES

$/per	Survey %	Average	Typical	U.S. Avg.	U.S. Typ	U.S. Max
Text	3.0%	150.00	150.00	298.46	60.00	1500.00
w/Graphics	3.0%	150.00	150.00	413.50	65.00	2000.00
Hour	42.4%	46.10	40.00	47.05	45.00	100.00

DIRECTORY

$/per	Survey %	Average	Typical	U.S. Avg.	U.S. Typ	U.S. Max
Text	3.0%	125.00	125.00	38.72	30.00	150.00
w/Graphics	3.0%	125.00	125.00	73.53	40.00	500.00
Hour	60.6%	39.57	36.00	43.08	40.00	125.00

DISPLAY ADVERTISING

$/per	Survey %	Average	Typical	U.S. Avg.	U.S. Typ	U.S. Max
Text	0.0%			109.28	30.00	1000.00
w/Graphics	0.0%			304.64	45.00	2500.00
Hour	48.5%	46.71	40.00	48.23	45.00	115.00

DISPLAY EXHIBITS

$/per	Survey %	Average	Typical	U.S. Avg.	U.S. Typ	U.S. Max
Text Panel	0.0%			858.57	90.00	5000.00
w/Graphics	0.0%			896.67	100.00	5000.00
Hour	27.3%	49.82	40.00	51.43	50.00	115.00

DOOR HANGERS

$/per	Survey %	Average	Typical	U.S. Avg.	U.S. Typ	U.S. Max
Text	0.0%			42.46	25.00	250.00
w/Graphics	0.0%			87.50	35.00	500.00
Hour	15.2%	49.00	40.00	47.19	45.00	100.00

DRAFTING

$/per	Survey %	Average	Typical	U.S. Avg.	U.S. Typ	U.S. Max
Page	0.0%			45.00	45.00	60.00
Hour	18.2%	46.06	40.00	46.62	45.00	100.00

FINANCIAL DOCUMENTS

$/per	Survey %	Average	Typical	U.S. Avg.	U.S. Typ	U.S. Max
Text Page	0.0%			45.33	33.00	150.00
w/Graphics	0.0%			92.00	60.00	150.00
Hour	21.2%	47.86	40.00	47.20	45.00	125.00

FLYERS

$/per	Survey %	Average	Typical	U.S. Avg.	U.S. Typ	U.S. Max
Text Page	9.1%	60.00	25.00	39.21	25.00	325.00
w/Graphics	6.1%	78.00	75.00	66.84	35.00	325.00
Hour	75.8%	38.69	35.00	42.22	40.00	100.00

FORMS

$/per	Survey %	Average	Typical	U.S. Avg.	U.S. Typ	U.S. Max
Text Page	9.1%	65.00	35.00	52.60	30.00	750.00
w/Graphics	6.1%	80.00	80.00	81.67	37.50	10000.00
Hour	66.7%	37.06	40.00	41.75	40.00	125.00

HANDBOOKS

$/per	Survey %	Average	Typical	U.S. Avg.	U.S. Typ	U.S. Max
Text Page	3.0%	125.00	125.00	38.22	25.00	150.00
w/Graphics	3.0%	125.00	125.00	62.46	35.00	250.00
Hour	69.7%	40.93	36.00	43.53	40.00	100.00

INSERTS

$/per	Survey %	Average	Typical	U.S. Avg.	U.S. Typ	U.S. Max
Text Page	3.0%	125.00	125.00	70.58	27.50	1000.00
w/Graphics	3.0%	125.00	125.00	193.50	35.00	2500.00
Hour	51.5%	40.02	40.00	43.99	40.00	100.00

INVITATIONS

$/per	Survey %	Average	Typical	U.S. Avg.	U.S. Typ	U.S. Max
Text	6.1%	82.50	80.00	35.01	25.00	250.00
w/Graphics	6.1%	87.50	87.00	73.16	35.00	750.00
Hour	66.7%	38.93	36.00	41.85	40.00	100.00

LABELS (Custom)

$/per	Survey %	Average	Typical	U.S. Avg.	U.S. Typ	U.S. Max
Text	3.2%	5.00	5.00	40.06	20.00	250.00
w/Graphics	3.1%	5.00	5.00	121.16	55.00	600.00
Hour	30.3%	40.79	35.00	43.55	40.00	100.00

LARGE FORMAT GRAPHICS

$/per	Survey %	Average	Typical	U.S. Avg.	U.S. Typ	U.S. Max
Text Page	0.0%			40.00	37.50	45.00
w/Graphics	0.0%			71.00	70.00	85.00
Hour	12.1%	65.09	75.00	47.95	45.00	90.00

LETTERHEAD & ENVELOPES

$/per	Survey %	Average	Typical	U.S. Avg.	U.S. Typ	U.S. Max
Text	0.0%			59.65	25.00	750.00
w/Graphics	0.0%			136.48	40.00	1000.00
Hour	72.7%	41.45	40.00	43.60	40.00	150.00

LINE ART & GENERAL ILLUSTRATIONS

$/per	Survey %	Average	Typical	U.S. Avg.	U.S. Typ	U.S. Max
Text Page	0.0%			64.17	47.50	135.00
w/Graphics	0.0%			221.89	100.00	1000.00
Hour	48.5%	44.58	40.00	46.24	43.50	115.00

LITIGATION GRAPHICS

$/per	Survey %	Average	Typical	U.S. Avg.	U.S. Typ	U.S. Max
Text Page	0.0%			75.00	75.00	75.00
w/Graphics	0.0%			100.00	100.00	100.00
Hour	9.1%	70.00	75.00	50.13	45.00	200.00

LOGOS

$/per	Survey %	Average	Typical	U.S. Avg.	U.S. Typ	U.S. Max
Each	3.0%	300.00	300.00	281.23	200.00	2000.00
Hour	72.7%	43.06	40.00	46.02	45.00	125.00

LOGOTYPE

$/per	Survey %	Average	Typical	U.S. Avg.	U.S. Typ	U.S. Max
Page	0.0%			304.36	300.00	1000.00
Hour	45.5%	46.02	40.00	48.68	45.00	125.00

MAGAZINES

$/per	Survey %	Average	Typical	U.S. Avg.	U.S. Typ	U.S. Max
Text Page	6.1%	130.00	130.00	60.49	35.00	250.00
w/Graphics	6.1%	162.50	165.00	90.89	40.00	500.00
Hour	33.3%	50.55	40.00	45.91	45.00	125.00

NOTES:
1. Multiple page prices converted to $/page.
2. Other prices noted for magazine design: $500 setup; $1,000 ea.

MAILERS

$/per	Survey %	Average	Typical	U.S. Avg.	U.S. Typ	U.S. Max
Text Page	0.0%			64.08	25.00	500.00
w/Graphics	0.0%			82.36	40.00	500.00
Hour	33.3%	43.67	40.00	46.11	42.00	100.00

MANUALS

$/per	Survey %	Average	Typical	U.S. Avg.	U.S. Typ	U.S. Max
Text Page	6.1%	67.50	65.00	42.06	17.50	500.00
w/Graphics	3.0%	125.00	125.00	58.10	30.00	500.00
Hour	63.6%	40.40	35.00	42.63	40.00	100.00

MAPS
(1C, 2C, Letter Size)

$/per	Survey %	Average	Typical	U.S. Avg.	U.S. Typ	U.S. Max
Simple	0.0%			76.25	70.00	250.00
Complex	3.0%	300.00	300.00	206.14	75.00	600.00
Hour	33.3%	51.94	45.00	46.90	45.00	100.00

MAPS
(4C, Larger Than Letter Size)

$/per	Survey %	Average	Typical	U.S. Avg.	U.S. Typ	U.S. Max
Simple	0.0%			168.75	72.50	500.00
Complex	3.0%	300.00	300.00	490.71	300.00	1600.00
Hour	33.3%	51.94	45.00	48.08	45.00	100.00

MARKETING PLANS

$/per	Survey %	Average	Typical	U.S. Avg.	U.S. Typ	U.S. Max
Text Page	0.0%			59.00	10.00	250.00
w/Graphics	0.0%			182.67	40.00	500.00
Hour	18.2%	66.67	75.00	47.80	45.00	100.00

MEMO PADS

$/per	Survey %	Average	Typical	U.S. Avg.	U.S. Typ	U.S. Max
Text	0.0%			20.14	14.50	100.00
w/Graphics	0.0%			31.79	17.50	150.00
Hour	27.3%	42.82	40.00	43.94	40.00	100.00

MENUS

$/per	Survey %	Average	Typical	U.S. Avg.	U.S. Typ	U.S. Max
Text Page	6.1%	140.00	25.00	75.65	35.00	500.00
w/Graphics	3.0%	25.00	25.00	125.25	45.00	1000.00
Hour	48.5%	43.77	40.00	44.35	40.00	150.00
Minimum	0.0%			233.75	200.00	500.00

NEWSLETTERS

$/per	Survey %	Average	Typical	U.S. Avg.	U.S. Typ	U.S. Max
Text Page	15.2%	60.50	50.00	62.86	45.00	200.00
w/Graphics	9.1%	73.33	50.00	76.16	50.00	200.00
Hour	93.9%	37.98	35.00	42.97	40.00	160.00

NOTEPADS

$/per	Survey %	Average	Typical	U.S. Avg.	U.S. Typ	U.S. Max
Text	3.0%	50.00	50.00	32.28	25.00	100.00
w/Graphics	3.0%	50.00	50.00	41.37	35.00	150.00
Hour	45.5%	41.69	40.00	43.72	40.00	100.00

PACKAGING

$/per	Survey %	Average	Typical	U.S. Avg.	U.S. Typ	U.S. Max
Text	0.0%			276.00	100.00	1000.00
w/Graphics	0.0%			478.18	250.00	2500.00
Hour	21.2%	62.29	75.00	51.64	50.00	150.00

PEN RULER

$/per	Survey %	Average	Typical	U.S. Avg.	U.S. Typ	U.S. Max
Page	0.0%			45.00	45.00	45.00
Hour	12.1%	56.25	75.00	48.81	50.00	85.00

PERIODICAL (OTHER)

$/per	Survey %	Average	Typical	U.S. Avg.	U.S. Typ	U.S. Max
Text Page	0.0%			36.00	25.00	150.00
w/Graphics	0.0%			58.00	35.00	250.00
Hour	27.3%	46.67	40.00	46.86	45.00	125.00

POINT-OF-PURCHASE DISPLAYS

$/per	Survey %	Average	Typical	U.S. Avg.	U.S. Typ	U.S. Max
Text Page	0.0%			650.00	600.00	1000.00
w/Graphics	0.0%			800.00	800.00	1000.00
Hour	15.2%	60.00	75.00	50.15	50.00	100.00

POST CARDS

$/per	Survey %	Average	Typical	U.S. Avg.	U.S. Typ	U.S. Max
Text Page	6.1%	217.50	225.00	45.18	20.00	400.00
w/Graphics	3.0%	400.00	400.00	64.31	30.00	500.00
Hour	57.6%	42.12	40.00	42.38	40.00	100.00

POSTERS

$/per	Survey %	Average	Typical	U.S. Avg.	U.S. Typ	U.S. Max
Text Page	3.0%	400.00	400.00	123.67	50.00	500.00
w/Graphics	3.1%	400.00	400.00	259.71	250.00	1000.00
Hour	39.4%	46.57	40.00	45.60	45.00	100.00

PRESENTATION MATERIALS

$/per	Survey %	Average	Typical	U.S. Avg.	U.S. Typ	U.S. Max
Text Page	3.0%	20.00	20.00	27.65	20.00	100.00
w/Graphics	3.0%	20.00	20.00	44.38	25.00	180.00
Hour	54.6%	38.96	31.00	45.04	45.00	100.00

PRICE LISTS

$/per	Survey %	Average	Typical	U.S. Avg.	U.S. Typ	U.S. Max
Text Page	3.0%	125.00	125.00	40.63	35.00	150.00
w/Graphics	3.1%	125.00	125.00	51.79	40.00	160.00
Hour	39.4%	43.87	40.00	42.68	40.00	100.00

PRINT ADS

$/per	Survey %	Average	Typical	U.S. Avg.	U.S. Typ	U.S. Max
Text	3.0%	200.00	200.00	107.09	45.00	1000.00
w/Graphics	3.0%	500.00	500.00	179.74	80.00	1100.00
Hour	48.5%	42.81	40.00	44.84	40.00	100.00

PROCEDURE GUIDES

$/per	Survey %	Average	Typical	U.S. Avg.	U.S. Typ	U.S. Max
Text Page	0.0%			60.00	15.00	300.00
w/Graphics	0.0%			93.21	25.00	500.00
Hour	21.2%	52.19	45.00	45.67	45.00	100.00

PRODUCT LITERATURE

$/per	Survey %	Average	Typical	U.S. Avg.	U.S. Typ	U.S. Max
Text Page	3.0%	125.00	125.00	67.97	30.00	500.00
w/Graphics	3.1%	125.00	125.00	118.81	40.00	1000.00
Hour	48.5%	46.63	40.00	45.43	42.00	100.00

PRODUCT SPECIFICATION SHEETS

$/per	Survey %	Average	Typical	U.S. Avg.	U.S. Typ	U.S. Max
Text Page	0.0%			70.95	25.00	500.00
w/Graphics	0.0%			168.89	35.00	1000.00
Hour	33.3%	44.58	40.00	46.44	45.00	100.00

PROGRAMS

$/per	Survey %	Average	Typical	U.S. Avg.	U.S. Typ	U.S. Max
Text Page	0.0%			43.92	25.00	200.00
w/Graphics	0.0%			95.94	35.00	500.00
Hour	24.2%	50.67	45.00	46.61	45.00	150.00

PUBLICATIONS (OTHER)

$/per	Survey %	Average	Typical	U.S. Avg.	U.S. Typ	U.S. Max
Text Page	3.0%	125.00	125.00	46.00	30.00	150.00
w/Graphics	3.0%	125.00	125.00	87.73	35.00	500.00
Hour	48.5%	40.40	35.00	44.63	40.00	125.00

RECORD BOOKS

$/per	Survey %	Average	Typical	U.S. Avg.	U.S. Typ	U.S. Max
Text Page	0.0%			20.67	15.00	45.00
w/Graphics	0.0%			35.00	35.00	45.00
Hour	12.1%	57.50	75.00	46.63	45.00	80.00

RESUMES

$/per	Survey %	Average	Typical	U.S. Avg.	U.S. Typ	U.S. Max
Each	18.2%	35.00	35.00	31.21	25.00	150.00
Page	18.2%	35.00	35.00	31.52	30.00	150.00
Hour	63.6%	39.76	40.00	40.96	40.00	150.00

RULERS

$/per	Survey %	Average	Typical	U.S. Avg.	U.S. Typ	U.S. Max
Each	0.0%			250.00	375.00	500.00
Hour	6.1%	75.00	75.00	49.08	50.00	100.00

SALES PRESENTATIONS

$/per	Survey %	Average	Typical	U.S. Avg.	U.S. Typ	U.S. Max
Text Page	0.0%			23.14	20.00	45.00
w/Graphics	0.0%			29.50	25.00	45.00
Hour	39.4%	47.38	36.00	46.13	45.00	100.00

SIGNAGE

$/per	Survey %	Average	Typical	U.S. Avg.	U.S. Typ	U.S. Max
Text	0.0%			27.50	35.00	55.00
w/Graphics	0.0%			159.06	35.00	575.00
Hour	30.3%	48.24	40.00	45.60	45.00	100.00

SLIDE DESIGN

$/per	Survey %	Average	Typical	U.S. Avg.	U.S. Typ	U.S. Max
Text	0.0%			25.00	20.00	75.00
w/Graphics	0.0%			30.11	25.00	100.00
Hour	24.2%	46.92	45.00	46.17	45.00	100.00

SLIDE SHOW DESIGN

$/per	Survey %	Average	Typical	U.S. Avg.	U.S. Typ	U.S. Max
Text Page	0.0%			30.00	25.00	75.00
w/Graphics	0.0%			40.00	30.00	100.00
Hour	21.2%	47.91	45.00	47.98	50.00	100.00

SPREADSHEET DESIGN

$/per	Survey %	Average	Typical	U.S. Avg.	U.S. Typ	U.S. Max
Text Page	0.0%			35.00	35.00	45.00
w/Graphics	0.0%			45.50	45.00	45.00
Hour	24.2%	42.50	40.00	45.82	45.00	125.00

TABLOIDS

$/per	Survey %	Average	Typical	U.S. Avg.	U.S. Typ	U.S. Max
Text Page	0.0%			70.71	45.00	200.00
w/Graphics	0.0%			67.50	50.00	120.00
Hour	33.3%	45.49	40.00	46.32	45.00	125.00

TABS

$/per	Survey %	Average	Typical	U.S. Avg.	U.S. Typ	U.S. Max
Text	0.0%			20.00	20.00	20.00
w/Graphics	0.0%			20.00	20.00	20.00
Hour	12.1%	52.59	75.00	47.58	45.00	100.00

TAGS

$/per	Survey %	Average	Typical	U.S. Avg.	U.S. Typ	U.S. Max
Each	0.0%			17.83	10.00	35.00
Hour	18.2%	53.39	75.00	44.69	42.00	80.00

TECHNICAL DOCUMENTS

$/per	Survey %	Average	Typical	U.S. Avg.	U.S. Typ	U.S. Max
Text Page	3.0%	125.00	125.00	72.69	40.00	250.00
w/Graphics	3.3%	125.00	125.00	87.50	45.00	500.00
Hour	33.3%	44.12	40.00	44.05	40.00	125.00

TECHNICAL ILLUSTRATIONS

$/per	Survey %	Average	Typical	U.S. Avg.	U.S. Typ	U.S. Max
Page	0.0%			70.45	75.00	200.00
Hour	33.3%	40.30	40.00	47.28	45.00	200.00

TICKETS

$/per	Survey %	Average	Typical	U.S. Avg.	U.S. Typ	U.S. Max
Text	3.0%	40.00	40.00	24.72	20.00	50.00
w/Graphics	3.0%	45.00	45.00	30.25	30.00	50.00
Hour	21.2%	39.34	35.00	42.53	40.00	100.00

TRANSPARENCY DESIGN (B&W)

$/per	Survey %	Average	Typical	U.S. Avg.	U.S. Typ	U.S. Max
Text Page	0.0%			34.00	25.00	130.00
w/Graphics	0.0%			92.50	45.00	250.00
Hour	57.6%	38.70	35.00	42.68	40.00	100.00

TRANSPARENCY DESIGN (COLOR)						
$/per	Survey %	Average	Typical	U.S. Avg.	U.S. Typ	U.S. Max
Text Page	0.0%			27.50	30.00	45.00
w/Graphics	0.0%			32.50	40.00	45.00
Hour	39.4%	41.18	40.00	44.69	45.00	100.00

OTHER DESIGN						
$/per	Survey %	Average	Typical	U.S. Avg.	U.S. Typ	U.S. Max
Hour	9.1%	45.12	40.00	48.76	45.00	100.00

LASER PRINTER OUTPUT

GENERAL NOTES:
1. Some shops bill as $ set-up fee plus price per page.
2. Some shops bill as $/hr plus $/page.
3. A few shops price at $/hr (typically same price as other services).
4. Some laser printer output priced as $/job plus $/pg.

LASER PRINTING (Up to 300 dpi)						
$/per	Survey %	Average	Typical	U.S. Avg.	U.S. Typ	U.S. Max
8.5 x 11	18.2%	1.21	2.00	1.64	1.00	15.00
8.5 x 14	6.1%	2.00	2.00	1.95	3.00	10.00
11 x 17	0.0%			3.13	2.25	6.00
Cost Plus	3.0%	25.00	25.00	31.25	30.00	50.00
Minimum	2.7%	15.00	15.00	15.00	5.00	25.00

LASER PRINTING (400 dpi)						
$/per	Survey %	Average	Typical	U.S. Avg.	U.S. Typ	U.S. Max
8.5 x 11	6.1%	1.88	2.00	3.03	1.93	15.50
8.5 x 14	6.1%	2.00	2.00	2.71	2.00	6.00
11 x 17	0.0%			6.75	4.50	20.00
Cost Plus	0.0%			28.00	20.00	50.00
Minimum	2.7%	15.00	15.00	15.00	5.00	25.00

LASER PRINTING (600 dpi)						
$/per	Survey %	Average	Typical	U.S. Avg.	U.S. Typ	U.S. Max
8.5 x 11	9.1%	0.87	2.00	1.88	1.00	15.00
8.5 x 14	3.0%	2.00	2.00	1.88	1.95	4.46
11 x 17	0.0%			4.12	5.16	6.00
Cost Plus	0.0%			28.00	20.00	50.00

LASER PRINTING **(800dpi)**						
$/per	Survey %	Average	Typical	U.S. Avg.	U.S. Typ	U.S. Max
8.5 x 11	0.0%			2.75	2.00	12.00
8.5 x 14	0.0%			2.94	4.00	5.00
11 x 17	0.0%			6.00	6.00	6.00
Cost Plus	0.0%			28.00	20.00	50.00
Minimum	2.7%	15.00	15.00	15.00	5.00	25.00

LASER PRINTING **(1000 dpi)**						
$/per	Survey %	Average	Typical	U.S. Avg.	U.S. Typ	U.S. Max
8.5 x 11	3.0%	2.50	2.50	3.10	3.00	7.00
8.5 x 14	3.0%	2.75	2.75	4.06	4.00	7.00
11 x 17	0.0%			6.00	6.00	6.00
Cost Plus	0.0%			28.00	20.00	50.00
Minimum	2.7%	15.00	15.00	15.00	10.00	25.00

LASER PRINTING **(1200 dpi)**						
$/per	Survey %	Average	Typical	U.S. Avg.	U.S. Typ	U.S. Max
8.5 x 11	0.0%			2.89	3.00	6.00
8.5 x 14	0.0%			4.82	6.00	6.43
11 x 17	0.0%			7.18	6.00	13.25
Cost Plus	0.0%			28.00	20.00	50.00
Minimum	2.7%	15.00	15.00	15.00	10.00	25.00

FOR PREPRESS AND OTHER SERVICES (INCLUDING IMAGESETTING OUTPUT), REFER TO THE SECTION MARKED "NATIONAL."

Price Distribution
NORTH CENTRAL
IA, IL, IN, KS, MI, MN, MO, ND, NE, OH, SD, WI

FILE CONVERSION

GENERAL NOTE: Survey responses listed as $/minute were converted to $/hr.

BOOKS ON DISK

$/per	Survey %	Average	Typical	U.S. Avg.	U.S. Typ	U.S. Max
Disk	1.3%	3.00	3.00	10.57	10.00	25.00
Page	1.3%	5.00	5.00	6.00	5.50	10.00
Hour	8.0%	28.50	30.00	40.11	35.00	95.00
Minimum	0.0%			15.00	15.00	15.00

CD-ROM

$/per	Survey %	Average	Typical	U.S. Avg.	U.S. Typ	U.S. Max
Page	0.0%			8.00	8.00	8.00
Disk	0.0%			25.00	25.00	25.00
Hour	2.7%	32.50	32.50	48.00	43.00	85.00
Minimum	0.0%			70.00	70.00	125.00

CROSS PLATFORM

$/per	Survey %	Average	Typical	U.S. Avg.	U.S. Typ	U.S. Max
Page	0.0%			3.83	2.88	8.00
File	1.3%	10.00	10.00	7.85	9.00	20.00
Disk	8.0%	10.00	10.00	11.85	10.00	50.00
Hour	21.3%	46.56	45.00	46.31	45.00	100.00
Minimum	1.3%	15.00	15.00	14.25	12.50	35.00

DATABASE FILES

$/per	Survey %	Average	Typical	U.S. Avg.	U.S. Typ	U.S. Max
Record	0.1%			0.16	0.15	0.25
File	1.3%	10.00	10.00	7.02	10.00	20.00
Disk	0.0%			21.67	15.00	50.00
Hour	13.3%	48.50	60.00	42.46	40.50	100.00
Minimum	2.7%	20.00	20.00	22.50	20.00	35.00

DOCUMENT FILES

$/per	Survey %	Average	Typical	U.S. Avg	U.S. Typ	U.S. Max
K byte	0.0%			5.25	5.25	5.25
Page	0.0%			2.71	2.75	3.50
File	5.3%	8.75	10.00	8.38	10.00	15.00
Disk	1.3%	7.50	7.50	15.73	15.00	50.00
Hour	22.7%	39.41	30.00	41.23	35.00	100.00
Minimum	2.7%	20.00	20.00	21.00	15.00	35.00

DOCUMENTS ON DISK

$/per	Survey %	Average	Typical	U.S. Avg	U.S. Typ	U.S. Max
Page	0.0%			6.17	7.00	15.00
File	0.0%			12.00	15.00	15.00
Disk	0.0%			14.00	10.00	50.00
Hour	5.3%	38.75	35.00	38.77	35.00	75.00
Minimum	0.0%			12.50	13.00	15.00

FORMS CONVERSION

$/per	Survey %	Average	Typical	U.S. Avg	U.S. Typ	U.S. Max
Page	1.3%	200.00	200.00	187.18	190.00	200.00
File	0.0%			26.00	10.00	50.00
Disk	0.0%			15.00	10.00	25.00
Hour	5.3%	53.75	50.00	47.68	40.00	100.00
Minimum	0.0%			12.50	15.00	15.00

GRAPHIC FORMAT FILES

$/per	Survey %	Average	Typical	U.S. Avg	U.S. Typ	U.S. Max
K byte	0.0%			5.25	5.25	5.25
Page	0.0%			18.32	20.00	20.00
File	4.0%	7.50	7.50	8.50	5.88	20.00
Disk	0.0%			15.36	15.00	50.00
Hour	17.3%	45.00	35.00	44.32	40.00	100.00
Minimum	2.7%	20.00	20.00	19.17	15.00	35.00

MEDIA CONVERSION

$/per	Survey %	Average	Typical	U.S. Avg	U.S. Typ	U.S. Max
File	2.7%	17.50	17.00	15.00	12.50	25.00
Disk	8.0%	10.00	10.00	13.05	10.00	50.00
Hour	16.0%	46.67	45.00	48.64	45.00	100.00
Minimum	1.3%	15.00	15.00	13.75	15.00	15.00

PAGE LAYOUT FILES

$/per	Survey %	Average	Typical	U.S. Avg	U.S. Typ	U.S. Max
500 K byte	0.0%			15.00	15.00	15.00
Page	1.3%	15.00	15.00	37.50	37.50	60.00
File	2.7%	12.50	12.50	12.70	12.50	25.00
Disk	0.0%			19.25	15.00	50.00
Hour	18.7%	43.21	35.00	42.91	40.00	100.00
Minimum	2.7%	20.00	20.00	20.00	15.00	35.00

SPREADSHEET FILES

$/per	Survey %	Average	Typical	U.S. Avg.	U.S. Typ	U.S. Max
25 K byte	0.%			7.50	7.50	7.50
Page	0.0%			2.88	2.88	2.00
File	2.7%	7.50	7.50	12.30	10.88	25.00
Disk	0.0%			26.25	20.00	50.00
Hour	10.7%	45.00	60.00	40.98	40.00	100.00
Minimum	2.7%	20.00	20.00	22.50	20.00	35.00

VIDEO TAPE TRANSFER

$/per	Survey %	Average	Typical	U.S. Avg.	U.S. Typ	U.S. Max
Disk	0.0%			25.00	25.00	25.00
Per Hour	0.0%			48.33	45.00	75.00
Minimum	0.0%			15.00	15.00	15.00

WORD PROCESSOR FILE TO SGML

$/per	Survey %	Average	Typical	U.S. Avg.	U.S. Typ	U.S. Max
Disk	0.0%			25.00	25.00	25.00
Hour	1.3%	25.00	25.00	45.00	40.00	75.00
Minimum	0.0%			15.00	15.00	15.00

TEXT CREATION

GENERAL COPY WRITING

$/per	Survey %	Average	Typical	U.S. Avg.	U.S. Typ	U.S. Max
Line	0.0%			0.20	0.20	0.20
Page	2.6%	20.00	20.00	30.38	20.00	87.50
Hour	39.0%	37.37	30.00	41.43	35.00	300.00
Minimum	0.0%			19.00	15.00	35.00

NEWSLETTER COPY

$/per	Survey %	Average	Typical	U.S. Avg.	U.S. Typ	U.S. Max
Column	1.3%	10.95	10.00	10.48	10.50	11.00
Page	9.1%	32.14	20.00	40.96	40.00	125.00
Hour	36.4%	39.11	35.00	39.31	35.00	300.00
Minimum	0.0%			283.33	125.00	800.00

PUBLICITY / ADVERTISING COPY

$/per	Survey %	Average	Typical	U.S. Avg.	U.S. Typ	U.S. Max
Page	2.6%	27.50	28.00	40.31	40.00	100.00
Piece	0.0%			260.00	300.00	425.00
Hour	27.3%	43.86	35.00	43.56	38.00	300.00
Minimum	0.0%			19.00	15.00	35.00

RESUME WRITING

$/per	Survey %	Average	Typical	U.S. Avg.	U.S. Typ	U.S. Max
Page	15.6%	30.75	30.00	32.43	25.00	100.00
Hour	37.7%	34.48	30.00	38.11	35.00	300.00
Minimum	0.0%			110.00	65.00	300.00

TECHNICAL WRITING

$/per	Survey %	Average	Typical	U.S. Avg.	U.S. Typ	U.S. Max
Page	3.9%	40.27	35.00	53.54	35.00	300.00
Hour	22.1%	40.94	35.00	45.99	35.00	300.00
Minimum	0.0%			35.00	35.00	55.00

DATA INPUT / EDITING

DATA ENTRY / KEYBOARDING

$/per	Survey %	Average	Typical	U.S. Avg.	U.S. Typ	U.S. Max
Character	0.0%			0.02	0.02	0.02
Page	3.9%	10.33	8.00	11.32	10.00	50.00
Hour	56.4%	31.02	25.00	32.64	28.00	100.00
Minimum	0.0%			20.00	15.00	35.00

COPY EDITING

$/per	Survey %	Average	Typical	U.S. Avg.	U.S. Typ	U.S. Max
Word	0.0%			0.06	0.06	0.11
Page	3.9%	4.33	5.00	9.47	7.00	50.00
Hour	48.7%	35.45	20.00	36.58	30.00	100.00
Minimum	0.0%			20.00	15.00	35.00

CONTENT EDITING

$/per	Survey %	Average	Typical	U.S. Avg.	U.S. Typ	U.S. Max
Word	0.0%			0.11	0.11	0.11
Page	3.9%	4.00	5.00	5.33	5.00	50.00
Hour	39.7%	33.94	35.00	37.44	36.00	100.00
Minimum	0.0%			33.50	35.00	35.00

PROOF READING

$/per	Survey %	Average	Typical	U.S. Avg.	U.S. Typ	U.S. Max
Page	3.9%	3.33	3.00	6.71	5.00	50.00
Hour	52.6%	34.22	30.00	35.63	30.00	100.00
Minimum	0.0%			33.50	35.00	35.00

REWRITING

$/per	Survey %	Average	Typical	U.S. Avg.	U.S. Typ	U.S. Max
Word	0.0%			0.07	0.03	0.11
Line	0.0%			0.25	0.20	1.00
Page	2.6%	6.00	6.00	22.67	13.50	50.00
Hour	34.6%	33.59	20.00	38.81	35.00	100.00
Minimum	0.0%			35.00	35.00	35.00

INDEXING

$/per	Survey %	Average	Typical	U.S. Avg.	U.S. Typ	U.S. Max
Page	1.3%	5.00	5.00	2.80	2.00	5.00
Hour	19.2%	34.33	30.00	38.60	35.00	100.00
Minimum	0.0%			87.50	87.50	140.00

MODEM INPUT

$/per	Survey %	Average	Typical	U.S. Avg.	U.S. Typ	U.S. Max
Page	1.3%	5.00	5.00	3.33	3.00	5.00
File	0.0%			10.00	10.00	10.00
K bytes	0.0%			1.32	1.40	1.50
Disk	0.0%			8.33	5.00	25.00
Minute	0.0%			1.50	1.50	2.00
Hour	18.0%	39.29	30.00	41.62	38.00	100.00
Minimum	0.0%			12.50	12.50	15.00

TEXT FILE IMPORTING

$/per	Survey %	Average	Typical	U.S. Avg.	U.S. Typ	U.S. Max
Page	1.9%	5.00	5.00	14.60	5.00	50.00
File	0.0%			11.00	10.00	25.00
K bytes	0.0%			1.32	1.40	1.50
Disk	0.0%			10.00	10.00	15.00
Minute	0.0%			1.50	1.50	2.00
Hour	34.6%	34.96	25.00	39.10	35.00	100.00
Minimum	0.0%			21.25	22.00	35.00

TRANSCRIPTION

$/per	Survey %	Average	Typical	U.S. Avg.	U.S. Typ	U.S. Max
Line	0.0%			0.17	0.17	0.25
Page	1.9%	5.00	5.00	4.79	4.25	8.00
File	0.0%			10.57	10.57	25.00
Disk	0.0%			25.00	25.00	25.00
Hour	25.6%	28.10	30.00	31.64	30.00	75.00
Minimum	0.0%			25.00	25.00	35.00

TRANSLATION

$/per	Survey %	Average	Typical	U.S. Avg	U.S. Typ	U.S. Max
Word	0.0%			0.17	0.17	0.20
Page	1.9%	5.00	5.00	24.17	22.50	50.00
Hour	9.0%	35.71	30.00	44.49	40.00	150.00
Minimum	0.0%			35.00	35..00	35.00

TYPOGRAPHY (General)

$/per	Survey %	Average	Typical	U.S. Avg	U.S. Typ	U.S. Max
Line	1.9%	0.25	0.25	0.25	0.25	0.25
Page	6.4%	19.20	15.00	21.48	15.00	75.00
Hour	52.6%	41.01	25.00	39.27	35.00	100.00
Minimum	0.0%			18.83	15.00	35.00

TYPOGRAPHY (Spreadsheet)

$/per	Survey %	Average	Typical	U.S. Avg	U.S. Typ	U.S. Max
Line	0.0%			0.25	0.25	0.25
Page	5.1%	18.00	15.00	24.06	17.00	75.00
Hour	38.5%	43.73	40.00	41.47	36.00	150.00
Minimum	0.0%			35.00	35.00	35.00

WORD PROCESSSING

$/per	Survey %	Average	Typical	U.S. Avg	U.S. Typ	U.S. Max
Line	2.6%	0.10	0.10	0.13	0.10	0.20
Page	5.1%	9.50	10.00	8.67	8.25	25.00
Hour	47.4%	29.03	25.00	32.90	25.00	100.00
Minimum	0.0%			21.67	15.00	35.00

DATA MANAGEMENT

GENERAL NOTES:
1. Assume customer pays for cost of media extra.
2. On $/word, assume 2K words per page.
3. Per file cost assumed to be for 1 year.
4. Assume $/file same as $/image.

ARCHIVING SERVICE

$/per	Survey %	Average	Typical	U.S. Avg	U.S. Typ	U.S. Max
Page	0.0%			7.50	7.50	7.50
File	3.9%	1.67	5.00	9.63	15.00	25.00
Tape	3.9%	16.67	20.00	37.50	20.00	150.00
Hour	3.9%	43.33	25.00	46.05	40.00	95.00
Minimum	0.0%			14.17	10.00	25.00

IMAGE MANAGEMENT

$/per	Survey %	Average	Typical	U.S. Avg.	U.S. Typ	U.S. Max
Page	0.0%			6.50	5.50	10.00
File	0.0%			16.67	15.00	50.00
Disk	3.9%	16.67	20.00	30.00	30.00	50.00
Hour	2.6%	12.50	12.50	44.81	40.00	110.00
Minimum	0.0%			14.17	10.00	25.00

NOTE: Assume $/.file same as $/image.

TEXT MANAGEMENT

$/per	Survey %	Average	Typical	U.S. Avg.	U.S. Typ	U.S. Max
Page	0.0%			8.67	6.00	15.00
File	0.0%			16.67	15.00	50.00
Disk	3.9%	16.67	20.00	23.33	15.00	50.00
Hour	3.9%	16.67	25.00	44.51	35.00	95.00
Minimum	0.0%			14.17	10.00	25.00

IMAGING SERVICES

DOCUMENT CAPTURE

$/per	Survey %	Average	Typical	U.S. Avg.	U.S. Typ	U.S. Max
Page	0.0%			3.65	3.00	7.50
File	1.3%	5.00	5.00	6.50	5.00	10.00
Hour	1.3%	35.00	35.00	39.41	35.00	95.00
Minimum	1.3%	25.00	25.00	16.25	16.25	25.00

DOCUMENT RETRIEVAL

$/per	Survey %	Average	Typical	U.S. Avg.	U.S. Typ	U.S. Max
Page	0.0%			1.50	1.50	2.00
File	2.6%	2.75	2.75	5.03	5.00	10.00
Hour	1.3%	50.00	50.00	38.82	39.00	85.00
Minimum	1.3%	25.00	25.00	16.25	16.25	25.00

GRAPHICS FILE IMPORTING

$/per	Survey %	Average	Typical	U.S. Avg.	U.S. Typ	U.S. Max
File	2.6%	5.25	5.00	6.98	5.00	15.00
Disk	0.0%			5.00	5.00	5.00
Hour	19.5%	39.33	35.00	43.35	36.00	100.00
Minimum	1.3%	25.00	25.00	14.17	14.17	35.00

PHOTO CD-ROM IMPORTING

$/per	Survey %	Average	Typical	U.S. Avg.	U.S. Typ	U.S. Max
Image	1.3%	10.00	10.00	10.02	7.25	45.00
Stock Fee	0.0%			75.00	75.00	75.00
Hour	3.9%	28.33	25.00	48.60	45.00	100.00
Minimum	1.3%	25.00	25.00	16.25	15.00	25.00

SCANNING (B&W Grey Scale)

$/per	Survey %	Average	Typical	U.S. Avg.	U.S. Typ	U.S. Max
Hour	18.2%	44.50	50.00	42.82	40.00	100.00
75-200 dpi	7.8%	6.58	6.50	10.10	9.00	75.00
300-400 dpi	35.1%	12.26	10.00	11.93	10.00	75.00
600-800 dpi	10.4%	13.25	12.00	13.51	11.00	75.00
1200 dpi	1.3%	15.00	15.00	20.20	12.00	75.00
2400 dpi	1.3%	30.00	30.00	36.86	30.00	75.00

SCANNING (B&W Line Art)

$/per	Survey %	Average	Typical	U.S. Avg.	U.S. Typ	U.S. Max
Hour	18.2%	40.21	48.00	40.94	40.00	100.00
75-200 dpi	7.8%	8.50	8.00	10.59	9.00	75.00
300-400 dpi	31.2%	9.62	8.00	11.92	10.00	75.00
600-800 dpi	9.1%	12.86	10.00	12.51	10.00	75.00
1200 dpi	2.6%	20.00	20.00	15.59	11.00	75.00
2400 dpi	1.3%	25.00	25.00	35.75	27.50	75.00
Per K	0.0%			51.67	50.00	75.00

SCANNING (B&W Photo)

$/per	Survey %	Average	Typical	U.S. Avg.	U.S. Typ	U.S. Max
Hour	13.0%	45.50	60.00	45.16	40.00	100.00
75-200 dpi	3.9%	8.33	8.00	12.28	10.00	75.00
300-400 dpi	24.7%	11.72	10.00	13.92	12.40	75.00
600-800 dpi	9.1%	13.86	12.00	14.79	12.60	75.00
1200 dpi	1.3%	15.00	15.00	19.88	17.50	75.00
2400 dpi	2.6%	27.50	27.50	35.56	31.00	75.00
Per K	0.0%			62.50	62.50	75.00

SCANNING (Color Illustration)

$/per	Survey %	Average	Typical	U.S. Avg.	U.S. Typ	U.S. Max
Hour	7.8%	47.50	60.00	49.23	50.00	125.00
75-200 dpi	3.9%	6.67	6.00	19.08	15.00	75.00
300-400 dpi	11.7%	24.00	20.00	21.03	19.00	82.00
600-800 dpi	6.5%	13.20	10.00	22.36	21.50	75.00
1200 dpi	1.3%	15.00	15.00	26.47	23.00	75.00
2400 dpi	2.6%	30.00	30.00	46.22	50.00	75.00

SCANNING (Color Photo)						
$/per	Survey %	Average	Typical	U.S. Avg.	U.S. Typ	U.S. Max
Hour	9.1%	49.29	60.00	49.23	50.00	125.00
75-200 dpi	2.6%	7.00	7.00	20.44	15.00	75.00
300-400 dpi	14.3%	22.00	20.00	20.97	17.75	82.00
600-800 dpi	7.8%	12.67	10.00	19.75	15.00	75.00
1200 dpi	1.3%	15.00	15.00	30.13	30.00	75.00
2400 dpi	2.6%	30.00	30.00	61.54	60.00	137.00

SCANNING (HIGH END) (Loose Scan)				
$/per	Survey %	U.S. Avg.	U.S. Typ	U.S. Max
2 x 3	0.1%	13.33	10.00	25.00
3 x 5	0.1%	11.25	10.00	20.00
4 x 5	0.1%	16.00	10.00	33.00
5 x 7	0.1%	18.00	10.00	37.00
5.5 x 8.5	0.1%	17.33	10.00	39.00
6 x 9	0.1%	24.67	15.00	49.00
8 x 10	0.1%	41.60	50.00	70.00
10 x 12	0.1%	47.80	60.00	84.00
11 x 14	0.1%	81.67	70.00	105.00
12 x 18	0.1%	90.67	80.00	122.00
16 x 20	0.1%	162.00	162.00	162.00
20 x 24	0.1%	199.00	199.00	199.00
Hour	0.1%	47.00	45.00	60.00

SCANNING (HIGH END) (Drum Scan)				
$/per	Survey %	U.S. Avg.	U.S. Typ	U.S. Max
2 x 3	0.1%	56..92	54.25	71.50
4 x 5	0.1%	57.21	55.00	94.50
5 x 7	0.1%	65.75	70.00	106.00
6 x 8	0.1%	103.13	102.50	117.50
6 x 9	0.1%	57.00	45.00	85.00
8 x 10	0.1%	51.25	50.00	60.00
10 x 12	0.1%	58.33	60.00	60.00
11 x 14	0.1%	71.25	72.50	75.00
12 x 18	0.1%	86.67	85.00	100.00
24 x 27	0.1%	600.00	600.00	600.00

SCANNING (HIGH END) (High Res Scan to Disk)				
$/per	Survey %	U.S. Avg.	U.S. Typ	U.S. Max
2 x 3	0.1%	20..50	19.50	25.00
4 x 5	0.1%	26.17	27.50	30.00
5 x 7	0.1%	34.00	35.00	41.00
6 x 9	0.1%	39.80	39.00	50.00

SCANNING (HIGH END) (High Res Scan to Disk)				
$/per	Survey %	U.S. Avg.	U.S. Typ	U.S. Max
8 x 10	0.1%	45.50	45.00	60.00
10 x 12	0.1%	56.83	59.00	70.00
11 x 14	0.1%	65.08	64.00	89.00
12 x 18	0.1%	78.90	75.00	100.00
16 x 20	0.1%	96.33	99.00	130.00
20 x 24	0.1%	128.00	134.00	160.00
24 x 27	0.1%	156.25	156.25	200.00

SCANNING (Transparency)						
$/per	Survey %	Average	Typical	U.S. Avg.	U.S. Typ	U.S. Max
Each	3.9%	8.33	10.00	18.70	16.00	45.00
Hour	2.6%	55.00	55.00	65.29	55.00	137.00

SCANNING (Slide)						
$/per	Survey %	Average	Typical	U.S. Avg.	U.S. Typ	U.S. Max
Each	3.9%	10.00	10.00	23.00	16.99	65.00
Hour	2.6%	55.00	55.00	68.42	55.00	137.00

COLOR CORRECTION						
$/per	Survey %	Average	Typical	U.S. Avg.	U.S. Typ	U.S. Max
Hour	5.2%	65.00	80.00	65.80	50.00	300.00

IMAGE EDITING						
$/per	Survey %	Average	Typical	U.S. Avg.	U.S. Typ	U.S. Max
Each	0.0%			20.75	15.00	50.00
Hour	14.3%	42.73	40.00	55.47	45.00	300.00

IMAGE ENHANCEMENT						
$/per	Survey %	Average	Typical	U.S. Avg.	U.S. Typ	U.S. Max
Hour	11.7%	50.56	50.00	57.60	50.00	300.00

RETOUCHING						
$/per	Survey %	Average	Typical	U.S. Avg.	U.S. Typ	U.S. Max
Each	0.0%			27.67	40.00	50.00
Hour	27.3%	52.86	45.00	58.60	50.00	300.00
Minimum	1.3%	25.00	25.00	26.08	25.00	35.00

TEXT SCAN (OCR)						
$/per	Survey %	Average	Typical	U.S. Avg.	U.S. Typ	U.S. Max
Page	16.9%	7.63	8.00	7.82	5.00	95.00

TEXT SCAN (OCR)

$/per	Survey %	Average	Typical	U.S. Avg.	U.S. Typ	U.S. Max
Hour	11.7%	27.78	30.00	36.33	30.00	75.00
Minimum	0.0%			19.08	16.90	35.00

NOTE:

1. Prices assume spell check conducted on scanned text.

2. Assumes 2 Kb per page, so $1/Kb response incorporated as $2/page.

NEGATIVE CREATION

$/per	Survey %	Average	Typical	U.S. Avg.	U.S. Typ	U.S. Max
Each	0.0%			22.00	22.00	40.00
Hour	0.0%			56.71	56.71	100.00
Minimum	1.3%	25.00	25.00	16.67	16.67	25.00

DESIGN SERVICES

ANNOUNCEMENTS

$/per	Survey %	Average	Typical	U.S. Avg.	U.S. Typ	U.S. Max
Text Page	3.9%	19.00	18.00	37.05	24.00	250.00
w/Graphics	2.6%	29.00	28.00	65.36	36.50	500.00
Hour	34.6%	44.04	40.00	42.21	40.00	100.00

ANNUAL REPORTS
(1C, 2C, Up To Letter Size Pages)

$/per	Survey %	Average	Typical	U.S. Avg.	U.S. Typ	U.S. Max
Text	2.6%	17.50	18.00	114.75	62.50	1000.00
w/Graphics	1.3%	30.00	30.00	222.00	100.00	7680.00
Hour	41.0%	42.34	40.00	46.58	45.00	100.00

ANNUAL REPORTS
(3C, 4C, Larger Size Pages)

$/per	Survey %	Average	Typical	U.S. Avg.	U.S. Typ	U.S. Max
Text	1.3%	15.00	15.00	214.55	100.00	1500.00
w/Graphics	0.0%			422.50	175.00	11520.00
Hour	39.7%	42.10	40.00	46.34	45.00	100.00

BAR CODING

$/per	Survey %	Average	Typical	U.S. Avg.	U.S. Typ	U.S. Max
Each	1.3%	25.00	25.00	13.25	11.00	150.00
Page	0.0%			29.00	29.00	50.00
Hour	15.4%	44.58	45.00	47.83	45.00	100.00

BOOKLETS

$/per	Survey %	Average	Typical	U.S. Avg.	U.S. Typ	U.S. Max
Text Page	5.1%	22.00	25.00	48.40	30.00	500.00
w/Graphics	5.1%	36.25	25.00	110.53	50.00	650.00
Hour	57.7%	44.13	40.00	43.87	25.00	100.00

BOOK COVERS

$/per	Survey %	Average	Typical	U.S. Avg.	U.S. Typ	U.S. Max
Text	3.9%	43.33	28.00	143.10	75.00	500.00
w/Graphics	1.3%	38.00	38.00	403.36	300.00	1800.00
Hour	38.5%	44.67	40.00	47.83	45.00	120.00

BOOK BODY

$/per	Survey %	Average	Typical	U.S. Avg.	U.S. Typ	U.S. Max
Text Page	3.9%	25.00	25.00	26.65	20.00	75.00
w/Graphics	2.6%	40.00	40.00	41.11	25.00	85.00
Hour	42.3%	41.36	45.00	44.26	40.00	100.00

BOOK JACKETS

$/per	Survey %	Average	Typical	U.S. Avg.	U.S. Typ	U.S. Max
Text	0.0%			161.54	175.00	500.00
w/Graphics	0.0%			491.00	325.00	1000.00
Hour	34.6%	45.00	45.00	48.63	45.00	120.00

BROCHURE
(1C, 2C, Up To Letter Size Sheet)

$/per	Survey %	Average	Typical	U.S. Avg.	U.S. Typ	U.S. Max
Text Page	7.7%	78.33	25.00	72.59	47.50	500.00
w/Graphics	6.4%	89.50	37.50	156.74	82.50	750.00
Hour	56.4%	44.11	40.00	42.85	40.00	125.00

BROCHURE
(3C, 4C, Larger Size Sheet)

$/per	Survey %	Average	Typical	U.S. Avg.	U.S. Typ	U.S. Max
Text Page	2.6%	125.00	150.00	123.79	60.00	1000.00
w/Graphics	2.6%	180.00	210.00	227.71	100.00	1500.00
Hour	57.7%	43.13	40.00	44.17	40.00	125.00

BULLETIN

$/per	Survey %	Average	Typical	U.S. Avg.	U.S. Typ	U.S. Max
Text Page	1.3%	25.00	25.00	32.75	25.00	150.00
w/Graphics	0.0%			47.81	35.00	200.00
Hour	32.1%	43.76	40.00	42.36	40.00	100.00

BUSINESS CARDS

$/per	Survey %	Average	Typical	U.S. Avg.	U.S. Typ	U.S. Max
Text Card	11.5%	22.56	20.00	38.81	25.00	500.00
w/Graphics	6.4%	24.20	25.00	91.70	40.00	1000.00
Hour	53.9%	42.48	40.00	43.19	40.00	150.00

BUSINESS REPLY CARDS

$/per	Survey %	Average	Typical	U.S. Avg.	U.S. Typ	U.S. Max
Text Card	1.3%	35.00	35.00	34.32	31.50	150.00
w/Graphics	0.0%			67.50	35.00	250.00
Hour	44.9%	44.26	40.00	43.79	40.00	100.00

BUSINESS LETTERS

$/per	Survey %	Average	Typical	U.S. Avg.	U.S. Typ	U.S. Max
Text Page	9.0%	10.25	10.00	17.23	12.25	90.00
w/Graphics	3.9%	19.33	18.00	27.08	18.75	100.00
Hour	43.6%	41.59	35.00	39.38	35.00	100.00

CALENDARS

$/per	Survey %	Average	Typical	U.S. Avg.	U.S. Typ	U.S. Max
Text Page	1.3%	20.00	20.00	82.50	50.00	500.00
w/Graphics	1.3%	20.00	20.00	53.18	45.00	150.00
Hour	38.5%	42.63	40.00	43.77	40.00	100.00

CALLIGRAPHY

$/per	Survey %	Average	Typical	U.S. Avg.	U.S. Typ	U.S. Max
Line	0.0%			1.00	1.00	60.00
Page	2.6%	15.00	20.00	40.00	35.00	100.00
Hour	20.5%	43.44	40.00	45.50	40.00	175.00

CARDS (FOLD-OVER)

$/per	Survey %	Average	Typical	U.S. Avg.	U.S. Typ	U.S. Max
Text Card	3.9%	23.33	20.00	31.45	25.00	60.00
w/Graphics	1.3%	25.00	25.00	65.47	46.40	250.00
Hour	24.4%	46.00	50.00	43.63	40.00	100.00

CARDS (ROLODEX)

$/per	Survey %	Average	Typical	U.S. Avg.	U.S. Typ	U.S. Max
Text Card	5.1%	16.88	21.00	37.34	25.00	150.00
w/Graphics	2.6%	36.50	36.00	63.00	48.00	250.00
Hour	23.1%	46.06	45.00	44.94	41.00	100.00

CARTOONS

$/per	Survey %	Average	Typical	U.S. Avg.	U.S. Typ	U.S. Max
Each	0.0%			119.29	60.00	400.00
Page	0.0%			163.33	65.00	400.00
Hour	21.8%	47.94	45.00	48.15	45.00	90.00

CATALOGS

$/per	Survey %	Average	Typical	U.S. Avg.	U.S. Typ	U.S. Max
Text Page	5.1%	17.00	15.00	69.03	40.00	500.00
w/Graphics	2.6%	19.00	20.00	129.05	67.50	1000.00
Hour	48.7%	42.87	45.00	45.68	45.00	125.00

CERTIFICATES

$/per	Survey %	Average	Typical	U.S. Avg.	U.S. Typ	U.S. Max
Text	5.1%	15.13	16.00	23.56	16.25	125.00
w/Graphics	3.9%	20.00	20.00	35.07	25.00	150.00
Hour	29.5%	44.96	40.00	42.15	40.00	100.00

CHARTS / DIAGRAMS

$/per	Survey %	Average	Typical	U.S. Avg.	U.S. Typ	U.S. Max
Text	2.6%	35.00	35.00	36.19	32.50	150.00
w/Graphics	1.3%	50.00	50.00	53.14	47.50	150.00
Hour	51.3%	44.84	45.00	44.29	40.00	100.00

COMIC BOOKS

$/per	Survey %	Average	Typical	U.S. Avg.	U.S. Typ	U.S. Max
Each Page	1.3%	35.00	35.00	65.00	60.00	100.00
Hour	10.3%	44.38	45.00	47.12	50.00	80.00

COMIC STRIPS

$/per	Survey %	Average	Typical	U.S. Avg.	U.S. Typ	U.S. Max
Each Strip	1.3%	25.00	25.00	38.33	30.00	60.00
Hour	10.3%	44.38	45.00	46.78	50.00	80.00

COMPUTER GENERATED ART

$/per	Survey %	Average	Typical	U.S. Avg.	U.S. Typ	U.S. Max
Page	1.3%	24.00	24.00	121.40	50.00	500.00
Hour	33.3%	44.38	40.00	46.70	42.00	175.00

CUSTOM DISPLAYS

$/per	Survey %	Average	Typical	U.S. Avg.	U.S. Typ	U.S. Max
Text	0.0%			192.14	60.00	1000.00
w/Graphics	0.0%			265.71	100.00	1000.00
Hour	20.5%	43.69	45.00	48.95	45.00	100.00

DATABASE DESIGN

$/per	Survey %	Average	Typical	U.S. Avg.	U.S. Typ	U.S. Max
Text	0.0%			38.33	30.00	60.00
w/Graphics	0.0%			43.33	40.00	60.00
Hour	15.4%	39.17	30.00	42.45	41.00	80.00

DIGITAL SLIDE PRESENTATIONS

$/per	Survey %	Average	Typical	U.S. Avg.	U.S. Typ	U.S. Max
Text	2.6%	22.50	22.00	27.13	27.50	60.00
w/Graphics	1.3%	20.00	20.00	35.00	32.50	60.00
Hour	16.7%	46.54	45.00	45.81	45.00	100.00

DIRECT MAIL PACKAGES

$/per	Survey %	Average	Typical	U.S. Avg.	U.S. Typ	U.S. Max
Text	1.3%	35.00	35.00	298.46	60.00	1500.00
w/Graphics	0.0%			413.50	65.00	2000.00
Hour	33.3%	45.73	45.00	47.05	45.00	100.00

DIRECTORY

$/per	Survey %	Average	Typical	U.S. Avg.	U.S. Typ	U.S. Max
Text	5.1%	24.25	25.00	38.72	30.00	150.00
w/Graphics	5.1%	25.00	25.00	73.53	40.00	500.00
Hour	43.6%	44.00	40.00	43.08	40.00	125.00

DISPLAY ADVERTISING

$/per	Survey %	Average	Typical	U.S. Avg.	U.S. Typ	U.S. Max
Text	5.1%	50.00	25.00	109.28	30.00	1000.00
w/Graphics	5.1%	87.50	35.00	304.64	45.00	2500.00
Hour	49.5%	45.26	45.00	48.23	45.00	115.00

DISPLAY EXHIBITS

$/per	Survey %	Average	Typical	U.S. Avg.	U.S. Typ	U.S. Max
Text Panel	0.0%			858.57	90.00	5000.00
w/Graphics	0.0%			896.67	100.00	5000.00
Hour	19.2%	44.93	45.00	51.43	50.00	115.00

DOOR HANGERS

$/per	Survey %	Average	Typical	U.S. Avg.	U.S. Typ	U.S. Max
Text	2.6%	20.00	20.00	42.46	25.00	250.00
w/Graphics	2.6%	35.00	35.00	87.50	35.00	500.00
Hour	24.4%	48.11	45.00	47.19	45.00	100.00

DRAFTING

$/per	Survey %	Average	Typical	U.S. Avg.	U.S. Typ	U.S. Max
Page	1.3%	25.00	25.00	45.00	45.00	60.00
Hour	11.5%	43.33	40.00	46.62	45.00	100.00

FINANCIAL DOCUMENTS

$/per	Survey %	Average	Typical	U.S. Avg.	U.S. Typ	U.S. Max
Text Page	2.6%	17.50	25.00	45.33	33.00	150.00
w/Graphics	0.0%			92.00	60.00	150.00
Hour	28.2%	47.45	50.00	47.20	45.00	125.00

FLYERS

$/per	Survey %	Average	Typical	U.S. Avg.	U.S. Typ	U.S. Max
Text Page	15.4%	29.00	25.00	39.21	25.00	325.00
w/Graphics	7.7%	33.33	35.00	66.84	35.00	325.00
Hour	59.0%	41.76	40.00	42.22	40.00	100.00

FORMS

$/per	Survey %	Average	Typical	U.S. Avg.	U.S. Typ	U.S. Max
Text Page	7.7%	25.00	25.00	52.60	30.00	750.00
w/Graphics	2.6%	30.00	35.00	81.67	37.50	10000.00
Hour	50.00%	42.97	40.00	41.75	40.00	125.00

HANDBOOKS

$/per	Survey %	Average	Typical	U.S. Avg.	U.S. Typ	U.S. Max
Text Page	1.3%	25.00	25.00	38.22	25.00	150.00
w/Graphics	0.0%			62.46	35.00	250.00
Hour	47.4%	44.57	45.00	43.53	40.00	100.00

INSERTS

$/per	Survey %	Average	Typical	U.S. Avg.	U.S. Typ	U.S. Max
Text Page	1.3%	25.00	25.00	70.58	27.50	1000.00
w/Graphics	0.0%			193.50	35.00	2500.00
Hour	47.4%	45.24	45.00	43.99	40.00	100.00

INVITATIONS

$/per	Survey %	Average	Typical	U.S. Avg.	U.S. Typ	U.S. Max
Text	5.1%	25.63	25.00	35.01	25.00	250.00
w/Graphics	0.0%			73.16	35.00	750.00
Hour	52.6%	43.68	40.00	41.85	40.00	100.00

LABELS (Custom)

$/per	Survey %	Average	Typical	U.S. Avg.	U.S. Typ	U.S. Max
Text	2.6%	45.50	45.00	40.06	20.00	250.00
w/Graphics	1.3%	75.00	75.00	121.16	55.00	600.00
Hour	29.9%	42.35	35.00	43.55	40.00	100.00

LARGE FORMAT GRAPHICS

$/per	Survey %	Average	Typical	U.S. Avg.	U.S. Typ	U.S. Max
Text Page	0.0%			40.00	37.50	45.00
w/Graphics	0.0%			71.00	70.00	85.00
Hour	15.6%	43.75	30.00	47.95	45.00	90.00

LETTERHEAD & ENVELOPES

$/per	Survey %	Average	Typical	U.S. Avg.	U.S. Typ	U.S. Max
Text	7.8%	32.00	18.00	59.65	25.00	750.00
w/Graphics	6.5%	44.50	45.00	136.48	40.00	1000.00
Hour	63.6%	41.45	40.00	43.60	40.00	150.00

LINE ART & GENERAL ILLUSTRATIONS

$/per	Survey %	Average	Typical	U.S. Avg.	U.S. Typ	U.S. Max
Text Page	0.0%			64.17	47.50	135.00
w/Graphics	1.3%	17.00	20.00	221.89	100.00	1000.00
Hour	45.5%	42.97	40.00	46.24	43.50	115.00

LITIGATION GRAPHICS

$/per	Survey %	Average	Typical	U.S. Avg.	U.S. Typ	U.S. Max
Text Page	0.0%			75.00	75.00	75.00
w/Graphics	0.0%			100.00	100.00	100.00
Hour	13.0%	38.00	35.00	50.13	45.00	200.00

LOGOS

$/per	Survey %	Average	Typical	U.S. Avg.	U.S. Typ	U.S. Max
Each	6.5%	144.59	62.50	281.23	200.00	2000.00
Hour	61.0%	43.86	40.00	46.02	45.00	125.00

LOGOTYPE

$/per	Survey %	Average	Typical	U.S. Avg.	U.S. Typ	U.S. Max
Page	1.3%	71.00	75.00	304.36	300.00	1000.00
Hour	45.5%	47.90	45.00	48.68	45.00	125.00

MAGAZINES

$/per	Survey %	Average	Typical	U.S. Avg.	U.S. Typ	U.S. Max
Text Page	3.9%	35.74	40.00	60.49	35.00	250.00
w/Graphics	3.9%	40.00	45.00	90.89	40.00	500.00
Hour	31.2%	40.83	40.00	45.91	45.00	125.00

NOTES:
1. Multiple page prices converted to $/page.
2. Other prices noted for magazine design: $500 setup; $1,000 ea.

MAILERS						
$/per	Survey %	Average	Typical	U.S. Avg.	U.S. Typ	U.S. Max
Text Page	1.3%	5.00	5.00	64.08	25.00	500.00
w/Graphics	0.0%			82.36	40.00	500.00
Hour	29.9%	43.00	40.00	46.11	42.00	100.00

MANUALS						
$/per	Survey %	Average	Typical	U.S. Avg.	U.S. Typ	U.S. Max
Text Page	5.2%	25.50	30.00	42.06	17.50	500.00
w/Graphics	2.6%	37.50	37.50	58.10	30.00	500.00
Hour	63.6%	40.29	35.00	42.63	40.00	100.00

MAPS (1C, 2C, Letter Size)						
$/per	Survey %	Average	Typical	U.S. Avg.	U.S. Typ	U.S. Max
Simple	0.0%			76.25	70.00	250.00
Complex	1.3%	37.50	37.50	206.14	75.00	600.00
Hour	32.5%	46.68	45.00	46.90	45.00	100.00

MAPS (4C, Larger Than Letter Size)						
$/per	Survey %	Average	Typical	U.S. Avg.	U.S. Typ	U.S. Max
Simple	0.0%			168.75	72.50	500.00
Complex	0.0%			490.71	300.00	1600.00
Hour	28.6%	48.86	45.00	48.08	45.00	100.00

MARKETING PLANS						
$/per	Survey %	Average	Typical	U.S. Avg.	U.S. Typ	U.S. Max
Text Page	0.0%			59.00	10.00	250.00
w/Graphics	0.0%			182.67	40.00	500.00
Hour	23.4%	44.39	40.00	47.80	45.00	100.00

MEMO PADS						
$/per	Survey %	Average	Typical	U.S. Avg.	U.S. Typ	U.S. Max
Text	3.9%	14.50	16.00	20.14	14.50	100.00
w/Graphics	1.3%	10.00	10.00	31.79	17.50	150.00
Hour	31.2%	42.67	40.00	43.94	40.00	100.00

MENUS						
$/per	Survey %	Average	Typical	U.S. Avg.	U.S. Typ	U.S. Max
Text Page	5.2%	32.50	30.00	75.65	35.00	500.00
w/Graphics	2.6%	45.00	45.00	125.25	45.00	1000.00
Hour	44.2%	41.88	35.00	44.35	40.00	150.00
Minimum	0.6	300.0	300.0	233.75	200.00	500.00

NEWSLETTERS

$/per	Survey %	Average	Typical	U.S. Avg.	U.S. Typ	U.S. Max
Text Page	9.1%	60.21	45.00	62.86	45.00	200.00
w/Graphics	6.5%	68.00	45.00	76.16	50.00	200.00
Hour	70.1%	41.35	40.00	42.97	40.00	160.00

NOTEPADS

$/per	Survey %	Average	Typical	U.S. Avg.	U.S. Typ	U.S. Max
Text	5.2%	22.75	16.00	32.28	25.00	100.00
w/Graphics	3.9%	31.00	28.00	41.37	35.00	150.00
Hour	44.2%	43.21	40.00	43.72	40.00	100.00

PACKAGING

$/per	Survey %	Average	Typical	U.S. Avg.	U.S. Typ	U.S. Max
Text	1.3%	45.00	45.00	276.00	100.00	1000.00
w/Graphics	1.3%	45.00	45.00	478.18	250.00	2500.00
Hour	32.5%	47.16	50.00	51.64	50.00	150.00

PEN RULER

$/per	Survey %	Average	Typical	U.S. Avg.	U.S. Typ	U.S. Max
Page	1.3%	45.00	45.00	45.00	45.00	45.00
Hour	20.8%	47.50	45.00	48.81	50.00	85.00

PERIODICAL (OTHER)

$/per	Survey %	Average	Typical	U.S. Avg.	U.S. Typ	U.S. Max
Text Page	2.6%	33.00	33.00	36.00	25.00	150.00
w/Graphics	2.6%	37.50	37.50	58.00	35.00	250.00
Hour	26.0%	46.20	45.00	46.86	45.00	125.00

POINT-OF-PURCHASE DISPLAYS

$/per	Survey %	Average	Typical	U.S. Avg.	U.S. Typ	U.S. Max
Text Page	0.0%			650.00	600.00	1000.00
w/Graphics	0.0%			800.00	800.00	1000.00
Hour	14.3%	41.27	40.00	50.15	50.00	100.00

POST CARDS

$/per	Survey %	Average	Typical	U.S. Avg.	U.S. Typ	U.S. Max
Text Page	9.1%	22.50	20.00	45.18	20.00	400.00
w/Graphics	7.8%	26.67	30.00	64.31	30.00	500.00
Hour	50.6%	41.77	35.00	42.38	40.00	100.00

POSTERS

$/per	Survey %	Average	Typical	U.S. Avg.	U.S. Typ	U.S. Max
Text Page	5.2%	38.75	45.00	123.67	50.00	500.00
w/Graphics	2.6%	60.00	60.00	259.71	250.00	1000.00
Hour	46.8%	42.06	40.00	45.60	45.00	100.00

PRESENTATION MATERIALS

$/per	Survey %	Average	Typical	U.S. Avg.	U.S. Typ	U.S. Max
Text Page	2.6%	30.00	30.00	27.65	20.00	100.00
w/Graphics	2.6%	31.00	31.00	44.38	25.00	180.00
Hour	53.3%	44.54	45.00	45.04	45.00	100.00

PRICE LISTS

$/per	Survey %	Average	Typical	U.S. Avg.	U.S. Typ	U.S. Max
Text Page	6.5%	29.00	30.00	40.63	35.00	150.00
w/Graphics	3.9%	33.33	30.00	51.79	40.00	160.00
Hour	55.8%	40.14	35.00	42.68	40.00	100.00

PRINT ADS

$/per	Survey %	Average	Typical	U.S. Avg.	U.S. Typ	U.S. Max
Text	9.1%	55.00	45.00	107.09	45.00	1000.00
w/Graphics	7.8%	85.83	80.00	179.74	80.00	1100.00
Hour	50.7%	40.94	40.00	44.84	40.00	100.00

PROCEDURE GUIDES

$/per	Survey %	Average	Typical	U.S. Avg.	U.S. Typ	U.S. Max
Text Page	1.3%	15.00	15.00	60.00	15.00	300.00
w/Graphics	1.3%	15.00	15.00	93.21	25.00	500.00
Hour	27.3%	40.90	30.00	45.67	45.00	100.00

PRODUCT LITERATURE

$/per	Survey %	Average	Typical	U.S. Avg.	U.S. Typ	U.S. Max
Text Page	2.6%	35.00	35.00	67.97	30.00	500.00
w/Graphics	3.9%	33.67	45.00	118.81	40.00	1000.00
Hour	41.6%	41.84	40.00	45.43	42.00	100.00

PRODUCT SPECIFICATION SHEETS

$/per	Survey %	Average	Typical	U.S. Avg.	U.S. Typ	U.S. Max
Text Page	1.3%	25.00	25.00	70.95	25.00	500.00
w/Graphics	0.0%			168.89	35.00	1000.00
Hour	22.1%	42.00	30.00	46.44	45.00	100.00

PROGRAMS

$/per	Survey %	Average	Typical	U.S. Avg.	U.S. Typ	U.S. Max
Text Page	2.6%	17.50	17.50	43.92	25.00	200.00
w/Graphics	0.0%			95.94	35.00	500.00
Hour	26.0%	45.20	45.00	46.61	45.00	150.00

PUBLICATIONS (OTHER)

$/per	Survey %	Average	Typical	U.S. Avg.	U.S. Typ	U.S. Max
Text Page	1.3%	45.00	45.00	46.00	30.00	150.00
w/Graphics	1.3%	45.00	45.00	87.73	35.00	500.00
Hour	42.9%	43.00	40.00	44.63	40.00	125.00

RECORD BOOKS

$/per	Survey %	Average	Typical	U.S. Avg.	U.S. Typ	U.S. Max
Text Page	1.3%	45.00	45.00	20.67	15.00	45.00
w/Graphics	1.3%	45.00	45.00	35.00	35.00	45.00
Hour	22.1%	42.65	40.00	46.63	45.00	80.00

RESUMES

$/per	Survey %	Average	Typical	U.S. Avg.	U.S. Typ	U.S. Max
Each	22.1%	32.24	25.00	31.21	25.00	150.00
Page	23.4%	32.11	30.00	31.52	30.00	150.00
Hour	66.2%	38.41	30.00	40.96	40.00	150.00

RULERS

$/per	Survey %	Average	Typical	U.S. Avg.	U.S. Typ	U.S. Max
Each	0.0%			250.00	375.00	500.00
Hour	11.7%	43.22	40.00	49.08	50.00	100.00

SALES PRESENTATIONS

$/per	Survey %	Average	Typical	U.S. Avg.	U.S. Typ	U.S. Max
Text Page	2.6%	37.50	37.50	23.14	20.00	45.00
w/Graphics	1.3%	45.00	45.00	29.50	25.00	45.00
Hour	36.4%	45.86	45.00	46.13	45.00	100.00

SIGNAGE

$/per	Survey %	Average	Typical	U.S. Avg.	U.S. Typ	U.S. Max
Text	0.0%			27.50	35.00	55.00
w/Graphics	0.0%			159.06	35.00	575.00
Hour	35.1%	45.78	40.00	45.60	45.00	100.00

SLIDE DESIGN

$/per	Survey %	Average	Typical	U.S. Avg.	U.S. Typ	U.S. Max
Text	2.6%	12.50	12.50	25.00	20.00	75.00
w/Graphics	2.6%	12.50	12.50	30.11	25.00	100.00
Hour	22.1%	44.71	40.00	46.17	45.00	100.00

SLIDE SHOW DESIGN

$/per	Survey %	Average	Typical	U.S. Avg.	U.S. Typ	U.S. Max
Text Page	0.0%			30.00	25.00	75.00
w/Graphics	0.0%			40.00	30.00	100.00
Hour	16.9%	41.15	30.00	47.98	50.00	100.00

SPREADSHEET DESIGN

$/per	Survey %	Average	Typical	U.S. Avg.	U.S. Typ	U.S. Max
Text Page	1.3%	45.00	45.00	35.00	35.00	45.00
w/Graphics	1.3%	45.00	45.00	45.50	45.00	45.00
Hour	24.7%	45.79	40.00	45.82	45.00	125.00

TABLOIDS

$/per	Survey %	Average	Typical	U.S. Avg.	U.S. Typ	U.S. Max
Text Page	1.3%	45.00	45.00	70.71	45.00	200.00
w/Graphics	1.3%	45.00	45.00	67.50	50.00	120.00
Hour	29.9%	41.96	30.00	46.32	45.00	125.00

TABS

$/per	Survey %	Average	Typical	U.S. Avg.	U.S. Typ	U.S. Max
Text	0.0%			20.00	20.00	20.00
w/Graphics	0.0%			20.00	20.00	20.00
Hour	18.2%	48.14	50.00	47.58	45.00	100.00

TAGS

$/per	Survey %	Average	Typical	U.S. Avg.	U.S. Typ	U.S. Max
Each	0.0%			17.83	10.00	35.00
Hour	16.9%	39.15	30.00	44.69	42.00	80.00

TECHNICAL DOCUMENTS

$/per	Survey %	Average	Typical	U.S. Avg.	U.S. Typ	U.S. Max
Text Page	2.6%	122.50	45.00	72.69	40.00	250.00
w/Graphics	1.3%	45.00	45.00	87.50	45.00	500.00
Hour	39.0%	43.80	40.00	44.05	40.00	125.00

TECHNICAL ILLUSTRATIONS

$/per	Survey %	Average	Typical	U.S. Avg.	U.S. Typ	U.S. Max
Page	2.6%	35.00	35.00	70.45	75.00	200.00
Hour	32.5%	43.56	40.00	47.28	45.00	200.00

TICKETS

$/per	Survey %	Average	Typical	U.S. Avg.	U.S. Typ	U.S. Max
Text	3.9%	35.00	30.00	24.72	20.00	50.00
w/Graphics	1.3%	30.00	30.00	30.25	30.00	50.00
Hour	28.6%	43.36	45.00	42.53	40.00	100.00

TRANSPARENCY DESIGN (B&W)

$/per	Survey %	Average	Typical	U.S. Avg.	U.S. Typ	U.S. Max
Text Page	5.2%	21.25	20.00	34.00	25.00	130.00
w/Graphics	5.2%	82.50	45.00	92.50	45.00	250.00
Hour	45.5%	44.54	40.00	42.68	40.00	100.00

TRANSPARENCY DESIGN (COLOR)						
$/per	Survey %	Average	Typical	U.S. Avg.	U.S. Typ	U.S. Max
Text Page	3.9%	25.00	20.00	27.50	30.00	45.00
w/Graphics	2.6%	32.50	32.50	32.50	40.00	45.00
Hour	33.8%	44.04	40.00	44.69	45.00	100.00

OTHER DESIGN						
$/per	Survey %	Average	Typical	U.S. Avg.	U.S. Typ	U.S. Max
Hour	3.9%	45.00	50.00	48.76	45.00	100.00

LASER PRINTER OUTPUT

GENERAL NOTES:
1. Some shops bill as $ set-up fee plus price per page.
2. Some shops bill as $/hr plus $/page.
3. A few shops price at $/hr (typically same price as other services).
4. Some laser printer output priced as $/job plus $/pg.

LASER PRINTING (Up to 300 dpi)						
$/per	Survey %	Average	Typical	U.S. Avg.	U.S. Typ	U.S. Max
8.5 x 11	29.5%	2.37	1.00	1.64	1.00	15.00
8.5 x 14	9.0%	2.72	1.50	1.95	3.00	10.00
11 x 17	2.6%	4.00	4.00	3.13	2.25	6.00
Cost Plus	0.0%			31.25	30.00	50.00
Minimum	2.7%	15.00	15.00	15.00	5.00	25.00

LASER PRINTING (400 dpi)						
$/per	Survey %	Average	Typical	U.S. Avg.	U.S. Typ	U.S. Max
8.5 x 11	5.1%	3.75	5.00	3.03	1.93	15.50
8.5 x 14	2.6%	5.50	5.50	2.71	2.00	6.00
11 x 17	0.0%			6.75	4.50	20.00
Cost Plus	1.3%	15.00	15.00	28.00	20.00	50.00
Minimum	2.7%	15.00	15.00	15.00	5.00	25.00

LASER PRINTING (600 dpi)						
$/per	Survey %	Average	Typical	U.S. Avg.	U.S. Typ	U.S. Max
8.5 x 11	10.3%	3.54	2.00	1.88	1.00	15.00
8.5 x 14	1.3%	3.00	3.00	1.88	1.95	4.46
11 x 17	1.3%	0.15	0.15	4.12	5.16	6.00
Cost Plus	1.3%	15.00	15.00	28.00	20.00	50.00

LASER PRINTING
(800dpi)

$/per	Survey %	Average	Typical	U.S. Avg.	U.S. Typ	U.S. Max
8.5 x 11	5.1%	5.59	6.00	2.75	2.00	12.00
8.5 x 14	0.0%			2.94	4.00	5.00
11 x 17	0.0%			6.00	6.00	6.00
Cost Plus	1.3%	15.00	15.00	28.00	20.00	50.00
Minimum	2.7%	15.00	15.00	15.00	5.00	25.00

LASER PRINTING
(1000 dpi)

$/per	Survey %	Average	Typical	U.S. Avg.	U.S. Typ	U.S. Max
8.5 x 11	2.6%	5.00	5.00	3.10	3.00	7.00
8.5 x 14	1.3%	7.00	7.00	4.06	4.00	7.00
11 x 17	0.0%			6.00	6.00	6.00
Cost Plus	1.3%	15.00	15.00	28.00	20.00	50.00
Minimum	2.7%	15.00	15.00	15.00	10.00	25.00

LASER PRINTING
(1200 dpi)

$/per	Survey %	Average	Typical	U.S. Avg.	U.S. Typ	U.S. Max
8.5 x 11	3.9%	3.12	3.00	2.89	3.00	6.00
8.5 x 14	1.3%	6.00	6.00	4.82	6.00	6.43
11 x 17	1.3%	5.00	5.00	7.18	6.00	13.25
Cost Plus	1.3%	15.00	15.00	28.00	20.00	50.00
Minimum	2.7%	15.00	15.00	15.00	10.00	25.00

FOR PREPRESS AND OTHER SERVICES (INCLUDING IMAGESETTING OUTPUT), REFER TO THE SECTION MARKED "NATIONAL."

Price Distribution
SOUTH CENTRAL
AL, AR, KY, LA, MS, OK, TN, TX

FILE CONVERSION

GENERAL NOTE: Survey responses listed as $/minute were converted to $/hr.

BOOKS ON DISK

$/per	Survey %	Average	Typical	U.S. Avg.	U.S. Typ	U.S. Max
Disk	1.9%	20.00	20.00	10.57	10.00	25.00
Page	1.9%	6.00	6.00	6.00	5.50	10.00
Hour	7.7%	47.50	50.00	40.11	35.00	95.00
Minimum	0.0%			15.00	15.00	15.00

CD-ROM

$/per	Survey %	Average	Typical	U.S. Avg.	U.S. Typ	U.S. Max
Page	0.0%			8.00	8.00	8.00
Disk	0.0%			25.00	25.00	25.00
Hour	1.9%	30.00	30.00	48.00	43.00	85.00
Minimum	0.0%			70.00	70.00	125.00

CROSS PLATFORM

$/per	Survey %	Average	Typical	U.S. Avg.	U.S. Typ	U.S. Max
Page	0.0%			3.83	2.88	8.00
File	3.9%	3.00	3.00	7.85	9.00	20.00
Disk	7.7%	7.75	5.00	11.85	10.00	50.00
Hour	21.2%	40.45	35.00	46.31	45.00	100.00
Minimum	3.9%	21.25	20.00	14.25	12.50	35.00

DATABASE FILES

$/per	Survey %	Average	Typical	U.S. Avg.	U.S. Typ	U.S. Max
Record	3.9%	0.25	0.25	0.16	0.15	0.25
File	3.9%	7.02	7.00	7.02	10.00	20.00
Disk	0.0%			21.67	15.00	50.00
Hour	13.5%	46.43	50.00	42.46	40.50	100.00
Minimum	1.9%	35.50	35.00	22.50	20.00	35.00

DOCUMENT FILES

$/per	Survey %	Average	Typical	U.S. Avg.	U.S. Typ	U.S. Max
K byte	0.0%			5.25	5.25	5.25
Page	0.0%			2.71	2.75	3.50
File	3.9%	5.00	5.00	8.38	10.00	15.00
Disk	1.9%	20.00	20.00	15.73	15.00	50.00
Hour	19.2%	44.50	45.00	41.23	35.00	100.00
Minimum	1.9%	35.00	35.00	21.00	15.00	35.00

DOCUMENTS ON DISK

$/per	Survey %	Average	Typical	U.S. Avg.	U.S. Typ	U.S. Max
Page	1.9%	6.66	6.50	6.17	7.00	15.00
File	1.9%	5.00	5.00	12.00	15.00	15.00
Disk	1.9%	20.00	20.00	14.00	10.00	50.00
Hour	11.5%	48.33	55.00	38.77	35.00	75.00
Minimum	0.0%			12.50	13.00	15.00

FORMS CONVERSION

$/per	Survey %	Average	Typical	U.S. Avg.	U.S. Typ	U.S. Max
Page	0.0%			187.18	190.00	200.00
File	0.0%			26.00	10.00	50.00
Disk	0.0%			15.00	10.00	25.00
Hour	5.8%	40.00	30.00	47.68	40.00	100.00
Minimum	0.0%			12.50	15.00	15.00

GRAPHIC FORMAT FILES

$/per	Survey %	Average	Typical	U.S. Avg.	U.S. Typ	U.S. Max
K byte	0.0%			5.25	5.25	5.25
Page	0.0%			18.32	20.00	20.00
File	1.9%	5.00	5.00	8.50	5.88	20.00
Disk	5.8%	13.33	10.00	15.36	15.00	50.00
Hour	23.1%	47.08	55.00	44.32	40.00	100.00
Minimum	1.9%	35.00	35.00	19.17	15.00	35.00

MEDIA CONVERSION

$/per	Survey %	Average	Typical	U.S. Avg.	U.S. Typ	U.S. Max
File	0.0%			15.00	12.50	25.00
Disk	3.9%	10.00	10.00	13.05	10.00	50.00
Hour	5.8%	41.67	35.00	48.64	45.00	100.00
Minimum	0.0%			13.75	15.00	15.00

PAGE LAYOUT FILES

$/per	Survey %	Average	Typical	U.S. Avg.	U.S. Typ	U.S. Max
500 K byte	0.0%			15.00	15.00	15.00
Page	0.0%			37.50	37.50	60.00
File	1.9%	5.00	5.00	12.70	12.50	25.00
Disk	1.9%	20.00	20.00	19.25	15.00	50.00
Hour	19.2%	46.50	55.00	42.91	40.00	100.00
Minimum	1.9%	35.00	35.00	20.00	15.00	35.00

SPREADSHEET FILES

$/per	Survey %	Average	Typical	U.S. Avg.	U.S. Typ	U.S. Max
25 K byte	0.0%			7.50	7.50	7.50
Page	0.0%			2.88	2.88	2.00
File	0.0%			12.30	10.88	25.00
Disk	0.0%			26.25	20.00	50.00
Hour	9.6%	40.00	40.00	40.98	40.00	100.00
Minimum	1.9%	35.00	35.00	22.50	20.00	35.00

VIDEO TAPE TRANSFER

$/per	Survey %	Average	Typical	U.S. Avg.	U.S. Typ	U.S. Max
Disk	0.0%			25.00	25.00	25.00
Per Hour	1.9%	30.00	30.00	48.33	45.00	75.00
Minimum	0.0%			15.00	15.00	15.00

WORD PROCESSOR FILE TO SGML

$/per	Survey %	Average	Typical	U.S. Avg.	U.S. Typ	U.S. Max
Disk	0.0%			25.00	25.00	25.00
Hour	0.0%			45.00	40.00	75.00
Minimum	0.0%			15.00	15.00	15.00

TEXT CREATION

GENERAL COPY WRITING

$/per	Survey %	Average	Typical	U.S. Avg.	U.S. Typ	U.S. Max
Line	0.0%			0.20	0.20	0.20
Page	5.8%	52.67	75.00	30.38	20.00	87.50
Hour	50.0%	44.69	45.00	41.43	35.00	300.00
Minimum	1.9%	35.00	35.00	19.00	15.00	35.00

NEWSLETTER COPY

$/per	Survey %	Average	Typical	U.S. Avg.	U.S. Typ	U.S. Max
Column	0.0%			10.48	10.50	11.00
Page	7.7%	49.00	80.00	40.96	40.00	125.00
Hour	48.1%	42.16	45.00	39.31	35.00	300.00
Minimum	1.9%	35.00	35.00	283.33	125.00	800.00

PUBLICITY / ADVERTISING COPY

$/per	Survey %	Average	Typical	U.S. Avg.	U.S. Typ	U.S. Max
Page	3.9%	41.50	41.50	40.31	40.00	100.00
Piece	1.9%	95.00	95.00	260.00	300.00	425.00
Hour	50.0%	44.81	50.00	43.56	38.00	300.00
Minimum	1.9%	35.00	35.00	19.00	15.00	35.00

RESUME WRITING

$/per	Survey %	Average	Typical	U.S. Avg.	U.S. Typ	U.S. Max
Page	7.7%	38.74	25.00	32.43	25.00	100.00
Hour	36.5%	36.84	35.00	38.11	35.00	300.00
Minimum	1.9%	35.00	35.00	110.00	65.00	300.00

TECHNICAL WRITING

$/per	Survey %	Average	Typical	U.S. Avg.	U.S. Typ	U.S. Max
Page	0.0%			53.54	35.00	300.00
Hour	30.8%	48.06	45.00	45.99	35.00	300.00
Minimum	0.0%			35.00	35.00	55.00

DATA INPUT / EDITING

DATA ENTRY / KEYBOARDING

$/per	Survey %	Average	Typical	U.S. Avg.	U.S. Typ	U.S. Max
Character	0.0%			0.02	0.02	0.02
Page	5.8%	7.67	10.00	11.32	10.00	50.00
Hour	55.8%	34.59	30.00	32.64	28.00	100.00
Minimum	3.9%	17.50	17.00	20.00	15.00	35.00

COPY EDITING

$/per	Survey %	Average	Typical	U.S. Avg.	U.S. Typ	U.S. Max
Word	0.0%			0.06	0.06	0.11
Page	1.9%	5.00	5.00	9.47	7.00	50.00
Hour	53.9%	36.75	30.00	36.58	30.00	100.00
Minimum	3.9%	17.50	17.00	20.00	15.00	35.00

CONTENT EDITING

$/per	Survey %	Average	Typical	U.S. Avg.	U.S. Typ	U.S. Max
Word	0.0%			0.11	0.11	0.11
Page	0.0%			5.33	5.00	50.00
Hour	48.1%	38.50	30.00	37.44	36.00	100.00
Minimum	3.9%	17.50	17.00	33.50	35.00	35.00

PROOF READING

$/per	Survey %	Average	Typical	U.S. Avg.	U.S. Typ	U.S. Max
Page	5.8%	6.00	5.00	6.71	5.00	50.00
Hour	55.8%	37.00	30.00	35.63	30.00	100.00
Minimum	3.9%	17.50	17.00	33.50	35.00	35.00

REWRITING

$/per	Survey %	Average	Typical	U.S. Avg.	U.S. Typ	U.S. Max
Word	0.0%			0.07	0.03	0.11
Line	0.0%			0.25	0.20	1.00
Page	0.0%			22.67	13.50	50.00
Hour	44.2%	42.91	30.00	38.81	35.00	100.00
Minimum	3.9%	17.50	17.00	35.00	35.00	35.00

INDEXING

$/per	Survey %	Average	Typical	U.S. Avg.	U.S. Typ	U.S. Max
Page	0.0%			2.80	2.00	5.00
Hour	36.5%	41.16	50.00	38.60	35.00	100.00
Minimum	5.8%	58.33	60.00	87.50	87.50	140.00

MODEM INPUT

$/per	Survey %	Average	Typical	U.S. Avg.	U.S. Typ	U.S. Max
Page	0.0%			3.33	3.00	5.00
File	0.0%			10.00	10.00	10.00
K bytes	0.0%			1.32	1.40	1.50
Disk	0.0%			8.33	5.00	25.00
Minute	1.9%	1.00	1.00	1.50	1.50	2.00
Hour	21.2%	49.55	50.00	41.62	38.00	100.00
Minimum	0.0%			12.50	12.50	15.00

TEXT FILE IMPORTING

$/per	Survey %	Average	Typical	U.S. Avg.	U.S. Typ	U.S. Max
Page	0.0%			14.60	5.00	50.00
File	0.0%			11.00	10.00	25.00
K bytes	0.0%			1.32	1.40	1.50
Disk	1.9%	15.00	15.00	10.00	10.00	15.00
Minute	0.0%			1.50	1.50	2.00
Hour	36.5%	39.89	30.00	39.10	35.00	100.00
Minimum	3.9%	21.25	22.00	21.25	22.00	35.00

TRANSCRIPTION

$/per	Survey %	Average	Typical	U.S. Avg.	U.S. Typ	U.S. Max
Line	0.0%			0.17	0.17	0.25
Page	0.0%			4.79	4.25	8.00
File	0.0%			10.57	10.57	25.00
Disk	0.0%			25.00	25.00	25.00
Hour	19.2%	32.10	30.00	31.64	30.00	75.00
Minimum	1.9%	35.00	35.00	25.00	25.00	35.00

SOUTH CENTRAL

TRANSLATION

$/per	Survey %	Average	Typical	U.S. Avg.	U.S. Typ	U.S. Max
Word	0.0%			0.17	0.17	0.20
Page	0.0%			24.17	22.50	50.00
Hour	13.5%	34.29	30.00	44.49	40.00	150.00
Minimum	1.9%	35.00	35.00	35.00	35..00	35.00

TYPOGRAPHY (General)

$/per	Survey %	Average	Typical	U.S. Avg.	U.S. Typ	U.S. Max
Line	0.0%			0.25	0.25	0.25
Page	7.7%	17.50	8.50	21.48	15.00	75.00
Hour	55.8%	40.21	40.00	39.27	35.00	100.00
Minimum	3.9%	17.50	17.00	18.83	15.00	35.00

TYPOGRAPHY (Spreadsheet)

$/per	Survey %	Average	Typical	U.S. Avg.	U.S. Typ	U.S. Max
Line	0.0%			0.25	0.25	0.25
Page	1.9%	4.00	4.00	24.06	17.00	75.00
Hour	48.1%	41.72	40.00	41.47	36.00	150.00
Minimum	1.9%	35.00	35.00	35.00	35.00	35.00

WORD PROCESSSING

$/per	Survey %	Average	Typical	U.S. Avg.	U.S. Typ	U.S. Max
Line	0.0%			0.13	0.10	0.20
Page	7.7%	6.50	6.50	8.67	8.25	25.00
Hour	44.2%	32.17	15.00	32.90	25.00	100.00
Minimum	3.8%	25.00	25.00	21.67	15.00	35.00

DATA MANAGEMENT

GENERAL NOTES:
1. Assume customer pays for cost of media extra.
2. On $/word, assume 2K words per page.
3. Per file cost assumed to be for 1 month.
4. Assume $/file same as $/image.

ARCHIVING SERVICE

$/per	Survey %	Average	Typical	U.S. Avg.	U.S. Typ	U.S. Max
Page	5.8%	2.50	7.50	7.50	7.50	7.50
File	5.8%	7.50	7.50	9.63	15.00	25.00
Tape	7.7%	9.96	10.00	37.50	20.00	150.00
Hour	11.5%	37.50	35.00	46.05	40.00	95.00
Minimum	0.0%			14.17	10.00	25.00

IMAGE MANAGEMENT

$/per	Survey %	Average	Typical	U.S. Avg.	U.S. Typ	U.S. Max
Page	0.6%			6.50	5.50	10.00
File	1.9%	5.00	5.00	16.67	15.00	50.00
Disk	0.0%			30.00	30.00	50.00
Hour	9.6%	45.00	45.00	44.81	40.00	110.00
Minimum	0.0%			14.17	10.00	25.00

NOTE: Assume $/.file same as $/image.

TEXT MANAGEMENT

$/per	Survey %	Average	Typical	U.S. Avg.	U.S. Typ	U.S. Max
Page	0.0%			8.67	6.00	15.00
File	1.9%	5.00	5.00	16.67	15.00	50.00
Disk	0.0%			23.33	15.00	50.00
Hour	7.7%	46.25	47.50	44.51	35.00	95.00
Minimum	0.0%			14.17	10.00	25.00

IMAGING SERVICES

DOCUMENT CAPTURE

$/per	Survey %	Average	Typical	U.S. Avg.	U.S. Typ	U.S. Max
Page	0.0%			3.65	3.00	7.50
File	2.0%	5.00	5.00	6.50	5.00	10.00
Hour	9.8%	36.00	45.00	39.41	35.00	95.00
Minimum	0.0%			16.25	16.25	25.00

DOCUMENT RETRIEVAL

$/per	Survey %	Average	Typical	U.S. Avg.	U.S. Typ	U.S. Max
Page	0.0%			1.50	1.50	2.00
File	0.0%			5.03	5.00	10.00
Hour	5.9%	40.00	45.00	38.82	39.00	85.00
Minimum	0.0%			16.25	16.25	25.00

GRAPHICS FILE IMPORTING

$/per	Survey %	Average	Typical	U.S. Avg.	U.S. Typ	U.S. Max
File	3.9%	5.00	5.00	6.98	5.00	15.00
Disk	0.0%			5.00	5.00	5.00
Hour	19.6%	47.00	45.00	43.35	36.00	100.00
Minimum	5.9%	14.03	15.00	14.17	14.17	35.00

PHOTO CD-ROM IMPORTING

$/per	Survey %	Average	Typical	U.S. Avg.	U.S. Typ	U.S. Max
Image	3.9%	3.00	3.00	10.02	7.25	45.00
Stock Fee	0.0%			75.00	75.00	75.00
Hour	7.8%	51.251	60.00	48.60	45.00	100.00
Minimum	0.0%			16.25	15.00	25.00

SCANNING (B&W Grey Scale)

$/per	Survey %	Average	Typical	U.S. Avg.	U.S. Typ	U.S. Max
Hour	17.7%	48.33	45.00	42.82	40.00	100.00
75-200 dpi	5.9%	14.50	10.00	10.10	9.00	75.00
300-400 dpi	31.4%	9.19	10.00	11.93	10.00	75.00
600-800 dpi	19.6%	7.35	8.00	13.51	11.00	75.00
1200 dpi	2.0%	10.00	10.00	20.20	12.00	75.00
2400 dpi	0.0%			36.86	30.00	75.00

SCANNING (B&W Line Art)

$/per	Survey %	Average	Typical	U.S. Avg.	U.S. Typ	U.S. Max
Hour	17.7%	48.33	45.00	40.94	40.00	100.00
75-200 dpi	5.9%	14.50	10.00	10.59	9.00	75.00
300-400 dpi	37.3%	10.82	10.00	11.92	10.00	75.00
600-800 dpi	23.5%	9.29	10.00	12.51	10.00	75.00
1200 dpi	2.0%	10.00	10.00	15.59	11.00	75.00
2400 dpi	0.0%			35.75	27.50	75.00
Per K	0.0%			51.67	50.00	75.00

SCANNING (B&W Photo)

$/per	Survey %	Average	Typical	U.S. Avg.	U.S. Typ	U.S. Max
Hour	13.7%	52.14	60.00	45.16	40.00	100.00
75-200 dpi	7.8%	12.13	10.00	12.28	10.00	75.00
300-400 dpi	23.5%	13.21	10.00	13.92	12.40	75.00
600-800 dpi	17.7%	7.94	10.00	14.79	12.60	75.00
1200 dpi	2.0%	10.00	10.00	19.88	17.50	75.00
2400 dpi	0.0%			35.56	31.00	75.00
Per K	0.0%			62.50	62.50	75.00

SCANNING (Color Illustration)

$/per	Survey %	Average	Typical	U.S. Avg.	U.S. Typ	U.S. Max
Hour	7.8%	48.75	60.00	49.23	50.00	125.00
75-200 dpi	5.9%	19.50	15.00	19.08	15.00	75.00
300-400 dpi	17.7%	16.06	15.00	21.03	19.00	82.00
600-800 dpi	9.8%	14.60	10.00	22.36	21.50	75.00
1200 dpi	2.0%	10.00	10.00	26.47	23.00	75.00
2400 dpi	0.0%			46.22	50.00	75.00

SCANNING (Color Photo)

$/per	Survey %	Average	Typical	U.S. Avg.	U.S. Typ	U.S. Max
Hour	7.8%	48.75	60.00	49.23	50.00	125.00
75-200 dpi	5.9%	19.50	15.00	20.44	15.00	75.00
300-400 dpi	13.7%	16.21	10.00	20.97	17.75	82.00
600-800 dpi	9.8%	14.60	10.00	19.75	15.00	75.00
1200 dpi	2.0%	10.00	10.00	30.13	30.00	75.00
2400 dpi	0.0%			61.54	60.00	137.00

SCANNING (HIGH END)
(Loose Scan)

$/per	Survey %	U.S. Avg.	U.S. Typ	U.S. Max
2 x 3	0.1%	13.33	10.00	25.00
3 x 5	0.1%	11.25	10.00	20.00
4 x 5	0.1%	16.00	10.00	33.00
5 x 7	0.1%	18.00	10.00	37.00
5.5 x 8.5	0.1%	17.33	10.00	39.00
6 x 9	0.1%	24.67	15.00	49.00
8 x 10	0.1%	41.60	50.00	70.00
10 x 12	0.1%	47.80	60.00	84.00
11 x 14	0.1%	81.67	70.00	105.00
12 x 18	0.1%	90.67	80.00	122.00
16 x 20	0.1%	162.00	162.00	162.00
20 x 24	0.1%	199.00	199.00	199.00
Hour	0.1%	47.00	45.00	60.00

SCANNING (HIGH END)
(Drum Scan)

$/per	Survey %	U.S. Avg.	U.S. Typ	U.S. Max
2 x 3	0.1%	56..92	54.25	71.50
4 x 5	0.1%	57.21	55.00	94.50
5 x 7	0.1%	65.75	70.00	106.00
6 x 8	0.1%	103.13	102.50	117.50
6 x 9	0.1%	57.00	45.00	85.00
8 x 10	0.1%	51.25	50.00	60.00
10 x 12	0.1%	58.33	60.00	60.00
11 x 14	0.1%	71.25	72.50	75.00
12 x 18	0.1%	86.67	85.00	100.00
24 x 27	0.1%	600.00	600.00	600.00

SCANNING (HIGH END)
(High Res Scan to Disk)

$/per	Survey %	U.S. Avg.	U.S. Typ	U.S. Max
2 x 3	0.1%	20..50	19.50	25.00
4 x 5	0.1%	26.17	27.50	30.00
5 x 7	0.1%	34.00	35.00	41.00
6 x 9	0.1%	39.80	39.00	50.00

SCANNING (HIGH END)
(High Res Scan to Disk)

$/per	Survey %	U.S. Avg.	U.S. Typ	U.S. Max
8 x 10	0.1%	45.50	45.00	60.00
10 x 12	0.1%	56.83	59.00	70.00
11 x 14	0.1%	65.08	64.00	89.00
12 x 18	0.1%	78.90	75.00	100.00
16 x 20	0.1%	96.33	99.00	130.00
20 x 24	0.1%	128.00	134.00	160.00
24 x 27	0.1%	156.25	156.25	200.00

SCANNING (Transparency)

$/per	Survey %	Average	Typical	U.S. Avg.	U.S. Typ	U.S. Max
Each	1.9%	10.00	10.00	18.70	16.00	45.00
Hour	2.0%	30.00	30.00	65.29	55.00	137.00

SCANNING (Slide)

$/per	Survey %	Average	Typical	U.S. Avg.	U.S. Typ	U.S. Max
Each	0.0%			23.00	16.99	65.00
Hour	2.0%	30.00	30.00	68.42	55.00	137.00

COLOR CORRECTION

$/per	Survey %	Average	Typical	U.S. Avg.	U.S. Typ	U.S. Max
Hour	11.8%	44.17	50.00	65.80	50.00	300.00

IMAGE EDITING

$/per	Survey %	Average	Typical	U.S. Avg.	U.S. Typ	U.S. Max
Each	0.0%			20.75	15.00	50.00
Hour	27.5%	44.93	50.00	55.47	45.00	300.00

IMAGE ENHANCEMENT

$/per	Survey %	Average	Typical	U.S. Avg.	U.S. Typ	U.S. Max
Hour	21.6%	45.45	45.00	57.60	50.00	300.00

RETOUCHING

$/per	Survey %	Average	Typical	U.S. Avg.	U.S. Typ	U.S. Max
Each	2.0%	30.00	30.00	27.67	40.00	50.00
Hour	35.3%	41.89	45.00	58.60	50.00	300.00
Minimum	3.9%	17.50	20.00	26.08	25.00	35.00

TEXT SCAN (OCR)

$/per	Survey %	Average	Typical	U.S. Avg.	U.S. Typ	U.S. Max
Page	3.9%	6.00	6.00	7.82	5.00	95.00

TEXT SCAN (OCR)

$/per	Survey %	Average	Typical	U.S. Avg.	U.S. Typ	U.S. Max
Hour	27.5%	32.50	35.00	36.33	30.00	75.00
Minimum	5.9%	14.17	15.00	19.08	16.90	35.00

NOTE:
1. Prices assume spell check conducted on scanned text.
2. Assumes 2 Kb per page, so $1/Kb response incorporated as $2/page.

NEGATIVE CREATION

$/per	Survey %	Average	Typical	U.S. Avg.	U.S. Typ	U.S. Max
Each	0.0%			22.00	22.00	40.00
Hour	2.1%	30.00	30.00	56.71	56.71	100.00
Minimum	0.0%			16.67	16.67	25.00

DESIGN SERVICES

ANNOUNCEMENTS

$/per	Survey %	Average	Typical	U.S. Avg.	U.S. Typ	U.S. Max
Text Page	7.7%	31.25	15.00	37.05	24.00	250.00
w/Graphics	3.9%	16.00	20.00	65.36	36.50	500.00
Hour	44.2%	47.72	50.00	42.21	40.00	100.00

ANNUAL REPORTS
(1C, 2C, Up To Letter Size Pages)

$/per	Survey %	Average	Typical	U.S. Avg.	U.S. Typ	U.S. Max
Text	1.9%	15.00	15.00	114.75	62.50	1000.00
w/Graphics	1.9%	15.00	15.00	222.00	100.00	7680.00
Hour	50.0%	51.83	50.00	46.58	45.00	100.00

ANNUAL REPORTS
(3C, 4C, Larger Size Pages)

$/per	Survey %	Average	Typical	U.S. Avg.	U.S. Typ	U.S. Max
Text	1.9%	15.00	15.00	214.55	100.00	1500.00
w/Graphics	1.9%	15.00	15.00	422.50	175.00	11520.00
Hour	50.0%	51.83	50.00	46.34	45.00	100.00

BAR CODING

$/per	Survey %	Average	Typical	U.S. Avg.	U.S. Typ	U.S. Max
Each	1.9%	3.00	3.00	13.25	11.00	150.00
Page	0.0%			29.00	29.00	50.00
Hour	15.4%	57.50	55.00	47.83	45.00	100.00

BOOKLETS

$/per	Survey %	Average	Typical	U.S. Avg.	U.S. Typ	U.S. Max
Text Page	5.8%	13.33	15.00	48.40	30.00	500.00
w/Graphics	1.9%	15.00	15.00	110.53	50.00	650.00
Hour	67.3%	48.43	50.00	43.87	25.00	100.00

BOOK COVERS

$/per	Survey %	Average	Typical	U.S. Avg.	U.S. Typ	U.S. Max
Text	3.9%	207.50	200.00	143.10	75.00	500.00
w/Graphics	1.9%	800.00	800.00	403.36	300.00	1800.00
Hour	44.2%	53.91	55.00	47.83	45.00	120.00

BOOK BODY

$/per	Survey %	Average	Typical	U.S. Avg.	U.S. Typ	U.S. Max
Text Page	3.9%	15.00	15.00	26.65	20.00	75.00
w/Graphics	3.9%	15.00	15.00	41.11	25.00	85.00
Hour	36.5%	50.13	50.00	44.26	40.00	100.00

BOOK JACKETS

$/per	Survey %	Average	Typical	U.S. Avg.	U.S. Typ	U.S. Max
Text	3.9%	207.50	400.00	161.54	175.00	500.00
w/Graphics	1.9%	800.00	800.00	491.00	325.00	1000.00
Hour	40.4%	54.29	55.00	48.63	45.00	120.00

BROCHURE
(1C, 2C, Up To Letter Size Sheet)

$/per	Survey %	Average	Typical	U.S. Avg.	U.S. Typ	U.S. Max
Text Page	13.5%	58.00	45.00	72.59	47.50	500.00
w/Graphics	5.8%	166.67	80.00	156.74	82.50	750.00
Hour	71.2%	49.15	50.00	42.85	40.00	125.00

BROCHURE
(3C, 4C, Larger Size Sheet)

$/per	Survey %	Average	Typical	U.S. Avg.	U.S. Typ	U.S. Max
Text Page	7.7%	42.75	50.00	123.79	60.00	1000.00
w/Graphics	3.9%	55.00	75.00	227.71	100.00	1500.00
Hour	67.3%	50.81	50.00	44.17	40.00	125.00

BULLETIN

$/per	Survey %	Average	Typical	U.S. Avg.	U.S. Typ	U.S. Max
Text Page	3.9%	15.50	16.00	32.75	25.00	150.00
w/Graphics	0.0%			47.81	35.00	200.00
Hour	38.5%	9.63	50.00	42.36	40.00	100.00

BUSINESS CARDS

$/per	Survey %	Average	Typical	U.S. Avg.	U.S. Typ	U.S. Max
Text Card	19.2%	20.50	20.00	38.81	25.00	500.00
w/Graphics	3.9%	29.50	30.00	91.70	40.00	1000.00
Hour	69.2%	50.00	50.00	43.19	40.00	150.00

BUSINESS REPLY CARDS

$/per	Survey %	Average	Typical	U.S. Avg.	U.S. Typ	U.S. Max
Text Card	3.9%	22.50	30.00	34.32	31.50	150.00
w/Graphics	0.0%			67.50	35.00	250.00
Hour	50.0%	51.92	50.00	43.79	40.00	100.00

BUSINESS LETTERS

$/per	Survey %	Average	Typical	U.S. Avg.	U.S. Typ	U.S. Max
Text Page	7.7%	30.75	15.00	17.23	12.25	90.00
w/Graphics	1.9%	10.00	10.00	27.08	18.75	100.00
Hour	46.2%	44.79	45.00	39.38	35.00	100.00

CALENDARS

$/per	Survey %	Average	Typical	U.S. Avg.	U.S. Typ	U.S. Max
Text Page	9.6%	41.00	25.00	82.50	50.00	500.00
w/Graphics	1.9%	25.00	25.00	53.18	45.00	150.00
Hour	46.2%	49.79	50.00	43.77	40.00	100.00

CALLIGRAPHY

$/per	Survey %	Average	Typical	U.S. Avg.	U.S. Typ	U.S. Max
Line	0.0%			1.00	1.00	60.00
Page	0.0%			40.00	35.00	100.00
Hour	25.0%	51.54	55.00	45.50	40.00	175.00

CARDS (FOLD-OVER)

$/per	Survey %	Average	Typical	U.S. Avg.	U.S. Typ	U.S. Max
Text Card	1.9%	12.00	12.00	31.45	25.00	60.00
w/Graphics	1.9%	15.00	15.00	65.47	46.40	250.00
Hour	32.7%	50.44	55.00	43.63	40.00	100.00

CARDS (ROLODEX)

$/per	Survey %	Average	Typical	U.S. Avg.	U.S. Typ	U.S. Max
Text Card	1.9%	30.00	30.00	37.34	25.00	150.00
w/Graphics	0.0%			63.00	48.00	250.00
Hour	26.9%	52.68	55.00	44.94	41.00	100.00

CARTOONS

$/per	Survey %	Average	Typical	U.S. Avg.	U.S. Typ	U.S. Max
Each	1.9%	125.00	125.00	119.29	60.00	400.00
Page	0.0%			163.33	65.00	400.00
Hour	34.6%	54.58	55.00	48.15	45.00	90.00

CATALOGS

$/per	Survey %	Average	Typical	U.S. Avg.	U.S. Typ	U.S. Max
Text Page	7.7%	52.50	50.00	69.03	40.00	500.00
w/Graphics	1.9%	75.00	75.00	129.05	67.50	1000.00
Hour	61.5%	50.86	50.00	45.68	45.00	125.00

CERTIFICATES

$/per	Survey %	Average	Typical	U.S. Avg.	U.S. Typ	U.S. Max
Text	7.7%	18.00	20.00	23.56	16.25	125.00
w/Graphics	1.9%	16.00	16.00	35.07	25.00	150.00
Hour	38.5%	48.63	50.00	42.15	40.00	100.00

CHARTS / DIAGRAMS

$/per	Survey %	Average	Typical	U.S. Avg.	U.S. Typ	U.S. Max
Text	1.9%	35.00	35.00	36.19	32.50	150.00
w/Graphics	0.0%			53.14	47.50	150.00
Hour	53.9%	50.27	50.00	44.29	40.00	100.00

COMIC BOOKS

$/per	Survey %	Average	Typical	U.S. Avg.	U.S. Typ	U.S. Max
Each Page	0.0%			65.00	60.00	100.00
Hour	11.5%	55.00	55.00	47.12	50.00	80.00

COMIC STRIPS

$/per	Survey %	Average	Typical	U.S. Avg.	U.S. Typ	U.S. Max
Each Strip	0.0%			38.33	30.00	60.00
Hour	11.5%	55.00	55.00	46.78	50.00	80.00

COMPUTER GENERATED ART

$/per	Survey %	Average	Typical	U.S. Avg.	U.S. Typ	U.S. Max
Page	0.0%			121.40	50.00	500.00
Hour	57.7%	50.83	55.00	46.70	42.00	175.00

CUSTOM DISPLAYS

$/per	Survey %	Average	Typical	U.S. Avg.	U.S. Typ	U.S. Max
Text	1.9%	15.00	15.00	192.14	60.00	1000.00
w/Graphics	0.0%			265.71	100.00	1000.00
Hour	38.5%	58.50	55.00	48.95	45.00	100.00

DATABASE DESIGN

$/per	Survey %	Average	Typical	U.S. Avg.	U.S. Typ	U.S. Max
Text	0.0%			38.33	30.00	60.00
w/Graphics	0.0%			43.33	40.00	60.00
Hour	23.1%	52.29	55.00	42.45	41.00	80.00

DIGITAL SLIDE PRESENTATIONS

$/per	Survey %	Average	Typical	U.S. Avg.	U.S. Typ	U.S. Max
Text	0.0%			27.13	27.50	60.00
w/Graphics	0.0%			35.00	32.50	60.00
Hour	19.2%	53.75	55.00	45.81	45.00	100.00

DIRECT MAIL PACKAGES

$/per	Survey %	Average	Typical	U.S. Avg.	U.S. Typ	U.S. Max
Text	1.9%	10.00	10.00	298.46	60.00	1500.00
w/Graphics	1.9%	15.00	15.00	413.50	65.00	2000.00
Hour	48.1%	55.00	50.00	47.05	45.00	100.00

DIRECTORY

$/per	Survey %	Average	Typical	U.S. Avg.	U.S. Typ	U.S. Max
Text	1.9%	25.00	25.00	38.72	30.00	150.00
w/Graphics	1.9%	25.00	25.00	73.53	40.00	500.00
Hour	44.2%	47.61	50.00	43.08	40.00	125.00

DISPLAY ADVERTISING

$/per	Survey %	Average	Typical	U.S. Avg.	U.S. Typ	U.S. Max
Text	7.7%	40.00	25.00	109.28	30.00	1000.00
w/Graphics	0.0%			304.64	45.00	2500.00
Hour	51.9%	56.85	55.00	48.23	45.00	115.00

DISPLAY EXHIBITS

$/per	Survey %	Average	Typical	U.S. Avg.	U.S. Typ	U.S. Max
Text Panel	0.0%			858.57	90.00	5000.00
w/Graphics	0.0%			896.67	100.00	5000.00
Hour	34.6%	60.56	60.00	51.43	50.00	115.00

DOOR HANGERS

$/per	Survey %	Average	Typical	U.S. Avg.	U.S. Typ	U.S. Max
Text	0.0%			42.46	25.00	250.00
w/Graphics	0.0%			87.50	35.00	500.00
Hour	26.9%	54.64	55.00	47.19	45.00	100.00

DRAFTING

$/per	Survey %	Average	Typical	U.S. Avg.	U.S. Typ	U.S. Max
Page	0.0%			45.00	45.00	60.00
Hour	19.2%	55.50	55.00	46.62	45.00	100.00

FINANCIAL DOCUMENTS

$/per	Survey %	Average	Typical	U.S. Avg.	U.S. Typ	U.S. Max
Text Page	1.9%	15.00	15.00	45.33	33.00	150.00
w/Graphics	0.0%			92.00	60.00	150.00
Hour	32.7%	48.24	50.00	47.20	45.00	125.00

FLYERS

$/per	Survey %	Average	Typical	U.S. Avg.	U.S. Typ	U.S. Max
Text Page	17.3%	39.00	25.00	39.21	25.00	325.00
w/Graphics	5.8%	115.00	25.00	66.84	35.00	325.00
Hour	69.2%	49.93	50.00	42.22	40.00	100.00

FORMS

$/per	Survey %	Average	Typical	U.S. Avg.	U.S. Typ	U.S. Max
Text Page	9.6%	52.00	35.00	52.60	30.00	750.00
w/Graphics	1.9%	35.00	35.00	81.67	37.50	10000.00
Hour	65.4%	46.84	50.00	41.75	40.00	125.00

HANDBOOKS

$/per	Survey %	Average	Typical	U.S. Avg.	U.S. Typ	U.S. Max
Text Page	1.9%	10.00	10.00	38.22	25.00	150.00
w/Graphics	0.0%			62.46	35.00	250.00
Hour	53.9%	49.91	50.00	43.53	40.00	100.00

INSERTS

$/per	Survey %	Average	Typical	U.S. Avg.	U.S. Typ	U.S. Max
Text Page	9.6%	43.40	35.00	70.58	27.50	1000.00
w/Graphics	1.9%	16.00	16.00	193.50	35.00	2500.00
Hour	51.9%	49.54	50.00	43.99	40.00	100.00

INVITATIONS

$/per	Survey %	Average	Typical	U.S. Avg.	U.S. Typ	U.S. Max
Text	9.6%	34.40	15.00	35.01	25.00	250.00
w/Graphics	3.9%	23.00	25.00	73.16	35.00	750.00
Hour	63.5%	47.35	50.00	41.85	40.00	100.00

LABELS (Custom)

$/per	Survey %	Average	Typical	U.S. Avg.	U.S. Typ	U.S. Max
Text	1.9%	12.00	12.00	40.06	20.00	250.00
w/Graphics	1.9%	16.00	16.00	121.16	55.00	600.00
Hour	30.8%	50.78	50.00	43.55	40.00	100.00

LARGE FORMAT GRAPHICS

$/per	Survey %	Average	Typical	U.S. Avg.	U.S. Typ	U.S. Max
Text Page	0.0%			40.00	37.50	45.00
w/Graphics	0.0%			71.00	70.00	85.00
Hour	25.0%	51.35	55.00	47.95	45.00	90.00

LETTERHEAD & ENVELOPES

$/per	Survey %	Average	Typical	U.S. Avg.	U.S. Typ	U.S. Max
Text	11.5%	24.00	25.00	59.65	25.00	750.00
w/Graphics	5.8%	24.33	25.00	136.48	40.00	1000.00
Hour	78.9%	49.09	50.00	43.60	40.00	150.00

LINE ART & GENERAL ILLUSTRATIONS

$/per	Survey %	Average	Typical	U.S. Avg.	U.S. Typ	U.S. Max
Text Page	3.9%	32.50	35.00	64.17	47.50	135.00
w/Graphics	0.2%	1000.00	1000.00	221.89	100.00	1000.00
Hour	59.6%	51.85	55.00	46.24	43.50	115.00

LITIGATION GRAPHICS

$/per	Survey %	Average	Typical	U.S. Avg.	U.S. Typ	U.S. Max
Text Page	0.0%			75.00	75.00	75.00
w/Graphics	0.0%			100.00	100.00	100.00
Hour	30.8%	49.22	55.00	50.13	45.00	200.00

LOGOS

$/per	Survey %	Average	Typical	U.S. Avg.	U.S. Typ	U.S. Max
Each	7.7%	108.75	150.00	281.23	200.00	2000.00
Hour	78.9%	51.10	50.00	46.02	45.00	125.00

LOGOTYPE

$/per	Survey %	Average	Typical	U.S. Avg.	U.S. Typ	U.S. Max
Page	1.9%	60.00	60.00	304.36	300.00	1000.00
Hour	55.8%	53.19	50.00	48.68	45.00	125.00

MAGAZINES

$/per	Survey %	Average	Typical	U.S. Avg.	U.S. Typ	U.S. Max
Text Page	1.9%	10.00	10.00	60.49	35.00	250.00
w/Graphics	0.0%			90.89	40.00	500.00
Hour	40.4%	51.19	50.00	45.91	45.00	125.00

NOTES:
1. Multiple page prices converted to $/page.
2. Other prices noted for magazine design: $500 setup; $1,000 ea.

MAILERS

$/per	Survey %	Average	Typical	U.S. Avg.	U.S. Typ	U.S. Max
Text Page	1.9%	12.00	12.00	64.08	25.00	500.00
w/Graphics	1.9%	16.00	16.00	82.36	40.00	500.00
Hour	34.6%	54.31	55.00	46.11	42.00	100.00

MANUALS

$/per	Survey %	Average	Typical	U.S. Avg.	U.S. Typ	U.S. Max
Text Page	5.8%	10.00	10.00	42.06	17.50	500.00
w/Graphics	1.9%	10.00	10.00	58.10	30.00	500.00
Hour	57.7%	45.75	50.00	42.63	40.00	100.00

MAPS
(1C, 2C, Letter Size)

$/per	Survey %	Average	Typical	U.S. Avg.	U.S. Typ	U.S. Max
Simple	0.0%			76.25	70.00	250.00
Complex	0.0%			206.14	75.00	600.00
Hour	44.2%	52.61	50.00	46.90	45.00	100.00

MAPS
(4C, Larger Than Letter Size)

$/per	Survey %	Average	Typical	U.S. Avg.	U.S. Typ	U.S. Max
Simple	0.0%			168.75	72.50	500.00
Complex	0.0%			490.71	300.00	1600.00
Hour	44.2%	52.61	50.00	48.08	45.00	100.00

MARKETING PLANS

$/per	Survey %	Average	Typical	U.S. Avg.	U.S. Typ	U.S. Max
Text Page	1.9%	10.00	10.00	59.00	10.00	250.00
w/Graphics	0.0%			182.67	40.00	500.00
Hour	23.1%	54.79	55.00	47.80	45.00	100.00

MEMO PADS

$/per	Survey %	Average	Typical	U.S. Avg.	U.S. Typ	U.S. Max
Text	3.9%	8.00	8.00	20.14	14.50	100.00
w/Graphics	3.9%	12.50	13.00	31.79	17.50	150.00
Hour	32.7%	48.68	50.00	43.94	40.00	100.00

MENUS

$/per	Survey %	Average	Typical	U.S. Avg.	U.S. Typ	U.S. Max
Text Page	3.9%	22.50	22.50	75.65	35.00	500.00
w/Graphics	0.0%			125.25	45.00	1000.00
Hour	57.7%	50.50	50.00	44.35	40.00	150.00
Minimum	0.6%	35.00	35.00	233.75	200.00	500.00

NEWSLETTERS

$/per	Survey %	Average	Typical	U.S. Avg.	U.S. Typ	U.S. Max
Text Page	9.6%	76.00	75.00	62.86	45.00	200.00
w/Graphics	3.9%	117.50	125.00	76.16	50.00	200.00
Hour	78.9%	48.11	50.00	42.97	40.00	160.00

NOTEPADS

$/per	Survey %	Average	Typical	U.S. Avg.	U.S. Typ	U.S. Max
Text	1.9%	100.00	100.00	32.28	25.00	100.00
w/Graphics	0.0%			41.37	35.00	150.00
Hour	48.1%	48.10	45.00	43.72	40.00	100.00

PACKAGING

$/per	Survey %	Average	Typical	U.S. Avg.	U.S. Typ	U.S. Max
Text	0.0%			276.00	100.00	1000.00
w/Graphics	0.0%			478.18	250.00	2500.00
Hour	38.5%	55.50	55.00	51.64	50.00	150.00

PEN RULER

$/per	Survey %	Average	Typical	U.S. Avg.	U.S. Typ	U.S. Max
Page	0.0%			45.00	45.00	45.00
Hour	17.3%	54.44	55.00	48.81	50.00	85.00

PERIODICAL (OTHER)

$/per	Survey %	Average	Typical	U.S. Avg.	U.S. Typ	U.S. Max
Text Page	1.9%	35.00	35.00	36.00	25.00	150.00
w/Graphics	1.9%	50.00	50.00	58.00	35.00	250.00
Hour	36.5%	51.18	50.00	46.86	45.00	125.00

POINT-OF-PURCHASE DISPLAYS

$/per	Survey %	Average	Typical	U.S. Avg.	U.S. Typ	U.S. Max
Text Page	0.0%			650.00	600.00	1000.00
w/Graphics	0.0%			800.00	800.00	1000.00
Hour	23.1%	61.46	60.00	50.15	50.00	100.00

POST CARDS

$/per	Survey %	Average	Typical	U.S. Avg.	U.S. Typ	U.S. Max
Text Page	5.8%	27.33	20.00	45.18	20.00	400.00
w/Graphics	3.9%	22.50	22.50	64.31	30.00	500.00
Hour	55.8%	47.33	50.00	42.38	40.00	100.00

POSTERS

$/per	Survey %	Average	Typical	U.S. Avg.	U.S. Typ	U.S. Max
Text Page	1.9%	20.00	20.00	123.67	50.00	500.00
w/Graphics	1.9%	20.00	20.00	259.71	250.00	1000.00
Hour	53.9%	51.52	50.00	45.60	45.00	100.00

PRESENTATION MATERIALS

$/per	Survey %	Average	Typical	U.S. Avg.	U.S. Typ	U.S. Max
Text Page	0.0%			27.65	20.00	100.00
w/Graphics	0.0%			44.38	25.00	180.00
Hour	40.4%	51.79	55.00	45.04	45.00	100.00

PRICE LISTS

$/per	Survey %	Average	Typical	U.S. Avg.	U.S. Typ	U.S. Max
Text Page	1.9%	10.00	10.00	40.63	35.00	150.00
w/Graphics	0.0%			51.79	40.00	160.00
Hour	50.0%	47.212	50.00	42.68	40.00	100.00

PRINT ADS

$/per	Survey %	Average	Typical	U.S. Avg.	U.S. Typ	U.S. Max
Text	5.8%	46.67	30.00	107.09	45.00	1000.00
w/Graphics	1.9%	25.00	25.00	179.74	80.00	1100.00
Hour	67.3%	50.00	50.00	44.84	40.00	100.00

PROCEDURE GUIDES

$/per	Survey %	Average	Typical	U.S. Avg.	U.S. Typ	U.S. Max
Text Page	0.0%			60.00	15.00	300.00
w/Graphics	0.0%			93.21	25.00	500.00
Hour	23.1%	52.71	45.00	45.67	45.00	100.00

PRODUCT LITERATURE

$/per	Survey %	Average	Typical	U.S. Avg.	U.S. Typ	U.S. Max
Text Page	1.9%	45.00	45.00	67.97	30.00	500.00
w/Graphics	1.9%	45.00	45.00	118.81	40.00	1000.00
Hour	53.9%	51.43	50.00	45.43	42.00	100.00

PRODUCT SPECIFICATION SHEETS

$/per	Survey %	Average	Typical	U.S. Avg.	U.S. Typ	U.S. Max
Text Page	0.0%			70.95	25.00	500.00
w/Graphics	0.0%			168.89	35.00	1000.00
Hour	25.0%	53.27	45.00	46.44	45.00	100.00

PROGRAMS

$/per	Survey %	Average	Typical	U.S. Avg.	U.S. Typ	U.S. Max
Text Page	3.9%	107.50	120.00	43.92	25.00	200.00
w/Graphics	0.0%			95.94	35.00	500.00
Hour	32.7%	48.68	45.00	46.61	45.00	150.00

PUBLICATIONS (OTHER)

$/per	Survey %	Average	Typical	U.S. Avg.	U.S. Typ	U.S. Max
Text Page	1.9%	25.00	25.00	46.00	30.00	150.00
w/Graphics	1.9%	65.00	65.00	87.73	35.00	500.00
Hour	46.2%	52.08	50.00	44.63	40.00	125.00

RECORD BOOKS

$/per	Survey %	Average	Typical	U.S. Avg.	U.S. Typ	U.S. Max
Text Page	0.0%			20.67	15.00	45.00
w/Graphics	0.0%			35.00	35.00	45.00
Hour	28.9%	52.67	50.00	46.63	45.00	80.00

RESUMES

$/per	Survey %	Average	Typical	U.S. Avg.	U.S. Typ	U.S. Max
Each	9.6%	52.40	35.00	31.21	25.00	150.00
Page	13.5%	43.14	30.00	31.52	30.00	150.00
Hour	61.5%	47.03	50.00	40.96	40.00	150.00

RULERS

$/per	Survey %	Average	Typical	U.S. Avg.	U.S. Typ	U.S. Max
Each	0.0%			250.00	375.00	500.00
Hour	15.4%	59.69	60.00	49.08	50.00	100.00

SALES PRESENTATIONS

$/per	Survey %	Average	Typical	U.S. Avg.	U.S. Typ	U.S. Max
Text Page	0.0%			23.14	20.00	45.00
w/Graphics	0.0%			29.50	25.00	45.00
Hour	34.6%	56.67	55.00	46.13	45.00	100.00

SIGNAGE

$/per	Survey %	Average	Typical	U.S. Avg.	U.S. Typ	U.S. Max
Text	0.0%			27.50	35.00	55.00
w/Graphics	0.0%			159.06	35.00	575.00
Hour	44.2%	53.26	52.50	45.60	45.00	100.00

SLIDE DESIGN

$/per	Survey %	Average	Typical	U.S. Avg.	U.S. Typ	U.S. Max
Text	0.0%			25.00	20.00	75.00
w/Graphics	0.0%			30.11	25.00	100.00
Hour	19.2%	52.25	55.00	46.17	45.00	100.00

SLIDE SHOW DESIGN

$/per	Survey %	Average	Typical	U.S. Avg.	U.S. Typ	U.S. Max
Text Page	0.0%			30.00	25.00	75.00
w/Graphics	0.0%			40.00	30.00	100.00
Hour	17.3%	61.94	55.00	47.98	50.00	100.00

SPREADSHEET DESIGN

$/per	Survey %	Average	Typical	U.S. Avg.	U.S. Typ	U.S. Max
Text Page	0.0			35.00	35.00	45.00
w/Graphics	0.0%			45.50	45.00	45.00
Hour	23.1%	50.21	50.00	45.82	45.00	125.00

TABLOIDS

$/per	Survey %	Average	Typical	U.S. Avg.	U.S. Typ	U.S. Max
Text Page	3.9%	117.50	125.00	70.71	45.00	200.00
w/Graphics	0.0%			67.50	50.00	120.00
Hour	40.4%	51.43	50.00	46.32	45.00	125.00

TABS

$/per	Survey %	Average	Typical	U.S. Avg.	U.S. Typ	U.S. Max
Text	0.0%			20.00	20.00	20.00
w/Graphics	0.0%			20.00	20.00	20.00
Hour	25.0%	52.88	55.00	47.58	45.00	100.00

TAGS

$/per	Survey %	Average	Typical	U.S. Avg.	U.S. Typ	U.S. Max
Each	0.0%			17.83	10.00	35.00
Hour	19.2%	56.25	55.00	44.69	42.00	80.00

TECHNICAL DOCUMENTS

$/per	Survey %	Average	Typical	U.S. Avg.	U.S. Typ	U.S. Max
Text Page	1.9%	45.00	45.00	72.69	40.00	250.00
w/Graphics	1.9%	45.00	45.00	87.50	45.00	500.00
Hour	38.5%	47.63	50.00	44.05	40.00	125.00

TECHNICAL ILLUSTRATIONS

$/per	Survey %	Average	Typical	U.S. Avg.	U.S. Typ	U.S. Max
Page	0.0%			70.45	75.00	200.00
Hour	36.6%	55.39	55.00	47.28	45.00	200.00

TICKETS

$/per	Survey %	Average	Typical	U.S. Avg.	U.S. Typ	U.S. Max
Text	3.9%	16.00	20.00	24.72	20.00	50.00
w/Graphics	0.0%			30.25	30.00	50.00
Hour	26.9%	46.96	50.00	42.53	40.00	100.00

TRANSPARENCY DESIGN (B&W)

$/per	Survey %	Average	Typical	U.S. Avg.	U.S. Typ	U.S. Max
Text Page	0.0%			34.00	25.00	130.00
w/Graphics	0.0%			92.50	45.00	250.00
Hour	25.0%	44.42	45.00	42.68	40.00	100.00

TRANSPARENCY DESIGN (COLOR)

$/per	Survey %	Average	Typical	U.S. Avg.	U.S. Typ	U.S. Max
Text Page	0.0%			27.50	30.00	45.00
w/Graphics	0.0%			32.50	40.00	45.00
Hour	23.1%	49.38	50.00	44.69	45.00	100.00

OTHER DESIGN

$/per	Survey %	Average	Typical	U.S. Avg.	U.S. Typ	U.S. Max
Hour	5.7%	63.33	60.00	48.76	45.00	100.00

LASER PRINTER OUTPUT

GENERAL NOTES:
1. Some shops bill as $ set-up fee plus price per page.
2. Some shops bill as $/hr plus $/page.
3. A few shops price at $/hr (typically same price as other services).
4. Some laser printer output priced as $/job plus $/pg.

LASER PRINTING
(Up to 300 dpi)

$/per	Survey %	Average	Typical	U.S. Avg.	U.S. Typ	U.S. Max
8.5 x 11	30.8%	1.38	2.00	1.64	1.00	15.00
8.5 x 14	13.5%	2.00	3.00	1.95	3.00	10.00
11 x 17	1.9%	2.00	2.00	3.13	2.25	6.00
Cost Plus	1.9%	50.00	50.00	31.25	30.00	50.00
Minimum	2.7%	15.00	15.00	15.00	5.00	25.00

LASER PRINTING
(400 dpi)

$/per	Survey %	Average	Typical	U.S. Avg.	U.S. Typ	U.S. Max
8.5 x 11	0.0%			3.03	1.93	15.50
8.5 x 14	0.0%			2.71	2.00	6.00
11 x 17	0.0%			6.75	4.50	20.00
Cost Plus	1.9%	50.00	50.00	28.00	20.00	50.00
Minimum	2.7%	15.00	15.00	15.00	5.00	25.00

LASER PRINTING
(600 dpi)

$/per	Survey %	Average	Typical	U.S. Avg.	U.S. Typ	U.S. Max
8.5 x 11	3.9%	1.25	1.50	1.88	1.00	15.00
8.5 x 14	3.9%	1.25	1.50	1.88	1.95	4.46
11 x 17	0.0%			4.12	5.16	6.00
Cost Plus	1.9%	50.00	50.00	28.00	20.00	50.00

SOUTH CENTRAL

LASER PRINTING
(800dpi)

$/per	Survey %	Average	Typical	U.S. Avg.	U.S. Typ	U.S. Max
8.5 x 11	3.9%	2.00	2.00	2.75	2.00	12.00
8.5 x 14	1.9%	3.00	3.00	2.94	4.00	5.00
11 x 17	0.0%			6.00	6.00	6.00
Cost Plus	1.9%	50.00	50.00	28.00	20.00	50.00
Minimum	2.7%	15.00	15.00	15.00	5.00	25.00

LASER PRINTING
(1000 dpi)

$/per	Survey %	Average	Typical	U.S. Avg.	U.S. Typ	U.S. Max
8.5 x 11	1.9%	5.00	5.00	3.10	3.00	7.00
8.5 x 14	0.0%			4.06	4.00	7.00
11 x 17	0.0%			6.00	6.00	6.00
Cost Plus	1.9%	50.00	50.00	28.00	20.00	50.00
Minimum	2.7%	15.00	15.00	15.00	10.00	25.00

LASER PRINTING
(1200 dpi)

$/per	Survey %	Average	Typical	U.S. Avg.	U.S. Typ	U.S. Max
8.5 x 11	1.9%	3.00	3.00	2.89	3.00	6.00
8.5 x 14	1.9%	4.50	4.50	4.82	6.00	6.43
11 x 17	1.9%	10.00	10.00	7.18	6.00	13.25
Cost Plus	1.9%	50.00	50.00	28.00	20.00	50.00
Minimum	2.7%	15.00	15.00	15.00	10.00	25.00

FOR PREPRESS AND OTHER SERVICES (INCLUDING IMAGESETTING OUTPUT), REFER TO THE SECTION MARKED "NATIONAL."

Price Distribution
MOUNTAIN
AZ, CO, ID, MT, NM, NV, UT, WY

FILE CONVERSION

GENERAL NOTE: Survey responses listed as $/minute were converted to $/hr.

BOOKS ON DISK

$/per	Survey %	Average	Typical	U.S. Avg.	U.S. Typ	U.S. Max
Disk	0.0%			10.57	10.00	25.00
Page	0.0%			6.00	5.50	10.00
Hour	6.3%	34.50	35.00	40.11	35.00	95.00
Minimum	0.0%			15.00	15.00	15.00

CD-ROM

$/per	Survey %	Average	Typical	U.S. Avg.	U.S. Typ	U.S. Max
Page	0.0%			8.00	8.00	8.00
Disk	0.0%			25.00	25.00	25.00
Hour	0.0%			48.00	43.00	85.00
Minimum	0.0%			70.00	70.00	125.00

CROSS PLATFORM

$/per	Survey %	Average	Typical	U.S. Avg.	U.S. Typ	U.S. Max
Page	0.0%			3.83	2.88	8.00
File	0.0%			7.85	9.00	20.00
Disk	12.5%	6.88	10.00	11.85	10.00	50.00
Hour	25.1%	43.63	45.00	46.31	45.00	100.00
Minimum	0.0%			14.25	12.50	35.00

DATABASE FILES

$/per	Survey %	Average	Typical	U.S. Avg.	U.S. Typ	U.S. Max
Record	0.0%			0.16	0.15	0.25
File	3.1%	1.50	1.50	7.02	10.00	20.00
Disk	0.0%			21.67	15.00	50.00
Hour	9.4%	33.00	36.00	42.46	40.50	100.00
Minimum	0.0%			22.50	20.00	35.00

DOCUMENT FILES

$/per	Survey %	Average	Typical	U.S. Avg.	U.S. Typ	U.S. Max
K byte	0.0%			5.25	5.25	5.25
Page	0.0%			2.71	2.75	3.50
File	6.3%	3.25	3.50	8.38	10.00	15.00
Disk	0.0%			15.73	15.00	50.00
Hour	18.8%	40.67	36.00	41.23	35.00	100.00
Minimum	0.0%			21.00	15.00	35.00

DOCUMENTS ON DISK

$/per	Survey %	Average	Typical	U.S. Avg.	U.S. Typ	U.S. Max
Page	0.0%			6.17	7.00	15.00
File	0.0%			12.00	15.00	15.00
Disk	6.3%	10.03	10.00	14.00	10.00	50.00
Hour	18.8%	34.83	35.00	38.77	35.00	75.00
Minimum	0.0%			12.50	13.00	15.00

FORMS CONVERSION

$/per	Survey %	Average	Typical	U.S. Avg.	U.S. Typ	U.S. Max
Page	0.0%			187.18	190.00	200.00
File	0.0%			26.00	10.00	50.00
Disk	0.0%			15.00	10.00	25.00
Hour	0.0%			47.68	40.00	100.00
Minimum	0.0%			12.50	15.00	15.00

GRAPHIC FORMAT FILES

$/per	Survey %	Average	Typical	U.S. Avg.	U.S. Typ	U.S. Max
K byte	0.0%			5.25	5.25	5.25
Page	0.0%			18.32	20.00	20.00
File	6.3%	3.25	3.50	8.50	5.88	20.00
Disk	0.0%			15.36	15.00	50.00
Hour	21.9%	38.00	30.00	44.32	40.00	100.00
Minimum	0.0%			19.17	15.00	35.00

MEDIA CONVERSION

$/per	Survey %	Average	Typical	U.S. Avg.	U.S. Typ	U.S. Max
File	0.0%			15.00	12.50	25.00
Disk	3.1%	2.50	2.50	13.05	10.00	50.00
Hour	12.5%	40.25	40.00	48.64	45.00	100.00
Minimum	0.0%			13.75	15.00	15.00

PAGE LAYOUT FILES

$/per	Survey %	Average	Typical	U.S. Avg.	U.S. Typ	U.S. Max
500 K byte	0.0%			15.00	15.00	15.00
Page	0.0%			37.50	37.50	60.00
File	3.1%	3.00	3.00	12.70	12.50	25.00
Disk	0.0%			19.25	15.00	50.00
Hour	12.5%	31.50	36.00	42.91	40.00	100.00
Minimum	0.0%			20.00	15.00	35.00

SPREADSHEET FILES

$/per	Survey %	Average	Typical	U.S. Avg.	U.S. Typ	U.S. Max
25 K byte	0.0%			7.50	7.50	7.50
Page	0.0%			2.88	2.88	2.00
File	3.1%	1.50	1.50	12.30	10.88	25.00
Disk	0.0%			26.25	20.00	50.00
Hour	12.5%	49.00	45.00	40.98	40.00	100.00
Minimum	0.0%			22.50	20.00	35.00

VIDEO TAPE TRANSFER

$/per	Survey %	Average	Typical	U.S. Avg.	U.S. Typ	U.S. Max
Disk	0.0%			25.00	25.00	25.00
Per Hour	0.0%			48.33	45.00	75.00
Minimum	0.0%			15.00	15.00	15.00

WORD PROCESSOR FILE TO SGML

$/per	Survey %	Average	Typical	U.S. Avg.	U.S. Typ	U.S. Max
Disk	0.0%			25.00	25.00	25.00
Hour	3.1%	45.00	45.00	45.00	40.00	75.00
Minimum	0.0%			15.00	15.00	15.00

TEXT CREATION

GENERAL COPY WRITING

$/per	Survey %	Average	Typical	U.S. Avg.	U.S. Typ	U.S. Max
Line	0.0%			0.20	0.20	0.20
Page	3.1%	15.00	15.00	30.38	20.00	87.50
Hour	59.4%	33.11	25.00	41.43	35.00	300.00
Minimum	0.0%			19.00	15.00	35.00

NEWSLETTER COPY

$/per	Survey %	Average	Typical	U.S. Avg.	U.S. Typ	U.S. Max
Column	0.0%			10.48	10.50	11.00
Page	6.3%	55.00	55.00	40.96	40.00	125.00
Hour	43.8%	31.57	25.00	39.31	35.00	300.00
Minimum	0.0%			283.33	125.00	800.00

PUBLICITY / ADVERTISING COPY

$/per	Survey %	Average	Typical	U.S. Avg.	U.S. Typ	U.S. Max
Page	3.1%	20.00	20.00	40.31	40.00	100.00
Piece	0.0%			260.00	300.00	425.00
Hour	56.3%	33.22	25.00	43.56	38.00	300.00
Minimum	0.0%			19.00	15.00	35.00

RESUME WRITING

$/per	Survey %	Average	Typical	U.S. Avg.	U.S. Typ	U.S. Max
Page	21.9%	24.29	25.00	32.43	25.00	100.00
Hour	37.5%	30.67	24.00	38.11	35.00	300.00
Minimum	3.1%	30.46	30.00	110.00	65.00	300.00

TECHNICAL WRITING

$/per	Survey %	Average	Typical	U.S. Avg.	U.S. Typ	U.S. Max
Page	6.3%	13.50	15.00	53.54	35.00	300.00
Hour	37.50%	33.75	25.00	45.99	35.00	300.00
Minimum	0.0%			35.00	35.00	55.00

DATA INPUT / EDITING

DATA ENTRY / KEYBOARDING

$/per	Survey %	Average	Typical	U.S. Avg.	U.S. Typ	U.S. Max
Character	3.1%	0.02	0.02	0.02	0.02	0.02
Page	9.4%	10.00	10.00	11.32	10.00	50.00
Hour	50.0%	24.38	25.00	32.64	28.00	100.00
Minimum	0.0%			20.00	15.00	35.00

COPY EDITING

$/per	Survey %	Average	Typical	U.S. Avg.	U.S. Typ	U.S. Max
Word	6.3%	0.06	0.06	0.06	0.06	0.11
Page	6.3%	7.50	7.50	9.47	7.00	50.00
Hour	53.1%	33.35	25.00	36.58	30.00	100.00
Minimum	0.0%			20.00	15.00	35.00

CONTENT EDITING

$/per	Survey %	Average	Typical	U.S. Avg.	U.S. Typ	U.S. Max
Word	3.1%	0.11	0.11	0.11	0.11	0.11
Page	3.1%	12.00	12.00	5.33	5.00	50.00
Hour	50.0%	34.38	35.00	37.44	36.00	100.00
Minimum	0.0%			33.50	35.00	35.00

PROOF READING

$/per	Survey %	Average	Typical	U.S. Avg.	U.S. Typ	U.S. Max
Page	9.4%	8.33	10.00	6.71	5.00	50.00
Hour	50.00%	29.75	25.00	35.63	30.00	100.00
Minimum	0.0%			33.50	35.00	35.00

REWRITING

$/per	Survey %	Average	Typical	U.S. Avg.	U.S. Typ	U.S. Max
Word	6.4%	0.07	0.07	0.07	0.03	0.11
Line	0.0%			0.25	0.20	1.00
Page	3.1%	12.00	12.00	22.67	13.50	50.00
Hour	37.5%	33.17	25.00	38.81	35.00	100.00
Minimum	0.0%			35.00	35.00	35.00

INDEXING

$/per	Survey %	Average	Typical	U.S. Avg.	U.S. Typ	U.S. Max
Page	6.3%	2.00	2.00	2.80	2.00	5.00
Hour	21.9%	44.00	24.00	38.60	35.00	100.00
Minimum	0.0%			87.50	87.50	140.00

MODEM INPUT

$/per	Survey %	Average	Typical	U.S. Avg.	U.S. Typ	U.S. Max
Page	0.0%			3.33	3.00	5.00
File	0.0%			10.00	10.00	10.00
K bytes	0.0%			1.32	1.40	1.50
Disk	0.0%			8.33	5.00	25.00
Minute	0.0%			1.50	1.50	2.00
Hour	18.8%	28.17	25.00	41.62	38.00	100.00
Minimum	0.0%			12.50	12.50	15.00

TEXT FILE IMPORTING

$/per	Survey %	Average	Typical	U.S. Avg.	U.S. Typ	U.S. Max
Page	0.0%			14.60	5.00	50.00
File	0.0%			11.00	10.00	25.00
K bytes	0.0%			1.32	1.40	1.50
Disk	0.0%			10.00	10.00	15.00
Minute	0.0%			1.50	1.50	2.00
Hour	37.5%	39.33	35.00	39.10	35.00	100.00
Minimum	0.0%			21.25	22.00	35.00

TRANSCRIPTION

$/per	Survey %	Average	Typical	U.S. Avg.	U.S. Typ	U.S. Max
Line	3.1%	0.12	0.12	0.17	0.17	0.25
Page	0.0%			4.79	4.25	8.00
File	0.0%			10.57	10.57	25.00
Disk	0.0%			25.00	25.00	25.00
Hour	18.8%	21.67	18.00	31.64	30.00	75.00
Minimum	0.0%			25.00	25.00	35.00

TRANSLATION

$/per	Survey %	Average	Typical	U.S. Avg.	U.S. Typ	U.S. Max
Word	3.1%	0.20	0.20	0.17	0.17	0.20
Page	0.0%			24.17	22.50	50.00
Hour	3.1%	45.00	45.00	44.49	40.00	150.00
Minimum	0.0%			35.00	35..00	35.00

TYPOGRAPHY (General)

$/per	Survey %	Average	Typical	U.S. Avg.	U.S. Typ	U.S. Max
Line	0.0%			0.25	0.25	0.25
Page	6.3%	16.00	16.00	21.48	15.00	75.00
Hour	53.1%	34.53	25.00	39.27	35.00	100.00
Minimum	0.0%			18.83	15.00	35.00

TYPOGRAPHY (Spreadsheet)

$/per	Survey %	Average	Typical	U.S. Avg.	U.S. Typ	U.S. Max
Line	0.0%	0.25	0.25	0.25	0.25	0.25
Page	0.0%			24.06	17.00	75.00
Hour	43.8%	39.86	35.00	41.47	36.00	150.00
Minimum	0.0%			35.00	35.00	35.00

WORD PROCESSSING

$/per	Survey %	Average	Typical	U.S. Avg.	U.S. Typ	U.S. Max
Line	0.0%			0.13	0.10	0.20
Page	0.0%			8.67	8.25	25.00
Hour	59.4%	28.79	25.00	32.90	25.00	100.00
Minimum	0.0%			21.67	15.00	35.00

DATA MANAGEMENT

GENERAL NOTES:
1. Assume customer pays for cost of media extra.
2. On $/word, assume 2K words per page.
3. Per file cost assumed to be for 1 month.
4. Assume $/file same as $/image.

ARCHIVING SERVICE

$/per	Survey %	Average	Typical	U.S. Avg.	U.S. Typ	U.S. Max
Page	0.0%			7.50	7.50	7.50
File	0.0%			9.63	15.00	25.00
Tape	0.0%			37.50	20.00	150.00
Hour	6.3%	39.00	39.00	46.05	40.00	95.00
Minimum	0.2%			14.17	10.00	25.00

IMAGE MANAGEMENT

$/per	Survey %	Average	Typical	U.S. Avg.	U.S. Typ	U.S. Max
Page	0.0%			6.50	5.50	10.00
File	0.0%			16.67	15.00	50.00
Disk	0.0%			30.00	30.00	50.00
Hour	6.3%	35.00	35.00	44.81	40.00	110.00
Minimum	0.0%			14.17	10.00	25.00

NOTE: Assume $/.file same as $/image.

TEXT MANAGEMENT

$/per	Survey %	Average	Typical	U.S. Avg.	U.S. Typ	U.S. Max
Page	0.0%			8.67	6.00	15.00
File	0.0%			16.67	15.00	50.00
Disk	0.0%			23.33	15.00	50.00
Hour	3.1%	18.00	18.00	44.51	35.00	95.00
Minimum	0.0%			14.17	10.00	25.00

IMAGING SERVICES

DOCUMENT CAPTURE

$/per	Survey %	Average	Typical	U.S. Avg.	U.S. Typ	U.S. Max
Page	0.0%			3.65	3.00	7.50
File	0.0%			6.50	5.00	10.00
Hour	15.6%	25.60	28.00	39.41	35.00	95.00
Minimum	0.0%			16.25	16.25	25.00

DOCUMENT RETRIEVAL

$/per	Survey %	Average	Typical	U.S. Avg.	U.S. Typ	U.S. Max
Page	0.0%			1.50	1.50	2.00
File	0.0%			5.03	5.00	10.00
Hour	12.5%	20.50	24.00	38.82	39.00	85.00
Minimum	0.0%			16.25	16.25	25.00

GRAPHICS FILE IMPORTING

$/per	Survey %	Average	Typical	U.S. Avg.	U.S. Typ	U.S. Max
File	3.1%	10.00	10.00	6.98	5.00	15.00
Disk	0.0%			5.00	5.00	5.00
Hour	31.3%	37.90	35.00	43.35	36.00	100.00
Minimum	3.1%	10.00	10.00	14.17	14.17	35.00

MOUNTAIN

PHOTO CD-ROM IMPORTING

$/per	Survey %	Average	Typical	U.S. Avg.	U.S. Typ	U.S. Max
Image	3.1%	5.00	5.00	10.02	7.25	45.00
Stock Fee	0.0%			75.00	75.00	75.00
Hour	9.4%	53.33	45.00	48.60	45.00	100.00
Minimum	0.0%			16.25	15.00	25.00

SCANNING (B&W Grey Scale)

$/per	Survey %	Average	Typical	U.S. Avg.	U.S. Typ	U.S. Max
Hour	28.1%	42.56	35.00	42.82	40.00	100.00
75-200 dpi	9.4%	8.33	10.00	10.10	9.00	75.00
300-400 dpi	31.3%	10.30	10.00	11.93	10.00	75.00
600-800 dpi	6.3%	10.00	10.00	13.51	11.00	75.00
1200 dpi	3.1%	10.00	10.00	20.20	12.00	75.00
2400 dpi	3.1%	15.00	15.00	36.86	30.00	75.00

SCANNING (B&W Line Art)

$/per	Survey %	Average	Typical	U.S. Avg.	U.S. Typ	U.S. Max
Hour	28.1%	39.78	35.00	40.94	40.00	100.00
75-200 dpi	6.3%	7.50	7.50	10.59	9.00	75.00
300-400 dpi	31.3%	8.55	10.00	11.92	10.00	75.00
600-800 dpi	6.3%	10.00	10.00	12.51	10.00	75.00
1200 dpi	3.1%	10.00	10.00	15.59	11.00	75.00
2400 dpi	0.0%			35.75	27.50	75.00
Per K	0.0%			51.67	50.00	75.00

SCANNING (B&W Photo)

$/per	Survey %	Average	Typical	U.S. Avg.	U.S. Typ	U.S. Max
Hour	28.1%	42.56	35.00	45.16	40.00	100.00
75-200 dpi	9.4%	10.00	10.00	12.28	10.00	75.00
300-400 dpi	28.1%	10.89	10.00	13.92	12.40	75.00
600-800 dpi	6.3%	10.00	10.00	14.79	12.60	75.00
1200 dpi	3.1%	10.00	10.00	19.88	17.50	75.00
2400 dpi	3.1%	15.00	15.00	35.56	31.00	75.00
Per K	0.0%			62.50	62.50	75.00

SCANNING (Color Illustration)

$/per	Survey %	Average	Typical	U.S. Avg.	U.S. Typ	U.S. Max
Hour	12.5%	55.00	75.00	49.23	50.00	125.00
75-200 dpi	9.4%	11.67	10.00	19.08	15.00	75.00
300-400 dpi	15.6%	12.50	10.00	21.03	19.00	82.00
600-800 dpi	6.3%	15.00	15.00	22.36	21.50	75.00
1200 dpi	6.3%	14.00	14.00	26.47	23.00	75.00
2400 dpi	3.1%	58.00	58.00	46.22	50.00	75.00

SCANNING (Color Photo)

$/per	Survey %	Average	Typical	U.S. Avg.	U.S. Typ	U.S. Max
Hour	15.6%	51.00	35.00	49.23	50.00	125.00
75-200 dpi	9.4%	11.67	10.00	20.44	15.00	75.00
300-400 dpi	15.6%	12.50	10.00	20.97	17.75	82.00
600-800 dpi	6.3%	15.00	15.00	19.75	15.00	75.00
1200 dpi	6.3%	15.00	15.00	30.13	30.00	75.00
2400 dpi	3.1%	58.00	58.00	61.54	60.00	137.00

SCANNING (HIGH END)
(Loose Scan)

$/per	Survey %	U.S. Avg.	U.S. Typ	U.S. Max
2 x 3	0.1%	13.33	10.00	25.00
3 x 5	0.1%	11.25	10.00	20.00
4 x 5	0.1%	16.00	10.00	33.00
5 x 7	0.1%	18.00	10.00	37.00
5.5 x 8.5	0.1%	17.33	10.00	39.00
6 x 9	0.1%	24.67	15.00	49.00
8 x 10	0.1%	41.60	50.00	70.00
10 x 12	0.1%	47.80	60.00	84.00
11 x 14	0.1%	81.67	70.00	105.00
12 x 18	0.1%	90.67	80.00	122.00
16 x 20	0.1%	162.00	162.00	162.00
20 x 24	0.1%	199.00	199.00	199.00
Hour	0.1%	47.00	45.00	60.00

SCANNING (HIGH END)
(Drum Scan)

$/per	Survey %	U.S. Avg.	U.S. Typ	U.S. Max
2 x 3	0.1%	56..92	54.25	71.50
4 x 5	0.1%	57.21	55.00	94.50
5 x 7	0.1%	65.75	70.00	106.00
6 x 8	0.1%	103.13	102.50	117.50
6 x 9	0.1%	57.00	45.00	85.00
8 x 10	0.1%	51.25	50.00	60.00
10 x 12	0.1%	58.33	60.00	60.00
11 x 14	0.1%	71.25	72.50	75.00
12 x 18	0.1%	86.67	85.00	100.00
24 x 27	0.1%	600.00	600.00	600.00

SCANNING (HIGH END)
(High Res Scan to Disk)

$/per	Survey %	U.S. Avg.	U.S. Typ	U.S. Max
2 x 3	0.1%	20..50	19.50	25.00
4 x 5	0.1%	26.17	27.50	30.00
5 x 7	0.1%	34.00	35.00	41.00
6 x 9	0.1%	39.80	39.00	50.00

SCANNING (HIGH END) (High Res Scan to Disk)				
$/per	Survey %	U.S. Avg.	U.S. Typ	U.S. Max
8 x 10	0.1%	45.50	45.00	60.00
10 x 12	0.1%	56.83	59.00	70.00
11 x 14	0.1%	65.08	64.00	89.00
12 x 18	0.1%	78.90	75.00	100.00
16 x 20	0.1%	96.33	99.00	130.00
20 x 24	0.1%	128.00	134.00	160.00
24 x 27	0.1%	156.25	156.25	200.00

SCANNING (Transparency)						
$/per	Survey %	Average	Typical	U.S. Avg.	U.S. Typ	U.S. Max
Each	0.0%			18.70	16.00	45.00
Hour	0.0%			65.29	55.00	137.00

SCANNING (Slide)						
$/per	Survey %	Average	Typical	U.S. Avg.	U.S. Typ	U.S. Max
Each	0.0%			23.00	16.99	65.00
Hour	0.0%			68.42	55.00	137.00

COLOR CORRECTION						
$/per	Survey %	Average	Typical	U.S. Avg.	U.S. Typ	U.S. Max
Hour	25.0%	62.00	60.00	65.80	50.00	300.00

IMAGE EDITING						
$/per	Survey %	Average	Typical	U.S. Avg.	U.S. Typ	U.S. Max
Each	0.0%			20.75	15.00	50.00
Hour	37.5%	43.83	40.00	55.47	45.00	300.00

IMAGE ENHANCEMENT						
$/per	Survey %	Average	Typical	U.S. Avg.	U.S. Typ	U.S. Max
Hour	34.4%	54.18	45.00	57.60	50.00	300.00

RETOUCHING						
$/per	Survey %	Average	Typical	U.S. Avg.	U.S. Typ	U.S. Max
Each	0.0%			27.67	40.00	50.00
Hour	31.3%	47.10	45.00	58.60	50.00	300.00
Minimum	0.0%			26.08	25.00	35.00

TEXT SCAN (OCR)						
$/per	Survey %	Average	Typical	U.S. Avg.	U.S. Typ	U.S. Max
Page	18.8%	5.04	5.00	7.82	5.00	95.00

TEXT SCAN (OCR)						
$/per	Survey %	Average	Typical	U.S. Avg.	U.S. Typ	U.S. Max
Hour	21.9%	34.14	30.00	36.33	30.00	75.00
Minimum	0.0%			19.08	16.90	35.00

NOTE:
1. Prices assume spell check conducted on scanned text.
2. Assumes 2 Kb per page, so $1/Kb response incorporated as $2/page.

NEGATIVE CREATION						
$/per	Survey %	Average	Typical	U.S. Avg.	U.S. Typ	U.S. Max
Each	0.0%			22.00	22.00	40.00
Hour	3.1%	60.00	60.00	56.71	56.71	100.00
Minimum	3.1%	25.00	25.00	16.67	16.67	25.00

DESIGN SERVICES

ANNOUNCEMENTS						
$/per	Survey %	Average	Typical	U.S. Avg.	U.S. Typ	U.S. Max
Text Page	6.3%	20.00	20.00	37.05	24.00	250.00
w/Graphics	6.3%	32.50	32.50	65.36	36.50	500.00
Hour	31.3%	36.80	25.00	42.21	40.00	100.00

ANNUAL REPORTS (1C, 2C, Up To Letter Size Pages)						
$/per	Survey %	Average	Typical	U.S. Avg.	U.S. Typ	U.S. Max
Text	0.0%			114.75	62.50	1000.00
w/Graphics	3.1%	100.00	100.00	222.00	100.00	7680.00
Hour	21.9%	33.29	25.00	46.58	45.00	100.00

ANNUAL REPORTS (3C, 4C, Larger Size Pages)						
$/per	Survey %	Average	Typical	U.S. Avg.	U.S. Typ	U.S. Max
Text	0.0%			214.55	100.00	1500.00
w/Graphics	0.0%			422.50	175.00	11520.00
Hour	21.9%	33.29	25.00	46.34	45.00	100.00

BAR CODING						
$/per	Survey %	Average	Typical	U.S. Avg.	U.S. Typ	U.S. Max
Each	3.1%	8.00	8.00	13.25	11.00	150.00
Page	3.1%	8.00	8.00	29.00	29.00	50.00
Hour	6.3%	34.50	34.50	47.83	45.00	100.00

BOOKLETS

$/per	Survey %	Average	Typical	U.S. Avg.	U.S. Typ	U.S. Max
Text Page	12.5%	18.25	25.99	48.40	30.00	500.00
w/Graphics	9.4%	37.50	35.00	110.53	50.00	650.00
Hour	53.1%	39.00	35.00	43.87	25.00	100.00

BOOK COVERS

$/per	Survey %	Average	Typical	U.S. Avg.	U.S. Typ	U.S. Max
Text	0.0%			143.10	75.00	500.00
w/Graphics	0.0%			403.36	300.00	1800.00
Hour	40.6%	44.15	40.00	47.83	45.00	120.00

BOOK BODY

$/per	Survey %	Average	Typical	U.S. Avg.	U.S. Typ	U.S. Max
Text Page	6.3%	11.50	11.50	26.65	20.00	75.00
w/Graphics	0.0%			41.11	25.00	85.00
Hour	40.6%	43.31	45.00	44.26	40.00	100.00

BOOK JACKETS

$/per	Survey %	Average	Typical	U.S. Avg.	U.S. Typ	U.S. Max
Text	0.0%			161.54	175.00	500.00
w/Graphics	0.0%			491.00	325.00	1000.00
Hour	28.1%	41.00	40.00	48.63	45.00	120.00

BROCHURE
(1C, 2C, Up To Letter Size Sheet)

$/per	Survey %	Average	Typical	U.S. Avg.	U.S. Typ	U.S. Max
Text Page	15.6%	45.00	40.00	72.59	47.50	500.00
w/Graphics	15.6%	66.00	70.00	156.74	82.50	750.00
Hour	56.3%	41.28	35.00	42.85	40.00	125.00

BROCHURE
(3C, 4C, Larger Size Sheet)

$/per	Survey %	Average	Typical	U.S. Avg.	U.S. Typ	U.S. Max
Text Page	12.5%	48.75	60.00	123.79	60.00	1000.00
w/Graphics	12.5%	98.75	100.00	227.71	100.00	1500.00
Hour	53.1%	41.94	36.00	44.17	40.00	125.00

BULLETIN

$/per	Survey %	Average	Typical	U.S. Avg.	U.S. Typ	U.S. Max
Text Page	3.1%	10.00	10.00	32.75	25.00	150.00
w/Graphics	3.1%	15.00	15.00	47.81	35.00	200.00
Hour	40.6%	40.08	35.00	42.36	40.00	100.00

BUSINESS CARDS

$/per	Survey %	Average	Typical	U.S. Avg.	U.S. Typ	U.S. Max
Text Card	21.9%	23.71	25.00	38.81	25.00	500.00
w/Graphics	15.6%	45.00	30.00	91.70	40.00	1000.00
Hour	50.0%	36.75	36.00	43.19	40.00	150.00

BUSINESS REPLY CARDS

$/per	Survey %	Average	Typical	U.S. Avg.	U.S. Typ	U.S. Max
Text Card	9.4%	18.33	20.00	34.32	31.50	150.00
w/Graphics	9.4%	23.33	25.00	67.50	35.00	250.00
Hour	28.1%	35.89	35.00	43.79	40.00	100.00

BUSINESS LETTERS

$/per	Survey %	Average	Typical	U.S. Avg.	U.S. Typ	U.S. Max
Text Page	0.0%			17.23	12.25	90.00
w/Graphics	0.0%			27.08	18.75	100.00
Hour	37.5%	36.50	28.00	39.38	35.00	100.00

CALENDARS

$/per	Survey %	Average	Typical	U.S. Avg.	U.S. Typ	U.S. Max
Text Page	0.0%			82.50	50.00	500.00
w/Graphics	3.1%	45.00	45.00	53.18	45.00	150.00
Hour	21.9%	36.71	40.00	43.77	40.00	100.00

CALLIGRAPHY

$/per	Survey %	Average	Typical	U.S. Avg.	U.S. Typ	U.S. Max
Line	0.0%			1.00	1.00	60.00
Page	0.0%			40.00	35.00	100.00
Hour	6.3%	30.00	30.00	45.50	40.00	175.00

CARDS (FOLD-OVER)

$/per	Survey %	Average	Typical	U.S. Avg.	U.S. Typ	U.S. Max
Text Card	3.1%	20.00	20.00	31.45	25.00	60.00
w/Graphics	3.1%	25.00	25.00	65.47	46.40	250.00
Hour	25.0%	42.38	45.00	43.63	40.00	100.00

CARDS (ROLODEX)

$/per	Survey %	Average	Typical	U.S. Avg.	U.S. Typ	U.S. Max
Text Card	0.0%			37.34	25.00	150.00
w/Graphics	0.0%			63.00	48.00	250.00
Hour	28.1%	34.11	35.00	44.94	41.00	100.00

CARTOONS

$/per	Survey %	Average	Typical	U.S. Avg.	U.S. Typ	U.S. Max
Each	0.0%			119.29	60.00	400.00
Page	3.1%	30.00	30.00	163.33	65.00	400.00
Hour	18.8%	36.83	40.00	48.15	45.00	90.00

CATALOGS

$/per	Survey %	Average	Typical	U.S. Avg.	U.S. Typ	U.S. Max
Text Page	9.4%	21.00	25.00	69.03	40.00	500.00
w/Graphics	9.4%	43.67	35.00	129.05	67.50	1000.00
Hour	31.3%	51.80	45.00	45.68	45.00	125.00

CERTIFICATES

$/per	Survey %	Average	Typical	U.S. Avg.	U.S. Typ	U.S. Max
Text	12.5%	23.75	25.00	23.56	16.25	125.00
w/Graphics	9.4%	41.67	40.00	35.07	25.00	150.00
Hour	31.3%	38.30	35.00	42.15	40.00	100.00

CHARTS / DIAGRAMS

$/per	Survey %	Average	Typical	U.S. Avg.	U.S. Typ	U.S. Max
Text	12.5%	26.25	30.00	36.19	32.50	150.00
w/Graphics	9.4%	40.00	35.00	53.14	47.50	150.00
Hour	40.6%	39.54	35.00	44.29	40.00	100.00

COMIC BOOKS

$/per	Survey %	Average	Typical	U.S. Avg.	U.S. Typ	U.S. Max
Each Page	3.1%	100.00	100.00	65.00	60.00	100.00
Hour	3.1%	45.00	45.00	47.12	50.00	80.00

COMIC STRIPS

$/per	Survey %	Average	Typical	U.S. Avg.	U.S. Typ	U.S. Max
Each Strip	3.1%	30.00	30.00	38.33	30.00	60.00
Hour	6.3%	30.00	30.00	46.78	50.00	80.00

COMPUTER GENERATED ART

$/per	Survey %	Average	Typical	U.S. Avg.	U.S. Typ	U.S. Max
Page	0.0%			121.40	50.00	500.00
Hour	40.6%	37.31	36.00	46.70	42.00	175.00

CUSTOM DISPLAYS

$/per	Survey %	Average	Typical	U.S. Avg.	U.S. Typ	U.S. Max
Text	0.0%			192.14	60.00	1000.00
w/Graphics	0.0%			265.71	100.00	1000.00
Hour	28.1%	39.11	35.00	48.95	45.00	100.00

DATABASE DESIGN

$/per	Survey %	Average	Typical	U.S. Avg.	U.S. Typ	U.S. Max
Text	3.1%	25.00	25.00	38.33	30.00	60.00
w/Graphics	3.1%	30.00	30.00	43.33	40.00	60.00
Hour	15.6%	34.80	30.00	42.45	41.00	80.00

DIGITAL SLIDE PRESENTATIONS

$/per	Survey %	Average	Typical	U.S. Avg.	U.S. Typ	U.S. Max
Text	6.3%	18.50	18.50	27.13	27.50	60.00
w/Graphics	3.1%	40.00	40.00	35.00	32.50	60.00
Hour	18.8%	37.67	40.00	45.81	45.00	100.00

DIRECT MAIL PACKAGES

$/per	Survey %	Average	Typical	U.S. Avg.	U.S. Typ	U.S. Max
Text	3.1%	30.00	30.00	298.46	60.00	1500.00
w/Graphics	3.1%	35.00	35.00	413.50	65.00	2000.00
Hour	25.0%	38.13	35.00	47.05	45.00	100.00

DIRECTORY

$/per	Survey %	Average	Typical	U.S. Avg.	U.S. Typ	U.S. Max
Text	9.4%	25.00	25.00	38.72	30.00	150.00
w/Graphics	3.1%	30.00	30.00	73.53	40.00	500.00
Hour	34.4%	39.64	30.00	43.08	40.00	125.00

DISPLAY ADVERTISING

$/per	Survey %	Average	Typical	U.S. Avg.	U.S. Typ	U.S. Max
Text	0.0%			109.28	30.00	1000.00
w/Graphics	0.0%			304.64	45.00	2500.00
Hour	34.4%	47.18	40.00	48.23	45.00	115.00

DISPLAY EXHIBITS

$/per	Survey %	Average	Typical	U.S. Avg.	U.S. Typ	U.S. Max
Text Panel	0.0%			858.57	90.00	5000.00
w/Graphics	0.0%			896.67	100.00	5000.00
Hour	12.5%	39.50	45.00	51.43	50.00	115.00

DOOR HANGERS

$/per	Survey %	Average	Typical	U.S. Avg.	U.S. Typ	U.S. Max
Text	12.3%	25.00	25.00	42.46	25.00	250.00
w/Graphics	3.1%	35.00	35.000	87.50	35.00	500.00
Hour	18.8%	42.33	45.00	47.19	45.00	100.00

DRAFTING

$/per	Survey %	Average	Typical	U.S. Avg.	U.S. Typ	U.S. Max
Page	0.0%			45.00	45.00	60.00
Hour	18.8%	33.00	35.00	46.62	45.00	100.00

FINANCIAL DOCUMENTS

$/per	Survey %	Average	Typical	U.S. Avg.	U.S. Typ	U.S. Max
Text Page	0.0%			45.33	33.00	150.00
w/Graphics	0,0%			92.00	60.00	150.00
Hour	28.1%	49.67	40.00	47.20	45.00	125.00

FLYERS

$/per	Survey %	Average	Typical	U.S. Avg.	U.S. Typ	U.S. Max
Text Page	12.5%	26.25	30.00	39.21	25.00	325.00
w/Graphics	6.3%	35.00	35.00	66.84	35.00	325.00
Hour	56.3%	38.50	35.00	42.22	40.00	100.00

FORMS

$/per	Survey %	Average	Typical	U.S. Avg.	U.S. Typ	U.S. Max
Text Page	15.6%	32.00	30.00	52.60	30.00	750.00
w/Graphics	12.5%	45.00	35.00	81.67	37.50	10000.00
Hour	50.0%	41.13	35.00	41.75	40.00	125.00

HANDBOOKS

$/per	Survey %	Average	Typical	U.S. Avg.	U.S. Typ	U.S. Max
Text Page	9.4%	18.67	20.00	38.22	25.00	150.00
w/Graphics	6.3%	18.50	18.50	62.46	35.00	250.00
Hour	46.9%	40.60	35.00	43.53	40.00	100.00

INSERTS

$/per	Survey %	Average	Typical	U.S. Avg.	U.S. Typ	U.S. Max
Text Page	6.3%	30.00	30.00	70.58	27.50	1000.00
w/Graphics	6.3%	42.50	42.50	193.50	35.00	2500.00
Hour	25.0%	38.00	35.00	43.99	40.00	100.00

INVITATIONS

$/per	Survey %	Average	Typical	U.S. Avg.	U.S. Typ	U.S. Max
Text	12.5%	21.25	20.00	35.01	25.00	250.00
w/Graphics	9.4%	26.67	25.00	73.16	35.00	750.00
Hour	34.4%	35.00	25.00	41.85	40.00	100.00

LABELS (Custom)

$/per	Survey %	Average	Typical	U.S. Avg.	U.S. Typ	U.S. Max
Text	3.1%	20.00	20.00	40.06	20.00	250.00
w/Graphics	3.1%	100.00	50.00	121.16	55.00	600.00
Hour	31.2%	34.30	25.00	43.55	40.00	100.00

LARGE FORMAT GRAPHICS

$/per	Survey %	Average	Typical	U.S. Avg.	U.S. Typ	U.S. Max
Text Page	0.0%			40.00	37.50	45.00
w/Graphics	0.0%			71.00	70.00	85.00
Hour	6.3%	32.50	32.50	47.95	45.00	90.00

LETTERHEAD & ENVELOPES

$/per	Survey %	Average	Typical	U.S. Avg.	U.S. Typ	U.S. Max
Text	15.6%	25.00	30.00	59.65	25.00	750.00
w/Graphics	15.6%	30.00	30.00	136.48	40.00	1000.00
Hour	53.1%	40.88	36.00	43.60	40.00	150.00

LINE ART & GENERAL ILLUSTRATIONS

$/per	Survey %	Average	Typical	U.S. Avg.	U.S. Typ	U.S. Max
Text Page	0.0%			64.17	47.50	135.00
w/Graphics	0.0%			221.89	100.00	1000.00
Hour	43.8%	40.79	40.00	46.24	43.50	115.00

LITIGATION GRAPHICS

$/per	Survey %	Average	Typical	U.S. Avg.	U.S. Typ	U.S. Max
Text Page	0.0%			75.00	75.00	75.00
w/Graphics	0.0%			100.00	100.00	100.00
Hour	9.4%	43.33	45.00	50.13	45.00	200.00

LOGOS

$/per	Survey %	Average	Typical	U.S. Avg.	U.S. Typ	U.S. Max
Each	12.5%	230.00	100.00	281.23	200.00	2000.00
Hour	53.1%	46.18	40.00	46.02	45.00	125.00

LOGOTYPE

$/per	Survey %	Average	Typical	U.S. Avg.	U.S. Typ	U.S. Max
Page	6.3%	412.50	400.00	304.36	300.00	1000.00
Hour	34.4%	50.91	35.00	48.68	45.00	125.00

MAGAZINES

$/per	Survey %	Average	Typical	U.S. Avg.	U.S. Typ	U.S. Max
Text Page	3.1%	8.00	8.00	60.49	35.00	250.00
w/Graphics	3.1%	12.00	12.00	90.89	40.00	500.00
Hour	25.0%	47.50	40.00	45.91	45.00	125.00

NOTES:
1. Multiple page prices converted to $/page.
2. Other prices noted for magazine design: $500 setup; $1,000 ea.

MAILERS

$/per	Survey %	Average	Typical	U.S. Avg.	U.S. Typ	U.S. Max
Text Page	3.1%	45.00	45.00	64.08	25.00	500.00
w/Graphics	3.1%	50.00	50.00	82.36	40.00	500.00
Hour	25.0%	48.13	45.00	46.11	42.00	100.00

MANUALS

$/per	Survey %	Average	Typical	U.S. Avg.	U.S. Typ	U.S. Max
Text Page	6.3%	11.00	11.00	42.06	17.50	500.00
w/Graphics	3.1%	15.00	15.00	58.10	30.00	500.00
Hour	46.9%	39.60	35.00	42.63	40.00	100.00

MAPS
(1C, 2C, Letter Size)

$/per	Survey %	Average	Typical	U.S. Avg.	U.S. Typ	U.S. Max
Simple	0.0%			76.25	70.00	250.00
Complex	0.0%			206.14	75.00	600.00
Hour	18.8%	37.17	40.00	46.90	45.00	100.00

MAPS
(4C, Larger Than Letter Size)

$/per	Survey %	Average	Typical	U.S. Avg.	U.S. Typ	U.S. Max
Simple	0.0%			168.75	72.50	500.00
Complex	0.0%			490.71	300.00	1600.00
Hour	15.6%	39.60	40.00	48.08	45.00	100.00

MARKETING PLANS

$/per	Survey %	Average	Typical	U.S. Avg.	U.S. Typ	U.S. Max
Text Page	0.0%			59.00	10.00	250.00
w/Graphics	0.0%			182.67	40.00	500.00
Hour	12.5%	33.50	35.00	47.80	45.00	100.00

MEMO PADS

$/per	Survey %	Average	Typical	U.S. Avg.	U.S. Typ	U.S. Max
Text	6.3%	27.50	27.50	20.14	14.50	100.00
w/Graphics	6.3%	32.50	32.50	31.79	17.50	150.00
Hour	18.8%	36.67	35.00	43.94	40.00	100.00

MENUS

$/per	Survey %	Average	Typical	U.S. Avg.	U.S. Typ	U.S. Max
Text Page	9.4%	35.00	30.00	75.65	35.00	500.00
w/Graphics	6.3%	30.00	30.00	125.25	45.00	1000.00
Hour	37.5%	45.33	45.00	44.35	40.00	150.00
Minimum	0.0%			233.75	200.00	500.00

NEWSLETTERS

$/per	Survey %	Average	Typical	U.S. Avg.	U.S. Typ	U.S. Max
Text Page	12.5%	71.25	50.00	62.86	45.00	200.00
w/Graphics	15.6%	72.00	50.00	76.16	50.00	200.00
Hour	68.8%	41.45	36.00	42.97	40.00	160.00

NOTEPADS

$/per	Survey %	Average	Typical	U.S. Avg.	U.S. Typ	U.S. Max
Text	9.4%	20.00	15.00	32.28	25.00	100.00
w/Graphics	9.4%	26.67	20.00	41.37	35.00	150.00
Hour	21.9%	40.00	40.00	43.72	40.00	100.00

PACKAGING

$/per	Survey %	Average	Typical	U.S. Avg.	U.S. Typ	U.S. Max
Text	0.0%			276.00	100.00	1000.00
w/Graphics	0.0%			478.18	250.00	2500.00
Hour	21.9%	55.00	40.00	51.64	50.00	150.00

PEN RULER

$/per	Survey %	Average	Typical	U.S. Avg.	U.S. Typ	U.S. Max
Page	0.0%			45.00	45.00	45.00
Hour	6.3%	52.50	52.50	48.81	50.00	85.00

PERIODICAL (OTHER)

$/per	Survey %	Average	Typical	U.S. Avg.	U.S. Typ	U.S. Max
Text Page	3.1%	8.00	8.00	36.00	25.00	150.00
w/Graphics	3.1%	12.00	12.00	58.00	35.00	250.00
Hour	25.0%	47.00	40.00	46.86	45.00	125.00

POINT-OF-PURCHASE DISPLAYS

$/per	Survey %	Average	Typical	U.S. Avg.	U.S. Typ	U.S. Max
Text Page	0.0%			650.00	600.00	1000.00
w/Graphics	0.0%			800.00	800.00	1000.00
Hour	6.3%	30.00	30.00	50.15	50.00	100.00

POST CARDS

$/per	Survey %	Average	Typical	U.S. Avg.	U.S. Typ	U.S. Max
Text Page	9.4%	18.33	15.00	45.18	20.00	400.00
w/Graphics	9.4%	25.00	25.00	64.31	30.00	500.00
Hour	37.5%	32.17	35.00	42.38	40.00	100.00

POSTERS

$/per	Survey %	Average	Typical	U.S. Avg.	U.S. Typ	U.S. Max
Text Page	0.0%			123.67	50.00	500.00
w/Graphics	0.0%			259.71	250.00	1000.00
Hour	31.3%	44.00	40.00	45.60	45.00	100.00

PRESENTATION MATERIALS

$/per	Survey %	Average	Typical	U.S. Avg.	U.S. Typ	U.S. Max
Text Page	3.1%	40.00	40.00	27.65	20.00	100.00
w/Graphics	3.1%	45.00	45.00	44.38	25.00	180.00
Hour	40.6%	44.08	40.00	45.04	45.00	100.00

PRICE LISTS

$/per	Survey %	Average	Typical	U.S. Avg.	U.S. Typ	U.S. Max
Text Page	9.4%	28.33	25.00	40.63	35.00	150.00
w/Graphics	6.3%	22.50	22.50	51.79	40.00	160.00
Hour	43.8%	41.07	35.00	42.68	40.00	100.00

PRINT ADS

$/per	Survey %	Average	Typical	U.S. Avg.	U.S. Typ	U.S. Max
Text	9.4%	23.33	25.00	107.09	45.00	1000.00
w/Graphics	9.4%	56.67	30.00	179.74	80.00	1100.00
Hour	43.8%	41.50	36.00	44.84	40.00	100.00

PROCEDURE GUIDES

$/per	Survey %	Average	Typical	U.S. Avg.	U.S. Typ	U.S. Max
Text Page	3.1%	40.00	40.00	60.00	15.00	300.00
w/Graphics	3.1%	45.00	45.00	93.21	25.00	500.00
Hour	31.3%	43.00	35.00	45.67	45.00	100.00

PRODUCT LITERATURE

$/per	Survey %	Average	Typical	U.S. Avg.	U.S. Typ	U.S. Max
Text Page	3.1%	40.00	40.00	67.97	30.00	500.00
w/Graphics	3.1%	45.00	45.00	118.81	40.00	1000.00
Hour	31.3%	47.50	45.00	45.43	42.00	100.00

PRODUCT SPECIFICATION SHEETS

$/per	Survey %	Average	Typical	U.S. Avg.	U.S. Typ	U.S. Max
Text Page	3.1%	40.00	40.00	70.95	25.00	500.00
w/Graphics	3.1%	45.00	45.00	168.89	35.00	1000.00
Hour	25.0%	48.13	45.00	46.44	45.00	100.00

PROGRAMS

$/per	Survey %	Average	Typical	U.S. Avg.	U.S. Typ	U.S. Max
Text Page	3.1%	35.00	35.00	43.92	25.00	200.00
w/Graphics	3.1%	40.00	40.00	95.94	35.00	500.00
Hour	21.9%	49.14	45.00	46.61	45.00	150.00

PUBLICATIONS (OTHER)

$/per	Survey %	Average	Typical	U.S. Avg.	U.S. Typ	U.S. Max
Text Page	3.1%	30.00	30.00	46.00	30.00	150.00
w/Graphics	3.1%	35.00	35.00	87.73	35.00	500.00
Hour	40.6%	46.69	36.00	44.63	40.00	125.00

RECORD BOOKS

$/per	Survey %	Average	Typical	U.S. Avg.	U.S. Typ	U.S. Max
Text Page	0.0%			20.67	15.00	45.00
w/Graphics	0.0%			35.00	35.00	45.00
Hour	6.3%	37.50	37.50	46.63	45.00	80.00

RESUMES

$/per	Survey %	Average	Typical	U.S. Avg.	U.S. Typ	U.S. Max
Each	18.8%	26.67	25.00	31.21	25.00	150.00
Page	18.8%	26.67	25.00	31.52	30.00	150.00
Hour	37.5%	35.08	35.00	40.96	40.00	150.00

RULERS

$/per	Survey %	Average	Typical	U.S. Avg.	U.S. Typ	U.S. Max
Each	0.0%			250.00	375.00	500.00
Hour	0.0%			49.08	50.00	100.00

SALES PRESENTATIONS

$/per	Survey %	Average	Typical	U.S. Avg.	U.S. Typ	U.S. Max
Text Page	3.1%	40.00	40.00	23.14	20.00	45.00
w/Graphics	3.1%	45.00	45.00	29.50	25.00	45.00
Hour	34.4%	42.09	45.00	46.13	45.00	100.00

SIGNAGE

$/per	Survey %	Average	Typical	U.S. Avg.	U.S. Typ	U.S. Max
Text	3.1%	15.00	15.00	27.50	35.00	55.00
w/Graphics	3.1%	15.00	15.00	159.06	35.00	575.00
Hour	21.9%	33.00	35.00	45.60	45.00	100.00

SLIDE DESIGN

$/per	Survey %	Average	Typical	U.S. Avg.	U.S. Typ	U.S. Max
Text	6.3%	21.00	21.00	25.00	20.00	75.00
w/Graphics	6.3%	21.00	21.00	30.11	25.00	100.00
Hour	18.8%	36.83	40.00	46.17	45.00	100.00

SLIDE SHOW DESIGN

$/per	Survey %	Average	Typical	U.S. Avg.	U.S. Typ	U.S. Max
Text Page	3.1%	10.00	10.00	30.00	25.00	75.00
w/Graphics	3.1%	10.00	10.00	40.00	30.00	100.00
Hour	12.5%	35.25	35.00	47.98	50.00	100.00

SPREADSHEET DESIGN

$/per	Survey %	Average	Typical	U.S. Avg.	U.S. Typ	U.S. Max
Text Page	0.0%			35.00	35.00	45.00
w/Graphics	0.0%			45.50	45.00	45.00
Hour	28.1%	49.22	48.00	45.82	45.00	125.00

TABLOIDS

$/per	Survey %	Average	Typical	U.S. Avg.	U.S. Typ	U.S. Max
Text Page	3.1%	40.00	40.00	70.71	45.00	200.00
w/Graphics	3.1%	45.00	45.00	67.50	50.00	120.00
Hour	18.8%	57.50	45.00	46.32	45.00	125.00

TABS

$/per	Survey %	Average	Typical	U.S. Avg.	U.S. Typ	U.S. Max
Text	3.1%	20.00	20.00	20.00	20.00	20.00
w/Graphics	3.1%	20.00	20.00	20.00	20.00	20.00
Hour	15.6%	33.80	35.00	47.58	45.00	100.00

TAGS

$/per	Survey %	Average	Typical	U.S. Avg.	U.S. Typ	U.S. Max
Each	0.0%		5	17.83	10.00	35.00
Hour	12.5%	32.50	30.00	44.69	42.00	80.00

TECHNICAL DOCUMENTS

$/per	Survey %	Average	Typical	U.S. Avg.	U.S. Typ	U.S. Max
Text Page	3.1%	40.00	40.00	72.69	40.00	250.00
w/Graphics	3.1%	45.00	45.00	87.50	45.00	500.00
Hour	56.3%	40.78	35.00	44.05	40.00	125.00

TECHNICAL ILLUSTRATIONS

$/per	Survey %	Average	Typical	U.S. Avg.	U.S. Typ	U.S. Max
Page	0.0%			70.45	75.00	200.00
Hour	34.4%	41.00	35.00	47.28	45.00	200.00

TICKETS

$/per	Survey %	Average	Typical	U.S. Avg.	U.S. Typ	U.S. Max
Text	3.1%	20.00	20.00	24.72	20.00	50.00
w/Graphics	3.1%	25.00	25.00	30.25	30.00	50.00
Hour	12.5%	38.50	45.00	42.53	40.00	100.00

TRANSPARENCY DESIGN (B&W)

$/per	Survey %	Average	Typical	U.S. Avg.	U.S. Typ	U.S. Max
Text Page	9.4%	20.00	20.00	34.00	25.00	130.00
w/Graphics	6.3%	30.00	30.00	92.50	45.00	250.00
Hour	40.6%	40.38	36.00	42.68	40.00	100.00

TRANSPARENCY DESIGN (COLOR)						
$/per	Survey %	Average	Typical	U.S. Avg.	U.S. Typ	U.S. Max
Text Page	6.3%	25.00	25.00	27.50	30.00	45.00
w/Graphics	3.1%	40.00	40.00	32.50	40.00	45.00
Hour	31.3%	47.00	45.00	44.69	45.00	100.00

OTHER DESIGN						
$/per	Survey %	Average	Typical	U.S. Avg.	U.S. Typ	U.S. Max
Hour	18.8%	54.67	60.00	48.76	45.00	100.00

LASER PRINTER OUTPUT

GENERAL NOTES:
1. Some shops bill as $ set-up fee plus price per page.
2. Some shops bill as $/hr plus $/page.
3. A few shops price at $/hr (typically same price as other services).
4. Some laser printer output priced as $/job plus $/pg.

LASER PRINTING (Up to 300 dpi)						
$/per	Survey %	Average	Typical	U.S. Avg.	U.S. Typ	U.S. Max
8.5 x 11	28.1%	1.58	1.00	1.64	1.00	15.00
8.5 x 14	12.5%	1.20	0.95	1.95	3.00	10.00
11 x 17	6.3%	1.73	1.75	3.13	2.25	6.00
Cost Plus	3.1%	40.00	40.00	31.25	30.00	50.00
Minimum	2.7%	15.00	15.00	15.00	5.00	25.00

LASER PRINTING (400 dpi)						
$/per	Survey %	Average	Typical	U.S. Avg.	U.S. Typ	U.S. Max
8.5 x 11	9.4%	1.02	1.00	3.03	1.93	15.50
8.5 x 14	6.3%	1.03	1.05	2.71	2.00	6.00
11 x 17	3.1%	2.50	2.50	6.75	4.50	20.00
Cost Plus	3.1%	40.00	40.00	28.00	20.00	50.00
Minimum	2.7%	15.00	15.00	15.00	5.00	25.00

LASER PRINTING (600 dpi)						
$/per	Survey %	Average	Typical	U.S. Avg.	U.S. Typ	U.S. Max
8.5 x 11	12.5%	1.29	1.10	1.88	1.00	15.00
8.5 x 14	12.5%	1.36	1.25	1.88	1.95	4.46
11 x 17	0.0%			4.12	5.16	6.00
Cost Plus	3.1%	40.00	40.00	28.00	20.00	50.00

LASER PRINTING (800dpi)						
$/per	Survey %	Average	Typical	U.S. Avg.	U.S. Typ	U.S. Max
8.5 x 11	9.4%	0.77	0.95	2.75	2.00	12.00
8.5 x 14	6.3%	1.03	1.05	2.94	4.00	5.00
11 x 17	0.0%			6.00	6.00	6.00
Cost Plus	3.1%	40.00	40.00	28.00	20.00	50.00
Minimum	2.7%	15.00	15.00	15.00	5.00	25.00

LASER PRINTING (1000 dpi)						
$/per	Survey %	Average	Typical	U.S. Avg.	U.S. Typ	U.S. Max
8.5 x 11	0.0%			3.10	3.00	7.00
8.5 x 14	0.0%			4.06	4.00	7.00
11 x 17	0.0%			6.00	6.00	6.00
Cost Plus	3.1%	40.00	40.00	28.00	20.00	50.00
Minimum	2.7%	15.00	15.00	15.00	10.00	25.00

LASER PRINTING (1200 dpi)						
$/per	Survey %	Average	Typical	U.S. Avg.	U.S. Typ	U.S. Max
8.5 x 11	3.1%	4.00	4.00	2.89	3.00	6.00
8.5 x 14	3.1%	6.00	6.00	4.82	6.00	6.43
11 x 17	0.0%			7.18	6.00	13.25
Cost Plus	3.1%	40.00	40.00	28.00	20.00	50.00
Minimum	2.7%	15.00	15.00	15.00	10.00	25.00

FOR PREPRESS AND OTHER SERVICES (INCLUDING IMAGESETTING OUTPUT), REFER TO THE SECTION MARKED "NATIONAL."

Price Distribution
PACIFIC
AK, CA, HI, OR, WA

FILE CONVERSION

GENERAL NOTE: Survey responses listed as $/minute were converted to $/hr.

BOOKS ON DISK

$/per	Survey %	Average	Typical	U.S. Avg.	U.S. Typ	U.S. Max
Disk	2.9%	10.20	10.00	10.57	10.00	25.00
Page	0.6%	2.00	2.00	6.00	5.50	10.00
Hour	8.24%	45.57	35.00	40.11	35.00	95.00
Minimum	0.0%			15.00	15.00	15.00

CD-ROM

$/per	Survey %	Average	Typical	U.S. Avg.	U.S. Typ	U.S. Max
Page	0.0%			8.00	8.00	8.00
Disk	0.6%	25.00	25.00	25.00	25.00	25.00
Hour	3.5%	50.00	50.00	48.00	43.00	85.00
Minimum	0.6%	125.00	75.00	70.00	70.00	125.00

CROSS PLATFORM

$/per	Survey %	Average	Typical	U.S. Avg.	U.S. Typ	U.S. Max
Page	1.2%	0.75	0.75	3.83	2.88	8.00
File	7.7%	8.23	10.00	7.85	9.00	20.00
Disk	5.9%	16.50	10.00	11.85	10.00	50.00
Hour	25.88%	47.89	45.00	46.31	45.00	100.00
Minimum	1.8%	10.00	10.00	14.25	12.50	35.00

DATABASE FILES

$/per	Survey %	Average	Typical	U.S. Avg.	U.S. Typ	U.S. Max
Record	0.1%	0.05	0.05	0.16	0.15	0.25
File	2.9%	11.01	10.00	7.02	10.00	20.00
Disk	1.8%	30.00	25.00	21.67	15.00	50.00
Hour	12.9%	40.82	45.00	42.46	40.50	100.00
Minimum	0.0%			22.50	20.00	35.00

DOCUMENT FILES

$/per	Survey %	Average	Typical	U.S. Avg.	U.S. Typ	U.S. Max
K byte	0.0%	5.25	5.25	5.25	5.25	5.25
Page	0.6%	2.00	2.00	2.71	2.75	3.50
File	5.9%	10.20	10.00	8.38	10.00	15.00
Disk	2.9%	21.40	15.00	15.73	15.00	50.00
Hour	22.9%	40.08	35.00	41.23	35.00	100.00
Minimum	0.0%			21.00	15.00	35.00

DOCUMENTS ON DISK

$/per	Survey %	Average	Typical	U.S. Avg.	U.S. Typ	U.S. Max
Page	0.6%	1.50	6.16	6.17	7.00	15.00
File	2.4%	13.75	15.00	12.00	15.00	15.00
Disk	4.1%	11.14	10.57	14.00	10.00	50.00
Hour	0.6%	41.78	40.11	38.77	35.00	75.00
Minimum	0.0%			12.50	13.00	15.00

FORMS CONVERSION

$/per	Survey %	Average	Typical	U.S. Avg.	U.S. Typ	U.S. Max
Page	0.0%			187.18	190.00	200.00
File	2.4%	30.00	50.00	26.00	10.00	50.00
Disk	1.2%	17.75	17.50	15.00	10.00	25.00
Hour	5.3%	48.89	50.00	47.68	40.00	100.00
Minimum	0.0%			12.50	15.00	15.00

GRAPHIC FORMAT FILES

$/per	Survey %	Average	Typical	U.S. Avg.	U.S. Typ	U.S. Max
K byte	0.1%	5.25	5.25	5.25	5.25	5.25
Page	0.0%			18.32	20.00	20.00
File	8.8%	10.33	10.00	8.50	5.88	20.00
Disk	2.4%	25.00	25.00	15.36	15.00	50.00
Hour	23.5%	42.33	40.00	44.32	40.00	100.00
Minimum	0.6%	10.00	10.00	19.17	15.00	35.00

MEDIA CONVERSION

$/per	Survey %	Average	Typical	U.S. Avg.	U.S. Typ	U.S. Max
File	0.6%	15.00	15.00	15.00	12.50	25.00
Disk	4.7%	14.94	10.00	13.05	10.00	50.00
Hour	11.8%	50.60	50.00	48.64	45.00	100.00
Minimum	0.6%	10.00	10.00	13.75	15.00	15.00

PAGE LAYOUT FILES

$/per	Survey %	Average	Typical	U.S. Avg.	U.S. Typ	U.S. Max
500 K byte	0.1%	5.25	5.25	15.00	15.00	15.00
Page	0.6%	2.00	2.00	37.50	37.50	60.00
File	3.5%	15.67	15.00	12.70	12.50	25.00
Disk	2.4%	23.00	25.00	19.25	15.00	50.00
Hour	21.2%	42.11	40.00	42.91	40.00	100.00
Minimum	0.6%	10.00	10.00	20.00	15.00	35.00

SPREADSHEET FILES

$/per	Survey %	Average	Typical	U.S. Avg.	U.S. Typ	U.S. Max
25 K byte	0.1%	7.50	7.50	7.50	7.50	7.50
Page	0.6%	2.00	2.00	2.88	2.88	2.00
File	3.5%	17.08	25.00	12.30	10.88	25.00
Disk	1.2%	37.50	35.00	26.25	20.00	50.00
Hour	11.2%	41.00	40.00	40.98	40.00	100.00
Minimum	0.0%			22.50	20.00	35.00

VIDEO TAPE TRANSFER

$/per	Survey %	Average	Typical	U.S. Avg.	U.S. Typ	U.S. Max
Disk	0.6%	25.00	25.00	25.00	25.00	25.00
Per Hour	2.9%	52.00	55.00	48.33	45.00	75.00
Minimum	0.0%			15.00	15.00	15.00

WORD PROCESSOR FILE TO SGML

$/per	Survey %	Average	Typical	U.S. Avg.	U.S. Typ	U.S. Max
Disk	0.6%	25.00	25.00	25.00	25.00	25.00
Hour	2.4%	50.00	55.00	45.00	40.00	75.00
Minimum	0.0%			15.00	15.00	15.00

TEXT CREATION

GENERAL COPY WRITING

$/per	Survey %	Average	Typical	U.S. Avg.	U.S. Typ	U.S. Max
Line	0.0%			0.20	0.20	0.20
Page	5.9%	29.25	15.00	30.38	20.00	87.50
Hour	46.8%	44.43	35.00	41.43	35.00	300.00
Minimum	1.2%	30.00	30.00	19.00	15.00	35.00

NEWSLETTER COPY

$/per	Survey %	Average	Typical	U.S. Avg.	U.S. Typ	U.S. Max
Column	0.0%			10.48	10.50	11.00
Page	8.3%	44.29	30.00	40.96	40.00	125.00
Hour	41.4%	43.71	35.00	39.31	35.00	300.00
Minimum	0.7%	114.25	300.00	283.33	125.00	800.00

PUBLICITY / ADVERTISING COPY

$/per	Survey %	Average	Typical	U.S. Avg.	U.S. Typ	U.S. Max
Page	4.7%	46.31	50.00	40.31	40.00	100.00
Piece	0.6%	425.00	425.00	260.00	300.00	425.00
Hour	35.5%	47.38	40.00	43.56	38.00	300.00
Minimum	0.6%	7.00	10.00	19.00	15.00	35.00

RESUME WRITING

$/per	Survey %	Average	Typical	U.S. Avg.	U.S. Typ	U.S. Max
Page	15.4%	31.06	30.00	32.43	25.00	100.00
Hour	34.9%	41.01	35.00	38.11	35.00	300.00
Minimum	0.6%	50.00	50.00	110.00	65.00	300.00

TECHNICAL WRITING

$/per	Survey %	Average	Typical	U.S. Avg.	U.S. Typ	U.S. Max
Page	1.2%	30.00	30.00	53.54	35.00	300.00
Hour	30.2%	49.61	42.00	45.99	35.00	300.00
Minimum	0.0%			35.00	35.00	55.00

DATA INPUT / EDITING

DATA ENTRY / KEYBOARDING

$/per	Survey %	Average	Typical	U.S. Avg.	U.S. Typ	U.S. Max
Character	0.0%			0.02	0.02	0.02
Page	5.9%	8.60	7.00	11.32	10.00	50.00
Hour	51.2%	33.13	30.00	32.64	28.00	100.00
Minimum	0.6%	10.00	10.00	20.00	15.00	35.00

COPY EDITING

$/per	Survey %	Average	Typical	U.S. Avg.	U.S. Typ	U.S. Max
Word	0.0%			0.06	0.06	0.11
Page	3.5%	6.33	7.00	9.47	7.00	50.00
Hour	48.8%	37.45	35.00	36.58	30.00	100.00
Minimum	0.6%	10.00	10.00	20.00	15.00	35.00

CONTENT EDITING

$/per	Survey %	Average	Typical	U.S. Avg.	U.S. Typ	U.S. Max
Word	0.0%			0.11	0.11	0.11
Page	1.2%	7.13	7.00	5.33	5.00	50.00
Hour	40.6%	40.24	35.00	37.44	36.00	100.00
Minimum	0.0%			33.50	35.00	35.00

PROOF READING

$/per	Survey %	Average	Typical	U.S. Avg.	U.S. Typ	U.S. Max
Page	2.9%	5.20	5.00	6.71	5.00	50.00
Hour	51.2%	36.93	35.00	35.63	30.00	100.00
Minimum	0.6%	10.00	10.00	33.50	35.00	35.00

REWRITING

$/per	Survey %	Average	Typical	U.S. Avg.	U.S. Typ	U.S. Max
Word	0.0%			0.07	0.03	0.11
Line	1.2%	0.40	0.55	0.25	0.20	1.00
Page	1.2%	26.57	26.50	22.67	13.50	50.00
Hour	41.8%	41.51	35.00	38.81	35.00	100.00
Minimum	0.6%	7.00	7.00	35.00	35.00	35.00

INDEXING

$/per	Survey %	Average	Typical	U.S. Avg.	U.S. Typ	U.S. Max
Page	1.2%	2.47	2.50	2.80	2.00	5.00
Hour	21.2%	38.53	35.00	38.60	35.00	100.00
Minimum	0.0%			87.50	87.50	140.00

MODEM INPUT

$/per	Survey %	Average	Typical	U.S. Avg.	U.S. Typ	U.S. Max
Page	0.6%	2.97	3.00	3.33	3.00	5.00
File	0.0%			10.00	10.00	10.00
K bytes	0.0%			1.32	1.40	1.50
Disk	0.0%			8.33	5.00	25.00
Minute	1.7%	1.22	2.00	1.50	1.50	2.00
Hour	17.1%	41.66	40.00	41.62	38.00	100.00
Minimum	0.0%			12.50	12.50	15.00

TEXT FILE IMPORTING

$/per	Survey %	Average	Typical	U.S. Avg.	U.S. Typ	U.S. Max
Page	1.2%	4.00	4.00	14.60	5.00	50.00
File	1.8%	15.00	10.00	11.00	10.00	25.00
K bytes	0.0%			1.32	1.40	1.50
Disk	0.0%			10.00	10.00	15.00
Minute	0.0%			1.50	1.50	2.00
Hour	31.8%	37.57	35.00	39.10	35.00	100.00
Minimum	0.0%			21.25	22.00	35.00

TRANSCRIPTION

$/per	Survey %	Average	Typical	U.S. Avg.	U.S. Typ	U.S. Max
Line	1.2%	0.16	0.17	0.17	0.17	0.25
Page	1.8%	4.08	3.25	4.79	4.25	8.00
File	0.0%			10.57	10.57	25.00
Disk	0.0%			25.00	25.00	25.00
Hour	17.7%	35.68	35.00	31.64	30.00	75.00
Minimum	0.0%			25.00	25.00	35.00

TRANSLATION

$/per	Survey %	Average	Typical	U.S. Avg.	U.S. Typ	U.S. Max
Word	0.6%	0.16	0.15	0.17	0.17	0.20
Page	1.8%	23.33	25.00	24.17	22.50	50.00
Hour	10.6%	53.67	50.00	44.49	40.00	150.00
Minimum	0.0%			35.00	35..00	35.00

TYPOGRAPHY (General)

$/per	Survey %	Average	Typical	U.S. Avg.	U.S. Typ	U.S. Max
Line	0.0%			0.25	0.25	0.25
Page	3.5%	18.92	15.00	21.48	15.00	75.00
Hour	53.5%	38.40	35.00	39.27	35.00	100.00
Minimum	0.6%	6.50	6.50	18.83	15.00	35.00

TYPOGRAPHY (Spreadsheet)

$/per	Survey %	Average	Typical	U.S. Avg.	U.S. Typ	U.S. Max
Line	0.0%			0.25	0.25	0.25
Page	4.7%	32.13	25.00	24.06	17.00	75.00
Hour	38.2%	41.34	35.00	41.47	36.00	150.00
Minimum	0.0%			35.00	35.00	35.00

WORD PROCESSSING

$/per	Survey %	Average	Typical	U.S. Avg.	U.S. Typ	U.S. Max
Line	0.0%			0.13	0.10	0.20
Page	6.5%	10.61	8.50	8.67	8.25	25.00
Hour	52.9%	32.58	30.00	32.90	25.00	100.00
Minimum	0.0%			21.67	15.00	35.00

DATA MANAGEMENT

GENERAL NOTES:
1. Assume customer pays for cost of media extra.
2. On $/word, assume 2K words per page.
3. Per file cost assumed to be for 1 year.
4. Assume $/file same as $/image.

ARCHIVING SERVICE

$/per	Survey %	Average	Typical	U.S. Avg.	U.S. Typ	U.S. Max
Page	0.0%			7.50	7.50	7.50
File	0.6%	25.00	25.00	9.63	15.00	25.00
Tape	1.8%	11.67	10.00	37.50	20.00	150.00
Hour	7.1%	47.50	45.00	46.05	40.00	95.00
Minimum	0.0%			14.17	10.00	25.00

IMAGE MANAGEMENT

$/per	Survey %	Average	Typical	U.S. Avg.	U.S. Typ	U.S. Max
Page	0.0%			6.50	5.50	10.00
File	1.2%	7.50	7.50	16.67	15.00	50.00
Disk	0.6%	10.00	10.00	30.00	30.00	50.00
Hour	5.9%	44.50	35.00	44.81	40.00	110.00
Minimum	0.0%			14.17	10.00	25.00

NOTE: Assume $/.file same as $/image.

TEXT MANAGEMENT

$/per	Survey %	Average	Typical	U.S. Avg.	U.S. Typ	U.S. Max
Page	0.0%			8.67	6.00	15.00
File	0.6%	15.00	15.00	16.67	15.00	50.00
Disk	1.2%	10.00	10.00	23.33	15.00	50.00
Hour	6.5%	49.09	35.00	44.51	35.00	95.00
Minimum	0.0%			14.17	10.00	25.00

IMAGING SERVICES

DOCUMENT CAPTURE

$/per	Survey %	Average	Typical	U.S. Avg.	U.S. Typ	U.S. Max
Page	0.0%			3.65	3.00	7.50
File	1.8%	7.50	7.50	6.50	5.00	10.00
Hour	3.6%	44.17	35.00	39.41	35.00	95.00
Minimum	0.0%			16.25	16.25	25.00

DOCUMENT RETRIEVAL

$/per	Survey %	Average	Typical	U.S. Avg.	U.S. Typ	U.S. Max
Page	0.0%			1.50	1.50	2.00
File	3.0%	5.94	5.00	5.03	5.00	10.00
Hour	2.4%	35.00	35.00	38.82	39.00	85.00
Minimum	0.0%			16.25	16.25	25.00

GRAPHICS FILE IMPORTING

$/per	Survey %	Average	Typical	U.S. Avg.	U.S. Typ	U.S. Max
File	7.7%	7.04	7.00	6.98	5.00	15.00
Disk	0.0%			5.00	5.00	5.00
Hour	11.8%	41.15	55.00	43.35	36.00	100.00
Minimum	0.0%			14.17	14.17	35.00

PHOTO CD-ROM IMPORTING

$/per	Survey %	Average	Typical	U.S. Avg.	U.S. Typ	U.S. Max
Image	7.7%	8.04	7.50	10.02	7.25	45.00
Stock Fee	0.0%			75.00	75.00	75.00
Hour	5.3%	51.11	45.00	48.60	45.00	100.00
Minimum	0.0%			16.25	15.00	25.00

SCANNING (B&W Grey Scale)

$/per	Survey %	Average	Typical	U.S. Avg.	U.S. Typ	U.S. Max
Hour	16.6%	39.68	35.00	42.82	40.00	100.00
75-200 dpi	5.9%	12.92	15.00	10.10	9.00	75.00
300-400 dpi	27.8%	12.14	10.00	11.93	10.00	75.00
600-800 dpi	8.9%	13.27	10.00	13.51	11.00	75.00
1200 dpi	7.7%	17.62	12.00	20.20	12.00	75.00
2400 dpi	2.4%	34.50	30.00	36.86	30.00	75.00

SCANNING (B&W Line Art)

$/per	Survey %	Average	Typical	U.S. Avg.	U.S. Typ	U.S. Max
Hour	16.6%	37.96	35.00	40.94	40.00	100.00
75-200 dpi	8.3%	10.55	10.00	10.59	9.00	75.00
300-400 dpi	31.9%	10.36	10.00	11.92	10.00	75.00
600-800 dpi	12.4%	11.93	10.00	12.51	10.00	75.00
1200 dpi	7.7%	10.38	10.00	15.59	11.00	75.00
2400 dpi	1.2%	21.50	22.00	35.75	27.50	75.00
Per K	0.0%			51.67	50.00	75.00

SCANNING (B&W Photo)

$/per	Survey %	Average	Typical	U.S. Avg.	U.S. Typ	U.S. Max
Hour	14.2%	44.00	35.00	45.16	40.00	100.00
75-200 dpi	7.1%	13.17	15.00	12.28	10.00	75.00
300-400 dpi	23.7%	12.55	10.00	13.92	12.40	75.00
600-800 dpi	10.7%	12.86	10.00	14.79	12.60	75.00
1200 dpi	5.9%	17.25	10.00	19.88	17.50	75.00
2400 dpi	2.4%	31.25	30.00	35.56	31.00	75.00
Per K	0.0%			62.50	62.50	75.00

SCANNING (Color Illustration)

$/per	Survey %	Average	Typical	U.S. Avg.	U.S. Typ	U.S. Max
Hour	8.8%	52.67	50.00	49.23	50.00	125.00
75-200 dpi	3.6%	19.33	20.00	19.08	15.00	75.00
300-400 dpi	10.1%	21.09	20.00	21.03	19.00	82.00
600-800 dpi	4.1%	19.29	20.00	22.36	21.50	75.00
1200 dpi	5.3%	24.67	20.00	26.47	23.00	75.00
2400 dpi	2.4%	43.25	60.00	46.22	50.00	75.00

SCANNING (Color Photo)

$/per	Survey %	Average	Typical	U.S. Avg.	U.S. Typ	U.S. Max
Hour	8.3%	52.14	55.00	49.23	50.00	125.00
75-200 dpi	3.0%	21.20	20.00	20.44	15.00	75.00
300-400 dpi	9.5%	21.22	20.00	20.97	17.75	82.00
600-800 dpi	4.1%	19.57	20.00	19.75	15.00	75.00
1200 dpi	3.6%	29.50	25.00	30.13	30.00	75.00
2400 dpi	3.6%	60.00	65.00	61.54	60.00	137.00

SCANNING (HIGH END)
(Loose Scan)

$/per	Survey %	U.S. Avg.	U.S. Typ	U.S. Max
2 x 3	0.1%	13.33	10.00	25.00
3 x 5	0.1%	11.25	10.00	20.00
4 x 5	0.1%	16.00	10.00	33.00
5 x 7	0.1%	18.00	10.00	37.00
5.5 x 8.5	0.1%	17.33	10.00	39.00
6 x 9	0.1%	24.67	15.00	49.00
8 x 10	0.1%	41.60	50.00	70.00
10 x 12	0.1%	47.80	60.00	84.00
11 x 14	0.1%	81.67	70.00	105.00
12 x 18	0.1%	90.67	80.00	122.00
16 x 20	0.1%	162.00	162.00	162.00
20 x 24	0.1%	199.00	199.00	199.00
Hour	0.1%	47.00	45.00	60.00

SCANNING (HIGH END)
(Drum Scan)

$/per	Survey %	U.S. Avg.	U.S. Typ	U.S. Max
2 x 3	0.1%	56..92	54.25	71.50
4 x 5	0.1%	57.21	55.00	94.50
5 x 7	0.1%	65.75	70.00	106.00
6 x 8	0.1%	103.13	102.50	117.50
6 x 9	0.1%	57.00	45.00	85.00
8 x 10	0.1%	51.25	50.00	60.00
10 x 12	0.1%	58.33	60.00	60.00
11 x 14	0.1%	71.25	72.50	75.00
12 x 18	0.1%	86.67	85.00	100.00
24 x 27	0.1%	600.00	600.00	600.00

SCANNING (HIGH END)
(High Res Scan to Disk)

$/per	Survey %	U.S. Avg.	U.S. Typ	U.S. Max
2 x 3	0.1%	20..50	19.50	25.00
4 x 5	0.1%	26.17	27.50	30.00
5 x 7	0.1%	34.00	35.00	41.00
6 x 9	0.1%	39.80	39.00	50.00

SCANNING (HIGH END)
(High Res Scan to Disk)

$/per	Survey %	U.S. Avg.	U.S. Typ	U.S. Max
8 x 10	0.1%	45.50	45.00	60.00
10 x 12	0.1%	56.83	59.00	70.00
11 x 14	0.1%	65.08	64.00	89.00
12 x 18	0.1%	78.90	75.00	100.00
16 x 20	0.1%	96.33	99.00	130.00
20 x 24	0.1%	128.00	134.00	160.00
24 x 27	0.1%	156.25	156.25	200.00

SCANNING (Transparency)

$/per	Survey %	Average	Typical	U.S. Avg.	U.S. Typ	U.S. Max
Each	3.0%	25.40	25.00	18.70	16.00	45.00
Hour	1.2%	75.00	70.00	65.29	55.00	137.00

SCANNING (Slide)

$/per	Survey %	Average	Typical	U.S. Avg.	U.S. Typ	U.S. Max
Each	3.6%	29.17	25.00	23.00	16.99	65.00
Hour	1.2%	87.50	85.00	68.42	55.00	137.00

COLOR CORRECTION

$/per	Survey %	Average	Typical	U.S. Avg.	U.S. Typ	U.S. Max
Hour	13.6%	79.43	60.00	65.80	50.00	300.00

IMAGE EDITING

$/per	Survey %	Average	Typical	U.S. Avg.	U.S. Typ	U.S. Max
Each	1.2%	26.50	25.00	20.75	15.00	50.00
Hour	24.9%	69.33	50.00	55.47	45.00	300.00

IMAGE ENHANCEMENT

$/per	Survey %	Average	Typical	U.S. Avg.	U.S. Typ	U.S. Max
Hour	18.3%	67.32	50.00	57.60	50.00	300.00

RETOUCHING

$/per	Survey %	Average	Typical	U.S. Avg.	U.S. Typ	U.S. Max
Each	1.2%	26.50	25.00	27.67	40.00	50.00
Hour	27.8%	66.47	50.00	58.60	50.00	300.00
Minimum	0.0%			26.08	25.00	35.00

TEXT SCAN (OCR)

$/per	Survey %	Average	Typical	U.S. Avg.	U.S. Typ	U.S. Max
Page	13.6%	9.03	3.00	7.82	5.00	95.00

TEXT SCAN (OCR)

$/per	Survey %	Average	Typical	U.S. Avg.	U.S. Typ	U.S. Max
Hour	16.0%	38.07	35.00	36.33	30.00	75.00
Minimum	0.6%	15.80	15.00	19.08	16.90	35.00

NOTE:

1. Prices assume spell check conducted on scanned text.
2. Assumes 2 Kb per page, so $1/Kb response incorporated as $2/page.

NEGATIVE CREATION

$/per	Survey %	Average	Typical	U.S. Avg.	U.S. Typ	U.S. Max
Each	3.0%	18.40	16.00	22.00	22.00	40.00
Hour	3.6%	70.00	80.00	56.71	56.71	100.00
Minimum	0.0%			16.67	16.67	25.00

DESIGN SERVICES

ANNOUNCEMENTS

$/per	Survey %	Average	Typical	U.S. Avg.	U.S. Typ	U.S. Max
Text Page	10.5%	49.22	30.00	37.05	24.00	250.00
w/Graphics	10.5%	87.71	40.00	65.36	36.50	500.00
Hour	32.8%	42.30	40.00	42.21	40.00	100.00

ANNUAL REPORTS
(1C, 2C, Up To Letter Size Pages)

$/per	Survey %	Average	Typical	U.S. Avg.	U.S. Typ	U.S. Max
Text	7.0%	153.33	100.00	114.75	62.50	1000.00
w/Graphics	5.9%	313.00	200.00	222.00	100.00	7680.00
Hour	35.7%	49.17	45.00	46.58	45.00	100.00

ANNUAL REPORTS
(3C, 4C, Larger Size Pages)

$/per	Survey %	Average	Typical	U.S. Avg.	U.S. Typ	U.S. Max
Text	4.1%	311.43	100.00	214.55	100.00	1500.00
w/Graphics	2.9%	504.00	250.00	422.50	175.00	11520.00
Hour	31.0%	49.10	45.00	46.34	45.00	100.00

BAR CODING

$/per	Survey %	Average	Typical	U.S. Avg.	U.S. Typ	U.S. Max
Each	2.3%	48.25	30.00	13.25	11.00	150.00
Page	0.6%	50.00	50.00	29.00	29.00	50.00
Hour	10.5%	46.78	45.00	47.83	45.00	100.00

BOOKLETS

$/per	Survey %	Average	Typical	U.S. Avg.	U.S. Typ	U.S. Max
Text Page	11.7%	64.10	45.00	48.40	30.00	500.00
w/Graphics	11.1%	154.47	55.00	110.53	50.00	650.00
Hour	59.1%	44.88	40.00	43.87	25.00	100.00

BOOK COVERS

$/per	Survey %	Average	Typical	U.S. Avg.	U.S. Typ	U.S. Max
Text	7.0%	175.42	200.00	143.10	75.00	500.00
w/Graphics	7.0%	465.42	350.00	403.36	300.00	1800.00
Hour	36.8%	50.15	45.00	47.83	45.00	120.00

BOOK BODY

$/per	Survey %	Average	Typical	U.S. Avg.	U.S. Typ	U.S. Max
Text Page	5.3%	87.61	60.00	26.65	20.00	75.00
w/Graphics	4.1%	250.00	100.00	41.11	25.00	85.00
Hour	34.5%	45.22	40.00	44.26	40.00	100.00

BOOK JACKETS

$/per	Survey %	Average	Typical	U.S. Avg.	U.S. Typ	U.S. Max
Text	5.9%	165.50	180.00	161.54	175.00	500.00
w/Graphics	4.7%	476.25	350.00	491.00	325.00	1000.00
Hour	32.2%	51.05	45.00	48.63	45.00	120.00

BROCHURE
(1C, 2C, Up To Letter Size Sheet)

$/per	Survey %	Average	Typical	U.S. Avg.	U.S. Typ	U.S. Max
Text Page	11.7%	85.85	60.00	72.59	47.50	500.00
w/Graphics	13.5%	206.41	100.00	156.74	82.50	750.00
Hour	64.9%	44.25	40.00	42.85	40.00	125.00

BROCHURE
(3C, 4C, Larger Size Sheet)

$/per	Survey %	Average	Typical	U.S. Avg.	U.S. Typ	U.S. Max
Text Page	5.3%	207.22	60.00	123.79	60.00	1000.00
w/Graphics	7.0%	342.08	300.00	227.71	100.00	1500.00
Hour	58.5%	44.20	40.00	44.17	40.00	125.00

BULLETIN

$/per	Survey %	Average	Typical	U.S. Avg.	U.S. Typ	U.S. Max
Text Page	5.9%	30.20	35.00	32.75	25.00	150.00
w/Graphics	5.9%	57.50	60.00	47.81	35.00	200.00
Hour	24.6%	41.60	40.00	42.36	40.00	100.00

BUSINESS CARDS

$/per	Survey %	Average	Typical	U.S. Avg.	U.S. Typ	U.S. Max
Text Card	20.5%	58.57	30.00	38.81	25.00	500.00
w/Graphics	19.9%	111.99	45.00	91.70	40.00	1000.00
Hour	72.5%	43.96	40.00	43.19	40.00	150.00

BUSINESS REPLY CARDS

$/per	Survey %	Average	Typical	U.S. Avg.	U.S. Typ	U.S. Max
Text Card	6.4%	49.09	40.00	34.32	31.50	150.00
w/Graphics	6.4%	91.36	60.00	67.50	35.00	250.00
Hour	43.3%	43.99	37.50	43.79	40.00	100.00

BUSINESS LETTERS

$/per	Survey %	Average	Typical	U.S. Avg.	U.S. Typ	U.S. Max
Text Page	9.9%	20.66	22.50	17.23	12.25	90.00
w/Graphics	4.7%	42.50	40.00	27.08	18.75	100.00
Hour	44.4%	37.75	35.00	39.38	35.00	100.00

CALENDARS

$/per	Survey %	Average	Typical	U.S. Avg.	U.S. Typ	U.S. Max
Text Page	4.1%	107.86	50.00	82.50	50.00	500.00
w/Graphics	2.9%	87.00	75.00	53.18	45.00	150.00
Hour	29.8%	44.45	40.00	43.77	40.00	100.00

CALLIGRAPHY

$/per	Survey %	Average	Typical	U.S. Avg.	U.S. Typ	U.S. Max
Line	0.6%	1.50	1.00	1.00	1.00	60.00
Page	2.3%	61.25	60.00	40.00	35.00	100.00
Hour	18.7%	43.91	40.00	45.50	40.00	175.00

CARDS (FOLD-OVER)

$/per	Survey %	Average	Typical	U.S. Avg.	U.S. Typ	U.S. Max
Text Card	5.9%	36.00	35.00	31.45	25.00	60.00
w/Graphics	5.9%	81.25	50.00	65.47	46.40	250.00
Hour	29.4%	42.25	40.00	43.63	40.00	100.00

CARDS (ROLODEX)

$/per	Survey %	Average	Typical	U.S. Avg.	U.S. Typ	U.S. Max
Text Card	4.7%	45.63	35.00	37.34	25.00	150.00
w/Graphics	4.7%	68.13	50.00	63.00	48.00	250.00
Hour	19.3%	44.97	42.00	44.94	41.00	100.00

CARTOONS

$/per	Survey %	Average	Typical	U.S. Avg.	U.S. Typ	U.S. Max
Each	3.5%	118.33	60.00	119.29	60.00	400.00
Page	1.2%	230.00	225.00	163.33	65.00	400.00
Hour	21.1%	47.71	45.00	48.15	45.00	90.00

CATALOGS

$/per	Survey %	Average	Typical	U.S. Avg.	U.S. Typ	U.S. Max
Text Page	6.4%	120.91	60.00	69.03	40.00	500.00
w/Graphics	5.9%	196.50	100.00	129.05	67.50	1000.00
Hour	42.7%	45.00	42.00	45.68	45.00	125.00

CERTIFICATES

$/per	Survey %	Average	Typical	U.S. Avg.	U.S. Typ	U.S. Max
Text	7.0%	36.00	27.00	23.56	16.25	125.00
w/Graphics	5.9%	46.20	32.00	35.07	25.00	150.00
Hour	28.7%	41.81	40.00	42.15	40.00	100.00

CHARTS / DIAGRAMS

$/per	Survey %	Average	Typical	U.S. Avg.	U.S. Typ	U.S. Max
Text	7.6%	35.23	35.00	36.19	32.50	150.00
w/Graphics	7.0%	56.58	50.00	53.14	47.50	150.00
Hour	42.7%	43.36	40.00	44.29	40.00	100.00

COMIC BOOKS

$/per	Survey %	Average	Typical	U.S. Avg.	U.S. Typ	U.S. Max
Each Page	0.6%	60.00	60.00	65.00	60.00	100.00
Hour	5.3%	46.11	60.00	47.12	50.00	80.00

COMIC STRIPS

$/per	Survey %	Average	Typical	U.S. Avg.	U.S. Typ	U.S. Max
Each Strip	0.6%	60.00	60.00	38.33	30.00	60.00
Hour	4.7%	48.75	60.00	46.78	50.00	80.00

COMPUTER GENERATED ART

$/per	Survey %	Average	Typical	U.S. Avg.	U.S. Typ	U.S. Max
Page	2.9%	50.00	50.00	121.40	50.00	500.00
Hour	46.8%	48.29	45.00	46.70	42.00	175.00

CUSTOM DISPLAYS

$/per	Survey %	Average	Typical	U.S. Avg.	U.S. Typ	U.S. Max
Text	3.5%	221.67	100.00	192.14	60.00	1000.00
w/Graphics	3.5%	226.67	100.00	265.71	100.00	1000.00
Hour	21.1%	50.31	45.00	48.95	45.00	100.00

DATABASE DESIGN

$/per	Survey %	Average	Typical	U.S. Avg.	U.S. Typ	U.S. Max
Text	1.2%	45.00	45.00	38.33	30.00	60.00
w/Graphics	1.2%	50.00	50.00	43.33	40.00	60.00
Hour	9.4%	41.06	40.00	42.45	41.00	80.00

DIGITAL SLIDE PRESENTATIONS

$/per	Survey %	Average	Typical	U.S. Avg.	U.S. Typ	U.S. Max
Text	1.8%	35.00	35.00	27.13	27.50	60.00
w/Graphics	1.8%	40.00	35.00	35.00	32.50	60.00
Hour	9.9%	45.82	45.00	45.81	45.00	100.00

DIRECT MAIL PACKAGES

$/per	Survey %	Average	Typical	U.S. Avg.	U.S. Typ	U.S. Max
Text	3.5%	344.17	400.00	298.46	60.00	1500.00
w/Graphics	3.5%	650.83	750.00	413.50	65.00	2000.00
Hour	36.3%	45.63	40.00	47.05	45.00	100.00

DIRECTORY

$/per	Survey %	Average	Typical	U.S. Avg.	U.S. Typ	U.S. Max
Text	5.9%	43.45	40.00	38.72	30.00	150.00
w/Graphics	5.3%	104.44	50.00	73.53	40.00	500.00
Hour	32.2%	42.40	40.00	43.08	40.00	125.00

DISPLAY ADVERTISING

$/per	Survey %	Average	Typical	U.S. Avg.	U.S. Typ	U.S. Max
Text	4.7%	192.13	60.00	109.28	30.00	1000.00
w/Graphics	4.1%	477.86	60.00	304.64	45.00	2500.00
Hour	39.2%	46.75	42.00	48.23	45.00	115.00

DISPLAY EXHIBITS

$/per	Survey %	Average	Typical	U.S. Avg.	U.S. Typ	U.S. Max
Text Panel	3.5%	896.67	100.00	858.57	90.00	5000.00
w/Graphics	3.5%	918.33	100.00	896.67	100.00	5000.00
Hour	22.8%	53.31	50.00	51.43	50.00	115.00

DOOR HANGERS

$/per	Survey %	Average	Typical	U.S. Avg.	U.S. Typ	U.S. Max
Text	4.1%	57.43	25.00	42.46	25.00	250.00
w/Graphics	3.5%	113.75	47.50	87.50	35.00	500.00
Hour	18.1%	44.48	42.00	47.19	45.00	100.00

DRAFTING

$/per	Survey %	Average	Typical	U.S. Avg.	U.S. Typ	U.S. Max
Page	1.2%	45.00	45.00	45.00	45.00	60.00
Hour	14.6%	49.88	45.00	46.62	45.00	100.00

FINANCIAL DOCUMENTS

$/per	Survey %	Average	Typical	U.S. Avg.	U.S. Typ	U.S. Max
Text Page	2.3%	73.75	60.00	45.33	33.00	150.00
w/Graphics	2.3%	4105.00	150.00	92.00	60.00	150.00
Hour	19.9%	44.51	50.00	47.20	45.00	125.00

FLYERS

$/per	Survey %	Average	Typical	U.S. Avg.	U.S. Typ	U.S. Max
Text Page	17.0%	40.33	25.00	39.21	25.00	325.00
w/Graphics	15.2%	73.65	35.00	66.84	35.00	325.00
Hour	69.6%	41.66	37.50	42.22	40.00	100.00

FORMS

$/per	Survey %	Average	Typical	U.S. Avg.	U.S. Typ	U.S. Max
Text Page	10.5%	78.17	35.00	52.60	30.00	750.00
w/Graphics	9.9%	116.76	60.00	81.67	37.50	10000.00
Hour	57.3%	41.59	36.00	41.75	40.00	125.00

HANDBOOKS

$/per	Survey %	Average	Typical	U.S. Avg.	U.S. Typ	U.S. Max
Text Page	3.5%	48.67	35.00	38.22	25.00	150.00
w/Graphics	3.5%	85.00	60.00	62.46	35.00	250.00
Hour	42.1%	43.05	40.00	43.53	40.00	100.00

INSERTS

$/per	Survey %	Average	Typical	U.S. Avg.	U.S. Typ	U.S. Max
Text Page	5.3%	133.83	30.00	70.58	27.50	1000.00
w/Graphics	4.7%	345.94	35.00	193.50	35.00	2500.00
Hour	39.2%	43.88	40.00	43.99	40.00	100.00

INVITATIONS

$/per	Survey %	Average	Typical	U.S. Avg.	U.S. Typ	U.S. Max
Text	11.1%	35.68	20.00	35.01	25.00	250.00
w/Graphics	8.2%	98.39	35.00	73.16	35.00	750.00
Hour	55.6%	41.03	36.00	41.85	40.00	100.00

LABELS (Custom)

$/per	Survey %	Average	Typical	U.S. Avg.	U.S. Typ	U.S. Max
Text	6.4%	52.80	35.00	40.06	20.00	250.00
w/Graphics	5.2%	180.33	75.00	121.16	55.00	600.00
Hour	29.7%	44.53	42.00	43.55	40.00	100.00

LARGE FORMAT GRAPHICS

$/per	Survey %	Average	Typical	U.S. Avg.	U.S. Typ	U.S. Max
Text Page	1.7%	40.00	45.00	40.00	37.50	45.00
w/Graphics	1.2%	70.00	70.00	71.00	70.00	85.00
Hour	14.5%	46.28	45.00	47.95	45.00	90.00

LETTERHEAD & ENVELOPES

$/per	Survey %	Average	Typical	U.S. Avg.	U.S. Typ	U.S. Max
Text	13.4%	83.29	35.00	59.65	25.00	750.00
w/Graphics	11.6%	166.95	50.00	136.48	40.00	1000.00
Hour	66.3%	44.93	45.00	43.60	40.00	150.00

LINE ART & GENERAL ILLUSTRATIONS

$/per	Survey %	Average	Typical	U.S. Avg.	U.S. Typ	U.S. Max
Text Page	1.7%	93.33	100.00	64.17	47.50	135.00
w/Graphics	2.9%	116.00	100.00	221.89	100.00	1000.00
Hour	45.9%	48.48	45.00	46.24	43.50	115.00

LITIGATION GRAPHICS

$/per	Survey %	Average	Typical	U.S. Avg.	U.S. Typ	U.S. Max
Text Page	0.6%	75.00	75.00	75.00	75.00	75.00
w/Graphics	0.6%	100.00	100.00	100.00	100.00	100.00
Hour	12.2%	56.07	50.00	50.13	45.00	200.00

LOGOS

$/per	Survey %	Average	Typical	U.S. Avg.	U.S. Typ	U.S. Max
Each	16.3%	294.38	200.00	281.23	200.00	2000.00
Hour	61.6%	47.23	45.00	46.02	45.00	125.00

LOGOTYPE

$/per	Survey %	Average	Typical	U.S. Avg.	U.S. Typ	U.S. Max
Page	3.5%	427.50	500.00	304.36	300.00	1000.00
Hour	34.3%	48.29	50.00	48.68	45.00	125.00

MAGAZINES

$/per	Survey %	Average	Typical	U.S. Avg.	U.S. Typ	U.S. Max
Text Page	3.5%	80.00	40.00	60.49	35.00	250.00
w/Graphics	4.7%	119.38	40.00	90.89	40.00	500.00
Hour	29.7%	44.81	40.00	45.91	45.00	125.00

NOTES:
1. Multiple page prices converted to $/page.
2. Other prices noted for magazine design: $500 setup; $1,000 ea.

MAILERS

$/per	Survey %	Average	Typical	U.S. Avg.	U.S. Typ	U.S. Max
Text Page	4.7	85.25	35.00	64.08	25.00	500.00
w/Graphics	6.7%	101.88	45.00	82.36	40.00	500.00
Hour	32.6%	45.75	40.00	46.11	42.00	100.00

MANUALS

$/per	Survey %	Average	Typical	U.S. Avg.	U.S. Typ	U.S. Max
Text Page	6.4%	69.50	25.00	42.06	17.50	500.00
w/Graphics	6.4%	82.05	40.00	58.10	30.00	500.00
Hour	48.9%	44.41	40.00	42.63	40.00	100.00

MAPS
(1C, 2C, Letter Size)

$/per	Survey %	Average	Typical	U.S. Avg.	U.S. Typ	U.S. Max
Simple	4.7%	76.25	70.00	76.25	70.00	250.00
Complex	5.2%	214.44	75.00	206.14	75.00	600.00
Hour	28.5%	44.46	40.00	46.90	45.00	100.00

MAPS
(4C, Larger Than Letter Size)

$/per	Survey %	Average	Typical	U.S. Avg.	U.S. Typ	U.S. Max
Simple	2.3%	163.55	100.00	168.75	72.50	500.00
Complex	3.5%	522.50	600.00	490.71	300.00	1600.00
Hour	26.2%	45.50	45.00	48.08	45.00	100.00

MARKETING PLANS

$/per	Survey %	Average	Typical	U.S. Avg.	U.S. Typ	U.S. Max
Text Page	2.3%	71.25	25.00	59.00	10.00	250.00
w/Graphics	1.7%	182.67	40.00	182.67	40.00	500.00
Hour	15.7%	45.85	40.00	47.80	45.00	100.00

MEMO PADS

$/per	Survey %	Average	Typical	U.S. Avg.	U.S. Typ	U.S. Max
Text	5.2%	26.17	15.00	20.14	14.50	100.00
w/Graphics	4.1%	45.71	35.00	31.79	17.50	150.00
Hour	28.5%	43.69	42.00	43.94	40.00	100.00

MENUS

$/per	Survey %	Average	Typical	U.S. Avg.	U.S. Typ	U.S. Max
Text Page	5.2%	90.56	30.00	75.65	35.00	500.00
w/Graphics	5.8%	156.00	45.00	125.25	45.00	1000.00
Hour	44.2%	44.02	40.00	44.35	40.00	150.00
Minimum	0.0			233.75	200.00	500.00

NEWSLETTERS

$/per	Survey %	Average	Typical	U.S. Avg.	U.S. Typ	U.S. Max
Text Page	12.8%	67.59	55.00	62.86	45.00	200.00
w/Graphics	13.4%	82.72	65.00	76.16	50.00	200.00
Hour	69.8%	43.54	40.00	42.97	40.00	160.00

NOTEPADS

$/per	Survey %	Average	Typical	U.S. Avg.	U.S. Typ	U.S. Max
Text	4.1%	35.00	25.00	32.28	25.00	100.00
w/Graphics	4.1%	53.93	45.00	41.37	35.00	150.00
Hour	39.0%	43.31	40.00	43.72	40.00	100.00

PACKAGING

$/per	Survey %	Average	Typical	U.S. Avg.	U.S. Typ	U.S. Max
Text	2.3%	297.50	100.00	276.00	100.00	1000.00
w/Graphics	2.9%	738.00	100.00	478.18	250.00	2500.00
Hour	26.2%	52.32	55.00	51.64	50.00	150.00

PEN RULER

$/per	Survey %	Average	Typical	U.S. Avg.	U.S. Typ	U.S. Max
Page	0.0%			45.00	45.00	45.00
Hour	14.0%	46.33	50.00	48.81	50.00	85.00

PERIODICAL (OTHER)

$/per	Survey %	Average	Typical	U.S. Avg.	U.S. Typ	U.S. Max
Text Page	3.5%	46.17	35.00	36.00	25.00	150.00
w/Graphics	2.9%	77.00	35.00	58.00	35.00	250.00
Hour	23.8%	45.87	45.00	46.86	45.00	125.00

POINT-OF-PURCHASE DISPLAYS

$/per	Survey %	Average	Typical	U.S. Avg.	U.S. Typ	U.S. Max
Text Page	1.2%	650.00	650.00	650.00	600.00	1000.00
w/Graphics	1.2%	800.00	800.00	800.00	800.00	1000.00
Hour	18.6%	48.66	50.00	50.15	50.00	100.00

POST CARDS

$/per	Survey %	Average	Typical	U.S. Avg.	U.S. Typ	U.S. Max
Text Page	6.4%	46.00	20.00	45.18	20.00	400.00
w/Graphics	7.6%	72.50	35.00	64.31	30.00	500.00
Hour	46.5%	42.25	36.00	42.38	40.00	100.00

POSTERS

$/per	Survey %	Average	Typical	U.S. Avg.	U.S. Typ	U.S. Max
Text Page	5.2%	142.22	50.00	123.67	50.00	500.00
w/Graphics	7.0%	281.25	250.00	259.71	250.00	1000.00
Hour	43.0%	45.24	42.00	45.60	45.00	100.00

PRESENTATION MATERIALS

$/per	Survey %	Average	Typical	U.S. Avg.	U.S. Typ	U.S. Max
Text Page	2.9%	37.40	20.00	27.65	20.00	100.00
w/Graphics	2.9%	76.00	50.00	44.38	25.00	180.00
Hour	39.5%	44.93	45.00	45.04	45.00	100.00

PRICE LISTS

$/per	Survey %	Average	Typical	U.S. Avg.	U.S. Typ	U.S. Max
Text Page	7.6%	46.31	35.00	40.63	35.00	150.00
w/Graphics	7.0%	57.71	40.00	51.79	40.00	160.00
Hour	52.3%	42.66	40.00	42.68	40.00	100.00

PRINT ADS

$/per	Survey %	Average	Typical	U.S. Avg.	U.S. Typ	U.S. Max
Text	7.6%	154.77	45.00	107.09	45.00	1000.00
w/Graphics	7.0%	212.08	90.00	179.74	80.00	1100.00
Hour	52.3%	45.73	40.00	44.84	40.00	100.00

PROCEDURE GUIDES

$/per	Survey %	Average	Typical	U.S. Avg.	U.S. Typ	U.S. Max
Text Page	1.7%	113.33	25.00	60.00	15.00	300.00
w/Graphics	1.7%	185.00	30.00	93.21	25.00	500.00
Hour	20.4%	46.54	45.00	45.67	45.00	100.00

PRODUCT LITERATURE

$/per	Survey %	Average	Typical	U.S. Avg.	U.S. Typ	U.S. Max
Text Page	4.1%	97.43	30.00	67.97	30.00	500.00
w/Graphics	4.1%	213.57	35.00	118.81	40.00	1000.00
Hour	43.6%	45.73	42.00	45.43	42.00	100.00

PRODUCT SPECIFICATION SHEETS

$/per	Survey %	Average	Typical	U.S. Avg.	U.S. Typ	U.S. Max
Text Page	2.9%	115.40	25.00	70.95	25.00	500.00
w/Graphics	2.9%	278.00	35.00	168.89	35.00	1000.00
Hour	27,3%	46.81	45.00	46.44	45.00	100.00

PROGRAMS

$/per	Survey %	Average	Typical	U.S. Avg.	U.S. Typ	U.S. Max
Text Page	2.3%	48.00	25.00	43.92	25.00	200.00
w/Graphics	2.3%	165.00	100.00	95.94	35.00	500.00
Hour	26.7%	47.76	45.00	46.61	45.00	150.00

PUBLICATIONS (OTHER)

$/per	Survey %	Average	Typical	U.S. Avg.	U.S. Typ	U.S. Max
Text Page	3.5%	45.33	35.00	46.00	30.00	150.00
w/Graphics	2.9%	128.00	35.00	87.73	35.00	500.00
Hour	31.4%	44.23	40.00	44.63	40.00	125.00

RECORD BOOKS

$/per	Survey %	Average	Typical	U.S. Avg.	U.S. Typ	U.S. Max
Text Page	1.2%	8.50	8.50	20.67	15.00	45.00
w/Graphics	0.6%	25.00	25.00	35.00	35.00	45.00
Hour	19.2%	45.30	45.00	46.63	45.00	80.00

RESUMES

$/per	Survey %	Average	Typical	U.S. Avg.	U.S. Typ	U.S. Max
Each	11.6%	27.57	25.00	31.21	25.00	150.00
Page	14.5%	28.26	27.00	31.52	30.00	150.00
Hour	50.0%	42.12	36.00	40.96	40.00	150.00

RULERS

$/per	Survey %	Average	Typical	U.S. Avg.	U.S. Typ	U.S. Max
Each	0.6%	250.00	250.00	250.00	375.00	500.00
Hour	13.4%	46.17	45.00	49.08	50.00	100.00

SALES PRESENTATIONS

$/per	Survey %	Average	Typical	U.S. Avg.	U.S. Typ	U.S. Max
Text Page	0.6%	20.00	20.00	23.14	20.00	45.00
w/Graphics	0.0%			29.50	25.00	45.00
Hour	25.0%	43.94	55.00	46.13	45.00	100.00

SIGNAGE

$/per	Survey %	Average	Typical	U.S. Avg.	U.S. Typ	U.S. Max
Text	1.7%	41.67	35.00	27.50	35.00	55.00
w/Graphics	2.9%	244.90	75.00	159.06	35.00	575.00
Hour	30.2%	46.36	45.00	45.60	45.00	100.00

SLIDE DESIGN

$/per	Survey %	Average	Typical	U.S. Avg.	U.S. Typ	U.S. Max
Text	2.3%	35.75	35.00	25.00	20.00	75.00
w/Graphics	2.3%	43.50	35.00	30.11	25.00	100.00
Hour	15.1%	45.65	45.00	46.17	45.00	100.00

SLIDE SHOW DESIGN

$/per	Survey %	Average	Typical	U.S. Avg.	U.S. Typ	U.S. Max
Text Page	1.7%	36.67	25.00	30.00	25.00	75.00
w/Graphics	1.2%	55.00	55.00	40.00	30.00	100.00
Hour	13.4%	49.65	50.00	47.98	50.00	100.00

SPREADSHEET DESIGN

$/per	Survey %	Average	Typical	U.S. Avg.	U.S. Typ	U.S. Max
Text Page	0.6%	25.00	25.00	35.00	35.00	45.00
w/Graphics	0.0%			45.50	45.00	45.00
Hour	18.0%	44.27	40.00	45.82	45.00	125.00

TABLOIDS

$/per	Survey %	Average	Typical	U.S. Avg.	U.S. Typ	U.S. Max
Text Page	1.7%	58.33	50.00	70.71	45.00	200.00
w/Graphics	1.7%	65.00	50.00	67.50	50.00	120.00
Hour	25.6%	45.17	45.00	46.32	45.00	125.00

TABS

$/per	Survey %	Average	Typical	U.S. Avg.	U.S. Typ	U.S. Max
Text	0.0%			20.00	20.00	20.00
w/Graphics	0.0%			20.00	20.00	20.00
Hour	15.1%	45.15	45.00	47.58	45.00	100.00

TAGS

$/per	Survey %	Average	Typical	U.S. Avg.	U.S. Typ	U.S. Max
Each	1.2%	22.50	20.00	17.83	10.00	35.00
Hour	16.9%	44.03	45.00	44.69	42.00	80.00

TECHNICAL DOCUMENTS

$/per	Survey %	Average	Typical	U.S. Avg.	U.S. Typ	U.S. Max
Text Page	2.9%	83.00	50.00	72.69	40.00	250.00
w/Graphics	4.1%	123.57	60.00	87.50	45.00	500.00
Hour	33.7%	45.30	42.00	44.05	40.00	125.00

TECHNICAL ILLUSTRATIONS

$/per	Survey %	Average	Typical	U.S. Avg.	U.S. Typ	U.S. Max
Page	2.9%	92.00	75.00	70.45	75.00	200.00
Hour	30.8%	46.39	45.00	47.28	45.00	200.00

TICKETS

$/per	Survey %	Average	Typical	U.S. Avg.	U.S. Typ	U.S. Max
Text	2.9%	31.00	35.00	24.72	20.00	50.00
w/Graphics	2.3%	37.50	45.00	30.25	30.00	50.00
Hour	23.8%	42.37	40.00	42.53	40.00	100.00

TRANSPARENCY DESIGN (B&W)

$/per	Survey %	Average	Typical	U.S. Avg.	U.S. Typ	U.S. Max
Text Page	1.2%	85.00	85.00	34.00	25.00	130.00
w/Graphics	1.2%	175.00	175.00	92.50	45.00	250.00
Hour	30.2%	43.25	45.0	42.68	40.00	100.00

TRANSPARENCY DESIGN (COLOR)

$/per	Survey %	Average	Typical	U.S. Avg.	U.S. Typ	U.S. Max
Text Page	0.6%	40.00	40.00	27.50	30.00	45.00
w/Graphics	0.6%	25.00	25.00	32.50	40.00	45.00
Hour	23.3%	44.48	45.00	44.69	45.00	100.00

OTHER DESIGN

$/per	Survey %	Average	Typical	U.S. Avg.	U.S. Typ	U.S. Max
Hour	8.1%	45.00	50.00	48.76	45.00	100.00

LASER PRINTER OUTPUT

GENERAL NOTES:
1. Some shops bill as $ set-up fee plus price per page.
2. Some shops bill as $/hr plus $/page.
3. A few shops price at $/hr (typically same price as other services).
4. Some laser printer output priced as $/job plus $/pg.

LASER PRINTING
(Up to 300 dpi)

$/per	Survey %	Average	Typical	U.S. Avg.	U.S. Typ	U.S. Max
8.5 x 11	26.5%	1.30	1.00	1.64	1.00	15.00
8.5 x 14	8.8%	1.28	1.00	1.95	3.00	10.00
11 x 17	0.6%	20.00	20.00	3.13	2.25	6.00
Cost Plus	1.8%	7.03	1.00	31.25	30.00	50.00
Minimum	0.6%	5.00	5.00	15.00	5.00	25.00

LASER PRINTING
(400 dpi)

$/per	Survey %	Average	Typical	U.S. Avg.	U.S. Typ	U.S. Max
8.5 x 11	2.4%	5.25	3.00	3.03	1.93	15.50
8.5 x 14	0.0%			2.71	2.00	6.00
11 x 17	1.2%	12.00	12.00	6.75	4.50	20.00
Cost Plus	0.6%	20.00	20.00	28.00	20.00	50.00
Minimum	0.6%	5.00	5.00	15.00	5.00	25.00

LASER PRINTING
(600 dpi)

$/per	Survey %	Average	Typical	U.S. Avg.	U.S. Typ	U.S. Max
8.5 x 11	8.2%	1.62	1.00	1.88	1.00	15.00
8.5 x 14	0.0%			1.88	1.95	4.46
11 x 17	0.6%	6.00	6.00	4.12	5.16	6.00
Cost Plus	0.6%	20.00	20.00	28.00	20.00	50.00

LASER PRINTING
(800dpi)

$/per	Survey %	Average	Typical	U.S. Avg.	U.S. Typ	U.S. Max
8.5 x 11	2.4%	2.56	3.25	2.75	2.00	12.00
8.5 x 14	1.2%	4.50	4.50	2.94	4.00	5.00
11 x 17	0.0%			6.00	6.00	6.00
Cost Plus	0.6%	20.00	20.00	28.00	20.00	50.00
Minimum	2.7%	10.00	10.00	15.00	5.00	25.00

LASER PRINTING
(1000 dpi)

$/per	Survey %	Average	Typical	U.S. Avg.	U.S. Typ	U.S. Max
8.5 x 11	1.8%	2.00	2.00	3.10	3.00	7.00
8.5 x 14	0.6%	2.50	2.50	4.06	4.00	7.00
11 x 17	0.0%			6.00	6.00	6.00
Cost Plus	0.6%	20.00	20.00	28.00	20.00	50.00
Minimum	2.7%	10.00	10.00	15.00	10.00	25.00

LASER PRINTING
(1200 dpi)

$/per	Survey %	Average	Typical	U.S. Avg.	U.S. Typ	U.S. Max
8.5 x 11	2.4%	2.46	2.50	2.89	3.00	6.00
8.5 x 14	0.6%	2.00	2.00	4.82	6.00	6.43
11 x 17	1.8%	5.33	4.00	7.18	6.00	13.25
Cost Plus	0.6%	20.00	20.00	28.00	20.00	50.00
Minimum	2.7%	8.33	10.00	15.00	10.00	25.00

FOR PREPRESS AND OTHER SERVICES (INCLUDING IMAGESETTING OUTPUT), REFER TO THE SECTION MARKED "NATIONAL."

Price Distribution
CANADA

GENERAL NOTE: Survey responses listed as $/minute were converted to $/hr.

BOOKS ON DISK

$/per	Survey %	Average	Typical	U.S. Avg.	U.S. Typ	U.S. Max
Disk	0.0%			10.57	10.00	25.00
Page	0.0%			6.00	5.50	10.00
Hour	0.0%			40.11	35.00	95.00
Minimum	0.0%			15.00	15.00	15.00

CD-ROM

$/per	Survey %	Average	Typical	U.S. Avg.	U.S. Typ	U.S. Max
Page	0.0%			8.00	8.00	8.00
Disk	0.0%			25.00	25.00	25.00
Hour	0.0%			48.00	43.00	85.00
Minimum	0.0%			70.00	70.00	125.00

CROSS PLATFORM

$/per	Survey %	Average	Typical	U.S. Avg.	U.S. Typ	U.S. Max
Page	0.0%			3.83	2.88	8.00
File	0.0%			7.85	9.00	20.00
Disk	20.0%	15.00	15.00	11.85	10.00	50.00
Hour	40.0%	45.00	46.00	46.31	45.00	100.00
Minimum	0.0%			14.25	12.50	35.00

DATABASE FILES

$/per	Survey %	Average	Typical	U.S. Avg.	U.S. Typ	U.S. Max
Record	0.0%			0.16	0.15	0.25
File	0.0%			7.02	10.00	20.00
Disk	0.0%			21.67	15.00	50.00
Hour	0.0%			42.46	40.50	100.00
Minimum	0.0%			22.50	20.00	35.00

DOCUMENT FILES

$/per	Survey %	Average	Typical	U.S. Avg.	U.S. Typ	U.S. Max
K byte	0.0%			5.25	5.25	5.25
Page	0.0%			2.71	2.75	3.50
File	0.0%			8.38	10.00	15.00
Disk	20.0%	15.00	15.00	15.73	15.00	50.00
Hour	20.%	50.00	50.00	41.23	35.00	100.00
Minimum	0.0%			21.00	15.00	35.00

DOCUMENTS ON DISK

$/per	Survey %	Average	Typical	U.S. Avg.	U.S. Typ	U.S. Max
Page	0.0%			6.17	7.00	15.00
File	0.0%			12.00	15.00	15.00
Disk	0.0%			14.00	10.00	50.00
Hour	0.0%			38.77	35.00	75.00
Minimum	0.0%			12.50	13.00	15.00

FORMS CONVERSION

$/per	Survey %	Average	Typical	U.S. Avg.	U.S. Typ	U.S. Max
Page	0.0%			187.18	190.00	200.00
File	0.0%			26.00	10.00	50.00
Disk	0.0%			15.00	10.00	25.00
Hour	0.0%			47.68	40.00	100.00
Minimum	0.0%			12.50	15.00	15.00

GRAPHIC FORMAT FILES

$/per	Survey %	Average	Typical	U.S. Avg.	U.S. Typ	U.S. Max
K byte	0.0%			5.25	5.25	5.25
Page	0.0%			18.32	20.00	20.00
File	0.0%			8.50	5.88	20.00
Disk	40.0%	10.00	12.00	15.36	15.00	50.00
Hour	20.0%	50.00	50.00	44.32	40.00	100.00
Minimum	0.0%			19.17	15.00	35.00

MEDIA CONVERSION

$/per	Survey %	Average	Typical	U.S. Avg.	U.S. Typ	U.S. Max
File	0.0%			15.00	12.50	25.00
Disk	20.0%	15.00	15.00	13.05	10.00	50.00
Hour	20.0%	50.00	50.00	48.64	45.00	100.00
Minimum	0.0%			13.75	15.00	15.00

PAGE LAYOUT FILES

$/per	Survey %	Average	Typical	U.S. Avg.	U.S. Typ	U.S. Max
500 K byte	0.01%			15.00	15.00	15.00
Page	0.0%			37.50	37.50	60.00
File	0.0%			12.70	12.50	25.00
Disk	0.0%			19.25	15.00	50.00
Hour	0.0%			42.91	40.00	100.00
Minimum	0.0%			20.00	15.00	35.00

SPREADSHEET FILES

$/per	Survey %	Average	Typical	U.S. Avg	U.S. Typ	U.S. Max
25 K byte	0.0%			7.50	7.50	7.50
Page	0.0%			2.88	2.88	2.00
File	0.0%			12.30	10.88	25.00
Disk	0.0%			26.25	20.00	50.00
Hour	0.0%			40.98	40.00	100.00
Minimum	0.0%			22.50	20.00	35.00

VIDEO TAPE TRANSFER

$/per	Survey %	Average	Typical	U.S. Avg	U.S. Typ	U.S. Max
Disk	0.0%			25.00	25.00	25.00
Per Hour	0.0%			48.33	45.00	75.00
Minimum	0.0%			15.00	15.00	15.00

WORD PROCESSOR FILE TO SGML

$/per	Survey %	Average	Typical	U.S. Avg	U.S. Typ	U.S. Max
Disk	0.0%			25.00	25.00	25.00
Hour	0.0%			45.00	40.00	75.00
Minimum	0.0%			15.00	15.00	15.00

TEXT CREATION

GENERAL COPY WRITING

$/per	Survey %	Average	Typical	U.S. Avg	U.S. Typ	U.S. Max
Line	0.0%			0.20	0.20	0.20
Page	20.0%	24.89	30.00	30.38	20.00	87.50
Hour	20.0%	35.00	35.00	41.43	35.00	300.00
Minimum	0.0%			19.00	15.00	35.00

NEWSLETTER COPY

$/per	Survey %	Average	Typical	U.S. Avg	U.S. Typ	U.S. Max
Column	0.0%			10.48	10.50	11.00
Page	20.0%	23.67	25.00	40.96	40.00	125.00
Hour	20.0%	42.58	36.00	39.31	35.00	300.00
Minimum	0.0%			283.33	125.00	800.00

PUBLICITY / ADVERTISING COPY

$/per	Survey %	Average	Typical	U.S. Avg	U.S. Typ	U.S. Max
Page	20.0%	24.29	25.00	40.31	40.00	100.00
Piece	0.0%			260.00	300.00	425.00
Hour	20.0%	37.94	35.00	43.56	38.00	300.00
Minimum	0.0%			19.00	15.00	35.00

RESUME WRITING

$/per	Survey %	Average	Typical	U.S. Avg.	U.S. Typ	U.S. Max
Page	20.0%	21.57	20.00	32.43	25.00	100.00
Hour	0.0%			38.11	35.00	300.00
Minimum	0.0%			110.00	65.00	300.00

TECHNICAL WRITING

$/per	Survey %	Average	Typical	U.S. Avg.	U.S. Typ	U.S. Max
Page	20.0%	21.57	20.00	53.54	35.00	300.00
Hour	0.0%			45.99	35.00	300.00
Minimum	0.0%			35.00	35.00	55.00

DATA INPUT / EDITING

DATA ENTRY / KEYBOARDING

$/per	Survey %	Average	Typical	U.S. Avg.	U.S. Typ	U.S. Max
Character	0.0%			0.02	0.02	0.02
Page	0.0%			11.32	10.00	50.00
Hour	80.00%	21.25	25.00	32.64	28.00	100.00
Minimum	0.0%			20.00	15.00	35.00

COPY EDITING

$/per	Survey %	Average	Typical	U.S. Avg.	U.S. Typ	U.S. Max
Word	0.0%			0.06	0.06	0.11
Page	0.0%			9.47	7.00	50.00
Hour	20.0%	10.00	10.00	36.58	30.00	100.00
Minimum	0.0%			20.00	15.00	35.00

CONTENT EDITING

$/per	Survey %	Average	Typical	U.S. Avg.	U.S. Typ	U.S. Max
Word	0.0%			0.11	0.11	0.11
Page	0.0%			5.33	5.00	50.00
Hour	20.0%	10.00	10.00	37.44	36.00	100.00
Minimum	0.0%			33.50	35.00	35.00

PROOF READING

$/per	Survey %	Average	Typical	U.S. Avg.	U.S. Typ	U.S. Max
Page	0.0%			6.71	5.00	50.00
Hour	40.0%	17.50	17.50	35.63	30.00	100.00
Minimum	0.0%			33.50	35.00	35.00

REWRITING

$/per	Survey %	Average	Typical	U.S. Avg.	U.S. Typ	U.S. Max
Word	0.0%			0.07	0.03	0.11
Line	0.0%			0.25	0.20	1.00
Page	0.0%			22.67	13.50	50.00
Hour	20.0%	10.00	10.00	38.81	35.00	100.00
Minimum	0.0%			35.00	35.00	35.00

INDEXING

$/per	Survey %	Average	Typical	U.S. Avg.	U.S. Typ	U.S. Max
Page	0.0%			2.80	2.00	5.00
Hour	20.0%	10.00	10.00	38.60	35.00	100.00
Minimum	0.0%			87.50	87.50	140.00

MODEM INPUT

$/per	Survey %	Average	Typical	U.S. Avg.	U.S. Typ	U.S. Max
Page	20.0%	2.00	2.00	3.33	3.00	5.00
File	0.0%			10.00	10.00	10.00
K bytes	0.1%	10.57	10.57	1.32	1.40	1.50
Disk	0.0%			8.33	5.00	25.00
Minute	0.1%	10.57	10.57	1.50	1.50	2.00
Hour	0.0%			41.62	38.00	100.00
Minimum	0.0%			12.50	12.50	15.00

TEXT FILE IMPORTING

$/per	Survey %	Average	Typical	U.S. Avg.	U.S. Typ	U.S. Max
Page	0.0%			14.60	5.00	50.00
File	0.0%			11.00	10.00	25.00
K bytes	0.0%			1.32	1.40	1.50
Disk	0.0%			10.00	10.00	15.00
Minute	0.0%			1.50	1.50	2.00
Hour	20.0%	55.55	55.55	39.10	35.00	100.00
Minimum	0.0%			21.25	22.00	35.00

TRANSCRIPTION

$/per	Survey %	Average	Typical	U.S. Avg.	U.S. Typ	U.S. Max
Line	0.0%			0.17	0.17	0.25
Page	0.0%			4.79	4.25	8.00
File	0.1%	10.57	10.57	10.57	10.57	25.00
Disk	0.0%			25.00	25.00	25.00
Hour	20.00%	30.00	30.00	31.64	30.00	75.00
Minimum	0.0%			25.00	25.00	35.00

TRANSLATION

$/per	Survey %	Average	Typical	U.S. Avg.	U.S. Typ	U.S. Max
Word	0.0%			0.17	0.17	0.20
Page	0.0%			24.17	22.50	50.00
Hour	0.0%			44.49	40.00	150.00
Minimum	0.0%			35.00	35..00	35.00

TYPOGRAPHY (General)

$/per	Survey %	Average	Typical	U.S. Avg.	U.S. Typ	U.S. Max
Line	0.0%			0.25	0.25	0.25
Page	0.0%			21.48	15.00	75.00
Hour	40.0%	17.50	20.00	39.27	35.00	100.00
Minimum	0.0%			18.83	15.00	35.00

TYPOGRAPHY (Spreadsheet)

$/per	Survey %	Average	Typical	U.S. Avg.	U.S. Typ	U.S. Max
Line	0.0%			0.25	0.25	0.25
Page	0.0%			24.06	17.00	75.00
Hour	40.0%	17.50	20.00	41.47	36.00	150.00
Minimum	0.0%			35.00	35.00	35.00

WORD PROCESSSING

$/per	Survey %	Average	Typical	U.S. Avg.	U.S. Typ	U.S. Max
Line	0.0%			0.13	0.10	0.20
Page	0.0%			8.67	8.25	25.00
Hour	60.0%	23.33	25.00	32.90	25.00	100.00
Minimum	0.0%			21.67	15.00	35.00

DATA MANAGEMENT

GENERAL NOTES:
1. Assume customer pays for cost of media extra.
2. On $/word, assume 2K words per page.
3. Per file cost assumed to be for 1 year.
4. Assume $/file same as $/image.

ARCHIVING SERVICE

$/per	Survey %	Average	Typical	U.S. Avg.	U.S. Typ	U.S. Max
Page	0.0%			7.50	7.50	7.50
File	20.0%	1.00	1.00	9.63	15.00	25.00
Tape	0.0%			37.50	20.00	150.00
Hour	0.0%			46.05	40.00	95.00
Minimum	0.0%			14.17	10.00	25.00

IMAGE MANAGEMENT

$/per	Survey %	Average	Typical	U.S. Avg.	U.S. Typ	U.S. Max
Page	0.0%			6.50	5.50	10.00
File	0.0%			16.67	15.00	50.00
Disk	0.0%			30.00	30.00	50.00
Hour	20.0%	55.00	55.00	44.81	40.00	110.00
Minimum	0.0%			14.17	10.00	25.00

NOTE: Assume $/.file same as $/image.

TEXT MANAGEMENT

$/per	Survey %	Average	Typical	U.S. Avg.	U.S. Typ	U.S. Max
Page	0.0%			8.67	6.00	15.00
File	0.0%			16.67	15.00	50.00
Disk	0.0%			23.33	15.00	50.00
Hour	0.0%			44.51	35.00	95.00
Minimum	0.0%			14.17	10.00	25.00

IMAGING SERVICES

DOCUMENT CAPTURE

$/per	Survey %	Average	Typical	U.S. Avg.	U.S. Typ	U.S. Max
Page	0.0%			3.65	3.00	7.50
File	0.0%			6.50	5.00	10.00
Hour	0.0%			39.41	35.00	95.00
Minimum	0.0%			16.25	16.25	25.00

DOCUMENT RETRIEVAL

$/per	Survey %	Average	Typical	U.S. Avg.	U.S. Typ	U.S. Max
Page	0.0%			1.50	1.50	2.00
File	0.0%			5.03	5.00	10.00
Hour	0.0%			38.82	39.00	85.00
Minimum	0.0%			16.25	16.25	25.00

GRAPHICS FILE IMPORTING

$/per	Survey %	Average	Typical	U.S. Avg.	U.S. Typ	U.S. Max
File	20.0%	5.00	5.00	6.98	5.00	15.00
Disk	0.0%			5.00	5.00	5.00
Hour	0.0%			43.35	36.00	100.00
Minimum	0.0%			14.17	14.17	35.00

PHOTO CD-ROM IMPORTING

$/per	Survey %	Average	Typical	U.S. Avg.	U.S. Typ	U.S. Max
Image	0.0%			10.02	7.25	45.00
Stock Fee	0.0%			75.00	75.00	75.00
Hour	0.0%			48.60	45.00	100.00
Minimum	0.0%			16.25	15.00	25.00

SCANNING (B&W Grey Scale)

$/per	Survey %	Average	Typical	U.S. Avg.	U.S. Typ	U.S. Max
Hour	0.0%			42.82	40.00	100.00
75-200 dpi	40.0%	6.00	6.00	10.10	9.00	75.00
300-400 dpi	60.0%	12.33	15.00	11.93	10.00	75.00
600-800 dpi	40.0%	11.50	11.50	13.51	11.00	75.00
1200 dpi	0.0%			20.20	12.00	75.00
2400 dpi	0.0%			36.86	30.00	75.00

SCANNING (B&W Line Art)

$/per	Survey %	Average	Typical	U.S. Avg.	U.S. Typ	U.S. Max
Hour	0.0%			40.94	40.00	100.00
75-200 dpi	40.0%	6.00	6.00	10.59	9.00	75.00
300-400 dpi	60.0%	10.67	10.00	11.92	10.00	75.00
600-800 dpi	40.0%	9.00	9.00	12.51	10.00	75.00
1200 dpi	0.0%			15.59	11.00	75.00
2400 dpi	0.0%			35.75	27.50	75.00
Per K	0.0%			51.67	50.00	75.00

SCANNING (B&W Photo)

$/per	Survey %	Average	Typical	U.S. Avg.	U.S. Typ	U.S. Max
Hour	0.0%			45.16	40.00	100.00
75-200 dpi	40.0%	6.00	6.00	12.28	10.00	75.00
300-400 dpi	40.0%	11.00	11.00	13.92	12.40	75.00
600-800 dpi	20.0%	15.00	15.00	14.79	12.60	75.00
1200 dpi	0.0%			19.88	17.50	75.00
2400 dpi	0.0%			35.56	31.00	75.00
Per K	0.0%			62.50	62.50	75.00

SCANNING (Color Illustration)

$/per	Survey %	Average	Typical	U.S. Avg.	U.S. Typ	U.S. Max
Hour	0.0%			49.23	50.00	125.00
75-200 dpi	0.0%			19.08	15.00	75.00
300-400 dpi	40.0%	20.00	20.00	21.03	19.00	82.00
600-800 dpi	20.0%	25.00	25.00	22.36	21.50	75.00
1200 dpi	0.0%			26.47	23.00	75.00
2400 dpi	20.0%	50.00	50.00	46.22	50.00	75.00

SCANNING (Color Photo)

$/per	Survey %	Average	Typical	U.S. Avg.	U.S. Typ	U.S. Max
Hour	0.0%			49.23	50.00	125.00
75-200 dpi	0.0%			20.44	15.00	75.00
300-400 dpi	40.0%	20.00	20.00	20.97	17.75	82.00
600-800 dpi	20.0%	25.00	25.00	19.75	15.00	75.00
1200 dpi	0.0%			30.13	30.00	75.00
2400 dpi	20.0%	50.00	50.00	61.54	60.00	137.00

SCANNING (HIGH END)
(Loose Scan)

$/per	Survey %	U.S. Avg.	U.S. Typ	U.S. Max
2 x 3	0.1%	13.33	10.00	25.00
3 x 5	0.1%	11.25	10.00	20.00
4 x 5	0.1%	16.00	10.00	33.00
5 x 7	0.1%	18.00	10.00	37.00
5.5 x 8.5	0.1%	17.33	10.00	39.00
6 x 9	0.1%	24.67	15.00	49.00
8 x 10	0.1%	41.60	50.00	70.00
10 x 12	0.1%	47.80	60.00	84.00
11 x 14	0.1%	81.67	70.00	105.00
12 x 18	0.1%	90.67	80.00	122.00
16 x 20	0.1%	162.00	162.00	162.00
20 x 24	0.1%	199.00	199.00	199.00
Hour	0.1%	47.00	45.00	60.00

SCANNING (HIGH END)
(Drum Scan)

$/per	Survey %	U.S. Avg.	U.S. Typ	U.S. Max
2 x 3	0.1%	56..92	54.25	71.50
4 x 5	0.1%	57.21	55.00	94.50
5 x 7	0.1%	65.75	70.00	106.00
6 x 8	0.1%	103.13	102.50	117.50
6 x 9	0.1%	57.00	45.00	85.00
8 x 10	0.1%	51.25	50.00	60.00
10 x 12	0.1%	58.33	60.00	60.00
11 x 14	0.1%	71.25	72.50	75.00
12 x 18	0.1%	86.67	85.00	100.00
24 x 27	0.1%	600.00	600.00	600.00

SCANNING (HIGH END)
(High Res Scan to Disk)

$/per	Survey %	U.S. Avg.	U.S. Typ	U.S. Max
2 x 3	0.1%	20..50	19.50	25.00
4 x 5	0.1%	26.17	27.50	30.00
5 x 7	0.1%	34.00	35.00	41.00
6 x 9	0.1%	39.80	39.00	50.00

SCANNING (HIGH END) (High Res Scan to Disk)				
$/per	Survey %	U.S. Avg.	U.S. Typ	U.S. Max
8 x 10	0.1%	45.50	45.00	60.00
10 x 12	0.1%	56.83	59.00	70.00
11 x 14	0.1%	65.08	64.00	89.00
12 x 18	0.1%	78.90	75.00	100.00
16 x 20	0.1%	96.33	99.00	130.00
20 x 24	0.1%	128.00	134.00	160.00
24 x 27	0.1%	156.25	156.25	200.00

SCANNING (Transparency)						
$/per	Survey %	Average	Typical	U.S. Avg.	U.S. Typ	U.S. Max
Each	20.0%	25.00	25.00	18.70	16.00	45.00
Hour	0.0%			65.29	55.00	137.00

SCANNING (Slide)						
$/per	Survey %	Average	Typical	U.S. Avg.	U.S. Typ	U.S. Max
Each	20.0%	25.00	25.00	23.00	16.99	65.00
Hour	0.0%			68.42	55.00	137.00

COLOR CORRECTION						
$/per	Survey %	Average	Typical	U.S. Avg.	U.S. Typ	U.S. Max
Hour	40.0%	47.50	47.50	65.80	50.00	300.00

IMAGE EDITING						
$/per	Survey %	Average	Typical	U.S. Avg.	U.S. Typ	U.S. Max
Each	0.0%			20.75	15.00	50.00
Hour	40.0%	37.50	37.50	55.47	45.00	300.00

IMAGE ENHANCEMENT						
$/per	Survey %	Average	Typical	U.S. Avg.	U.S. Typ	U.S. Max
Hour	20.0%	40.00	40.00	57.60	50.00	300.00

RETOUCHING						
$/per	Survey %	Average	Typical	U.S. Avg.	U.S. Typ	U.S. Max
Each	0.0%			27.67	40.00	50.00
Hour	20.0%	40.00	40.00	58.60	50.00	300.00
Minimum	0.0%			26.08	25.00	35.00

TEXT SCAN (OCR)						
$/per	Survey %	Average	Typical	U.S. Avg.	U.S. Typ	U.S. Max
Page	0.0%			7.82	5.00	95.00

TEXT SCAN (OCR)

$/per	Survey %	Average	Typical	U.S. Avg.	U.S. Typ	U.S. Max
Hour	20.0%	10.00	10.00	36.33	30.00	75.00
Minimum	0.0%			19.08	16.90	35.00

NOTE:
1. Prices assume spell check conducted on scanned text.
2. Assumes 2 Kb per page, so $1/Kb response incorporated as $2/page.

NEGATIVE CREATION

$/per	Survey %	Average	Typical	U.S. Avg.	U.S. Typ	U.S. Max
Each	0.0%			22.00	22.00	40.00
Hour	0.0%			56.71	56.71	100.00
Minimum	0.0%			16.67	16.67	25.00

DESIGN SERVICES

ANNOUNCEMENTS

$/per	Survey %	Average	Typical	U.S. Avg.	U.S. Typ	U.S. Max
Text Page	40.0%	32.50	32.50	37.05	24.00	250.00
w/Graphics	20.0%	40.00	40.00	65.36	36.50	500.00
Hour	80.0%	47.50	50.00	42.21	40.00	100.00

ANNUAL REPORTS
(1C, 2C, Up To Letter Size Pages)

$/per	Survey %	Average	Typical	U.S. Avg.	U.S. Typ	U.S. Max
Text	0.0%			114.75	62.50	1000.00
w/Graphics	0.0%			222.00	100.00	7680.00
Hour	60.0%	41.67	50.00	46.58	45.00	100.00

ANNUAL REPORTS
(3C, 4C, Larger Size Pages)

$/per	Survey %	Average	Typical	U.S. Avg.	U.S. Typ	U.S. Max
Text	0.0%			214.55	100.00	1500.00
w/Graphics	0.0%			422.50	175.00	11520.00
Hour	60.0%	41.67	50.00	46.34	45.00	100.00

BAR CODING

$/per	Survey %	Average	Typical	U.S. Avg.	U.S. Typ	U.S. Max
Each	0.0%			13.25	11.00	150.00
Page	0.0%			29.00	29.00	50.00
Hour	20.0%	50.00	50.00	47.83	45.00	100.00

BOOKLETS

$/per	Survey %	Average	Typical	U.S. Avg.	U.S. Typ	U.S. Max
Text Page	40.0%	32.50	32.50	48.40	30.00	500.00
w/Graphics	20.0%	40.00	40.00	110.53	50.00	650.00
Hour	100.0%	41.00	40.00	43.87	25.00	100.00

BOOK COVERS

$/per	Survey %	Average	Typical	U.S. Avg.	U.S. Typ	U.S. Max
Text	0.0%			143.10	75.00	500.00
w/Graphics	0.0%			403.36	300.00	1800.00
Hour	60.0%	41.67	50.00	47.83	45.00	120.00

BOOK BODY

$/per	Survey %	Average	Typical	U.S. Avg.	U.S. Typ	U.S. Max
Text Page	20.0%	25.00	25.00	26.65	20.00	75.00
w/Graphics	20.0%	40.00	40.00	41.11	25.00	85.00
Hour	80.0%	41.25	50.00	44.26	40.00	100.00

BOOK JACKETS

$/per	Survey %	Average	Typical	U.S. Avg.	U.S. Typ	U.S. Max
Text	0.0%			161.54	175.00	500.00
w/Graphics	0.0%			491.00	325.00	1000.00
Hour	40.0%	32.50	35.00	48.63	45.00	120.00

BROCHURE
(1C, 2C, Up To Letter Size Sheet)

$/per	Survey %	Average	Typical	U.S. Avg.	U.S. Typ	U.S. Max
Text Page	20.0%	40.00	40.00	72.59	47.50	500.00
w/Graphics	0.0%			156.74	82.50	750.00
Hour	80.0%	41.25	50.00	42.85	40.00	125.00

BROCHURE
(3C, 4C, Larger Size Sheet)

$/per	Survey %	Average	Typical	U.S. Avg.	U.S. Typ	U.S. Max
Text Page	20.0%	40.00	40.00	123.79	60.00	1000.00
w/Graphics	0.0%			227.71	100.00	1500.00
Hour	80.0%	41.25	50.00	44.17	40.00	125.00

BULLETIN

$/per	Survey %	Average	Typical	U.S. Avg.	U.S. Typ	U.S. Max
Text Page	40.0%	32.50	32.00	32.75	25.00	150.00
w/Graphics	20.0%	40.00	40.00	47.81	35.00	200.00
Hour	100.0%	41.00	40.00	42.36	40.00	100.00

BUSINESS CARDS

$/per	Survey %	Average	Typical	U.S. Avg.	U.S. Typ	U.S. Max
Text Card	40.0%	32.50	32.50	38.81	25.00	500.00
w/Graphics	20.0%	40.00	40.00	91.70	40.00	1000.00
Hour	100.0%	41.00	40.00	43.19	40.00	150.00

BUSINESS REPLY CARDS

$/per	Survey %	Average	Typical	U.S. Avg.	U.S. Typ	U.S. Max
Text Card	0.0%			34.32	31.50	150.00
w/Graphics	0.0%			67.50	35.00	250.00
Hour	60.0%	41.67	50.00	43.79	40.00	100.00

BUSINESS LETTERS

$/per	Survey %	Average	Typical	U.S. Avg.	U.S. Typ	U.S. Max
Text Page	20.0%	25.00	25.00	17.23	12.25	90.00
w/Graphics	20.0%	40.00	40.00	27.08	18.75	100.00
Hour	80.0%	41.25	50.00	39.38	35.00	100.00

CALENDARS

$/per	Survey %	Average	Typical	U.S. Avg.	U.S. Typ	U.S. Max
Text Page	0.0%			82.50	50.00	500.00
w/Graphics	0.0%			53.18	45.00	150.00
Hour	40.0%	32.50	32.50	43.77	40.00	100.00

CALLIGRAPHY

$/per	Survey %	Average	Typical	U.S. Avg.	U.S. Typ	U.S. Max
Line	0.0%			1.00	1.00	60.00
Page	0.0%			40.00	35.00	100.00
Hour	40.0%	40.00	40.00	45.50	40.00	175.00

CARDS (FOLD-OVER)

$/per	Survey %	Average	Typical	U.S. Avg.	U.S. Typ	U.S. Max
Text Card	0.0%			31.45	25.00	60.00
w/Graphics	0.0%			65.47	46.40	250.00
Hour	20.0%	50.00	50.00	43.63	40.00	100.00

CARDS (ROLODEX)

$/per	Survey %	Average	Typical	U.S. Avg.	U.S. Typ	U.S. Max
Text Card	0.0%			37.34	25.00	150.00
w/Graphics	0.0%			63.00	48.00	250.00
Hour	20.0%	50.00	50.00	44.94	41.00	100.00

CARTOONS

$/per	Survey %	Average	Typical	U.S. Avg.	U.S. Typ	U.S. Max
Each	0.0%			119.29	60.00	400.00
Page	0.0%			163.33	65.00	400.00
Hour	20.0%	50.00	50.00	48.15	45.00	90.00

CATALOGS

$/per	Survey %	Average	Typical	U.S. Avg.	U.S. Typ	U.S. Max
Text Page	20.0%	30.00	30.00	69.03	40.00	500.00
w/Graphics	20.0%	40.00	40.00	129.05	67.50	1000.00
Hour	60.0%	50.00	50.00	45.68	45.00	125.00

CERTIFICATES

$/per	Survey %	Average	Typical	U.S. Avg.	U.S. Typ	U.S. Max
Text	0.0%			23.56	16.25	125.00
w/Graphics	0.0%			35.07	25.00	150.00
Hour	60.0%	41.67	50.00	42.15	40.00	100.00

CHARTS / DIAGRAMS

$/per	Survey %	Average	Typical	U.S. Avg.	U.S. Typ	U.S. Max
Text	20.0%	30.00	30.00	36.19	32.50	150.00
w/Graphics	20.0%	40.00	40.00	53.14	47.50	150.00
Hour	60.0%	35.00	40.00	44.29	40.00	100.00

COMIC BOOKS

$/per	Survey %	Average	Typical	U.S. Avg.	U.S. Typ	U.S. Max
Each Page	0.0%			65.00	60.00	100.00
Hour	20.0%	50.00	50.00	47.12	50.00	80.00

COMIC STRIPS

$/per	Survey %	Average	Typical	U.S. Avg.	U.S. Typ	U.S. Max
Each Strip	0.0%			38.33	30.00	60.00
Hour	20.0%	50.00	50.00	46.78	50.00	80.00

COMPUTER GENERATED ART

$/per	Survey %	Average	Typical	U.S. Avg.	U.S. Typ	U.S. Max
Page	0.0%			121.40	50.00	500.00
Hour	60.0%	45.00	45.00	46.70	42.00	175.00

CUSTOM DISPLAYS

$/per	Survey %	Average	Typical	U.S. Avg.	U.S. Typ	U.S. Max
Text	0.0%			192.14	60.00	1000.00
w/Graphics	0.0%			265.71	100.00	1000.00
Hour	20.0%	50.00	50.00	48.95	45.00	100.00

DATABASE DESIGN

$/per	Survey %	Average	Typical	U.S. Avg.	U.S. Typ	U.S. Max
Text	0.0%			38.33	30.00	60.00
w/Graphics	0.0%			43.33	40.00	60.00
Hour	20.0%	50.00	50.00	42.45	41.00	80.00

DIGITAL SLIDE PRESENTATIONS

$/per	Survey %	Average	Typical	U.S. Avg.	U.S. Typ	U.S. Max
Text	0.0%			27.13	27.50	60.00
w/Graphics	0.0%			35.00	32.50	60.00
Hour	20.0%	50.00	50.00	45.81	45.00	100.00

DIRECT MAIL PACKAGES

$/per	Survey %	Average	Typical	U.S. Avg.	U.S. Typ	U.S. Max
Text	0.0%			298.46	60.00	1500.00
w/Graphics	0.0%			413.50	65.00	2000.00
Hour	20.0%	50.00	50.00	47.05	45.00	100.00

DIRECTORY

$/per	Survey %	Average	Typical	U.S. Avg.	U.S. Typ	U.S. Max
Text	0.0%			38.72	30.00	150.00
w/Graphics	0.0%			73.53	40.00	500.00
Hour	20.0%	50.00	50.00	43.08	40.00	125.00

DISPLAY ADVERTISING

$/per	Survey %	Average	Typical	U.S. Avg.	U.S. Typ	U.S. Max
Text	0.0%			109.28	30.00	1000.00
w/Graphics	0.0%			304.64	45.00	2500.00
Hour	40.0%	55.00	55.00	48.23	45.00	115.00

DISPLAY EXHIBITS

$/per	Survey %	Average	Typical	U.S. Avg.	U.S. Typ	U.S. Max
Text Panel	0.0%			858.57	90.00	5000.00
w/Graphics	0.0%			896.67	100.00	5000.00
Hour	20.0%	50.00	50.00	51.43	50.00	115.00

DOOR HANGERS

$/per	Survey %	Average	Typical	U.S. Avg.	U.S. Typ	U.S. Max
Text	20.0%	40.00	40.00	42.46	25.00	250.00
w/Graphics	0.0%			87.50	35.00	500.00
Hour	60.0%	50.00	50.00	47.19	45.00	100.00

DRAFTING

$/per	Survey %	Average	Typical	U.S. Avg.	U.S. Typ	U.S. Max
Page	0.0%			45.00	45.00	60.00
Hour	40.0%	32.50	32.50	46.62	45.00	100.00

FINANCIAL DOCUMENTS

$/per	Survey %	Average	Typical	U.S. Avg.	U.S. Typ	U.S. Max
Text Page	20.0%	30.00	30.00	45.33	33.00	150.00
w/Graphics	20.0%	40.00	40.00	92.00	60.00	150.00
Hour	40.0%	45.00	45.00	47.20	45.00	125.00

FLYERS

$/per	Survey %	Average	Typical	U.S. Avg.	U.S. Typ	U.S. Max
Text Page	40.0%	32.50	32.50	39.21	25.00	325.00
w/Graphics	20.0%	40.00	40.00	66.84	35.00	325.00
Hour	100.0%	41.00	40.00	42.22	40.00	100.00

FORMS

$/per	Survey %	Average	Typical	U.S. Avg.	U.S. Typ	U.S. Max
Text Page	40.0%	32.50	32.50	52.60	30.00	750.00
w/Graphics	20.00%	40.00	40.00	81.67	37.50	10000.00
Hour	100.0%	41.00	40.00	41.75	40.00	125.00

HANDBOOKS

$/per	Survey %	Average	Typical	U.S. Avg.	U.S. Typ	U.S. Max
Text Page	40.0%	32.50	32.50	38.22	25.00	150.00
w/Graphics	20.0%	40.00	40.00	62.46	35.00	250.00
Hour	80.0%	36.25	40.00	43.53	40.00	100.00

INSERTS

$/per	Survey %	Average	Typical	U.S. Avg.	U.S. Typ	U.S. Max
Text Page	20.0%	25.00	25.00	70.58	27.50	1000.00
w/Graphics	20.0%	40.00	40.00	193.50	35.00	2500.00
Hour	60.0%	50.00	50.00	43.99	40.00	100.00

INVITATIONS

$/per	Survey %	Average	Typical	U.S. Avg.	U.S. Typ	U.S. Max
Text	40.0%	32.50	32.50	35.01	25.00	250.00
w/Graphics	20.0%	40.00	40.00	73.16	35.00	750.00
Hour	80.0%	47.50	50.00	41.85	40.00	100.00

LABELS (Custom)

$/per	Survey %	Average	Typical	U.S. Avg.	U.S. Typ	U.S. Max
Text	0.0%			40.06	20.00	250.00
w/Graphics	0.0%			121.16	55.00	600.00
Hour	60.0%	50.00	50.00	43.55	40.00	100.00

LARGE FORMAT GRAPHICS

$/per	Survey %	Average	Typical	U.S. Avg.	U.S. Typ	U.S. Max
Text Page	0.0%			40.00	37.50	45.00
w/Graphics	0.0%			71.00	70.00	85.00
Hour	20.0%	50.00	50.00	47.95	45.00	90.00

LETTERHEAD & ENVELOPES

$/per	Survey %	Average	Typical	U.S. Avg.	U.S. Typ	U.S. Max
Text	0.0%			59.65	25.00	750.00
w/Graphics	0.0%			136.48	40.00	1000.00
Hour	80.0%	41.25	50.00	43.60	40.00	150.00

LINE ART & GENERAL ILLUSTRATIONS

$/per	Survey %	Average	Typical	U.S. Avg.	U.S. Typ	U.S. Max
Text Page	0.0%			64.17	47.50	135.00
w/Graphics	0.0%			221.89	100.00	1000.00
Hour	80.0%	41.25	50.00	46.24	43.50	115.00

LITIGATION GRAPHICS

$/per	Survey %	Average	Typical	U.S. Avg.	U.S. Typ	U.S. Max
Text Page	0.0%			75.00	75.00	75.00
w/Graphics	0.0%			100.00	100.00	100.00
Hour	20.0%	50.00	50.00	50.13	45.00	200.00

LOGOS

$/per	Survey %	Average	Typical	U.S. Avg.	U.S. Typ	U.S. Max
Each	0.0%			281.23	200.00	2000.00
Hour	80.0%	41.25	50.00	46.02	45.00	125.00

LOGOTYPE

$/per	Survey %	Average	Typical	U.S. Avg.	U.S. Typ	U.S. Max
Page	0.0%			304.36	300.00	1000.00
Hour	20.0%	50.00	50.00	48.68	45.00	125.00

MAGAZINES

$/per	Survey %	Average	Typical	U.S. Avg.	U.S. Typ	U.S. Max
Text Page	0.0%			60.49	35.00	250.00
w/Graphics	0.0%			90.89	40.00	500.00
Hour	20.0%	50.00	50.00	45.91	45.00	125.00

NOTES:
1. Multiple page prices converted to $/page.
2. Other prices noted for magazine design: $500 setup; $1,000 ea.

MAILERS

$/per	Survey %	Average	Typical	U.S. Avg.	U.S. Typ	U.S. Max
Text Page	0.0%			64.08	25.00	500.00
w/Graphics	0.0%			82.36	40.00	500.00
Hour	40.0%	45.00	45.00	46.11	42.00	100.00

MANUALS

$/per	Survey %	Average	Typical	U.S. Avg.	U.S. Typ	U.S. Max
Text Page	0.0%			42.06	17.50	500.00
w/Graphics	0.0%			58.10	30.00	500.00
Hour	60.0%	35.00	40.00	42.63	40.00	100.00

MAPS
(1C, 2C, Letter Size)

$/per	Survey %	Average	Typical	U.S. Avg.	U.S. Typ	U.S. Max
Simple	0.0%			76.25	70.00	250.00
Complex	0.0%			206.14	75.00	600.00
Hour	20.0%	50.00	50.00	46.90	45.00	100.00

MAPS
(4C, Larger Than Letter Size)

$/per	Survey %	Average	Typical	U.S. Avg.	U.S. Typ	U.S. Max
Simple	0.0%			168.75	72.50	500.00
Complex	0.0%			490.71	300.00	1600.00
Hour	20.0%	50.00	50.00	48.08	45.00	100.00

MARKETING PLANS

$/per	Survey %	Average	Typical	U.S. Avg.	U.S. Typ	U.S. Max
Text Page	0.0%			59.00	10.00	250.00
w/Graphics	0.0%			182.67	40.00	500.00
Hour	20.0%	50.00	50.00	47.80	45.00	100.00

MEMO PADS

$/per	Survey %	Average	Typical	U.S. Avg.	U.S. Typ	U.S. Max
Text	0.0%			20.14	14.50	100.00
w/Graphics	0.0%			31.79	17.50	150.00
Hour	40.0%	55.00	55.00	43.94	40.00	100.00

MENUS

$/per	Survey %	Average	Typical	U.S. Avg.	U.S. Typ	U.S. Max
Text Page	0.0%			75.65	35.00	500.00
w/Graphics	0.0%			125.25	45.00	1000.00
Hour	80.0%	47.50	50.00	44.35	40.00	150.00
Minimum	0.0%			233.75	200.00	500.00

NEWSLETTERS

$/per	Survey %	Average	Typical	U.S. Avg.	U.S. Typ	U.S. Max
Text Page	0.0%			62.86	45.00	200.00
w/Graphics	0.0%			76.16	50.00	200.00
Hour	80.0%	47.50	50.00	42.97	40.00	160.00

NOTEPADS

$/per	Survey %	Average	Typical	U.S. Avg.	U.S. Typ	U.S. Max
Text	0.0%			32.28	25.00	100.00
w/Graphics	0.0%			41.37	35.00	150.00
Hour	40.0%	55.00	55.00	43.72	40.00	100.00

PACKAGING

$/per	Survey %	Average	Typical	U.S. Avg.	U.S. Typ	U.S. Max
Text	0.0%			276.00	100.00	1000.00
w/Graphics	0.0%			478.18	250.00	2500.00
Hour	20.0%	50.00	50.00	51.64	50.00	150.00

PEN RULER

$/per	Survey %	Average	Typical	U.S. Avg.	U.S. Typ	U.S. Max
Page	0.0%			45.00	45.00	45.00
Hour	20.0%	50.00	50.00	48.81	50.00	85.00

PERIODICAL (OTHER)

$/per	Survey %	Average	Typical	U.S. Avg.	U.S. Typ	U.S. Max
Text Page	0.0%			36.00	25.00	150.00
w/Graphics	0.0%			58.00	35.00	250.00
Hour	20.0%	50.00	50.00	46.86	45.00	125.00

POINT-OF-PURCHASE DISPLAYS

$/per	Survey %	Average	Typical	U.S. Avg.	U.S. Typ	U.S. Max
Text Page	0.0%			650.00	600.00	1000.00
w/Graphics	0.0%			800.00	800.00	1000.00
Hour	20.0%	50.00	50.00	50.15	50.00	100.00

POST CARDS

$/per	Survey %	Average	Typical	U.S. Avg.	U.S. Typ	U.S. Max
Text Page	0.0%			45.18	20.00	400.00
w/Graphics	0.0%			64.31	30.00	500.00
Hour	20.00%	50.00	50.00	42.38	40.00	100.00

POSTERS

$/per	Survey %	Average	Typical	U.S. Avg.	U.S. Typ	U.S. Max
Text Page	0.0%			123.67	50.00	500.00
w/Graphics	0.0%			259.71	250.00	1000.00
Hour	40.0%	55.00	55.00	45.60	45.00	100.00

PRESENTATION MATERIALS

$/per	Survey %	Average	Typical	U.S. Avg.	U.S. Typ	U.S. Max
Text Page	0.0%			27.65	20.00	100.00
w/Graphics	0.0%			44.38	25.00	180.00
Hour	40.0%	55.00	55.00	45.04	45.00	100.00

PRICE LISTS

$/per	Survey %	Average	Typical	U.S. Avg.	U.S. Typ	U.S. Max
Text Page	0.0%			40.63	35.00	150.00
w/Graphics	0.0%			51.79	40.00	160.00
Hour	80.0%	47.50	50.00	42.68	40.00	100.00

PRINT ADS

$/per	Survey %	Average	Typical	U.S. Avg.	U.S. Typ	U.S. Max
Text	0.0%			107.09	45.00	1000.00
w/Graphics	0.0%			179.74	80.00	1100.00
Hour	60.0%	50.00	50.00	44.84	40.00	100.00

PROCEDURE GUIDES

$/per	Survey %	Average	Typical	U.S. Avg.	U.S. Typ	U.S. Max
Text Page	0.0%			60.00	15.00	300.00
w/Graphics	0.0%			93.21	25.00	500.00
Hour	60.0%	50.00	50.00	45.67	45.00	100.00

PRODUCT LITERATURE

$/per	Survey %	Average	Typical	U.S. Avg.	U.S. Typ	U.S. Max
Text Page	0.0%			67.97	30.00	500.00
w/Graphics	0.0%			118.81	40.00	1000.00
Hour	40.0%	45.00	45.00	45.43	42.00	100.00

PRODUCT SPECIFICATION SHEETS

$/per	Survey %	Average	Typical	U.S. Avg.	U.S. Typ	U.S. Max
Text Page	0.0%			70.95	25.00	500.00
w/Graphics	0.0%			168.89	35.00	1000.00
Hour	20.0%	50.00	50.00	46.44	45.00	100.00

PROGRAMS

$/per	Survey %	Average	Typical	U.S. Avg.	U.S. Typ	U.S. Max
Text Page	0.0%			43.92	25.00	200.00
w/Graphics	0.0%			95.94	35.00	500.00
Hour	40.0%	55.00	55.00	46.61	45.00	150.00

PUBLICATIONS (OTHER)

$/per	Survey %	Average	Typical	U.S. Avg.	U.S. Typ	U.S. Max
Text Page	0.0%			46.00	30.00	150.00
w/Graphics	0.0%			87.73	35.00	500.00
Hour	20.0%	50.00	50.00	44.63	40.00	125.00

RECORD BOOKS

$/per	Survey %	Average	Typical	U.S. Avg.	U.S. Typ	U.S. Max
Text Page	0.0%			20.67	15.00	45.00
w/Graphics	0.0%			35.00	35.00	45.00
Hour	20.0%	50.00	50.00	46.63	45.00	80.00

RESUMES

$/per	Survey %	Average	Typical	U.S. Avg.	U.S. Typ	U.S. Max
Each	0.0%			31.21	25.00	150.00
Page	0.0%			31.52	30.00	150.00
Hour	80.0%	41.25	50.00	40.96	40.00	150.00

RULERS

$/per	Survey %	Average	Typical	U.S. Avg.	U.S. Typ	U.S. Max
Each	0.0%			250.00	375.00	500.00
Hour	20.0%	50.00	50.00	49.08	50.00	100.00

SALES PRESENTATIONS

$/per	Survey %	Average	Typical	U.S. Avg.	U.S. Typ	U.S. Max
Text Page	0.0%			23.14	20.00	45.00
w/Graphics	0.0%			29.50	25.00	45.00
Hour	40.0%	55.00	55.00	46.13	45.00	100.00

SIGNAGE

$/per	Survey %	Average	Typical	U.S. Avg.	U.S. Typ	U.S. Max
Text	0.0%			27.50	35.00	55.00
w/Graphics	0.0%			159.06	35.00	575.00
Hour	40.0%	32.50	35.00	45.60	45.00	100.00

SLIDE DESIGN

$/per	Survey %	Average	Typical	U.S. Avg.	U.S. Typ	U.S. Max
Text	0.0%			25.00	20.00	75.00
w/Graphics	0.0%			30.11	25.00	100.00
Hour	20.0%	50.00	50.00	46.17	45.00	100.00

SLIDE SHOW DESIGN

$/per	Survey %	Average	Typical	U.S. Avg.	U.S. Typ	U.S. Max
Text Page	0.0%			30.00	25.00	75.00
w/Graphics	0.0%			40.00	30.00	100.00
Hour	20.0%	50.00	50.00	47.98	50.00	100.00

SPREADSHEET DESIGN

$/per	Survey %	Average	Typical	U.S. Avg.	U.S. Typ	U.S. Max
Text Page	0.0%			35.00	35.00	45.00
w/Graphics	0.0%			45.50	45.00	45.00
Hour	20.0%	50.00	50.00	45.82	45.00	125.00

TABLOIDS

$/per	Survey %	Average	Typical	U.S. Avg.	U.S. Typ	U.S. Max
Text Page	0.0%			70.71	45.00	200.00
w/Graphics	0.0%			67.50	50.00	120.00
Hour	20.0%	50.00	50.00	46.32	45.00	125.00

TABS

$/per	Survey %	Average	Typical	U.S. Avg.	U.S. Typ	U.S. Max
Text	0.0%			20.00	20.00	20.00
w/Graphics	0.0%			20.00	20.00	20.00
Hour	20.0%	50.00	50.00	47.58	45.00	100.00

TAGS

$/per	Survey %	Average	Typical	U.S. Avg.	U.S. Typ	U.S. Max
Each	0.0%			17.83	10.00	35.00
Hour	40.0%	45.00	45.00	44.69	42.00	80.00

TECHNICAL DOCUMENTS

$/per	Survey %	Average	Typical	U.S. Avg.	U.S. Typ	U.S. Max
Text Page	0.0%			72.69	40.00	250.00
w/Graphics	0.0%			87.50	45.00	500.00
Hour	40.0%	32.50	35.00	44.05	40.00	125.00

TECHNICAL ILLUSTRATIONS

$/per	Survey %	Average	Typical	U.S. Avg.	U.S. Typ	U.S. Max
Page	0.0%			70.45	75.00	200.00
Hour	20.0%	50.00	50.00	47.28	45.00	200.00

TICKETS

$/per	Survey %	Average	Typical	U.S. Avg.	U.S. Typ	U.S. Max
Text	0.0%			24.72	20.00	50.00
w/Graphics	0.0%			30.25	30.00	50.00
Hour	40.0%	45.00	45.00	42.53	40.00	100.00

TRANSPARENCY DESIGN (B&W)

$/per	Survey %	Average	Typical	U.S. Avg.	U.S. Typ	U.S. Max
Text Page	0.0%			34.00	25.00	130.00
w/Graphics	0.0%			92.50	45.00	250.00
Hour	40.0%	55.00	55.00	42.68	40.00	100.00

TRANSPARENCY DESIGN (COLOR)

$/per	Survey %	Average	Typical	U.S. Avg.	U.S. Typ	U.S. Max
Text Page	0.0%			27.50	30.00	45.00
w/Graphics	0.0%			32.50	40.00	45.00
Hour	40.0%	55.00	55.00	44.69	45.00	100.00

OTHER DESIGN

$/per	Survey %	Average	Typical	U.S. Avg.	U.S. Typ	U.S. Max
Hour	0.0%			48.76	45.00	100.00

LASER PRINTER OUTPUT

GENERAL NOTES:
1. Some shops bill as $ set-up fee plus price per page.
2. Some shops bill as $/hr plus $/page.
3. A few shops price at $/hr (typically same price as other services).
4. Some laser printer output priced as $/job plus $/pg.

LASER PRINTING (Up to 300 dpi)

$/per	Survey %	Average	Typical	U.S. Avg.	U.S. Typ	U.S. Max
8.5 x 11	80.0%	3.63	1.00	1.64	1.00	15.00
8.5 x 14	40.0%	1.75	2.50	1.95	3.00	10.00
11 x 17	0.0%			3.13	2.25	6.00
Cost Plus	0.0%			31.25	30.00	50.00
Minimum	0.0%			15.00	5.00	25.00

LASER PRINTING (400 dpi)

$/per	Survey %	Average	Typical	U.S. Avg.	U.S. Typ	U.S. Max
8.5 x 11	0.0%			3.03	1.93	15.50
8.5 x 14	0.0%			2.71	2.00	6.00
11 x 17	0.0%			6.75	4.50	20.00
Cost Plus	0.0%			28.00	20.00	50.00
Minimum	0.0%			15.00	5.00	25.00

LASER PRINTING (600 dpi)

$/per	Survey %	Average	Typical	U.S. Avg.	U.S. Typ	U.S. Max
8.5 x 11	0.0%			1.88	1.00	15.00
8.5 x 14	0.0%			1.88	1.95	4.46
11 x 17	0.0%			4.12	5.16	6.00
Cost Plus	0.0%			28.00	20.00	50.00

LASER PRINTING
(800dpi)

$/per	Survey %	Average	Typical	U.S. Avg.	U.S. Typ	U.S. Max
8.5 x 11	20.0%	1.00	1.00	2.75	2.00	12.00
8.5 x 14	0.0%			2.94	4.00	5.00
11 x 17	0.0%			6.00	6.00	6.00
Cost Plus	0.0%			28.00	20.00	50.00
Minimum	0.0%			15.00	5.00	25.00

LASER PRINTING
(1000 dpi)

$/per	Survey %	Average	Typical	U.S. Avg.	U.S. Typ	U.S. Max
8.5 x 11	0.0%			3.10	3.00	7.00
8.5 x 14	0.0%			4.06	4.00	7.00
11 x 17	0.0%			6.00	6.00	6.00
Cost Plus	0.0%			28.00	20.00	50.00
Minimum	0.0%			15.00	10.00	25.00

LASER PRINTING
(1200 dpi)

$/per	Survey %	Average	Typical	U.S. Avg.	U.S. Typ	U.S. Max
8.5 x 11	20.0%	10.00	10.00	2.89	3.00	6.00
8.5 x 14	20.0%	12.00	12.00	4.82	6.00	6.43
11 x 17	20.0%	16.00	16.00	7.18	6.00	13.25
Cost Plus	0.0%			28.00	20.00	50.00
Minimum	0.0%			15.00	10.00	25.00

FOR PREPRESS AND OTHER SERVICES (INCLUDING IMAGESETTING OUTPUT), REFER TO THE SECTION MARKED "NATIONAL."

Additional Services
NATIONAL
Data Common to All Regions

GENERAL NOTE: The survey produced insufficient data to break out the following categories by region. Therefore the prices in this section represent a composite of all shops in North America. Percentages suggest the relative number of shops involved.

OTHER SERVICES

CAMERA WORK
(Photography)

$/per	Survey %	Average	Typical	Maximum
Hour	12.8%	53.85	50.00	150.00
Minimum	0.3%	10.00	10.00	10.00

CAMERA WORK
(Darkroom)

$/per	Survey %	Average	Typical	Maximum
Each	1.8%	12.40	13.50	25.00
Hour	9.3%	46.16	50.00	100.00

CHANGES & ALTERATIONS
(No Affect On Layout)

$/per	Survey %	Average	Typical	Maximum
Each	4.8%	6.14	5.00	25.00
Line	0.1%	2.48	0.75	8.00
Hour	63.5%	41.06	38.00	150.00
Job	2.2%	19.30	10.00	75.00
Minimum	0.3%	11.30	10.00	30.00

CHANGES & ALTERATIONS
(Revised Layout Required)

$/per	Survey %	Average	Typical	Maximum
Each	3.1%	7.04	5.00	25.00
Line	0.1%	1.00	1.00	1.00
Hour	65.9%	42.23	40.00	150.00
Job	1.8%	19.06	10.00	75.00
Minimum	3.2%	15.30	15.00	30.00

CHANGES & ALTERATIONS
(Typeface or Font Change)

$/per	Survey %	Average	Typical	Maximum
Each	3.3%	6.43	5.00	25.00
Line	0.1%	0.70	0.70	1.00
Hour	61.7%	41.28	35.00	150.00
Job	2.0%	16.72	10.00	75.00
Minimum	1.2%	13.68	15.00	20.00

CHANGES - UPDATE PREVIOUS WORK
(No Affect On Layout)

$/per	Survey %	Average	Typical	Maximum
Each	2.9%	6.85	3.50	25.00
Line	0.1%	1.00	1.00	1.00
Hour	63.3%	42.60	40.00	150.00
Job	1.1%	22.40	10.00	75.00
Minimum	3.2%	16.83	15.00	50.00

CHANGES - UPDATE PREVIOUS WORK
(Causes New Layout)

$/per	Survey %	Average	Typical	Maximum
Each	2.4%	7.86	5.00	25.00
Line	0.1%	1.00	1.00	1.00
Hour	61.5%	40.88	35.00	150.00
Job	1.6%	17.71	10.00	75.00
Minimum	3.2%	10.52	15.00	50.00

CONSULTING

$/per	Survey %	Average	Typical	Maximum
Hour	36.3%	49.50	45.00	1.50
Cost Plus %	0.4%	15.00	15.00	15.00

NOTE: Survey responses listed as $/minute, or $/day were converted to $/hr.

COORDINATING

$/per	Survey %	Average	Typical	Maximum
Hour	8.9%	46.68	40.00	125.00
Cost Plus %	0.9%	15.00	15.00	20.00

DATABASE PUBLISHING

$/per	Survey %	Average	Typical	Maximum
Hour	3.3%	39.60	35.00	75.00

DESKTOP VIDEO PRODUCTION

$/per	Survey %	Average	Typical	Maximum
Hour	3.1%	70.45	50.00	300.00

DIGITAL PHOTO COMPOSITION				
$/per	Survey %	Average	Typical	Maximum
Hour	10.8%	59.13	50.00	150.00

DIGITAL PHOTO ENHANCEMENT				
$/per	Survey %	Average	Typical	Maximum
Hour	13.5%	58.42	50.00	200.00

DIGITAL PHOTO PROCESSING				
$/per	Survey %	Average	Typical	Maximum
Hour	10.0%	56.90	50.00	250.00

PHOTO DESIGN				
$/per	Survey %	Average	Typical	Maximum
Hour	8.2%	59.12	50.00	175.00

MORPHING				
$/per	Survey %	Average	Typical	Maximum
Hour	0.4%	67.50	60.00	75.00

MULTIMEDIA (2-D Animation)				
$/per	Survey %	Average	Typical	Maximum
Hour	5.8%	53.38	50.00	87.50

MULTIMEDIA (3-D Animation)				
$/per	Survey %	Average	Typical	Maximum
Hour	5.5%	56.71	60.00	100.00

MULTIMEDIA (3-D Illustration - Rendering)				
$/per	Survey %	Average	Typical	Maximum
Hour	6.4%	57.17	55.00	100.00

MULTIMEDIA (3-D Modeling)				
$/per	Survey %	Average	Typical	Maximum
Hour	5.5%	56.91	55.00	100.00

MULTIMEDIA (Authoring)				
$/per	Survey %	Average	Typical	Maximum
Hour	5.5%	54.50	50.00	87.50

MULTIMEDIA (Dissolving Images)				
$/per	Survey %	Average	Typical	Maximum
Hour	4.7%	56.55	55.00	87.50

MULTIMEDIA (Non-Linear Editing)				
$/per	Survey %	Average	Typical	Maximum
Hour	4.9%	56.70	55.00	87.50

MULTIMEDIA (Title Design)				
$/per	Survey %	Average	Typical	Maximum
Hour	4.9%	57.39	55.00	87.50

MUSIC TYPESETTING				
$/per	Survey %	Average	Typical	Maximum
Line	0.2%	5.50	5.50	5.50
Page	0.4%	20.00	20.00	30.00
Hour	2.2%	51.50	45.00	85.00

SCRIPT FORMATTING				
$/per	Survey %	Average	Typical	Maximum
Hour	2.2%	53.50	50.00	100.00

SCRIPT WRITING				
$/per	Survey %	Average	Typical	Maximum
Page	0.2%	50.00	50.00	50.00
Hour	5.1%	48.49	50.00	100.00

STORYBOARDING				
$/per	Survey %	Average	Typical	Maximum
Hour	4.0%	54.28	50.00	100.00

PREPRESS SERVICES

BLUELINES				
$/per	Survey %	Average	Typical	Maximum
Page	5.3%	11.81	8.00	60.00
Hour	8.4%	53.11	55.00	125.00
Cost Plus %	2.2%	21.50	25.00	40.00

CHROMA TRANSFER

$/per	Survey %	Average	Typical	Maximum
Each	0.4%	25.50	30.00	39.00
Hour	0.7%	50.00	50.00	60.00
Cost Plus %	1.6%	22.86	25.00	40.00
Minimum	1.1%	30.00	30.00	30.00

COLOR CORRECTION

$/per	Survey %	Average	Typical	Maximum
Each	0.4%	67.50	50.00	95.00
Hour	5.1%	94.70	75.00	300.00
Cost Plus %	1.6%	22.80	25.00	40.00
Minimum	1.1%	60.00	60.00	60.00

COLOR PROOFS (DIGITAL)
(3M Digital Matchprint)

$/per	Survey %	Average	Typical	Maximum
8.5 x 11	0.1%	87.50	87.50	100.00

COLOR PROOFS (DIGITAL)
(Direct Digital Color Proof - DDCP)

$/per	Survey %	Average	Typical	Maximum
Each	0.1%	55.40	50.00	125.00
Cost Plus %	0.2%	31.67	30.00	40.00

COLOR PROOFS (DIGITAL)
(Iris Digital Proof)

$/per	Survey %	Average	Typical	Maximum
Each	0.0%			
Cost Plus %	0.1%	30.00	30.000	30.00

COLOR PROOFS (DIGITAL)
(Kodak Approval System)

$/per	Survey %	Average	Typical	Maximum
Each	0.0%			
Cost Plus %	0.1%	30.00	30.00	30.00

COLOR PROOFS (INTEGRAL)
(Agfaproof)

$/per	Survey %	Average	Typical	Maximum
9.5 x 15	0.1%	60.00	60.00	60.00
11 x 17	0.1%	100.00	100.00	100.00
15.7 x 22	0.1%	125.00	125.00	125.00
Cost Plus %	0.1%	28.12	30.00	40.00

COLOR PROOFS (INTEGRAL)
(Chromalin - Per Each)

$/per	Survey %	Average	Typical	Maximum
2 x 3	0.1%	11.00	11.00	11.00
4 x 5	0.1%	11.00	11.00	11.00
5 x 8	0.1%	12.00	12.00	12.00
6 x 9	0.1%	16.00	16.00	16.00
8 x 10	0.1%	20.00	20.00	20.00
10 x 12	0.1%	26.00	26.00	26.00
11 x 14	0.1%	33.00	33.00	33.00
12 x 18	0.1%	44.00	44.00	44.00
16 x 20	0.1%	61.00	61.00	61.00
20 x 24	0.1%	91.00	91.00	91.00
Cost Plus %	0.1%	31.67	30.00	40.00

COLOR PROOFS (INTEGRAL)
(Chromalin - Per Set)

$/per	Survey %	Average	Typical	Maximum
5 x 7	0.1%	45.00	45.00	45.00
8 x 10	0.1%	60.00	60.00	60.00
8.5 x 11	0.2%	85.36	75.00	150.00
10 x 12	0.1%	70.00	70.00	70.00
11 x 14	0.1%	80.00	80.00	80.00
11 x 17	0.1%	80.00	80.00	80.00
12 x 20	0.1%	100.00	100.00	100.00
16 x 20	0.1%	120.00	120.00	120.00
20 x 24	0.1%	140.00	140.00	140.00
Cost Plus %	0.1%	31.67	30.00	40.00

COLOR PROOFS (INTEGRAL)
(Color Art)

$/per	Survey %	Average	Typical	Maximum
Each	0.1%	65.00	75.00	80.00
Cost Plus %	0.1%	31.67	30.00	40.00

COLOR PROOFS (INTEGRAL)
(Matchprint)

$/per	Survey %	Average	Typical	Maximum
2 x 3	0.1%	37.00	37.00	37.00
4 x 5	0.1%	62.54	60.00	100.00
4 x 10	0.1%	67.50	67.50	75.00
5 x 7	0.1%	70.00	75.00	110.00
6 x 9	0.1%	102.50	102.00	130.00
8 x 10	0.2%	83.84	90.00	145.00
8.5 x 11	0.2%	63.58	68.00	140.00
10 x 12	0.2%	89.68	99.00	163.00
11 x 14	0.1%	103.69	75.00	189.00
11 x 17	0.1%	60.28	60.28	60.28
12 x 18	0.1%	136.75	155.00	225.00
14 x 17	0.1%	169.50	169.50	254.00
16 x 20	0.1%	172.33	180.00	295.00
20 x 24	0.1%	244.50	225.00	495.00
24 x 36	0.1%	140.00	140.00	140.00
25 x 38	0.1%	208.00	210.00	220.00
Cost Plus %	0.1%	31.67	30.00	40.00

COLOR PROOFS (INTEGRAL)
(Chromatec)

$/per	Survey %	Average	Typical	Maximum
5 x 7	0.1%	32.00	32.00	32.00
8 x 10	0.1%	36.00	36.00	36.00
10 x 12	0.1%	39.00	39.00	39.00
11 x 14	0.1%	43.00	43.00	43.00
12 x 18	0.1%	54.00	54.00	54.00
16 x 20	0.1%	62.00	62.00	62.00

COLOR PROOFS (INTEGRAL)
(Pressmatch - Each)

$/per	Survey %	Average	Typical	Maximum
2 x 3	0.1%	7.00	7.00	7.00
4 x 5	0.1%	7.00	7.00	7.00
5 x 8	0.1%	8.00	8.00	8.00
6 x 10	0.1%	11.00	11.00	11.00
10 x 12	0.1%	18.00	18.00	18.00
11 x 14	0.1%	22.00	22.00	22.00
12 x 18	0.1%	29.00	29.00	29.00
16 x 20	0.1%	41.00	41.00	41.00
20 x 24	0.1%	60.00	60.00	60.00

COLOR PROOFS (INTEGRAL) (Pressmatch - 4C)				
$/per	Survey %	Average	Typical	Maximum
2 x 3	0.1%	28.00	28.00	28.00
4 x 5	0.1%	30.50	30.00	33.00
5 x 7	0.1%	30.00	30.00	30.00
5 x 8	0.1%	42.00	42.00	42.00
6 x 9	0.1%	40.00	40.00	40.00
6 x 10	0.2%	41.33	40.00	40.00
8 x 10	0.2%	50.67	52.00	60.00
8.5 x 11	0.2%	50.00	50.00	50.00
8.5 x 14	0.1%	80.00	80.00	80.00
10 x 12	0.3%	63.60	60.00	76.00
11 x 14	0.3%	70.40	77.00	88.00
11 x 17	0.1%	80.00	80.00	100.00
12 x 18	0.3%	96.60	102.00	116.00
12 x 30	0.1%	160.00	160.00	160.00
14 x 17	0.1%	75.00	75.00	75.00
16 x 20	0.4%	118.83	114.00	164.00
20 x 24	0.4%	147.00	142.00	240.00
22 x 28	0.1%	265.00	265.00	265.00
24 x 30	0.1%	125.00	125.00	125.00
24 x 36	0.1%	360.00	360.00	360.00
25 x 38	0.1%	210.00	210.00	210.00
29 x 40	0.1%	500.00	500.00	500.00
Minimum	0.2%	60.00	60.00	60.00

COLOR PROOFS (INTEGRAL) (Signature)				
$/per	Survey %	Average	Typical	Maximum
Page	0.1%	60.00	60.00	80.00
Minimum	0.2%	31.67	30.00	40.00

COLOR PROOFS (OVERLAY) (Chroma Check)				
$/per	Survey %	Average	Typical	Maximum
5 x 7	0.1%	15.00	10.00	30.00
8.5 x 11	0.1%	21.67	20.00	40.00
10 x 12	0.1%	43.33	60.00	60.00
11 x 17	0.1%	35.00	35.00	60.00
20 x 24	0.1%	100.00	100.00	100.00
Cost Plus %	0.1%	31.67	30.00	40.00

COLOR PROOFS (OVERLAY) (Color-Key - Each)				
$/per	Survey %	Average	Typical	Maximum
4 x 5	0.1%	10.67	10.00	11.00
4 x 10	0.1%	8.00	8.00	8.00
5 x 7	0.1%	10.02	10.75	12.75
5 x 8	0.1%	8.00	8.00	8.00
8 x 10	0.1%	11.78	10.00	21.60
8.5 x 11	0.1%	19.87	20.00	27.00
10 x 12	0.1%	11.94	11.00	17.67
11 x 14	0.1%	14.24	12.00	26.78
12 x 18	0.1%	15.80	15.00	23.00
12 x 20	0.1%	15.13	15.00	16.25
14 x 17	0.1%	18.00	18.00	18.00
16 x 20	0.1%	19.33	20.00	30.00
20 x 24	0.1%	22.96	18.00	37.00
24 x 30	0.1%	22.00	22.00	22.00
24 x 36	0.1%	26.85	26.85	26.85
25 x 38	0.1%	30.75	30.75	37.50
Cost Plus %	0.1%	31.67	30.00	40.00

NOTE: Also listed as $/setup plus $/color.

COLOR PROOFS (OVERLAY) (Color-Key - 4C)				
$/per	Survey %	Average	Typical	Maximum
2 x 3	0.1%	35.00	35.00	45.00
4 x 5	0.1%	45.67	43.00	70.00
4 x 10	0.1%	35.00	35.00	45.00
5 x 7	0.1%	43.25	43.00	79.00
5 x 8	0.1%	35.00	35.00	45.00
6 x 9	0.1%	51.71	45.00	95.00
8 x 10	0.1%	56.45	56.00	105.00
8.5 x 11	0.1%	62.00	60.00	100.00
9 x 12	0.1%	63.00	63.00	81.00
10 x 12	0.1%	57.32	45.00	125.00
11 x 14	0.1%	71.05	65.00	137.00
11 x 17	0.1%	109.22	100.00	250.00
12 x 18	0.1%	91.90	90.00	180.00
14 x 17	0.1%	117.25	154.00	195.00
16 x 20	0.1%	124.73	150.00	225.00
20 x 24	0.1%	165.22	200.00	325.00
22 x 26	0.1%	260.00	260.00	265.00
23 x 38	0.1%	275.00	275.00	275.00
24 x 30	0.1%	196.00	200.00	300.00
24 x 36	0.1%	223.00	216.00	360.00
25 x 38	0.1%	215.00	220.00	340.00
29 x 40	0.1%	500.00	500.00	500.00

COLOR PROOFS (OVERLAY)
(Enco Film)

$/per	Survey %	Average	Typical	Maximum
8.5 x 11	0.1%	33.33	30.00	40.00
8.5 x 14	0.1%	60.00	60.00	60.00
11 x 17	0.1%	80.00	80.00	80.00
Cost Plus %	0.1%	31.67	30.00	40.00

COLOR PROOFS (PRESS)
(Press Proof)

$/per	Survey %	Average	Typical	Maximum
Each	0.1%	600.00	600.00	600.00
Hour	0.1%	400.00	400.00	500.00
Cost Plus %	0.1%	31.67	30.00	40.00

COLOR PROOFS (PRINTER OUTPUT)
(Iris Color Inkjet)

$/per	Survey %	Average	Typical	Maximum
8 x 10	0.1%	46.67	35.00	80.00
8.5 x 11	0.1%	29.00	35.00	80.00
9 x 12	0.1%	44.00	35.00	80.00
10 x 12	0.1%	62.50	35.00	80.00
10.6 x 17.2	0.1%	75.00	45.00	105.00
11 x 17	0.1%	41.25	45.00	45.00
12 x 18	0.1%	60.00	55.00	105.00
18 x 18	0.1%	100.00	100.00	125.00
18 x 24	0.1%	85.00	85.00	85.00
20 x 24	0.1%	95.00	95.00	95.00
23 x 23	0.1%	125.00	125.00	125.00
24 x 24	0.1%	98.00	95.00	124.00
34 x 47	0.1%	175.00	175.00	175.00
Cost Plus %	0.1%	31.67	30.00	40.00

COLOR PROOFS (PRINTER OUTPUT)
(QMS Color Inkjet)

$/per	Survey %	Average	Typical	Maximum
8 x 10	0.1%	14.50	14.50	16.00
8.5 x 11	0.1%	11.83	10.00	20.00
9 x 12	0.1%	16.00	16.00	16.00
11 x 17	0.1%	14.33	15.00	17.00
Cost Plus %	0.1%	31.67	30.00	40.00

COLOR PROOFS (PRINTER OUTPUT)
(300 dpi - Color Laser Printer)

$/per	Survey %	Average	Typical	Maximum
8.5x 11, 8.5 x 10.75	0.4%	10.41	10.00	20.00
8.5 x 14	0.1%	13.09	18.00	25.00
10.75 x 16.6	0.1%	16.14	15.00	21.00
11 x 17	0.1%	14.80	14.00	40.00
11.73 x 17.12	0.1%	18.40	18.00	21.00
Cost Plus %	0.1%	28.33	30.00	40.00

COLOR PROOFS (PRINTER OUTPUT)
(400 dpi - Color Laser Printer)

$/per	Survey %	Average	Typical	Maximum
8.5 x 11	0.1%	14.10	12.00	30.00
11 x 17	0.1%	29.33	17.00	90.00
Cost Plus %	0.1%	28.33	30.00	40.00

COLOR PROOFS (PRINTER OUTPUT)
(600 dpi - Color Laser Printer)

$/per	Survey %	Average	Typical	Maximum
8.5 x 11	0.1%	12.00	12.00	12.00
8.5 x 14	0.1%	12.00	12.00	12.00
Cost Plus %	0.1%	28.33	30.00	40.00

COLOR PROOFS (PRINTER OUTPUT)
(1200 dpi - Color Laser Printer)

$/per	Survey %	Average	Typical	Maximum
8.5 x 11	0.1%	12.00	12.00	12.00
8.5 x 14	0.1%	24.75	24.75	37.50
Cost Plus %	0.1%	2.59	2.59	2.59
8.5 x 14	3.2%	25.00	30.00	40.00

COLOR PROOFS (PRINTER OUTPUT)
(Canon CLC - Color Laser Printer)

$/per	Survey %	Average	Typical	Maximum
8.5 x 11	0.1%	15.00	15.00	15.00
11 x 17	0.1%	23.00	23.00	23.00
Cost Plus %	0.1%	25.00	30.00	40.00

NATIONAL

COLOR PROOFS (PRINTER OUTPUT)
(300 dpi - Dye Sublimation)

$/per	Survey %	Average	Typical	Maximum
8.5 x 11	0.1%	11.00	15.00	15.00
11 x 17	0.1%	44.00	45.00	50.00
Cost Plus %	0.1%	31.67	30.00	40.00

COLOR PROOFS (PRINTER OUTPUT)
(Solid Ink)

$/per	Survey %	Average	Typical	Maximum
8.5 x 11	0.1%	11.17	10.00	25.00
Cost Plus %	0.1%	31.25	30.00	40.00

COLOR PROOFS (PRINTER OUTPUT)
(300 dpi - Thermal Wax Printer)

$/per	Survey %	Average	Typical	Maximum
8.5 x 11	0.1%	10.96	10.00	20.00

NOTE: Some shops add $1/minute charge for over 5 minutes.

COLOR PROOFS (PRINTER OUTPUT)
(300 dpi - Seiko Color Thermal)

$/per	Survey %	Average	Typical	Maximum
8.5 x 11	0.1%	9.75	10.00	11.00
8.5 x 14	0.1%	10.00	10.00	12.00
11 x 17	0.1%	14.88	15.00	15.75
Cost Plus %	0.1%	31.67	30.00	40.00

COLOR SEPARATIONS
(Each Color)

$/per	Survey %	Average	Typical	Maximum
2 x 3	0.1%	25.40	25.00	33.00
4 x 5, 4 x 6	0.1%	36.73	35.00	82.00
5 x 7, 5.5 x 8.5	0.1%	44.61	40.00	93.00
6 x 8, 6 x 9	0.1%	49.02	50.00	70.00
7 x 10, 8 x 10	0.1%	58.12	60.00	83.00
9 x 12, 10 x 12	0.1%	74.78	73.00	91.00
11 x 14	0.1%	91.07	94.00	118.00
12 x 16, 12 x 18	0.1%	112.87	115.00	130.00
14 x 17	0.1%	116.00	116.00	122.00
16 x 20	0.1%	170.98	171.00	205.00
18 x 23	0.1%	219.00	219.00	219.00
20 x 24	0.1%	227.33	231.00	262.00
22 x 28	0.1%	250.00	250.00	250.00
24 x 36	0.1%	372.66	380.00	400.00
28 x 40	0.1%	519.00	510.00	588.00

COLOR SEPARATIONS (4C)				
$/per	Survey %	Average	Typical	Maximum
2 x 3	0.1%	54.40	55.00	120.00
4 x 5, 4 x 6	0.1%	135.00	137.00	148.00
5 x 7, 5.5 x 8.5	0.1%	119.33	120.00	168.00
6 x 8, 6 x 9	0.1%	129.25	125.00	192.00
7 x 10, 8 x 10	0.1%	162.50	162.50	205.00
10 x 12	0.1%	134.33	140.00	148.00
11 x 14	0.1%	157.00	157.00	179.00
12 x 16, 12 x 18	0.1%	190.00	190.00	204.00
14 x 17	0.1%	205.00	205.00	250.00
16 x 20	0.1%	275.66	275.00	310.00
18 x 24	0.1%	260.00	260.00	260.00
18 x 30	0.1%	300.00	300.00	300.00
18 x 36	0.1%	340.00	340.00	340.00
18 x 42	0.1%	380.00	380.00	380.00
18 x 48	0.1%	420.00	420.00	420.00
20 x 24	0.1%	465.00	465.00	480.00
22 x 28	0.1%	500.00	500.00	500.00
24 x 27	0.1%	600.00	600.00	600.00

COLOR SEPARATIONS (With Laminate Proof)				
$/per	Survey %	Average	Typical	Maximum
4 x 5	0.1%	93.00	93.00	93.00
5 x 7	0.1%	109.00	109.00	109.00
6 x 9	0.1%	127.00	127.00	127.00
8 x 10	0.1%	144.00	144.00	144.00
10 x 12	0.1%	171.00	171.00	171.00
11 x 14	0.1%	195.00	195.00	195.00
12 x 18	0.1%	224.00	224.00	224.00
16 x 20	0.1%	272.00	272.00	272.00
20 x 24	0.1%	366.00	366.00	366.00
22 x 28	0.1%	772.00	772.00	772.00
24 x 36	0.1%	1,131.00	1,131.00	1,131.00
25 x 38	0.1%	1,264.00	1,264.00	1,264.00
Cost Plus %	0.1%	25.00	25.00	25.00

COLOR SEPARATIONS
(With Overlay Proof)

$/per	Survey %	Average	Typical	Maximum
2 x 3	0.1%	29.72	30.00	50.00
4 x 5, 4 x 6	0.1%	42.58	45.00	69.00
5 x 7, 5.5 x 8.5	0.1%	49.98	50.00	80.00
6 x 8, 6 x 9	0.1%	50.14	51.00	97.00
7 x 10, 8 x 10	0.1%	65.60	66.00	121.00
9 x 12	0.1%	77.00	77.00	77.00
10 x 12	0.1%	83.89	85.00	145.00
11 x 14	0.2%	103.15	105.00	178.00
12 x 16, 12 x 18	0.1%	137.46	140.00	202.00
14 x 17	0.1%	156.90	157.00	195.00
16 x 20	0.1%	173.97	175.00	243.00
18 x 22, 18 x 23	0.1%	295.00	295.00	295.00
20 x 24	0.2%	243.13	245.00	325.00
22 x 28	0.1%	540.00	540.00	540.00
23 x 28	0.1%	250.00	250.00	250.00
24 x 30	0.1%	416.00	416.00	416.00
24 x 36	0.1%	588.50	562.50	850.00
25 x 38, 26 x 38	0.1%	950.00	950.00	950.00
28 x 40	0.1%	588.00	588.00	588.00
30 x 40	0.1%	709.00	709.00	900.00
30 x 42	0.1%	600.00	600.00	600.00
Minimum	0.1%	32.50	30.00	40.00

DUOTONE
(Each)

$/per	Survey %	Average	Typical	Maximum
2 x 3	0.1%	15.00	15.00	15.00
4 x 5, 4 x 6	0.1%	15.17	15.00	15.50
5 x 7, 5.5 x 8.5	0.1%	17.67	17.50	18.50
8 x 10	0.1%	20.47	20.00	22.40
10 x 12	0.1%	23.83	29.20	46.00
11 x 14	0.1%	38.70	35.50	52.00
12 x 18	0.1%	50.98	42.90	75.00
14 x 17	0.1%	90.00	90.00	90.00
16 x 20	0.1%	81.67	100.00	110.00
18 x 23	0.1%	130.00	130.00	130.00
20 x 24	0.1%	160.00	160.00	160.00

DUOTONE				
$/per	Survey %	Average	Typical	Maximum
2 x 3	0.1%	35.00	35.00	35.00
4 x 5	0.1%	37.50	37.50	40.00
5 x 7, 5 x 8	0.1%	39.25	41.00	45.00
8 x 10	0.1%	49.25	47.50	65.00
10 x 12	0.1%	68.50	68.50	75.00
11 x 14	0.1%	82.00	82.00	90.00
12 x 18	0.1%	115.00	100.00	130.00
14 x 17	0.1%	145.00	145.00	145.00
16 x 20	0.1%	159.50	159.50	195.00
20 x 24	0.1%	223.50	223.50	280.00
24 x 27	0.1%	375.00	375.00	375.00

ELECTRONIC IMPOSITION				
$/per	Survey %	Average	Typical	Maximum
Each	0.4%	10.00	10.00	10.00
Hour	2.2%	68.50	60.00	150.00

HALFTONE (Film Negative)				
$/per	Survey %	Average	Typical	Maximum
4 x 5	0.1%	7.81	6.75	12.00
4 x 10	0.1%	11.40	9.00	14.80
5 x 7	0.1%	9.07	10.00	12.00
5 x 8	0.1%	8.35	8.35	8.50
6 x 10	0.1%	12.43	12.40	15.50
8 x 10	0.1%	15.31	12.75	18.00
8.5 x 11	0.1%	15.62	13.00	25.00
10 x 12	0.1%	14.32	13.75	26.00
11 x 14	0.1%	17.44	15.90	27.00
12 x 14	0.1%	21.45	21.45	21.50
12 x 18	0.1%	20.18	22.00	25.00
12 x 20	0.1%	26.40	26.40	26.50
16 x 20	0.1%	29.60	31.00	34.00
20 x 24	0.1%	33.17	32.75	41.75
Cost Plus %	0.1%	32.50	32.50	40.00

NOTES:
1. Some shops charge additional $ per exposure for step-and-repeat exposures.
2. Some add $ for special screens and tints.

HALFTONE (Film Positive)				
$/per	Survey %	Average	Typical	Maximum
4 x 5	0.1%	9.20	10.00	12.00
4 x 10	0.1%	9.40	10.00	14.80
5 x 7	0.1%	7.73	11.00	12.00
6 x 10	0.1%	10.93	12.00	15.85
8 x 10	0.1%	11.61	12.33	18.00
8.5 x 11	0.1%	12.82	13.00	25.00
10 x 12	0.1%	16.86	13.20	36.00
11 x 14	0.1%	14.57	12.00	27.00
12 x 14	0.1%	21.45	21.45	21.45
12 x 18	0.1%	9.75	10.00	12.50
12 x 20	0.1%	26.40	26.40	26.40
16 x 20	0.1%	13.20	13.40	16.00
18 x 23	0.1%	12.90	12.90	12.90
20 x 24	0.1%	17.35	17.50	20.00
Cost Plus %	0.1%	32.50	32.50	40.00

HALFTONE (Print)				
$/per	Survey %	Average	Typical	Maximum
2 x 3	0.1%	20.00	20.00	20.00
4 x 5	0.1%	6.59	6.50	10.50
4 x 10	0.1%	9.25	9.25	10.50
5 x 7	0.1%	6.83	7.50	10.50
6 x 10	0.2%	9.75	9.75	10.50
8 x 10	0.1%	8.11	9.00	10.50
8.5 x 11	3.5%	14.50	11.00	15.00
9 x 12	0.1%	3.00	3.00	3.00
10 x 12	1.5%	10.14	11.00	12.00
11 x 14	1.1%	10.56	11.50	14.00
12 x 18	1.1%	13.24	15.00	17.00
12 x 20	0.1%	17.00	17.00	17.00
16 x 20	0.1%	21.00	21.00	21.00
20 x 24	0.1%	25.00	25.00	25.00
Cost Plus %	0.1%	32.50	32.50	40.00

HALFTONE (PMT)				
$/per	Survey %	Average	Typical	Maximum
4 x 5	0.1%	8.25	8.25	8.50
4 x 10	0.1%	8.45	8.45	10.90
5 x 7, 5 x 8	0.1%	6.83	9.50	10.00
6 x 10	0.1%	11.45	11.45	14.90
7 x 9	0.1%	11.25	11.25	11.25

HALFTONE (PMT)				
$/per	Survey %	Average	Typical	Maximum
4 x 10	0.1%	13.38	12.50	18.50
8.5 x 11	0.1%	6.00	6.00	6.00
10 x 12	1.0%	15.59	15.00	20.35
11 x 14	1.0%	16.17	16.00	18.50
11 x 15	0.1%	21.05	21.00	21.05
12 x 18	0.9%	19.83	21.50	22.00
15 x 23	0.1%	31.90	31.90	31.90
16 x 20	0.1%	27.00	27.00	34.00
20 x 24	0.1%	24.00	24.00	24.00

STATS (Film)				
$/per	Survey %	Average	Typical	Maximum
4 x 10	0.1%	7.50	7.50	8.00
6 x 10	0.1%	8.00	8.00	8.00
8.5 x 11	1.1%	9.98	9.00	15.00
10 x 12	0.5%	11.67	12.00	12.00
11 x 17	0.1%	12.00	12.00	12.00
Cost Plus %	0.1%	32.50	32.50	40.00

STATS (Print)				
$/per	Survey %	Average	Typical	Maximum
4 x 5	0.1%	4.05	4.00	4.05
4 x 10	0.1%	6.00	6.00	6.00
5 x 7	0.1%	7.80	7.80	7.80
6 x 10	0.1%	7.00	7.00	7.00
8 x 10	0.1%	8.40	8.40	8.40
8.5 x 11	2.3%	10.45	10.00	20.00
9 x 12	0.1%	9.00	9.00	9.00
10 x 12	0.2%	9.63	9.63	10.00
11 x 14	0.2%	11.50	11.50	12.00
12 x 18	0.2%	14.90	14.90	16.00
16 x 20	0.1%	17.50	17.50	17.50
20 x 24	0.1%	20.00	20.00	20.00
Hour	0.2%	32.50	32.50	35.00
Cost Plus %	0.2%	32.50	32.50	40.00

STATS (Positive Line Stat - PMT)				
$/per	Survey %	Average	Typical	Maximum
4 x 5	0.1%	4.40	4.40	4.40
4 x 10	0.3%	5.57	5.50	7.20
5 x 8	0.2%	5.08	5.08	5.50

NATIONAL

STATS
(Positive Line Stat - PMT)

$/per	Survey %	Average	Typical	Maximum
6 x 10	0.2%	7.13	7.13	9.25
8 x 10, 8.5 x 11	1.5%	7.16	6.00	12.35
10 x 12	1.1%	10.28	8.00	15.00
11 x 14	0.4%	10.65	9.10	15.00
11 x 15	0.2%	14.95	14.95	15.00
12 x 18	0.4%	12.65	11.00	18.00
14 x 17	0.2%	16.00	16.00	18.00
15 x 23	0.3%	22.58	24.75	25.00
16 x 20	0.3%	16.00	16.00	18.00
18 x 22	0.2%	22.50	22.50	25.00
20 x 24	0.2%	21.50	21.50	25.00
Hour	0.2%	32.50	32.50	35.00
Cost Plus %	0.2%	32.50	32.50	40.00

PASTE-UP (ELECTRONIC)

$/per	Survey %	Average	Typical	Maximum
Page	1.1%	51.00	50.00	150.00
Hour	23.0%	46.60	40.00	150.00
Minimum	0.2%	25.00	25.00	25.00

PASTE-UP (MANUAL)

$/per	Survey %	Average	Typical	Maximum
Page	1.6%	28.64	35.00	100.00
Hour	29.4%	38.35	35.00	100.00
Minimum	0.2%	25.00	25.00	25.00

STRIPPING (ELECTRONIC)

$/per	Survey %	Average	Typical	Maximum
Hour	6.8%	59.30	55.00	178.00
Cost Plus %	1.6%	22.86	25.00	40.00
Minimum	·0.0%			

STRIPPING (MANUAL)

$/per	Survey %	Average	Typical	Maximum
Hour	7.1%	49.35	50.00	75.00
Cost Plus %	1.6%	22.86	25.00	40.00
Minimum	0.0%			

VELOX (Contact Print)				
$/per	Survey %	Average	Typical	Maximum
4 x 5	0.1%	7.20	7.20	7.20
4 x 10	0.1%	7.92	7.92	7.92
5 x 7	0.3%	7.00	6.00	10.00
6 x 10	0.1%	9.80	9.80	9.80
8 x 10	0.3%	7.00	8.00	10.90
8.5 x 11	2.1%	9.05	8.00	18.00
10 x 12	0.7%	8.98	8.50	11.90
11 x 14	0.4%	10.00	10.00	11.00
12 x 14	0.1%	14.30	14.30	14.30
12 x 18	0.2%	14.00	14.00	14.00
12 x 20	0.2%	16.18	16.25	20.35
16 x 20	0.2%	17.00	17.00	20.00
20 x 24	0.4%	21.82	24.00	25.45
24 x 30	0.1%	30.00	30.00	30.00
30x 30	0.1%	35.00	35.00	35.00
30 x 40	0.1%	40.00	40.00	40.00
Hour	5.9%	45.90	45.90	95.00
Cost Plus %	0.2%	32.50	32.50	40.00

HIGH END PRINTER OUTPUT

GENERAL NOTES:
1. Some shops bill as $ set-up fee plus price per page.
2. Some shops bill as $/hr plus $/page.
3. A few shops price at $/hr (typically same price as other services).
4. Some imagesetting priced as $/job plus $/pg.
5. Some imagesetting priced as $/job plus $/foot (longest dimension).

IMAGESETTER (RC PAPER) (1200-1270 dpi)				
$/per	Survey %	Average	Typical	Maximum
8.5 x 11	12.6%	12.19	10.00	99.00
8.5 x 14	6.4%	12.87	12.00	25.00
9.5 x 12	0.9%	9.15	10.00	15.00
9.5 x 15	0.7%	6.90	7.00	13.20
10 x 14	0.9%	11.25	15.00	18.00
11 x 17	8.0%	15.92	16.00	25.00

IMAGESETTER (RC PAPER)
(1200-1270 dpi)

$/per	Survey %	Average	Typical	Maximum
11 x 18	0.4%	16.50	17.00	18.00
11.7 x 26	0.4%	25.00	25.00	25.00
12 x 15	0.2%	21.00	21.00	21.00
12 x 18	0.7%	19.67	19.00	25.00
12 x 23	0.9%	21.25	24.00	30.00
12 x 27	1.1%	28.10	28.00	34.00
18 x 24	0.2%	25.00	25.00	25.00
18 x 30	0.2%	35.00	35.00	35.00
18 x 36	0.2%	42.00	42.00	42.00
Cost Plus %	2.7%	27.33	30.00	60.00

IMAGESETTER (RC PAPER)
(2093, 2540 dpi)

$/per	Survey %	Average	Typical	Maximum
8.5 x 11	8.6%	11.86	12.00	20.00
8.5 x 14	5.1%	14.34	14.00	24.00
9.5 x 12	1.1%	13.02	10.50	21.00
9.5 x 15	1.1%	11.70	11.00	18.00
10 x 14	0.9%	11.63	13.00	15.00
11 x 17	5.7%	17.93	17.00	30.00
11 x 18	0.7%	12.17	11.00	18.00
11.7 x 26	0.9%	18.38	25.00	30.00
12 x 15	0.7%	14.17	15.00	24.00
12 x 18	1.1%	16.70	18.00	28.00
12 x 23	1.1%	16.90	17.00	30.00
12 x 27	1.3%	21.25	28.00	35.00
18 x 24	0.9%	21.63	28.00	40.00
18 x 30	0.9%	26.63	38.00	50.00
18 x 36	0.9%	30.88	45.00	60.00
Cost Plus %	2.4%	24.36	20.00	50.00

IMAGESETTER (RC PAPER)
(3000-3386 dpi)

$/per	Survey %	Average	Typical	Maximum
8.5 x 11	1.1%	11.50	11.00	16.00
8.5 x 14	0.7%	13.33	14.00	15.00
9.5 x 12	0.1%	13.00	13.00	13.00
9.5 x 15	0.1%	17.00	17.00	17.00
10 x 14	0.2%	18.00	18.00	18.00
11 x 17	0.9%	16.00	18.00	21.00
11 x 18	0.0%	17.00	17.00	17.00
11.7 x 26	0.0%			
12 x 15	0.1%	19.00	19.00	19.00
12 x 18	0.1%	19.00	19.00	19.00

IMAGESETTER (RC PAPER) **(3000-3386 dpi)**				
$/per	Survey %	Average	Typical	Maximum
12 x 23	0.0%			
12 x 27	0.0%			
18 x 24	0.2%	40.00	40.00	40.00
18 x 30	0.2%	50.00	50.00	50.00
18 x 36	0.2%	60.00	60.00	60.00
Cost Plus %	1.8%	24.13	20.00	50.00

ADDITIONAL NOTES
REGARDING IMAGESETTING SERVICES

A number of shops reported their rates as a price per job plus a price per page and cost plus a price per page

For example, we noted in the 1200 dpi area:

  (8.5 x 11) $10/job plus $1.50/pg
  (8.5 x 11) Cost + $5/pg
  (11 x 17) $10/job plus $2/pg

In the 2540 dpi area, we noted the following:

  (8.5 x 11) $10/job plus $8/pg
  (8.5 x 11) $4.50/job + $10.50/foot (length)

The dollars per job is a setup fee. This is standard in printing. It is common in prepress, and it is infrequent in desktop publishing (not that it shouldn't be implemented).

IMAGESETTER (FILM) **(1200-1270 dpi)**				
$/per	Survey %	Average	Typical	Maximum
8.5 x 11	9.5%	14.54	14.00	25.00
8.5 x 14	5.3%	18.13	18.00	30.00
9.5 x 12	0.7%	11.93	12.00	20.00
9.5 x 15	0.9%	15.00	18.00	30.00
10 x 14	1.1%	15.80	16.00	30.00
11 x 17	7.5%	23.08	23.00	40.00
11 x 18	0.4%	36.50	36.50	37.00
11.7 x 26	0.9%	43.50	45.00	54.00
12 x 15	0.2%	25.00	25.00	25.00
12 x 18	1.3%	26.58	31.00	38.00
12 x 23	1.1%	32.40	29.00	48.00
12 x 27	0.9%	39.50	37.00	56.00
18 x 24	0.7%	48.33	50.00	60.00
18 x 30	0.4%	52.50	52.50	60.00
18 x 36	0.9%	76.75	80.00	95.00
Cost Plus %	2.4%	24.36	20.00	50.00

IMAGESETTER (FILM)
(2093-2540 dpi)

$/per	Survey %	Average	Typical	Maximum
8.5 x 11	9.1%	16.54	15.00	31.50
8.5 x 14	4.6%	21.24	20.00	37.50
9.5 x 12	0.7%	21.07	20.00	24.00
9.5 x 15	0.4%	21.00	21.00	30.00
10 x 14	1.1%	19.60	20.00	30.00
11 x 17	6.0%	26.26	25.00	50.00
11 x 18	0.2%	38.00	38.00	38.00
11.7 x 26	0.4%	45.00	45.00	54.00
12 x 15	0.2%	28.00	28.00	28.00
12 x 18	0.7%	32.33	34.00	38.00
12 x 23	0.7%	36.67	42.00	48.00
12 x 27	0.4%	48.50	48.50	56.00
15 x 22	0.4%	32.00	32.00	37.00
18 x 24	0.7%	42.33	39.00	50.00
18 x 30	0.7%	51.67	48.00	60.00
18 x 36	0.7%	61.33	55.00	75.00
Cost Plus %	2.4%	24.36	20.00	50.00

IMAGESETTER (FILM)
(3000-3386 dpi)

$/per	Survey %	Average	Typical	Maximum
8.5 x 11	2.0%	17.14	20.00	25.00
8.5 x 14	0.9%	16.13	16.00	21.50
9.5 x 12	0.2%	16.00	16.00	16.00
9.5 x 15	0.4%	16.00	16.00	20.00
10 x 14	0.2%	20.00	20.00	20.00
11 x 17	1.3%	20.79	23.00	25.00
11 x 18	0.0%			
11.7 x 26	0.0%			
12 x 15	0.0%			
12 x 18	0.2%	29.00	29.00	29.00
12 x 23	0.2%	32.00	32.00	32.00
12 x 27	0.0%			
18 x 24	0.7%	43.67	42.00	50.00
18 x 30	0.4%	53.50	53.50	60.00
18 x 36	0.4%	64.50	64.50	75.00
Cost Plus %	2.2%	24.30	20.00	50.00

PRINTING SERVICES

PRINT BROKER

$/per	Survey %	Average	Typical	Maximum
Page	0.0%			
Hour	4.9%	48.27	40.00	100.00
Cost Plus %	15.5%	26.03	20.00	115.00

PRODUCTION EDITING

$/per	Survey %	Average	Typical	Maximum
Hour	7.1%	43.34	35.00	100.00
Cost Plus %	1.8%	25.00	15.00	50.00

PRODUCTION MANAGEMENT

$/per	Survey %	Average	Typical	Maximum
Page	0.0%			
Hour	8.8%	48.40	40.00	100.00
Cost Plus %	3.1%	21.79	20.00	50.00

IMAGING OUTPUT

TRANSPARENCY (FILM)
(Up to 300 dpi)

$/per	Survey %	Average	Typical	Maximum
8.5 x 11	5.3%	9.41	9.00	40.00
8.5 x 14	0.0%			
Cost Plus %	2.3%	21.80	20.00	50.00

TRANSPARENCY (FILM ONLY)
(600 dpi)

$/per	Survey %	Average	Typical	Maximum
8.5 x 11	1.4%	11.92	15.00	18.00
8.5 x 14	0.0%			
Cost Plus %	2.3%	20.40	20.00	50.00

TRANSPARENCY (FILM ONLY)
(1000 dpi)

$/per	Survey %	Average	Typical	Maximum
8.5 x 11	1.2%	17.20	15.00	40.00
8.5 x 14	0.0%			
Cost Plus %	2.3%	21.80	20.00	50.00

TRANSPARENCY (FILM ONLY)
(1200 dpi)

$/per	Survey %	Average	Typical	Maximum
8.5 x 11	1.2%	18.20	15.00	40.00
8.5 x 14	0.5%	19.50	20.00	27.00
11 x 17	0.0%			
Cost Plus %	2.3%	21.80	20.00	50.00

TRANSPARENCY (MOUNTED)
(up to 300 dpi)

$/per	Survey %	Average	Typical	Maximum
8.5 x 11	2.3%	15.83	15.00	40.00
8.5 x 14	0.0%			
11 x 17	0.0%			
Cost Plus %	2.3%	21.80	20.00	50.00

TRANSPARENCY (MOUNTED)
(600 dpi)

$/per	Survey %	Average	Typical	Maximum
8.5 x 11	1.2%	14.20	15.00	18.00
8.5 x 14	0.0%			
11 x 17	0.0%			
Cost Plus %	2.3%	21.80	20.00	50.00

TRANSPARENCY (MOUNTED)
(1000 dpi)

$/per	Survey %	Average	Typical	Maximum
8.5 x 11	0.9%	19.50	18.00	40.00
8.5 x 14	0.0%			
11 x 17	0.0%			
Cost Plus %	2.3%	21.80	20.00	50.00

TRANSPARENCY (MOUNTED)
(1200 dpi)

$/per	Survey %	Average	Typical	Maximum
8.5 x 11	0.7%	24.33	18.00	40.00
8.5 x 14	0.0%			
11 x 17	0.0%			
Cost Plus %	2.3%	21.80	20.00	50.00

TRANSPARENCY (COLOR-FILM ONLY)
(up to 300 dpi)

$/per	Survey %	Average	Typical	Maximum
8.2 x 10.7	1.4%	16.63	18.00	20.00
8.5 x 11	1.4%	13.50	18.00	20.00

TRANSPARENCY (COLOR - FILM ONLY) (up to 300 dpi)				
$/per	Survey %	Average	Typical	Maximum
11 x 17	1.0%			
Hourly	2.7%	63.75	2.59	100.00
Cost Plus %	3.2%	19.71	18.21	33.00

TRANSPARENCY (COLOR - MOUNTED) (up to 300 dpi)				
$/per	Survey %	Average	Typical	Maximum
8.2 x 10.7	1.4%	16.63	18.00	20.00
8.5 x 11	1.4%	16.63	18.00	20.00
8.5 x 14	0.0%			
10.75 x 16.6	0.7%	17.50	18.00	18.00
11 x 17	0.7%	22.50	24.00	27.00
Hourly	0.9%	58.75	60.00	100.00
Cost Plus %	2.3%	21.80	20.00	50.00

NOTE: One response listed as $0.23/sq inch with $48 minimum.

SLIDES (COLOR - FILM ONLY) (up to 4K, 35mm)				
$/per	Survey %	Average	Typical	Maximum
Each	1.6%	15.29	20.00	25.00
Hourly	0.2%	100.00	100.00	100.00
Cost Plus %	2.1%	20.56	15.00	50.00

SLIDES (COLOR - MOUNTED) (up to 4K, 35mm)				
$/per	Survey %	Average	Typical	Maximum
Each	1.8%	12.69	10.00	30.00
Hour	0.7%	91.67	100.00	100.00
Cost Plus %	2.1%	20.56	15.00	50.00

PHOTO CD-ROM				
$/per	Survey %	Average	Typical	Maximum
Each	0.2%	25.00	25.00	25.00
Hour	0.7%	111.67	110.00	125.00
Cost Plus %	0.9%	26.25	20.00	50.00

FINISHING SERVICES

BINDING (3-RING) (5.5 x 8.5)				
$/per	Survey %	Average	Typical	Maximum
100 Pages	0.1%	0.65	0.65	2.85
Each	0.2%	5.00	5.00	5.00
Hour	2.7%	35.70	35.00	100.00
Cost Plus %	3.4%	21.20	15.00	50.00

NOTES:
1. $/150 pages and $/200 pages converted to $/100 pages.
2. One response $0.15/100 pages if client supplies binder.

BINDING (3-RING) (8.5 x11)				
$/per	Survey %	Average	Typical	Maximum
Each	0.7%	3.28	2.85	5.00
Hour	2.4%	34.85	35.00	100.00
Cost Plus %	3.3%	21.20	15.00	50.00

BINDING (CASE) (5.5 x 8.5)				
$/per	Survey %	Average	Typical	Maximum
Hour	0.7%	31.78	35.00	40.00
Cost Plus %	2.9%	21.77	15.00	50.00

BINDING (CASE) (8.5 x11)				
$/per	Survey %	Average	Typical	Maximum
Hour	0.7%	31.78	35.00	40.00
Cost Plus %	2.9%	21.77	15.00	50.00

BINDING (CHANNEL) (5.5 x 8.5)				
$/per	Survey %	Average	Typical	Maximum
Hour	2.2%	35.00	35.00	35.00
Cost Plus %	2.9%	21.77	15.00	50.00

BINDING (CHANNEL) (8.5 x11)				
$/per	Survey %	Average	Typical	Maximum
Hour	0.2%	35.00	35.00	35.00
Cost Plus %	2.9%	21.77	15.00	50.00

BINDING (CHESHIRE)
(5.5 x 8.5)

$/per	Survey %	Average	Typical	Maximum
Each	0.2%	0.75	0.75	0.75
Hour	0.4%	25.00	25.00	35.00
Cost Plus %	2.9%	21.77	15.00	50.00

BINDING (CHESHIRE)
(8.5 x11)

$/per	Survey %	Average	Typical	Maximum
Each	0.2%	0.75	0.75	0.75
Hour	0.4%	25.00	25.00	35.00
Cost Plus %	2.9%	21.77	15.00	50.00

BINDING (COMB)
(5.5 x 8.5)

$/per	Survey %	Average	Typical	Maximum
Each	2.2%	1.18	1.00	2.00
Hour	1.8%	40.38	35.00	100.00
Cost Plus %	3.3%	21.20	15.00	50.00

BINDING (COMB)
(8.5 x11)

$/per	Survey %	Average	Typical	Maximum
Each	3.6%	1.75	1.50	5.00
Hour	1.8%	40.38	35.00	100.00
Cost Plus %	3.3%	21.20	15.00	50.00

BINDING (GLUE)
(5.5 x 8.5)

$/per	Survey %	Average	Typical	Maximum
Each	0.4%	2.63	2.65	5.00
Hour	0.7%	24.45	20.35	40.00
Cost Plus %	3.1%	20.23	15.00	50.00

BINDING (GLUE)
(8.5 x11)

$/per	Survey %	Average	Typical	Maximum
Each	0.7%	2.08	1.00	5.00
Hourly	0.7%	24.45	20.35	40.00
Cost Plus %	2.9%	21.77	15.00	50.00

BINDING (NOTCH)
(5.5 x 8.5)

$/per	Survey %	Average	Typical	Maximum
Cost Plus %	2.9%	21.77	15.00	50.00

BINDING (NOTCH)
(8.5 x11)

$/per	Survey %	Average	Typical	Maximum
Cost Plus %	2.9%	21.77	15.00	50.00

BINDING (OTABIND)
(5.5 x 8.5)

$/per	Survey %	Average	Typical	Maximum
Hour	0.2%	35.00	35.00	35.00
Cost Plus %	2.9%	21.77	15.00	50.00

BINDING (OTABIND)
(8.5 x11)

$/per	Survey %	Average	Typical	Maximum
Hour	0.2%	35.00	35.00	35.00
Cost Plus %	2.9%	21.77	15.00	50.00

BINDING (PAPERBACK)
(5.5 x 8.5)

$/per	Survey %	Average	Typical	Maximum
Each	0.2%	1.00	1.00	1.00
Hourly	0.4%	37.50	37.50	40.00
Cost Plus %	3.1%	21.29	15.00	50.00

BINDING (PAPERBACK)
(8.5 x11)

$/per	Survey %	Average	Typical	Maximum
Each	0.2%	1.00	1.00	1.00
Hourly	0.4%	37.50	37.50	40.00
Cost Plus %	3.1%	21.29	15.00	50.00

BINDING (PERFECT)
(5.5 x 8.5)

$/per	Survey %	Average	Typical	Maximum
Each	0.9%	1.19	1.00	2.00
Hourly	0.2%	40.00	40.00	40.00
Cost Plus %	2.9%	21.77	15.00	50.00

BINDING (PERFECT)
(8.5 x11)

$/per	Survey %	Average	Typical	Maximum
Each	1.1%	1.82	2.00	4.00
Hour	0.2%	40.00	40.00	40.00
Cost Plus %	2.9%	21.77	15.00	50.00

BINDING (PLASTIKOIL)
(5.5 x 8.5)

$/per	Survey %	Average	Typical	Maximum
Each	0.2%	1.25	1.25	1.25
Cost Plus %	2.9%	21.77	15.00	50.00

BINDING (PLASTIKOIL)
(8.5 x11)

$/per	Survey %	Average	Typical	Maximum
Each	0.4%	1.13	1.13	1.25
Cost Plus %	2.9%	21.77	15.00	50.00

BINDING (SADDLE STITCH)
(5.5 x 8.5)

$/per	Survey %	Average	Typical	Maximum
Staple	0.1%	0.01	0.01	0.01
Each Book	3.1%	0.09	0.06	0.33
Hourly	1.6%	53.71	40.00	126.00
Cost Plus %	3.1%	21.64	15.00	50.00

NOTE: $/M responses converted to $/Staple.

BINDING (SADDLE STITCH)
(8.5 x11)

$/per	Survey %	Average	Typical	Maximum
Staple	1.0%	0.01	0.01	0.01
Each Book	3.3%	0.09	0.06	0.33
Hourly	1.6%	53.71	40.00	126.00
Cost Plus %	3.1%	21.64	15.00	50.00

NOTE: $/M responses converted to $/Staple.

BINDING (SIDE SEWN)
(5.5 x 8.5)

$/per	Survey %	Average	Typical	Maximum
Each	0.2%	1.00	1.00	1.00
Hourly	0.2%	40.00	40.00	40.00
Cost Plus %	2.9%	21.77	15.00	50.00

BINDING (SIDE SEWN)
(8.5 x11)

$/per	Survey %	Average	Typical	Maximum
Each	0.2%	1.00	1.00	1.00
Hour	0.2%	40.00	40.00	40.00
Cost Plus %	2.9%	21.77	15.00	50.00

BINDING (SIDE STITCH)
(5.5 x 8.5)

$/per	Survey %	Average	Typical	Maximum
Each	10.7%	0.38	0.10	1.00
Hour	0.2%	35.00	35.00	35.00
Cost Plus %	2.9%	21.77	15.00	50.00

BINDING (SIDE STITCH)
(8.5 x11)

$/per	Survey %	Average	Typical	Maximum
Each	0.9%	0.30	0.10	1.00
Hour	0.4%	57.50	57.50	80.00
Cost Plus %	2.9%	21.77	15.00	50.00

BINDING (SMYTH SEWN)
(5.5 x 8.5)

$/per	Survey %	Average	Typical	Maximum
Hour	0.2%	40.00	40.00	40.00
Cost Plus %	2.9%	21.77	15.00	50.00

BINDING (SMYTH SEWN)
(8.5 x11)

$/per	Survey %	Average	Typical	Maximum
Each	0.2%	2.95	2.95	2.95
Hour	0.2%	40.00	40.00	40.00

BINDING (SPIRAL - PLASTIC)
(5.5 x 8.5)

$/per	Survey %	Average	Typical	Maximum
Each	2.0%	1.42	1.50	2.00
Hour	0.9%	23.34	28.00	35.00
Cost Plus %	3.1%	21.29	15.00	50.00

BINDING (SPIRAL - PLASTIC)
(8.5 x11)

$/per	Survey %	Average	Typical	Maximum
Each	2.9%	2.13	2.00	5.00
Hour	1.1%	26.67	25.00	35.00
Cost Plus %	3.1%	21.29	15.00	50.00

BINDING (SPIRAL - WIRE)
(5.5 x 8.5)

$/per	Survey %	Average	Typical	Maximum
Each	0.4%	1.50	1.50	2.00
Cost Plus %	2.9%	21.77	15.00	50.00

BINDING (SPIRAL - WIRE)
(8.5 x11)

$/per	Survey %	Average	Typical	Maximum
Each	0.4%	2.50	2.50	3.00
Cost Plus %	2.9%	21.77	15.00	50.00

BINDING (STRIP)
(5.5 x 8.5)

$/per	Survey %	Average	Typical	Maximum
Each	0.2%	1.00	1.00	1.00
Hour	0.2%	13.00	13.00	13.00
Cost Plus %	3.1%	21.64	15.00	50.00

BINDING (STRIP)
(8.5 x11)

$/per	Survey %	Average	Typical	Maximum
Each	0.2%	2.00	2.00	2.00
Hour	0.2%	13.00	13.00	13.00
Cost Plus %	3.1%	21.64	15.00	50.00

BINDING (THERMAL)
(5.5 x 8.5)

$/per	Survey %	Average	Typical	Maximum
Each	0.2%	2.00	2.00	2.00
Hour	0.4%	35.00	35.00	35.00
Cost Plus %	2.9%	21.77	15.00	50.00

BINDING (THERMAL)
(8.5 x11)

$/per	Survey %	Average	Typical	Maximum
Each	0.7%	1.58	1.75	2.00
Hour	0.4%	35.00	35.00	35.00
Cost Plus %	2.9%	21.77	15.00	50.00

BINDING (UNIBIND)
(5.5 x 8.5)

$/per	Survey %	Average	Typical	Maximum
Hour	0.2%	35.00	35.00	35.00
Cost Plus %	2.9%	21.77	15.00	50.00

BINDING (UNIBIND)
(8.5 x11)

$/per	Survey %	Average	Typical	Maximum
Each	0.4%	3.50	3.50	3.50
Hour	0.2%	35.00	35.00	35.00
Cost Plus %	2.9%	21.77	15.00	50.00

BINDING (VELOBIND)
(5.5 x 8.5)

$/per	Survey %	Average	Typical	Maximum
Each	0.7%	1.50	2.00	2.00
Hour	0.9%	28.75	35.00	35.00
Cost Plus %	3.1%	21.64	15.00	50.00

NOTE: Also priced as $/50 pages, and $/inch.

BINDING (VELOBIND)
(8.5 x11)

$/per	Survey %	Average	Typical	Maximum
Each	2.2%	1.62	2.00	2.50
Hour	0.9%	28.75	35.00	35.00
Cost Plus %	3.1%	21.64	15.00	50.00

BINDING (WIRE-O / TWIN WIRE)
(5.5 x 8.5)

$/per	Survey %	Average	Typical	Maximum
Each	0.2%	1.00	1.00	1.00
Hour	0.2%	40.00	40.00	40.00
Cost Plus %	2.9%	21.75	15.00	50.00

BINDING (WIRE-O / TWIN WIRE)
(8.5 x11)

$/per	Survey %	Average	Typical	Maximum
Each	0.2%	1.00	1.00	1.00
Hour	0.2%	40.00	40.00	40.00
Cost Plus %	2.9%	21.75	15.00	50.00

BINDING (OTHER - CERLOX, FASBACK)
(8.5 x 11)

$/per	Survey %	Average	Typical	Maximum
Each	0.4%	2.25	2.25	2.50
Hour	0.2%	40.00	40.00	40.00
Cost Plus %	2.9%	21.77	15.00	50.00

COLLATING

$/per	Survey %	Average	Typical	Maximum
M Sheets	4.2%	20.00	15.00	50.00
Hour	3.3%	38.33	30.00	150.00
Cost Plus %	3.1%	30.57	20.00	115.00

NOTE: Also listed as $/book (size specified).

CUT & TRIM (DIECUTTING)

$/per	Survey %	Average	Typical	Maximum
Each Cut	0.9%	0.42	0.60	1.00
Hour	2.0%	48.67	40.00	120.00
Cost Plus %	3.1%	30.57	20.00	115.00

NOTE: Also listed as $10/die and $1/inch/cut.

CUT & TRIM (PRINTED SHEETS)

$/per	Survey %	Average	Typical	Maximum
Each Cut	1.0%	0.010	0.014	0.02
Hour	2.2%	33.10	35.00	56.00
Cost Plus %	3.1%	30.57	20.00	115.00

NOTE: Also listed as $/job minimum, $/500 sheets and $/M sheets.

CUT & TRIM (ROUND CORNER)

$/per	Survey %	Average	Typical	Maximum
Each	0.7%	0.180	0.015	0.50
Hour	1.1%	35.00	40.00	40.00
Cost Plus %	3.1%	30.57	20.00	115.00

CUT & TRIM (TAB CUTTING)

$/per	Survey %	Average	Typical	Maximum
Each	0.2%	0.020	0.015	0.020
Hour	0.7%	33.33	40.00	40.00
Cost Plus %	2.9%	31.38	20.00	115.00

DRILLING

$/per	Survey %	Average	Typical	Maximum
Each Hole	2.0%	0.31	0.05	1.00
Hour	2.4%	27.30	34.00	40.00
Cost Plus %	2.9%	31.38	20.00	115.00

NOTE: Also listed as $/hole/inch.

EMBOSSING

$/per	Survey %	Average	Typical	Maximum
Cost Plus %	3.1%	30.57	20.00	115.00

FOLDING
(Machine - 1,2 folds)

$/per	Survey %	Average	Typical	Maximum
Each	5.1%	0.02	0.01	0.10
Hour	1.8%	40.25	40.00	80.00
Cost Plus %	3.3%	28.53	20.00	115.00

NOTE: Often listed as $/M sheets.

FOLDING
(Machine - 3 folds)

$/per	Survey %	Average	Typical	Maximum
Each	2.2%	0.010	0.013	0.023
Hour	1.6%	42.43	40.00	80.00
Cost Plus %	3.1%	30.57	20.00	115.00

NOTE: Often listed as $/M sheets.

FOLDING
(Manual - 1,2 folds)

$/per	Survey %	Average	Typical	Maximum
Each	3.1%	0.04	0.03	0.15
Hour	3.6%	28.52	30.00	80.00
Cost Plus %	2.9%	31.38	20.00	115.00

GLUING

$/per	Survey %	Average	Typical	Maximum
Each	0.2%	2.00	2.00	2.00
Hour	0.7%	65.00	40.00	120.00
Cost Plus %	2.9%	31.77	20.00	115.00

LAMINATING (ONE SIDE)

$/per	Survey %	Average	Typical	Maximum
Each	2.7%	1.72	1.50	3.00
Cost Plus %	2.9%	31.38	20.00	115.00

LAMINATING (DOUBLE SIDE)

$/per	Survey %	Average	Typical	Maximum
Each	3.1%	2.67	3.00	5.00
Hourly	0.4%	30.00	30.00	35.00
Cost Plus %	2.9%	31.38	20.00	115.00

NOTE: Also priced as $/job and $/100 sheets.

NUMBERING

$/per	Survey %	Average	Typical	Maximum
Each	1.6%	0.020	0.025	0.035
Hourly	2.0%	37.22	35.00	80.00
Cost Plus %	2.9%	31.38	20.00	115.00
Job	0.9%	17.00	20.00	20.00

NOTE: Also priced as $/ft/widthand $/sq inch.

PACKAGING (BAGGING & BOXING)

$/per	Survey %	Average	Typical	Maximum
Each	0.7%	2.13	3.00	3.00
Hourly	1.1%	30.60	35.00	40.00
Cost Plus %	2.9%	31.38	20.00	115.00

PADDING

$/per	Survey %	Average	Typical	Maximum
Each	2.0%	0.56	0.25	2.50
Hourly	2.0%	42.22	40.00	80.00
Cost Plus %	2.9%	31.38	20.00	115.00
Minimum	0.1%	3.00	3.00	3.00

PASTING

$/per	Survey %	Average	Typical	Maximum
Each	0.4%	2.00	2.00	3.00
Hourly	1.1%	28.00	25.00	40.00
Cost Plus %	2.9%	31.38	20.00	115.00
Minimum	0.1%	5.00	5.00	5.00

PERFORATING

$/per	Survey %	Average	Typical	Maximum
M	2.2%	20.00	19.00	30.00
Hourly	1.3%	44.17	40.00	80.00
Cost Plus %	2.9%	31.38	20.00	115.00
Minimum	0.1%	22.50	22.50	35.00

NOTE: Also listed as $/job plus $/M.

REINFORCING

$/per	Survey %	Average	Typical	Maximum
Hour	0.4%	37.50	37.50	40.00
Cost Plus %	2.9%	31.38	20.00	115.00

SCORING

$/per	Survey %	Average	Typical	Maximum
Each	1.8%	0.020	0.019	0.025
Hourly	1.6%	40.71	40.00	85.00
Cost Plus %	3.1%	30.57	20.00	115.00

SHRINK WRAPPING

$/per	Survey %	Average	Typical	Maximum
Each	0.4%	0.24	0.20	0.30
Hour	0.2%	20.00	20.00	20.00
Cost Plus %	0.4%	17.50	20.00	20.00

STAMPING (FOIL)

$/per	Survey %	Average	Typical	Maximum
Each	0.2%	10.00	10.00	10.00
Hour	0.2%	40.00	40.00	40.00
Cost Plus %	3.1%	30.57	20.00	115.00
NOTE: Also listed as $/setup plus $/each.				

STAPLING

$/per	Survey %	Average	Typical	Maximum
Each	3.6%	0.04	0.03	0.10
Hour	2.7%	26.92	30.00	40.00
Cost Plus %	2.9%	31.38	20.00	115.00

TAPING

$/per	Survey %	Average	Typical	Maximum
Each	0.2%	0.03	0.03	0.03
Hour	1.1%	30.00	25.00	40.00
Cost Plus %	2.9%	31.38	20.00	115.00

OTHER SERVICES

ANSWERING SERVICE

$/per	Survey %	Average	Typical	Maximum
Month	1.0%	50.00	50.00	55.00
Cost Plus %	3.2%	15.00	15.00	15.00

BAGGING (POLY)

$/per	Survey %	Average	Typical	Maximum
Hour	0.2%	40.00	40.00	40.00
Cost Plus %	0.2%	15.00	15.00	15.00

COPYING (B&W)

$/per	Survey %	Average	Typical	Maximum
Each	14.8%	0.09	0.08	0.30
Hour	2.4%	29.27	40.00	40.00
Cost Plus %	0.7%	16.67	15.00	20.00

COPYING (COLOR)

$/per	Survey %	Average	Typical	Maximum
Each	4.7%	1.36	1.25	4.00
Hour	1.8%	26.54	30.00	40.00
Cost Plus %	1.1%	22.00	20.00	40.00

DISTRIBUTION (Deliver for Customer)				
$/per	Survey %	Average	Typical	Maximum
Hourly	2.0%	25.89	20.00	50.00
Cost Plus %	0.4%	15.00	15.00	15.00

FAX SERVICE - SEND				
$/per	Survey %	Average	Typical	Maximum
Page	23.0%	1.76	2.00	5.00
Hour	1.1%	21.67	20.00	40.00
Cost Plus %	0.7%	16.67	15.00	20.00

NOTES:
1. Outgoing telephone connect charges billed extra.
2. Also found prices as $/hour + cents/minute (local call),
   and $/minute, or $/M characters.
3. All $/minute charges converted to $/hr for table listing.

FAX SERVICE - RECEIVE				
$/per	Survey %	Average	Typical	Maximum
Each	21.5%	1.04	1.00	4.00
Hour	1.1%	21.67	20.00	40.00
Cost Plus %	0.7%	16.67	15.00	20.00

INSERTING - SINGLE SHEET				
$/per	Survey %	Average	Typical	Maximum
M Sheets	4.7%	50.00	30.00	150.00
Hour	1.7%	19.86	13.00	35.00
Cost Plus %	0.4%	15.00	15.00	15.00

LABEL - ADDRESS				
$/per	Survey %	Average	Typical	Maximum
Each	7.1%	0.09	0.05	0.50
Hour	3.1%	29.86	25.00	75.00
Cost Plus %	0.4%	15.00	15.00	15.00

NOTE: Also listed as $10/M and $5 setup plus 5¢ each.

LABEL - BAR CODE (CODING)

$/per	Survey %	Average	Typical	Maximum
Each	1.1%	0.01	0.02	0.03
Hour	1.1%	35.60	35.00	50.00
Cost Plus %	0.4%	15.00	15.00	15.00

NOTE: $/M responses converted to $/each.

LABEL - BAR CODE (PRINTING)

$/per	Survey %	Average	Typical	Maximum
Each	1.1%	0.01	0.01	0.03
Hour	1.1%	35.60	35.00	50.00
Cost Plus %	0.4%	15.00	15.00	15.00

NOTE: $/M responses converted to $/each.

PICKUP & DELIVERY

$/per	Survey %	Average	Typical	Maximum
Each	7.1%	10.97	10.00	25.00
Mile	0.2%	0.50	0.50	0.50
Hour	6.2%	25.86	25.00	75.00
Cost Plus %	0.7%	16.67	15.00	20.00

MAIL MERGE

$/per	Survey %	Average	Typical	Maximum
Each	2.0%	1.37	1.50	3.00
Hour	8.4%	28.05	25.00	60.00
Cost Plus %	0.4%	15.00	15.00	15.00

NOTE: Also listed as $/setup plus $/line.

MAIL SERVICE (Carrier Route Sort)

$/per	Survey %	Average	Typical	Maximum
Each	1.6%	0.04	0.02	0.141
Hour	2.2%	24.30	25.00	45.00
Cost Plus %	0.9%	20.00	20.00	30.00

MAIL SERVICE (ZIP Code Sort)

$/per	Survey %	Average	Typical	Maximum
Each	2.4%	0.04	0.03	0.177
Hour	2.9%	24.31	25.00	55.00
Cost Plus %	0.9%	20.00	20.00	30.00

MAIL SERVICE (Mixed ZIP - Raw Sort)

$/per	Survey %	Average	Typical	Maximum
Each	1.6%	0.06	0.04	0.187
Hour	1.8%	28.05	25.00	65.00
Cost Plus %	0.9%	20.00	20.00	30.00

MAIL SERVICE
(Envelope Metering)

$/per	Survey %	Average	Typical	Maximum
Each	1.1%	0.05	0.02	0.15
M	0.1%	5.00	15.00	15.00
Hour	1.1%	25.00	25.00	30.00
Cost Plus %	0.9%	20.00	20.00	30.00

MAIL SERVICE
(Bulk Mail - Our Permit)

$/per	Survey %	Average	Typical	Maximum
Each	2.4%	0.03	0.03	0.0313
M	0.1%	20.00	25.65	31.30
Job	0.1%	20.00	20.00	25.00
Hour	2.9%	29.54	30.00	45.00
Cost Plus %	0.9%	20.00	20.00	30.00

MAIL SERVICE
(Bulk Mail - Client's Permit)

$/per	Survey %	Average	Typical	Maximum
Each	1.3%	0.04	0.02	0.15
M	0.1%	20.00	20.00	20.00
Job	0.1%	21.67	20.00	40.00
Hour	2.4%	26.36	25.00	45.00
Cost Plus %	0.9%	20.00	20.00	30.00

MAILING LIST
(Basic Address)

$/per	Survey %	Average	Typical	Maximum
Each	11.1%	0.28	0.25	1.33
Hour	7.5%	26.56	25.00	60.00
Cost Plus %	0.2%	15.00	15.00	15.00

NOTE: $/100 names converted to $/each.

MAILING LIST
(Additional Fields)

$/per	Survey %	Average	Typical	Maximum
Each, Field	2.1%	0.10	0.05	0.75
Hour	6.2%	27.50	25.00	60.00
Cost Plus %	0.2%	15.00	15.00	15.00

MAILING LIST
(Changes & Additions)

$/per	Survey %	Average	Typical	Maximum
Each	6.9%	0.24	0.15	1.00
Hour	7.5%	27.16	25.00	60.00
Cost Plus %	0.2%	15.00	15.00	15.00

MAILING LIST (Delete Address)				
$/per	Survey %	Average	Typical	Maximum
Each	6.4%	0.21	0.10	1.00
Hour	7.3%	26.92	25.00	60.00
Cost Plus %	0.2%	15.00	15.00	15.00

MAILING LIST (Entry With Verification)				
$/per	Survey %	Average	Typical	Maximum
Each	3.5%	0.22	0.23	0.40
Hour	6.6%	28.97	30.00	60.00
Cost Plus %	0.2%	15.00	15.00	15.00

SILK SCREENING				
$/per	Survey %	Average	Typical	Maximum
Each	0.4%	15.25	15.25	25.00
Hour	0.4%	44.07	45.00	75.00
Cost Plus %	0.7%	25.00	20.00	40.00

TRAINING - HARDWARE				
$/per	Survey %	Average	Typical	Maximum
Hour	11.5%	46.92	45.00	150.00

TRAINING - SOFTWARE				
$/per	Survey %	Average	Typical	Maximum
Hour	20.1%	46.70	40.00	237.50

TRAINING - PUBLISHING PROCESS				
$/per	Survey %	Average	Typical	Maximum
Hour	10.6%	49.66	45.00	150.00

APPENDIX

Other Useful Information

WHERE TO FIND IT

APPENDIX

TYPICAL NUMBER OF EMPLOYEES

In conducting the survey for this edition, we asked for profile information on each participating business. One of the many things that we were interested in analyzing is the number of full time, part time, and freelance employees working in the typical shop. As expected, we noted that the number varied by the size of the business. We decided to partition the worker data by income category. The following is a breakdown of our results.

INCOME	FULL TIME	PART TIME	FREELANCE
$500-$19,999	0.65	0.48	0.37
$20K - $49,999	1.00	0.33	0.57
$50K - $99,999	1.25	0.60	0.61
$100K - $249,999	2.07	0.79	1.40
$250K - $499,999	3.89	1.07	1.19
$500K - $999,999	11.26	1.43	1.26
> $1 million	27.41	6.59	2.69
All	3.03	0.89	1.19

INCOME DISTRIBUTION

The following chart describes how revenue is distributed across our survey population.

INCOME	% OF SURVEY PARTICIPANTS
$500-$19,999	41.4%
$20K - $49,999	23.9%
$50K - $99,999	11.7%
$100K - $249,999	9.2%
$250K - $499,999	5.3%
$500K - $999,999	4.9%
> $1 million	3.6%

EQUIPMENT
Used In The Business

The following list describes the most common equipment used by our survey participants. The list is prioritized by order of preference. Checkmarks indicate relative popularity.

BINDER

GBC
Ibco Standard comb binder - manual
Velo Bind - 40 sheets

CAMERA (Film, Paper)

Agfa 435
Film camera
Stat camera

CAMERA (Platemaker)
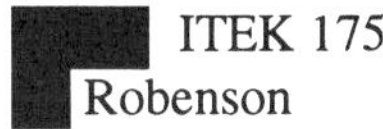
ITEK 175
Robenson

CAMERA (Digital)
Agfa RPS 2024 Super Automatic
Canon Zapshot
MicroDigital 480 (Log E)

CD ROM

CD ROM
NEC CD ROM
Texel 5024 CD ROM

COLLATOR/SORTER
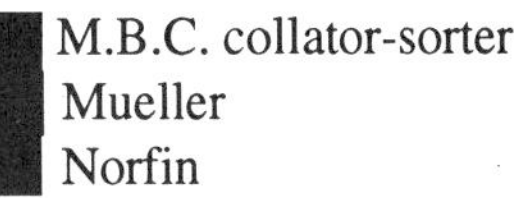
M.B.C. collator-sorter
Mueller
Norfin

APPENDIX

COMPUTERS

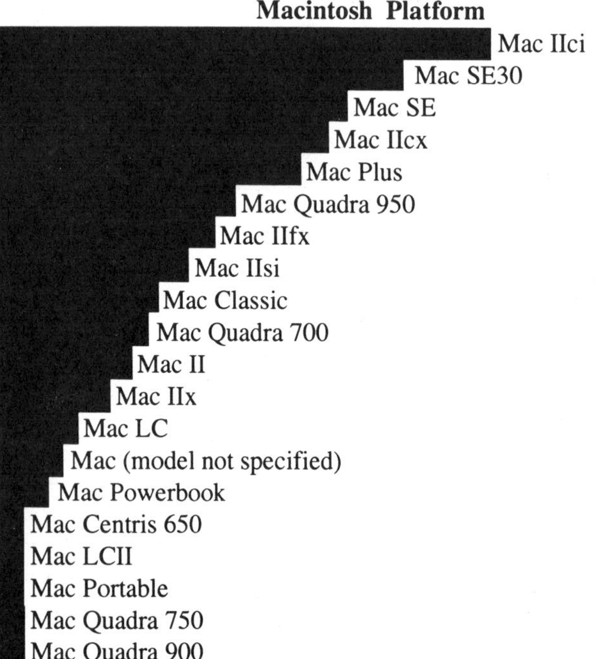

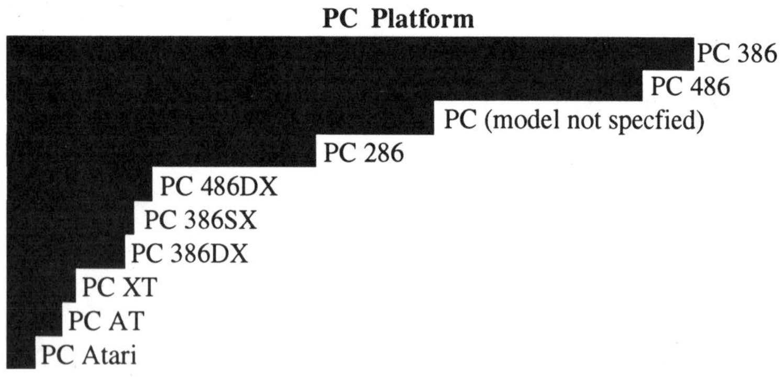

Other Platforms

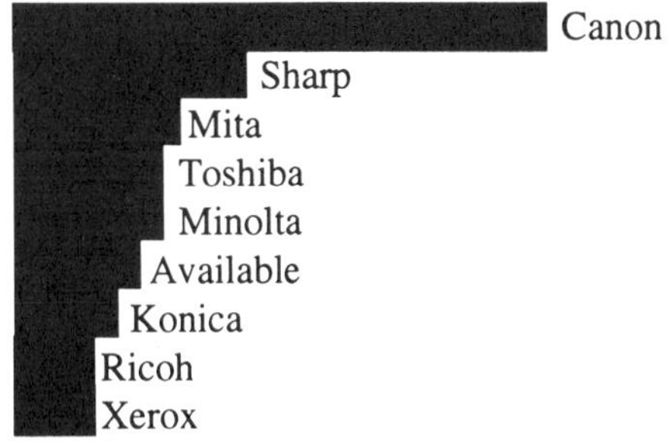

Workstation
Dainippon QT-220 Rapid Access Processor
Atari ST - 4/120, mono display, used as Mac
Compugraphic MCS 10/8400
Varityper

COPIER

Canon
Sharp
Mita
Toshiba
Minolta
Available
Konica
Ricoh
Xerox

CUTTER/TRIMMER

Manual
Boston
Challenge

DIGITAL CAMERA INPUT

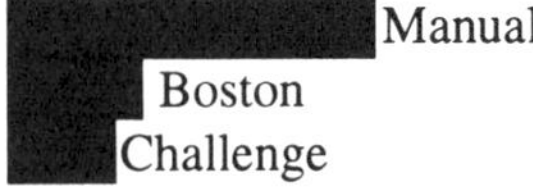

Computer Eyes Pro
Megavision

DIRECT DIGITAL COLOR PROOFER

Iris 3024
Canon CLC w/PS-1PU

DRILL PUNCH

Available (model not specified)
Challenge
M.B.C.

FAX MACHINE

Sharp
Zoom 2400/9600 fax

APPENDIX

FILM RECORDER

Agfa Forte
Dolev PS
Kodak
LFR
Masterpiece 8770
MGI Solitaire
PCR
ProColor Premier with Chromascript II P/S RIP

FOLDING MACHINE

Automatic
Manual
Baum 714

MODEM

Zoom
Unknown make
Hayes
U.S. Robotics
Hayes Ultra
Supra
Everex
Intel
Practical Peripherals
Prometheus
Xeba
Abaton
Internal Unk - PC card - internal
Interfax
Migent

Maximum Modem Baud Rate:

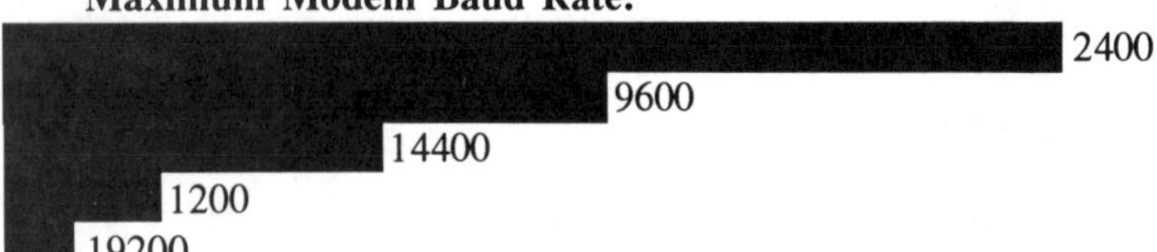

NUMBERER / PERFORATOR
Rossback
Wizard

PLOTTER
Agfa Selectset 7000 - 3600 dpi

PRINTER (Dot Matrix)
Epson
Panasonic
ImageWriter
Okidata
ImageWriter II
NEC
Star

PRINTER (Laser)
300 dpi
HP LaserJet III, IIIP
LaserWriter II NTX
LaserWriter II NT
NEC 95 SilentWriter
HP LaserJet II, IIP
HP LaserJet
Personal LaserWriter II NT
QMS 810
LaserWriter II
GCC PLP I
LaserWriter Plus
LaserWriter IIf
LaserWriter
Panasonic
LaserWriter IIg
TI Microlaser
Applewriter
Dataproducts LZR960
HP LaserJet IV
Texas Instruments Laser Printer
Okidata 840

400 dpi

Data Products 1560
LaserSmith
NuGen PS400P Turbo
Realtech 400

600 dpi

HP LaserJet IV
HP LaserJet III w/DpTek
Laserwriter II NTX w/Xante board
LaserWriter Plus w/Xante board

800 dpi

NewGen
HP LaserJet II w/LaserMaster controller
LaserMaster 800
HP LaserJet III w/LaserMaster controller
LaserMax 800

1000 dpi

LaserMaster - 1000

1200 dpi

HP LaserJet III w/controller
LaserMaster LM1200
HP LaserJet IV w/LaserMaster - 1200 dpi controller

PRINTER (Thermal)

AgfaMatrix TT200 - 200 dpi
Oce" Graphics - 300 dpi
Ole' - 300 dpi
Plotmaster Color - Calcomp - 200 dpi
QMS ColorScript color - 300 dpi
Tektronix Phaser IIPX Color

PRINTER (Inkjet B&W)

HP DeskJet 500 - 300 dpi
HP DeskJet Plus - 300 dpi
HP DeskWriter - 300 dpi

PRINTER (Color)

Tektronix Phaser - 300 dpi
Canon
QMS 100
Seiko Color Point - 300 dpi
HP

SCANNER (B&W)

300 dpi

HP ScanJet
Apple Scanner
Microtek
Abaton

400 dpi

Logitech Scanman 256
The Complete Half Page
HP IIC
Marstek Hand Scanner
Microtek 400G
Niscan GS hand scanner, BW
Pro-Scan

600 dpi

Microtek 600 Color/B&W
Dest PC Scan 3000
HP ScanJet

800 dpi

Microtek
Agfa Focus II

1000 and up

Arcus - up to 1270 dpi
Autoscan 1030 - 2000 dpi
ECRM - 1016 dpi
Kurzwell KDOS 4000

SCANNER (Color)

300 dpi
Microtek
Howtek ScanMaster 3

400 dpi
HP IIC
Logitech ScanMan 256

600 dpi
Microtek
Sharp
UMax

800 dpi
HP IIC
Microtek
Tamarach 8000
UMax UC 840

1200 dpi and up
Microtek
HP ScanJet
Agfa Arcus
Hell 399ERII
Scitex Smartscan
Crosfield 636 E
HP

SCANNER (Slide)
Leafscan
Arcus - 1270 dpi
Microtek 1850
Santos MIRA-35, 2700 dpi
Sharp JX-600
Umax UC630 adapter

SEWING MACHINE (for binding)
Singer

SHRINK WRAP MACHINE
- Available
- Heat gun - manual
- Sergeant

STITCHER
- Dexter
- M.B.C.
- Mueller Martini
- Rosback
- Sprint Bookletmaker

TYPESETTER / IMAGESETTER

1000 - 1800 dpi
- Lino L100-L300
- LaserMaster - 1000 dpi
- Varityper 5810
- XLI Laserpix - 1200 dpi

2000 - 3000 dpi
- Lino 300 series
- CG series - 12/2400 dpi
- Agfa series

> 3000 dpi
- Lino L-330

LOCAL AREA NETWORK
- AppleTalk/LocalTalk/PhoneNet
- AppleShare
- Ethernet (SW unknown)
- Novell
- TOPS
- Lantastic

SOFTWARE
Used In The Business

The following list describes the most popular software used by our survey participants. The list is prioritized by order of preference. Checkmarks indicate relative popularity.

WORD PROCESSING

Atari

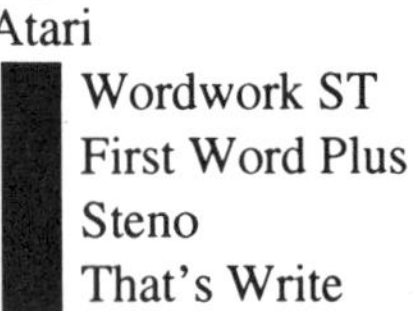

Mac

PC

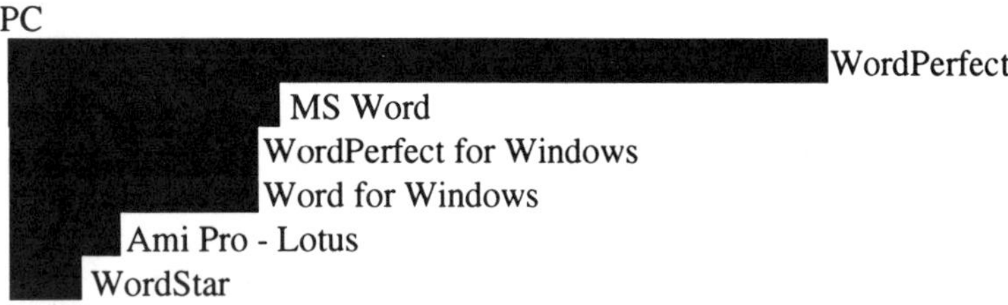

OCR SOFTWARE

Mac

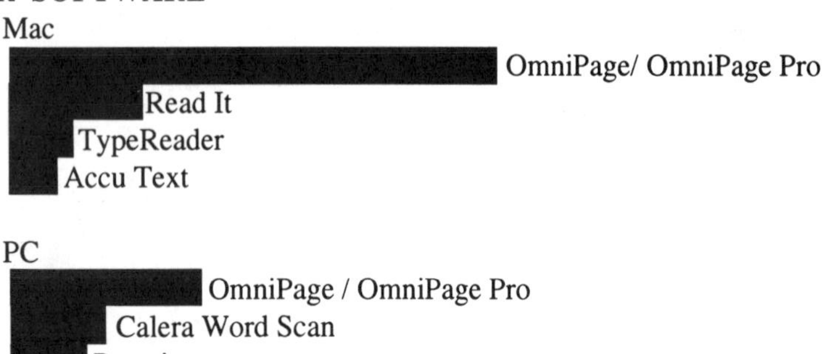

PC

Read Right
TypeReader

DRAW / PAINT

Atari
ST Degas
DT Paint
Touch Up

Mac
SuperPaint
MacDraw / MacDraw Pro
Canvas
DeskPaint
Painter
MacPaint
Color It

PC
Corel Draw
Arts & Letters - DOS/Windows
Paintbrush/Paintbrush Windows
Windows Paint
Draw Perfect
Publishers Paintbrush
PC Paintbrush
Designer
Draw

GRAPHICS

Mac
FreeHand
Illustrator
Gallery Effects
Dimension
Clip Art
Dynamic Graphics
Streamline

PC

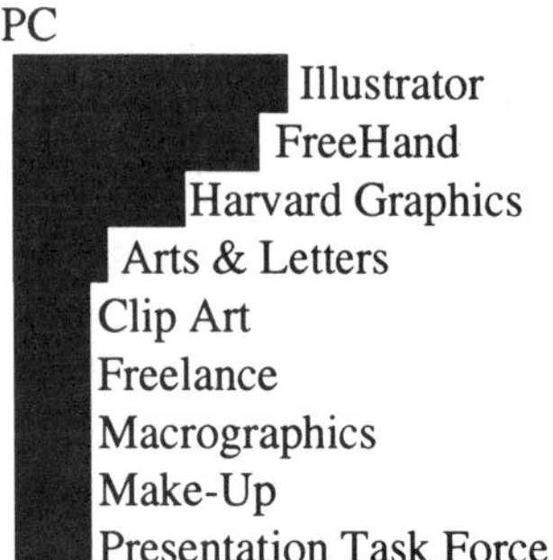

IMAGE/PHOTO EDITING

Mac

PC

FONT UTILITIES

Atari

Mac

PC

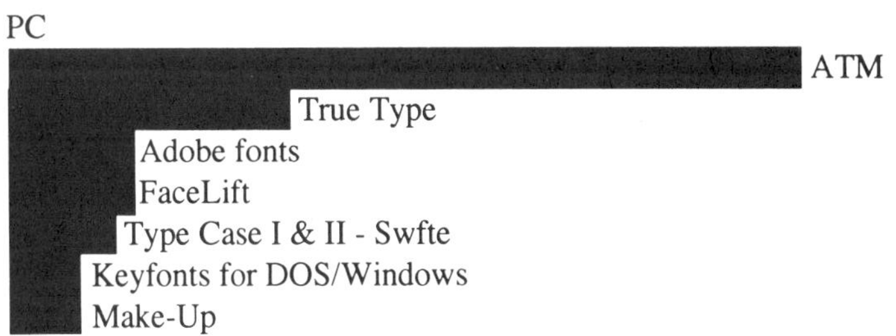

PAGE LAYOUT

Atari

Mac

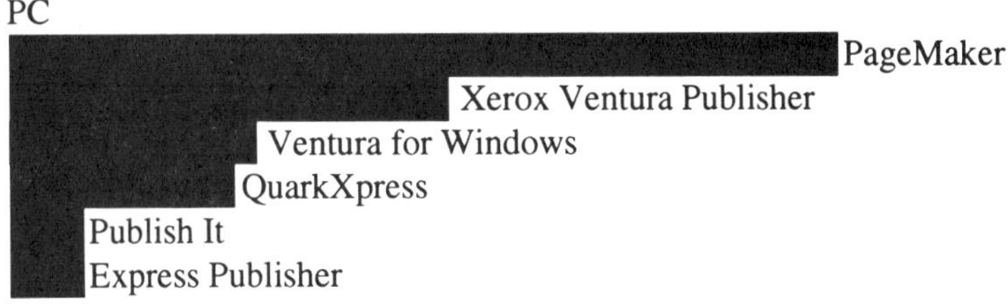

PC

PRESENTATION

Mac

PC

SPREADSHEET

Atari

Mac

Excel
MS Works
Lotus 123
Wingz

PC

Excel
Lotus 123
Quatro Pro

DATABASE

Atari

Mac

FileMaker / FileMaker Pro
MS Works
4th Dimension

PC

COMMUNICATION

Atari

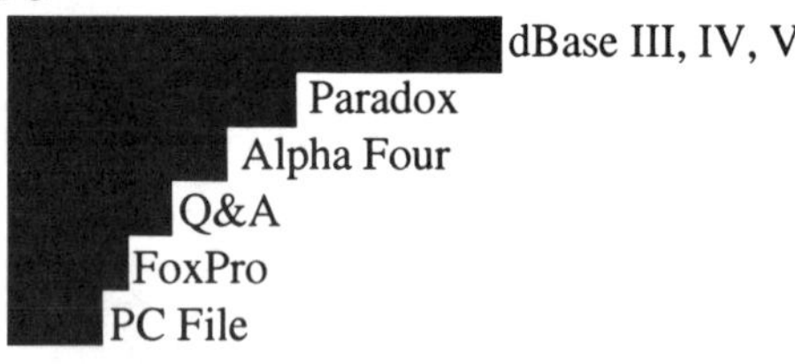

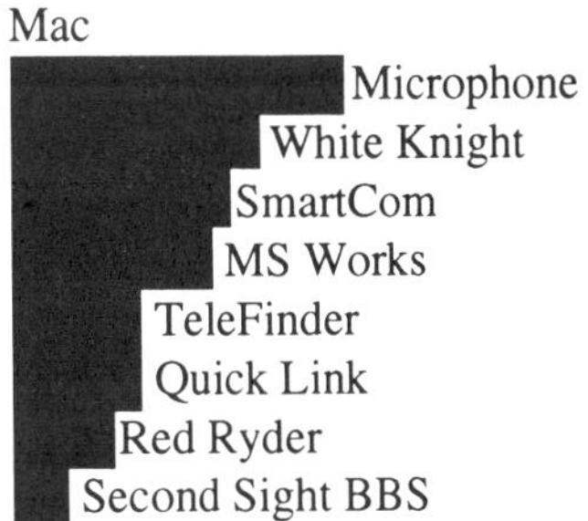

NETWORK

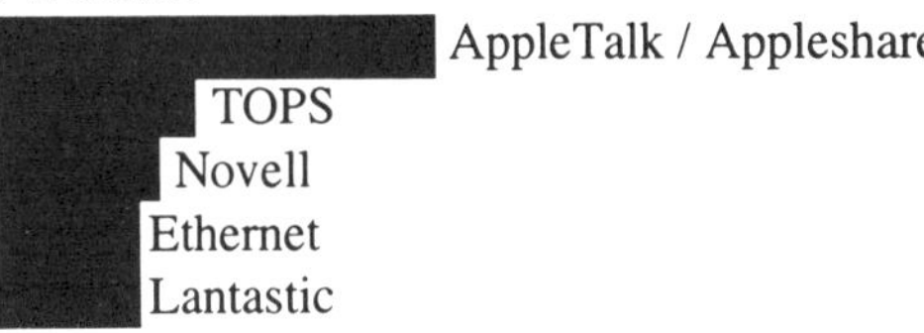

PROJECT MGMT

Mac

PC

CONTACT MGMT

Mac

PC

OTHER UTILITIES

Mac

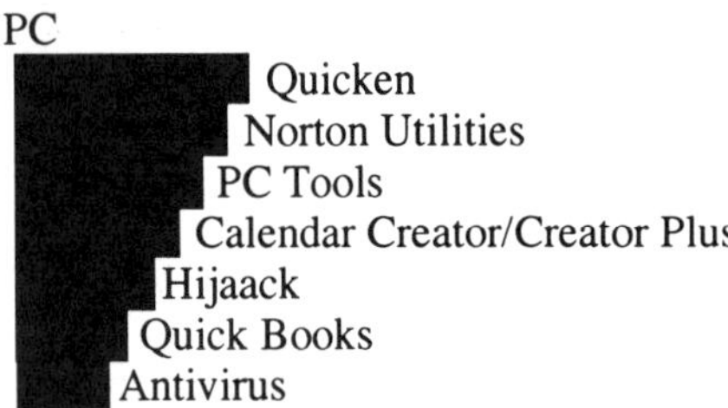

Norton Utilities
Quicken
After Dark
MacLink Plus
Quickeys
Stuff It

PC

Quicken
Norton Utilities
PC Tools
Calendar Creator/Creator Plus
Hijaack
Quick Books
Antivirus

HOW CUSTOMERS ARE FOUND

The following survey results show what lead generation methods seem to work best. The left column lists the methods used to generate leads. To the right of each method is the success rating on a priority scale of 1.00 to 5.00 (1.00 = best).

METHOD USED	SUCCESS RATING
Word of Mouth - Customer	1.86
Word of Mouth - Colleague	2.83
Word of Mouth - Vendor	3.30
Cold Calls - By Self	3.91
Direct Mail Advertising	4.10
Network at Professional Meetings	4.13
Yellow Pages Advertising	4.23
Association/Club Directory	4.42
Telemarketing	4.45
Newspaper Advertising	4.60
Business Directory Listing	4.61
Network at Trade Shows	4.65
Network at User Group Meetings	4.69
White Pages Listing	4.74
Advertise in Trade Publications	4.87
Magazine Advertising	4.90
Inserts	4.94
Windshielf Flyer	4.95
Door Hangers	4.96

What's This All Mean?

This data can be extremely valuable when planning your marketing and advertising budget. It also helps to know what strategies other DTP professionals feel work quite well for them. According to these colleagues, some techniques are just not worth the money. As you can see, a majority feel that the most successful business leads come from referrals by customers, business colleagues, and vendors.

These people feel that methods such as sticking flyers under car windshields in strip malls and placing inserts in various publications do not bring a satisfactory return on the investment in time and expense.

It's also interesting to note that our survey participants feel that newspaper advertising generates more response than magazine advertising and that direct mail beats them both.

As would be expected, good networking with your peers, and happy customers and vendors can make the difference between a $22,000 a year business and a $500,000 a year adventure.

PUBLICATIONS READ REGULARY

This section describes the most popular publications that others in our profession read on a regular basis. The mention of some publications was expected. However, the number and divertisty of publications being read each month is new information. Over 150 publications were mentioned in the survey returns. Only those publications mentioned most often are listed.

The wide range and number of publications indicates that owner-operators recognize the value in lateral thinking (getting ideas from diverse sources).

The check marks indicate relative importance. Most respondents regularly read about four publications each month. This is down from our last survey. Apparently, many owner-operators were too busy keeping their shops afloat during a down economy to have much time to tackle their "read" pile.

Publish
MacWorld
MacUser
PC Magazine
Home Office Computing
NADTP Journal
MacWeek
Electronic Publishing
PC Computing
PC World
Micro Publishing News
Graphic Arts Monthly
How Magazine
PC Publishing & Presn
I NC.
The Page
PC Week
Pre-
InfoWorld
Print
Step-by-Step
Desktop Communications
The Typographer

Helpful Addresses
(Publications)

Advertising Age
Subscription Dept.
965 E. Jefferson Ave.
Detroit, MI 48207-9901
fax (313) 446-0961

Aldus Magazine
Adobe Systems
411 First Avenue S.
Seattle, WA 98104-2871
(206) 628-2321

American Printer
29 North Wacker Drive
Chicago, IL 60606-3298
(312) 726-2802

Art & Design News
5783 Park Plaza Court
Indianapolis, IN 46220
(317) 849-6110 / fax (317) 576-5859

Artweek
12 S First Street, Ste. 520
San Jose, CA 95113
(800) 733-2916, (408) 279-2293

Beyond Computing
IBM Corporation,
590 Madison Ave., 32nd Floor
New York, NY 10022

Bottom Line Personal
Subscription Center
P.O. Box 58446
Boulder, CO 80322
(800) 274-5611

Business & Incentive Strategies
P.O. Box 1791
Riverton, NJ 08077-7391

Business Systems Dealer
14 W. South St.
Corry, PA 16407-1894

BusinessWeek
1221 Avenue of the Americas
New York, NY 10020
(212) 512-2000

BYTE
Subscription Dept.
P.O. Box 555
Hightstown, NJ 08520
(800) 257-9402

Communication Arts
P.O. Box 10300
Palo Alto, CA 94303
(415) 326-6040 / (800) 258-9111
fax (415) 326-1648

Communications Week
Circulation Dept.
P.O. Box 1094
Skokie, IL 60076
(708) 647-6834 / fax (708) 647-6838

Communication World
International Assn of Business Communicators
One Hallidie Plaza, Suite 600
San Francisco, CA 94102
(415) 433-3400 / fax (415) 362-8762

Compute!
Subscription Service Dept.
P.O. Box 10955
Des Moines, IA 50950
(800) 727-6937

Computer Currents
P.O. Box 2339
Berkeley, CA 94702
(415) 547-6800

Computer Graphics World
P.O. Box 122
Tulsa, OK 74101-9966
(918) 831-9400

Computer Pictures
701 Westchester Ave.
White Plains, NY 10604
(914) 328-9157 / fax (914) 328-9093

Computer Reseller News
CMP Publications Inc.
600 Community Dr.
Manhasset, NY 11030
(516) 562-5000

Computer Retail Week
Circulation Department
P.O. Box 4312
Manhasset, NY 11030
(516) 733-6800 / fax (516) 733-6960

Computer Retailing
1750 Peachtree Road
Atlanta, GA 30357
(404) 874-4462

Computer Shopper
One Park Avenue, 11th Floor
New York, NY 10016
(800) 274-6384

Computer Street Journal
P.O. Box 200516
Austin, TX 78720
(512) 263-9166

Computer Telephony
12 West 21 St.
New York, NY 10010
(212) 691-8215 / fax (212) 691-1191

Corelation Magazine
Assn of Corel Artists & Designers
1309 Riverside Dr.
Burbank, CA 91506
(818) 563-ACAD / fax (818) 955-5867

COSMEP Newsletter
The International Assn of Independent
Publishers
P.O. Box 420703
San Francisco, CA 94142-0703
(415) 922-9490 / fax (415) 922-5566

Cost Controller, The
Siefer Consultants, Inc.
525 Cayuga St.
Storm Lake, IA 50588
(800) 747-7342

Creative Business
275 Newbury Street
Boston, MA 02116
(617) 424-1368

CWIP Clips
Chicago Women in Publishing
43 E. Ohio St., Suite 1022
Chicago, IL 60611
(312) 645-0083

Design Tools Monthly
2111 30th St., Suite H
Boulder, CO 80301
(303) 444-6876 / fax (303) 440-3641

Editorial Eye
Editorial Experts
85 S Gragg St., Ste. 400
Alexandria, VA 22312
(703) 642-3040

Editor's Workshop
Lawrence Regan Communications
407 S. Dearborn St.
Chicago, IL 60605
(312) 922-8245

Electronic Business
Circulation Department
44 Cook St.
Denver, CO 80206
(303) 388-4511

Electronic BusinessBuyer
P.O. Box 7537
Highlands Ranch, CO 80126-9337

Electronic Buyers' News
Circulation Dept.
P.O. Box 9054
Jericho, NY 11753-8954

Electronic Engineering Times
Circulation Dept.
Box 2010
Manhasset, NY 11030
(516) 562-5000

Electronic Publishing
P.O. Box 170
Salem, NH 03079
(603) 898-2822

Entrepreneur
2392 Morse Avenue
Irvine, CA 92714
(800) 864-6864 / fax (714) 755-4211

Federal Computer Week
Circulation Department
P.O. Box 3023
Northbrook, IL 60065-3023
(708) 564-1385

Forecast
Faulkner & Gray, Inc.
Eleven Penn Plaza
New York, NY 10001
(212) 967-7000

Fortune
P.O. Box 60001
Tampa, FL 33660-0001
(800) 621-8000

Graphic Arts Monthly
Cahners Publishing Company
44 Cook St.
Denver, CO 80206-5800
(303) 388-4511

Graphics Arts Products News
Maclean-Hunter Publishing Corp.
300 W. Adams
Chicago, IL 60606
(312) 726-2802

Graphic Design USA
1556 Third Avenue
New York, NY

HEPC Syllabus
Subscription Services
1307 S. Mary Ave., Suite 211
Sunnyvale, CA 94087

High Volume Printing
425 Huehl Road
Bldg. 11, Box 368
Northbrook, IL 60065
(312) 564-5940

Home Office Computing
P.O. Box 51344
Boulder, CO 80321-1344
(800) 288-7812

How
P.O. Box 5250
Harlan, IA 51593-4750
(800) 333-1115

Imaging Magazine
12 West 21 Street
New York, NY 10010
(800) 677-3435

In-Plant Printer
425 Huehl Road
Bldg. 11, Box 368
Northbrook, IL 60065
(312) 564-5940

In-Plant Reproductions
401 N. Broad Street

Philadelphia, PA 19108
(215) 238-5300 / fax (215) 238-5457

INC.
P.O. Box 54129
Boulder, CO 80322-4129
(800) 234-0999

Incentive
355 Park Avenue S
New York, NY 10010
(212) 592-6493 / fax (212) 592-6499

InformationWeek
P.O. Box 1093
Skokie, IL 60076-8093
(516) 562-5000

InfoWorld
P.O. Box 1172
Skokie, IL 60076
(708) 647-7925 / fax (708) 647-0226

Instant & Small Commercial Printer
P.O. Box 1387
Northbrook, IL 60065-1387
(708) 564-5940 / fax (708) 564-8361

Larry Hunt's Color Copy News
5325 Kelly Road
Tampa, FL 33615
(813) 886-9107

Macazine
Subscription Service Dept.
P.O. Box 6815
Syracuse, NY 13217
(800) 624-2346

MacChicago
515 E. Golf Rd., Suite 201
Arlington Heights, IL 60005
(708) 439-6575

MacGuide
Subscription Dept.
P.O. Box 13067
Denver, CO 80201
(303) 935-8100

Macintosh Business Review
Subscription Service Dept.
10 Holland Drive
Hasbrouck Heights, NJ 07604
(201) 393-6474/6475

Macintosh Buyer's Guide, The
Redgate Communications Corp.
Circulation Dept.
660 Beachland Blvd.
Vero Beach, FL 32963-1794
(407) 231-6904

Macintosh Hands On
52 Domino Drive
Concord, MA 01742-9906

MacUser
P.O. Box 52461
Boulder, CO 80323-2461
(800) 627-2247

MacWEEK
Customer Service Dept
c/o JCI
P.O. Box 1766
Riverton, NJ 08077-7366
(609) 786-8230

Macworld
P.O. Box 51666
Boulder, CO 80321-1666
(800) 288-6848 / fax (415) 442-0766

Magazine Design & Production
Globecom Publishing
4551 W 107th St., Suite 343
Overland Park, KS 66207
(913) 642-6611

Marketing Computers
Adweek L.P.
1515 Broadway
New York, NY 10036
(212) 536-5336

Micro Publishing News
21150 Hawthorne Blvd. #104

Torrance, CA 90503
(310)371-5787

Microtimes
BAM Publications
5951 Canning
Oakland, CA 94609

Mobile Office
Circulation Department
911 Hope St., Bldg. 6
Stamford, CT 06907-0949
(203) 358-9900 / fax (203) 348-5792

Multimedia Monitor
P.O. Box 26
Falls Church, VA 22040
(800) 323-3472 / fax (703) 532-0529

Multimedia Today
IBM
4111 Northside Parkway
Internal Zip H4P-21
Atlanta, GA 30327
(800) 779-2062 / fax (404) 238-4298

NADTP Journal
462 Old Boston St.
Topsfield, MA 01983-1232
(508) 887-7900

NASS Newsletter
National Association of Secretarial
Services
3637 Fourth St., N, Suite 330
St. Petersburg, FL 33704
(800) 237-1462 / fax (813) 894-1277

Network Computing
600 Community Dr.
Manhasset, NY 11030
(708) 647-6834 / fax (708) 647-6838

New Media Magazine
P.O. Box 1771
Riverton, NJ 08077-7371
(609) 786-4430

OnLine Design
Subscription Department
20 Borica St.
San Francisco, CA 94127-2802
(415) 334-3800 / fax (415) 334-4458

Package Printing and Converting
P.O. Box 12829
Philadelphia, PA 19108-0829
fax (215) 238-5412

PC Computing
P.O. Box 58229
Boulder, CO 80322-8229
(800) 365-2770

PC Graphics & Video
201 E. Sandpointe Ave., Suite 600
Santa Ana, CA 92707
(714) 513-8400 / fax (714) 513-8612

PC Magazine
P.O. Box 54093
Boulder, CO 80321-4093
(800) 289-0429

PC Publishing & Presentations
P.O. Box 5050
Des Plaines, IL 60019-9435
(312) 296-0770

PC Resources
IDG Communications/Peterborough
P.O. Box 50302
Boulder, CO 80321-0302
(603) 924-9471

PC Week
P.O. Box 1767
Riverton, NJ 08077-9767

PC World
Subscriber Services
P.O. Box 55029
Boulder, CO 80322-5029
(800) 825-7595

Personal Computing
P.O. Box 359110
Palm Coast, FL 32035-9921
(800) 423-1780, (800) 858-0095

Personal Publishing
P.O. Box 3240
Harlan, IA 51593-2420
(515) 247-7540

Personal Selling Power
P.O. Box 5467
Fredericksburg, VA 22403
(800) 752-7355

Plan and Print
International Reprographic Assn.
611 E. Butterfield Rd., Suite 104
Lombard, IL 60148
(312) 852-3055

PMA Newsletter
Publishers Marketing Assn.
2401 Pacific Coast Hwy., Suite 102
Hermosa Beach, CA 90254
(310) 372-2732 / fax (310) 374-3342

Portable Office
80 Elm St.
Peterborough, NH 03458
(800) 245-0804

Post Gutenberg
Lee Publications Inc.
P.O. Box 121
Palatine Bridge, NY 13428
(518) 673-3237

Presentations
23410 Civic Center Way, Ste. E-10
Malibu, CA 90265
(310) 456-2283 / fax (310) 456-8686

Presentation Products
23410 Civic Center Way, Ste. E-10
Malibu, CA 90265
(310) 456-2283 / fax (310) 456-8686

APPENDIX

Presentations Magazine
50 S. Ninth St.
Minneapolis, MN 55402
(800) 328-4329

Print
320 Tower Oaks Blvd.
Rockville, MD 20852

Printing Impressions
401 N Broad St.
Philadelphia, PA 19108
(215) 238-5300

Printing Journal
1432 Duke St.
Alexandria, VA 22314-3436
(703) 683-8800 / fax (703) 683-8801

Printing Views
Midwest Publishing Co., Inc.
8328 N. Lincoln Avenue
Skokie, IL 60077
(312) 539-8540

Publish
Subscription Dept.
P.O. Box 55415
Boulder, CO 80321-5415
(800) 525-0643, (800) 685-3435

Publishers Weekly
P.O. Box 6547
Torrance, CA 90504-0457
(800) 278-2991

Publishing & Production Executive
North American Publishing Co.
401 N Broad St.
Philadelphia, PA 19108
(215) 238-5300 / fax (215) 238-5457

Reseller Management
P.O. Box 650
Morris Plains, NJ 07950-0650
(201) 292-5100

San Diego Writers' Monthly
3910 Chapman St.
San Diego, CA 92110
(619) 226-0896

Service & Support Management
Publications & Communications, Inc.
P.O. Box 399
Cedar Park, TX 78630-9820

Small Press
P.O. Box 3000
Denville, NJ 07834
(203) 226-6967

Small Publisher
c/o Nigel Maxey
P.O. Box 1620
Pineville, WV 24874-1620
(304) 732-8195

Southern Graphics
Zed Coast Center
1680 SW Bayshore Blvd.
Port St. Lucie, FL 34984-9985

Step-By-Step Graphics
Dynamic Graphics
6000 N. Forest Park Dr.
Peoria, IL 61614-3592
(800) 255-8800

St. Louis Computing
Wikman Publishing Inc.
1300 Hampton Ave., Suite 117
St. Louis, MO 63119
(314) 644-5854

Success
P.O. Box 10983
Des Moines, IA 50347-0983
(800) 234-7324

Target Marketing
P.O. Box 12827
Philadelphia, PA 19108-0827
fax (215) 238-5412

The Page
The Cobb Group
9420 Bunsen Pkwy, Suite 300
Louisville, KY 40220
(800) 223-8720

The Typographer
Typographers International Assn.
2262 Hall Place NW #101
Washington, DC 20007-1870
(202) 965-3400

The Writer
120 Boylston St.
Boston, MA 02116-4615

Upside
1159-B Triton Dr.
Foster City, CA 94404
(415) 377-0950 / fax (415) 377-1961

VARBusiness
Circulation Dept.
P.O. Box 2110
Manhasset, NY 11030-4309
(516) 733-6800 / fax (413) 637-4343

Word Perfect Magazine
Circulation Department
288 West Center Street
Orem, UT 84057

Writer's Digest
P.O. Box 2123
Harlan, IA 51593
(800) 333-0133

Writers' Journal
3585 N. Lexington Ave., Suite 328
Arden Hills, MN 55126-8056
(612) 486-7818

CLUB/ASSOCIATION MEMBERSHIP

Here we wanted to determine what associations and clubs we join. Many respondents called or wrote indicating amazement at the number of professional associations that are available to deskstop publishing shops and prepress service bureaus.

The spread of response data was too wide to be statistically relevant, but the absence of membership in some associations is interesting. It means that these groups are not making themselves known to DTP shop and service bureau owners and operators. An opportunity exists here for these organizations to gain membership and be of value to more people.

Since some respondents are members of more than one professional organization, the horizontal bars on the next page are only important in showing what associations are being represented in the survey responses and the relative number of respondents who are members.

Relative Membership Preference

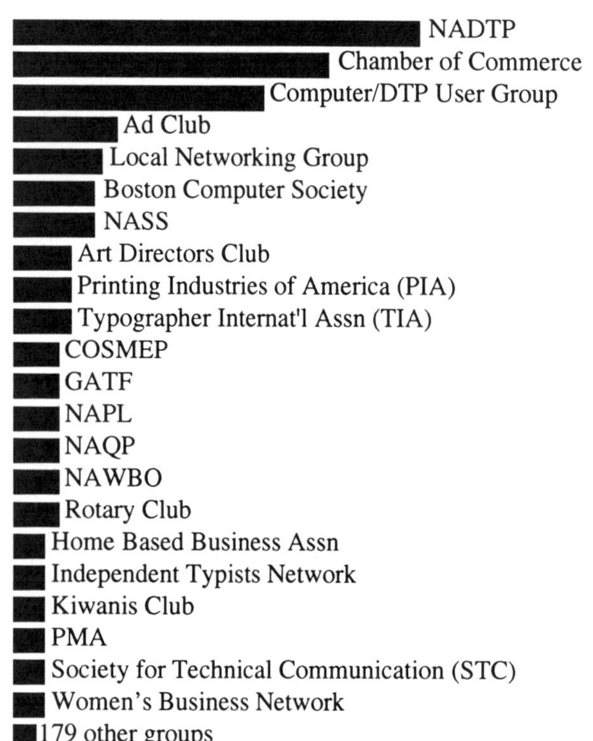

Helpful Addresses
(Organizations)

ABWA
P.O. Box 8728
Kansas City, MO 64114-0728
(816) 361-6621

Adobe Technology Exchange (ATX)
5201 Great America Pkwy, Ste. 441
Santa Clara, CA 95054
(800) 446-5622, (408) 562-6104

American Book Producers Association (ABPA)
New York, NY
(212) 683-0355

American Forest & Paper Association (AFPA)
1111 19th Street NW, Ste 800
Washington, DC 20036
(202) 463-2700

**American Institute of Graphic Arts
(AIGA)**
3748 22nd Street
San Francisco, CA 94114
(415) 647-4700

**American Institute of Technical
Illustrators**
2513 Forest Leaf Parkway, Ste 906
Ballwin, MO 63011
(314) 458-2248

**American Newspaper Publishers
Assn. (ANPA)**
P.O. Box 17407
Dulles International Airport
Washington, D.C. 20041
(703) 620-9500

American Paper Institute (API)
260 Madison Ave.
10th Floor
New York. NY 10016
(212) 340-0600

**American Society of Journalists &
Authors**
Northern CA Chapter
4603 Lincoln Drive
Concord CA 94521

**Association for Computing Machin-
ery (SIGGRAPH)**
1515 Broadway
New York, NY 10036
(212) 869-7440

**Association for Graphic Arts
Training (AGAT)**
c/o RIT T&E Center
P.O. Box 9887
Rochester, NY 14623
(716) 475-2737 / fax (716) 475-7050

**Association for Information and
Image Management (AIIM)**
1100 Wayne Ave., Suite 1100
Silver Springs, MD 20910
(301) 587-8202

**Association of American Publishers
(AAP)**
1718 Connecticut Avenue NW, Ste. 700
Washington, DC 20009-1148

**Association of College and University
Printers (ACUP)**
Cal State University-Long Beach
1250 Bellflower Rd
Long Beach. CA 90840
(213) 985-4501

**Association of College and University
Printers (ACUP)**
Pennsylvania State University
108 Business Services Bldg.
University Park, PA 16802
(814) 863-0580

**Association of Corel Artists &
Designers**
1309 Riverside Dr.
Burbank, CA 91506
(818) 563-ACAD / fax (818) 955-5867

Association of Electronic Cottagers
P.O. Box 1738
Davis, CA 95617
(916) 756-6430

**Association of Graphic Arts
Consultants (AGAC)**
P 0. Box 290249
Nashville, TN 37229
(615) 366-1094

**Association of Imaging Service
Bureaus (AISB)**
5601 Roanne Way, Suite 608
Greensboro, NC 27409
(800) 844-2472, (919) 855-0400

**Association of the Graphic Arts
(AGA)**
330 7th Avenue
New York, NY 10001-5010
(212) 279-2104

Baltimore Publishers Association (BPA)
Baltimore, MD
(410) 313-9338

Binders & Finishers Association
408 Eightth Ave., Suite 10-A
New York, NY 10001-1816
(212) 629-3232

Binding Industries of America (BIA/ PIA)
Printing Industries of America
70 E. Lake St.
Chicago, IL 60611
(312) 704-5000

Book Manufacturers' Institute (BMI)
Wellesley, MA
(617) 239-0103

Bookbuilders of Boston (BOB)
Woburn, MA
(617) 933-6878

Bookbuilders of Washington (BOW)
Washington, DC
(202) 287-3738

Bookbuilders West (BBW)
Box 883666
San Francisco, CA 94188
(415) 546-4991

Business & Professional Women (BPW)
Greater Londonderry Chapter
25 Orchard View Place, Suite 12
Londonderry, NH 03053
(603) 432-8967

Business Forms Management Association (BFMA)
519 SW 3rd Ave, Suite 712
Portland, OR 97204-2519
(503) 227-3393

Business Group Network
P.O. Box 12280
Richmond, VA 23241-2280
(804) 783-9307

Business/Professional Advertising Association (BPAA)
901 N. Washington, Suite 206
Alexandria, VA 22314

Cahners Expo Group
999 Summer St.
Stamford, CT 06905
(203) 964-0000

California Press Women
PO Box 19667
San Diego, CA 92119
(619) 460-9488

California Writers Club (CWC)
2214 Derby Street
Berkeley, CA 94705

Canadian Printing Industries Association (CPIA)
75 Albert St., Suite 906
Ottawa, Ontario K1P 5E7 Canada
(613) 236-7208

CAP International
One Longwater Circle
Norwell, MA 02061
(617) 982-9500

Chicago Book Clinic, The (CBC)
Chicago, IL
(312) 946-1700

Chicago Women in Publishing (CWIP)
43 E. Ohio St., Ste. 1022
Chicago, IL 60611
(312) 645-0083

Computer Electronics Marketing Association (CEMA)
8650 Gennessee Ave., Ste. 100-502
San Diego, CA 92122
(619) 549-8881

Corel Creative Club
Corel Corporation
The Corel Bldg., 1600 Carling Avenue
Ottawa, Ontario, K1Z 8R7 CANADA
U.S. (716) 423-8200
CAN (613) 728-8200

COSMEP (Assoc. of Independent Book Publishers)
Box 703
San Francisco, CA 94101
(415) 922-9490

Dallas Society of Visual Communications (DSVC)
3530 High Mesa
Dallas, TX 75234
(214) 241-2017

Dataquest Inc. (DTQ)
1290 Ridder Park Dr.
San Jose, CA 95131
(408) 437-8000

DDAP Association
(Digital Distribution of Advertising for Publications)
1855 E. Vista Way, Suite 16
Vista, CA 92084
(619) 758-9460

Demonstrative Evidence Specialists Association (DESA)
(800) 522-DESA

Dunn Technology, Inc. (DTI)
1855 E. Vista Way
Vista, CA 92084
(619) 758-9460

Dynamic Graphics Educational Foundation (DGEF)
6000 North Forest Park Dr.
Peoria, IL 61614
(800) 255-8800

Editorial Freelance Association
P.O. Box 2050
New York, NY 10159
(212) 677-3357

Electronic Graphic Artists of Dallas (EGAD)
6440 N. Central Expressway
University Tower, Suite 506
Dallas, TX 75206
(214) 360-9072

Electronic Prepress Section (EPS/PIA)
100 Daingerfield Rd.
Alexandria, VA 22314
(703) 519-8168

Flexographic Technical Association (FTA)
900 Marconi Ave.
Ronkonkoma, NY 11779-7212
(516) 737-6020

Freelance Editorial Association
P.O. Box 835
Cambridge, MA 02238
(617) 729-8164

Graphic Arts Association (GAA)
1900 Cherry St.
Philadelphia, PA 19103
(215) 299-3300

Graphic Arts Literacy Alliance (GALA)
Graphic Arts Technical Foundation
4615 Forbes Ave.
Pittsburgh, PA 15213
(412) 621-6941

Graphic Arts Sales Foundation
113 East Evans St.
Matlack Building
West Chester, PA 19380
(215) 436-9778

Graphic Arts Show Co. (GASC)
1899 Preston White Dr.
Reston, VA 22091-4367
(703) 264-7200

Graphic Arts Technical Foundation (GATF)
4615 Forbes Avenue
Pittsburgh, PA 15223-3796
(412) 621-6941 / fax (412) 621-3049

Graphic Arts Marketing Information Service (GCA/PIA)
Printing Industries of America
(703) 841-1879

Graphic Arts Suppliers Association
1900 Arch St.
Philadelphia, PA 19103-1498
(215) 564-3484

Graphic Communications Association (GCA-PIA)
100 Daingerfield Rd, 4th Floor
Alexandria, VA 22314
(703) 519-8160

Graphic Preparatory Association (GPA)
501 N. Wesley Ave
P.O. Box 2
Mount Morris, IL 61054
(815) 734-4178

Graphics of the Americas
PIA of South Florida
P.O. Box 170010
Hialeah, FL 33017
(305) 558-4855

Gravure Association of America
1200-A Scottsville Rd.
Rochester, NY 14623
(716) 436-2150 / fax (716) 436-7689

Gutenburg Expositions
P.O. Box 11712
Santa Ana, CA 92711
(714) 921-3120

Houston Association of In-Plant Printing (HAIP)
1324 West Clay St.
Houston, TX 77019
(713) 522-2046

IBFI
(The International Association Serving the Forms, Information Management, Systems Automation and Printed Communications Requirements of Business)
2111 Wilson Blvd., Suite 350
Arlington, VA 22201-3042
(703) 841-9191

International Network for Women in Enterprise and Trade (INET FOR WOMEN)
6819 Elm Street #3
McLean, VA 22101
(703) 893-8541

International Publishing Management Association (IPMA)
IPMA Building
1205 W. College Ave.
Liberty, MO 64068-3733
(816) 781-1111

Institute of Electrical & Electronic Enginers (IEEE) Computer Society
10662 Los Vaqueros Circle
P.O. Box 3014
Los Alamitos, CA 90720-1264

International Association of Business Communicators (IABC)
1 Hallidie Plaza, Suite 600
San Francisco, CA 94102
(800) 776-4222, (415) 433-3400

International Association of Printing House Craftsmen (IAPHC)
7042 Brooklyn Blvd.
Minneapolis, MN 55429-1370
(612) 560-1620

International Business Forms Industries (IBFI)
2111 Wilson Blvd., Ste. 350
Arlington, VA 22201
(703) 841-9191

International Graphic Arts Education Association (IGAEA)
4615 Forbes Ave.
Pittsburgh, PA 15213
(412) 682-5170

International Prepress Assn (IPA)
7200 France Ave. S., Suite 327
Edina, MN 55435
(800) 255-8141, (612) 896-1908
fax (612) 896-0181

International Television Association (ITVA)
6311 North O'Conner Rd., LB51
Irving TX 75039
(214) 869-1112

International Thermographers Association (ITA/PIA)
100 Daingerfield Rd.
Alexandria, VA 22314
(703) 519-8100/8122/8136

Kenex
575 E. 4500 S., Ste. B240
Salt Lake City, UT 84107
(801) 263-3276

Key Productions
94 Murphy Road
Hartford, CT 06114
(203) 247-8363

Last Monday Club
3871 Piedmont Avenue
Oakland, CA 94611
(510) 450-4800

Leads Club
P.O. Box 279
Carlsbad, CA 92018-0279
(800) 783-3761, (619) 434-3761

Macintosh Consultants Network (MCN)
3600 Sisk Rd., Ste. 3D
Modesto, CA 95356-0539
(209) 545-0569
CONNECT and AppleLink address is "MCN."

Marin Small Publishers Association
P.O. Box 1346
Ross, CA 94957

Mid-America Book Publishers (MABP)
Lincoln, NE
(402) 466-9665

Midwest Secretarial Services Network
795 Office Parkway, Suite 118
St. Louis, MO 63141
(314) 993-8588

National Association for Female Executives (NAFE)
127 W. 24th Street
New York, NY 10011-1914
(800) 927-NAFE, (212) 645-0770

National Association for the Cottage Industry
P.O. Box 14460
Chicago, Il 60614
(312) 472-8116

National Association for the Self-Employed (NASE)
2121 Precinct Line Rd.
Hurst, TX 76054
(800) 827-9990

National Association of Desktop Publishers (NADTP)
462 Old Boston Road
Suite 8
Topsfield, MA 01983
(508) 877-7900, (800) 874-4113

**National Association of Home Based
Businesses**
P.O. Box 30220
Baltimore, Md 21270
(301) 466-8070

**National Association of Litho Clubs
(NALC)**
P.O. Box 1258
Clifton, NJ 07012
(201) 777-6727

**National Association of Litho Clubs
(NALC)**
6550 Donjoy Dr.
Cincinnati, OH 45242
(513) 793-2532

**National Association of Printers and
Lithographers (NAPL)**
780 Palisades Avneue
Teaneck, NJ 07666
(201) 342-0705 / fax (201) 692-0286

**National Association of Printing Ink
Manufacturers (NAPIM)**
Heights Plaza, 777 Terrace Ave.
Hasbrouck Heights, NJ 07604
(201) 288-9454

**National Association of Quick
Printers (NAQP)**
401 N Michigan Ave.
Chicago, IL 60611
(312) 644-6610 ext. 4716 / fax (312)
245-1084

**National Association of Secretarial
Services (NASS)**
3637-4th Street North, Suite 330
St. Petersburg, FL 33704
(800) 237-1462, (813) 823-3646

**National Association of Women
Business Owners (NAWBO)**
600 S. Federal St. Suite 400
Chicago, Il 60605
(312) 922-0465

**National Business Forms Association
(NBFA)**
433 E. Monroe Avenue
Alexandria, VA 22301
(703) 836-6225

**National Computer Graphics
Association (NCGA)**
2722 Merrilee Dr., Ste. 200
Fairfax, VA 22031
(703) 698-9600

National Family Business Council
60 Revere Drive, Suite 500
Northbrook, IL 60062
(312) 480-9574

**National Foundation for Women
Business Owners (NFWBO)**
1001 Pennsylvania Avenue NW #435N
Washington, DC 20004
(202) 347-0978

**National League of American Pen
Women (NLAPW)**
1300 17th Street NW
Washington, D.C. 29936

**National Paper Trade Association
(NPTA)**
111 Great Neck Rd.
Great Neck, NY 11021
(516) 829-3070

National Small Business United
1155 15th St, NW, Ste 710
Washington, DC 20005
(202) 293-8830

**National State Printing Association
(NSPA)**
Council of State Governments
Iron Works Pike
P.O. Box 11910
Lexington, KY 40578
(606) 231-1871

National Writer's Union
873 Broadway, Suite 203
New York, NY 10003-1209

**Network of Entrepreneurial Women,
Inc. (NEW)**
P.O. Box 1100
Falls Church, VA 22041
(703) 435-4449

Network of Enterprising Women
P.O. Box 8324
Richmond, VA 23226

**New England Women Business
Owners (NEWBO)**
P.O. Box 67082
Chestnut Hill, MA 02167
(617) 566-3013

Newspaper Association of America
11600 Sunrise Valley Dr.
Reston, VA 22091
(703) 648-1000

**North American Bookdealers
Exchange (NABE)**
P.O. Box 606
Cottage Grove, OR 97424

**North American Graphic Arts
Suppliers Association (NAGASA)**
1720 Florida Ave., NW
Washington, DC 20009-2660
(202) 328-8441

**NPES, The Association for Suppliers
of Printing and Publishing Technolo-
gies**
1899 Preston White Dr
Reston VA 22091-4367
(703) 264-7200

Optical Publishing Association
P.O. Box 21268
Columbus, OH 43221
(614) 442-8805

Philadelphia Book Clinic (PBC)
Philadelphia, PA
(215) 664-2026

Print/New Jersey
75 Kearny Ave., PO Box 6
Kearny, NJ 07032
(201) 997-7468 / fax (201) 997-7063

**Print Production Club of Kansas City
(PPCKC)**
Kansas City, MO
(816) 432-2600

Printing Association of Florida (PAF)
P.O. Box 170010
Hialeah, FL 33017
(305 764-8808

Printing Industries of America (PIA)
100 Daingerfield Road
Arlington, VA 22314
(703) 519-8100/8158 / fax (703) 548-
3227

PIA of CT & Western Massachusetts
1 Regency Dr., P.O. Box 30
Bloomfield, CT 06002
(203) 242-8991 / fax (203) 286-0787

PIA of Georgia
5020 Highlands Pkwy.
Smyrna, GA 30082
(404) 433-3050   fax (404) 433-3062

PIA of Kansas City
702 Midland Bldg., 1221 Baltimore St.
Kansas City, MO 64105
(816) 421-7678 / fax (816) 421-7073

PIA of the Mountain States
900 E. Louisiana Avenue
Denver, CO 80210
(303) 744-6007 / fax (303) 698-1260

PIA of New York State
455 Commerce Drive
Amherst, NY 14228
(716) 691-3211 / fax (716) 691-4249

PIA of San Diego
3914 Murphy Canyon Rd., Ste A-107
San Diego, CA 92123
(619) 571-6555 / fax (619) 571-7935

PIA of the South
305 Plus Park Blvd.
Nashville, TN 37217
(615) 366-1091 / fax (615) 366-4192

PIA of Texas
910 W. Mockingbird Lane
Dallas TX 75247

Printing Industries of the Carolinas (PICA)
P.O. Box 19889
Charlotte, NC 28219
(704) 357-1150

Printing Industries of Maryland
2423 Maryland Avenue
Baltimore, MD 21218
(410) 366-0900 / fax (410) 366-1816

Printing Industries of Michigan
23815 Northwestern Hwy. #2700
Southfield, MI 48075-3366
(313) 354-9200 / fax (313) 354-1711

Printing Industries of the Midlands
11009 Aurora Avenue
Urbandale, IA 50322
(515) 270-1009 / fax (515) 270-8701

Printing Industries of Minnesota
450 N. Syndicate, Suite 200
St. Paul, MN 55104
(612) 646-4826 / fax (612) 646-8673

Printing Industries of New England
110 Tech Circle, PO Box 2009
Natick, MA 01760-0015
(508) 655-8700 / fax (508) 655-2586

Printing Industries of Oklahoma & Southwest Missouri
5200 S. Yale, Suite 101

Tulsa, OK 74135
(918) 496-1122 / fax (918) 496-2992

Printing Industries of Virginia
1108 E. Main Street, Ste. 300
Richmond, VA 23219
(804) 643-1800 / fax (804) 643-7482

Printing Industries of Wisconsin
P.O. Box 126
Elm Grove, WI 53122
(414) 785-9090 / fax (414) 785-7043

Printing Industry Association of the South
P.O. Box 290249
Nashville, TN 37229
(615) 366-1094

Printing Industry of the Carolinas (PICA)
P.O. Box 19889
Charlotte, NC 28219
(704) 357-1150

Printing Industry of Connecticut
P.O. Box 144
Milford, CT 06460
(203) 874-6793 / fax (203) 874-0291

Printing Industry of Illinois/Indiana Assn
70 E. Lake Street
Chicago, IL 60601
(312) 704-5000

Printing Industry of Metropolitan Washington, Inc., The
7 West Tower
1333 H Street NW
Washington, DC 20005
(202) 682-30001

Printing Industry of Ohio
88 Dorchester Sq., PO Box 819
Westerville, OH 43081
(614) 794-2300 / fax (614) 794-2049

Printing Industry of South Florida
P O Box 170010
Hialeah, FL 33017
(305) 764-8808

**Professional Association of
Secretarial Services (PASS)**
Premier Office Services, Inc.
1116 Lyford Lane
Wheaton, IL 60187
(908) 668-3652

Professional Referral Services
20123 Nordhoff Street
Chatsworth, CA 91311
(818) 998-0182

**Publishers' Marketing Association
(PMA)**
2401 Pacific Coast Hwy., Ste. 102
Hermosa Beach, CA 90254
(213) 372-2732

**Publication Production Association of
Southern California (PPASC)**
Long Beach, CA
(310) 425-1721

Publication Production Club (PPC)
Chicago, IL
(708) 323-9490

**Publication Production Group of
Northern California (PPGNC)**
Redwood City, CA
(415) 506-4763

Quad Cities Advertising Federation
P.O. Box 573
Moline, IL 61265
(309) 762-0732

**Quad Cities Club of Printing House
Craftsmen**
2216 W. 54th Street
Davenport, IA 52806
(319) 386-6325

Reed Exhibition Company
999 Summer St.
P.O. Box 3833
Stamford, CT 06905
(203) 964-0000

**Research & Engineering Council of
the Graphic Arts Industry**
Marshallton Bldg., P.O. Box 639
Chadds Ford, PA 19317
(215) 388-7394

Richmond Professional Network
P.O. Box 954
Richmond, VA 23207
(804) 355-7800

Rochester Institute of Technology
Technical & Educational Center
66 Lomb Memorial Dr.
Rochester, NY 14623-5604
(716) 475-5000

**Sacramento Women's Network
(SWN)**
P.O. Box 13085
Sacramento, CA 95813-3085

**Santa Cruz County Women's
Network (SCCWN)**
1822 Silvana Lane
Santa Cruz, CA 95062
(408) 479-0118

Screen Printing Association International (SPAI)
10015 Main St.
Fairfax, VA 22031
(703) 385-1335 / fax (703) 273-0456

Seybold Seminars
29160 Heathercliff Rd., Ste. 200
Malibu, CA 90265
(310) 457-5850

Society for Imaging Science & Technology
7003 Kilworth Lane
Springfield, VA 22151
(703) 642-9090

Society For Technical Writers
815 15th Street NW
Washington, DC 20005
(202) 737-0035

Society of Illustrators
128 E. 63rd Street
New York, NY 10021
(212) 838-2560

Society of Illustrators of Los Angeles
11480 Burbank Blvd.
North Hollywood, CA 91601-2301
(818) 784-0588

Society of Professional Journalists
P.O. Box 77
Greencastle, IN 46135-0077
(317) 653-3333

Society of Typographic Arts
233 E. Ontario, Suite 500
Chicago, IL 60611
(312) 787-2018

Southprint Printing Industry Association of the Southwest
P.O. Box 290249
Nashville, TN 37229
(615) 366-1094

State of New York Office of Minority & Business Development
P.O. Box 2072
Albany, NY 12220
(518) 474-6342

Technical Association of the Graphic Arts (TAGA)
68 Lomb Memorial Drive
Rochester, NY 14623-5604
(716) 475-7470

Technical Association of the Pulp & Paper Industry (TAPPI)
Technology Park
P.O. Box 105113
Atlanta, GA 30348
(404) 446-1400

The Creative Club
P.O. Box 983
Latham, NY 12110
(518) 449-4985

Type Directors Club
60 E. 42nd St, Ste 1130
New York NY 10165
(212) 983-6042

Typographers International Association (TIA)
2233 Wisconsin Avenue NW, Ste. 235
Washington, DC 20007
(202) 965-3400

Typographers International Association (TIA)
84 Park Avenue
Flemington, NJ 08822
(908) 782-4635

Ventura Users of Greater Boston
P.O. Box 517
Lexington, MA 02173
(617) 275-3592

Windows Prepublishing Association (WPS)
1804 Hayes St.
Nashville, TN 37203
(615) 320-9473

Wisconsin Publishers Production Club (WPPC)
North Lake, WI
(608) 838-9899

Women's Business Network (WBN)
P.O. Box 108
Berkeley, CA 94701
(510) 482-8583

Women for Women
849 23rd Street
Richmond, CA 94804
(415) 215-4202

Women in Business (WIB)
7358 N. Lincoln Ave., Ste. 150
Chicago, IL 60646
(708) 679-7800

Women in Communications
Georgia Chapter
P.O. Box 7763
Atlanta, GA 30357
(404) 482-0711

Women in Communications, Inc.
Portland Prof. Chapter
P.O. Box 3924
Portland, OR 97208

Women in Production (WIP)
New York, NY
(212) 481-7793

Xplor International
24238 Hawthorne Blvd.
Torrance, CA 90505-6505
(310) 373-3633

Other Books Related to Pricing

<u>Business of Graphics Design: A Sensible Approach,</u> Ed Gold, Watson-Guptill, New York, 1985 (ISBN 0-8230-0543-7).

<u>Desktop Dividends: Managing Electronic Prepress for Profit</u>, Philip K. Ruggles, Printing Management Services, San Luis Obispo, CA, 1993 (ISBN 0-9638203-0-3).

<u>Desktop Dollars & Sense Publishing</u>, Scott R. Anderson, Blue Heron Publishing, Hillsboro, OR 1992 (ISBN 0-936085-51-7).

<u>Handbook of Pricing & Ethetical Guidelines</u>, Graphic Arts Guild, ISBN 0-9321-02-07-7, 1991, $22.

<u>How to Set Your Fees and Get Them</u>, Kate Kelly, Visibility Enterprises, 11 Rockwood Drive, Larchmont, NY 10538. (914) 834-0602, 109 pp, $17.50.

<u>Negotiating Higher Design Fees</u>, Frank Stasiowski, Whitney Library of Design, 1515 Broadway, New York, NY 220 pp, $22.50.

<u>Pricing & Ethical Guidelines</u>, 6th Edition, 208 pp handbook by New York-based Graphic Artists Guild. North Light Books, $19.95.

APPENDIX